# The Reference Librarian's Bible

# The Reference Librarian's Bible

## Print and Digital Reference Resources Every Library Should Own

Steven W. Sowards and Juneal Chenoweth, Editors

LIBRARIES
UNLIMITED™

An Imprint of ABC-CLIO, LLC

Santa Barbara, California • Denver, Colorado

Library of Congress Cataloging in Publication Control Number: 2018023764

ISBN: 978-1-4408-6061-4 (paperback)
       978-1-4408-6062-1 (ebook)

22  21  20  19  18     1  2  3  4  5

This book is also available as an eBook.

Libraries Unlimited
An Imprint of ABC-CLIO, LLC

ABC-CLIO, LLC
130 Cremona Drive, P.O. Box 1911
Santa Barbara, California 93116-1911
www.abc-clio.com

This book is printed on acid-free paper ∞

Manufactured in the United States of America

# Contents

# Preface

## Why Reference Books (and Other Reference Tools)?

Not long ago, it was fashionable to claim that everything was on the Internet and therefore to claim that reference books and even libraries were obsolete. Both claims were wrong.

Our understanding of information on the Internet is more nuanced today. Yes, a great deal of valuable information is freely available, but it is mixed up with outdated information, ill-informed opinion, advertising disguised as information, and flat-out disinformation or "fake news." Readers and researchers want to discover, evaluate, and choose good sources, but doing so is challenging, confusing, time consuming, and tiring. In addition, high-quality information often comes from for-profit, copyrighted, licensed sources; most readers can't reach that information without paying for it or having someone pay for it on their behalf.

Libraries and librarians, of course, exist to solve these problems. Librarians evaluate information; choose, license, and buy high-quality resources on behalf of readers in their communities; and make resources both freely available and more easily discoverable. Those resources include reference tools: books, databases, annuals, maps, and more.

We turn to reference tools for reliable information—complete, balanced, objective, and accurate, and current—since the most up-to-date information is often the most accurate. Reference tools also save our time because they are designed to deliver answers clearly and directly. All of these characteristics contrast with the problems we meet when searching the Internet.

Authority is basic to reference resources. In a world of competing, contradictory, or misleading answers, we need to know the sources behind the answers. Why should we believe that an answer is true? Reference books—and other reference resources—highlight credentials so that readers can draw informed conclusions about the sources of the information they see, as well as the information itself. Reliable reference tools clearly identify authors and editors and state their expertise, experience, and affiliation. Reliable reference tools come from identifiable publishers and vendors—whether those are for-profit firms, nonprofit organizations, government bodies, or communities—and we can evaluate those publishers as part of the information-seeking process. Reference tools also are evaluated by reviewers in the pages of trusted sources like *Publishers Weekly*, *Choice*, and *American Reference Books Annual (ARBA)*. Finally, the reference tools in library reference collections have been evaluated by librarians when they select and acquire those tools based on local needs and professional standards of excellence.

## The "Best" of *ARBA*

The resources noted in this volume have passed all of these tests. The content was written by credentialed authors, published by reputable organizations, and selected by numerous libraries for their collections. These resources also were reviewed in *ARBA*. This is a collection of reviews originally written for the annual volume of *ARBA* or the *ARBAonline* database and repurposed here. These are the "best of *ARBA*" reviews or, more accurately, *ARBA*'s reviews of a core list of the "best" possible reference resources.

Recent information is a key element in accuracy and completeness, and so nearly all of the resources selected for this volume were published since the turn of the century in 2000. In many cases these works have a tradition of value, appearing in multiple editions, updated as needed. The *ARBA* reviews included here do not always reflect the latest editions, but later editions are noted.

There is an old saying: "You go to war with the army you have." In reference, you answer the questions with the resources you have. Even the best source will not be helpful if you can't put your hands on it, so access is another criterion for selection in this best collection. These are reviews of works widely provided by American libraries (in various editions) or freely available online.

## What You Will Find in This Book

For *The Reference Librarian's Bible*, the editors selected 500 reviews of significant reference tools out of some 29,000 reviews in the *ARBAonline* database or from earlier print volumes of *American Reference Books Annual*. These are the reviews as printed at the time: the names of the original review contributors appear at the end of those texts, along with their professional affiliations at the time of review. In a few cases, the editors wrote new reviews to fill gaps. Supplementary notes often follow, such as additional comments about the work, notes about newer editions that have appeared since the review was written, and mention of related works or works with similar titles. Library of Congress (LC) and Dewey classifications appear, as an aid to browsing for other works on the same topic. *ARBA* does not review every new edition of reference books, so reviews may reflect earlier editions (editions that in most cases remain on the shelves of libraries). Reviews or supplementary notes may mention earlier "classics" as well. Original reviews may or may not make purchase recommendations—nevertheless, we recommended each of these 500 titles for most public and academic libraries.

Entries are numbered, 1 to 500, and show the title or name of the resource, the authors or editors if stated, the publisher and year of publication; and the price. Price figures typically are those from the date of original publication. Given inflation and the healthy used book market, accurate current prices are fluid and elusive—at the same time, there is some utility in knowing that a particular book had an original cost of $25, as opposed to another book on the same topic that originally sold for $250. For digital resources, prices are often negotiated based on library size—other digital tools may be free online. Year of publication may not appear for online resources or recurring annuals.

The editors recommend these works as a core set of best reference sources to turn to, in a wide range of subject areas. Their recommendations also reflect a national consensus about quality and significance. These works attracted commitment and support from authors and editors, and then from editorial teams at publishing houses. After publication, *ARBA* and its librarian-reviewers regarded these works as important enough to review.

Finally, local librarians endorsed these sources when they selected and paid for them. With rare exceptions, the 500 publications noted in *The Reference Librarian's Bible* are among the most widely held titles in American libraries. Through the wisdom of crowds, librarians are saying that the subject matter, scope, and quality of these works address the most important needs and recurring interests of their library patrons.

These reviews tend to describe print-format publications, but the vast majority of these works also are available in digital form as e-books or through databases. Many of these works were not "born digital," and print versions are easier to describe in terms of length, date of publication, and price. About 100 digital resources are mentioned—as entries or in passing—and URLs appear for those items (but not simply for e-book versions). Continuously updated online versions sometimes complement their print counterparts: for those titles, the online version may be the one described. You will see references to CD-ROMs in some of the original reviews. Though this technology is outdated, it is important for librarians to know if a book included supplemental information on a CD-ROM at the time of publication.

## What You Will Not Find in This Book

This is not a list of the best reference works on all topics, regardless of date or availability. In some cases, high-quality books on particular topics have not been published or republished recently enough to be current (not since 2000). In other cases, books of high quality are not widely held: if only a few American libraries own the best book, it can't be used to answer a question at most local reference desks. In some cases, there is no up-to-date, high-quality work on a topic: the topic may be too obscure or too recent to have attracted an author and a publisher. There may be information on the Web—at which point the librarian's conversation with the user is about standards and credibility.

*The Reference Librarian's Bible* skips over some categories of reference tools, and here is why.

- Thanks to the ease of posting information on the Web, many directories have ceased publication, and others are no longer necessary. Some specialized directories remain useful—examples include *Writer's Market*, *Encyclopedia of Associations*, and *American Library Directory*—but few are included here (mainly for government and health-care entities).

- Bibliographies are another casualty of digital information. Library users create custom bibliographies about their topics as part of online searching. Few bibliographies remain of general interest. Of course, *The Reference Librarian's Bible* itself is a bibliography—the added value comes from title selection and annotation.

- Indexing and abstracting tools migrated from print to digital formats and then combined with full-text article tools, offering keyword searching to readers. For example, the printed *Psychological Abstracts* is now *PsycINFO* and *PsycARTICLES*. Those successor online tools are expensive, specialized, and numerous: a large college or university library might offer more than 50 databases of this kind for different academic disciplines. A comprehensive list is outside the scope of this book. That said, a good reference librarian will be aware of subject-specific indexes and general tools such as *Scopus*, *Web of Science*, *Google Scholar*, *PubMed*, and OCLC's *WorldCat*.

- Everyone—including reference librarians—uses search engines like Google, Bing, and Yahoo! but these arguably are not true reference resources. Too much retrieved content fails tests of objectivity, authority, balance, accuracy, and currency. There are unknowns about the relevance algorithms behind ranking of results, including advertisements and sponsored content. If a good reference tool delivers a few highly relevant answers, then these mass-retrieval tools don't fit the mold. Exceptions included here are a few specialized Web portals such as FDsys for government information.

- Library catalogs are in constant use by reference librarians but are not reference sources in the sense of *The Reference Librarian's Bible*. Librarians should understand the marketplace for integrated library systems and online public access catalogs, but those products are not covered here, nor are discovery layers.

## Why You Might Like This Book

The editors hope that this book will be helpful if you are

- a library and information science school graduate student learning about core reference tools. There are tens of thousands of reference resources in print and online, but nearly all fall into certain categories by format or purpose or subject matter. After learning about a representative list of widely held publications, one can look for similar works on other topics.

- a reference librarian seeking the best resource to help answer a patron's question. As already noted, these 500 resources are likely to be on library shelves (or found on the Web). When these specific titles don't provide the answer, similar resources may: *The Reference Librarian's Bible* supports browsing by providing Dewey and Library of Congress call numbers.

- a reference librarian evaluating a library's reference collection, whether for purchasing or weeding. Use *The Reference Librarian's Bible* as a checklist for categories of resources or specific works. When assessing gaps in a local collection, this list provides benchmarks based on the judgment of peers: these 500 titles are widely held. A given library may have alternative editions (older or newer) or alternative formats (print or digital)—other editions may be worth considering.

- a library user searching on your own for resources. Our list should suggest not only specific titles, but the kinds of works available in a reference collection. Browsing by Dewey or Library of Congress call number can lead to other useful books.

## Why You Might Not Like This Book and What to Do about It

Given that libraries own thousands of reference books, it's inevitable that our editorial choices may not be your choices. There are obvious objections to this kind of "top 500" list.

- Some categories of reference tools aren't included, such as most directories (for reasons cited earlier).

- Suggested sources on a given topic may be too old: where are the newer works or at least the newer editions?

- Coverage may seem unbalanced: too few books on some subjects, too many on others. (Why do American libraries collect more books on dogs and birds than on snakes and rodents?)

- Important languages have been left out of the list of bilingual dictionaries.

- Classic works are not on the list because they were not published during the past 20 years.

- Some social issues are included, but some are left out.
- The depth of treatment in selected books is too advanced for likely readers, or not advanced enough.

There is a simple solution to these objections: jot down your ideas about what to include or exclude, expand, or update, and act on your notes when selecting for your library's reference collection. Those notes are the starting point for a "collection development statement" that describes your ideal library reference collection.

- Will most of your library users want e-book access or print? State that preference in guidelines for purchases.
- Do selected directories need to be available? Fine, identify the ones that matter, and state why. Which users are served by these tools?
- If resources on a given topic are too old, what does "too old" mean? In an ideal library, should works on that topic be updated annually, every two years, every five years, and so on?
- Perhaps there are too many books on some topics and too few on others. List the key topics and shop for the best-available works. Listen to your users: what are they looking for and not finding on the shelf?
- Bilingual dictionaries in other languages may be crucial to meet your local needs: consult *ARBA* or other review sources, see what is good, see what is on the market, and buy to fill the gaps.
- If older classic works still matter for your users' needs, keep them on the shelf in reference. How old is "too old"? And how often should you look for updates and replacements?
- If recent social issues are not covered by your book set, look for new works and add them.
- Make sure the presentation of content on a topic is suitable for a likely set of readers.

There is no single best reference collection, of course: each library collection serves its own set of library users. If our list of the 500 best titles sparks an interest in crafting another list that is best for your library, then all is well.

## "Hot Stove League"

Before 24-hour sports television, and before fantasy statistical sports leagues—and especially for baseball—there was "hot stove league," the postseason rehash of the best and the worst. "Name the five best shortstops of all time." "Name the most valuable lineup of the year, the decade or the century." A list of the 500 best reference sources is a hot stove league exercise that can be entertaining, thought provoking, and useful. Think about titles that deserve high marks; compare strengths and weaknesses; and justify those choices. Your own best reference collection will reflect your knowledge of needs and opportunities.

# CHAPTER ONE

# General Reference Works

We use dictionaries, encyclopedias, almanacs, and atlases in our homes and offices, as well as our libraries. Many variations of these familiar publications are on the market. Some awareness of widely held titles—and the characteristics of the most well-regarded examples—can help when selecting materials for a library collection or recommending resources to library users.

## Dictionaries

Dictionaries are among the most widely used and fundamental reference tools: they record, explain, and sometimes influence the meanings behind the words we use. The decisions facing dictionary compilers go beyond simple recording of spelling and definitions. A descriptive dictionary will include nonstandard speech and usage, while a prescriptive dictionary will endorse certain forms and reject others. Dictionary makers also must decide which "new" words and meanings deserve recognition. As our spoken and written languages evolve and grow, so do the dictionaries that reflect those languages. For example, Noah Webster's classic nineteenth-century *American Dictionary of the English Language* helped to support and define the independent identity of the new United States through its language and its linguistic separation from British English.

### English-Language Dictionaries

#### Unabridged Dictionaries

An unabridged dictionary offers accurate, clearly stated, and especially comprehensive coverage of a language based on enormous archives that compile examples of the use of words. A complete new edition of an unabridged dictionary is the work of years or even decades, but updates are common in order to stay current with changes in speech. The average adult is said to know some 25,000 words; a collegiate dictionary typically includes more than 100,000 words; and an unabridged dictionary may define more than 500,000 words. This large total includes obscure and outdated words not in regular use and may include slang and nonstandard expressions. Dictionary editors have answered this key question in various ways: what are the appropriate (and practical) limits of comprehensive coverage of a living language?

1. *Webster's Third New International Dictionary of the English Language, Unabridged,* by Philip Babcock Gove

Publisher: Merriam-Webster, Springfield, MA (2002)

Price: $93.35

Review by Steven W. Sowards—Associate Director for Collections, Michigan State University Libraries, East Lansing.

The publication of *Webster's Third* in 1961 triggered a controversy about coverage. In a nutshell, the editor of *Webster's Third* adopted a descriptive—rather than prescriptive and normative—approach. Famously, the word "ain't" was included, while words that had not seen significant use in two hundred years were removed, along with biographical and geographical coverage (entries typical of so-called encyclopedic dictionaries). The authority of the dictionary now was applied to recording and explaining actual usage, rather than instructing about proper usage. *The American Heritage Dictionary of the English Language* (entry 5) appeared in 1969 as a conservative response, but over time, the descriptive approach has prevailed. Libraries today overwhelmingly own editions of *Webster's Third* to meet the need for an unabridged dictionary. Dictionary entries indicate spelling—including irregular plurals, capitalization, and verb forms—and pronunciation; identify parts of speech; trace the etymology of words and trends in usage, through identification of Middle English and other sources and illustrative dated quotations; signal the "status" of words, such as standard, slang, dialect, or obsolete; and provide one or more definitions. There are no biographical or geographical entries, but line illustrations and tables—such as the signs of the Zodiac, or the metric system—support the main text.

---

Classification: LC PE1625; Dewey 423.

---

2. *Random House Webster's Unabridged Dictionary*

Publisher: Random House Reference, New York, NY (2001)

Price: $238.25

Review by Steven W. Sowards—Associate Director for Collections, Michigan State University Libraries, East Lansing.

First published in 1966 as *The Random House Dictionary of the English Language: The Unabridged Edition*, and updated frequently. This unabridged dictionary adopts the descriptive rather than prescriptive model. As a so-called "encyclopedic dictionary," the text also includes short biographical and geographical entries, numerous maps, and some line illustrations. Dictionary entries indicate spelling, pronunciation, parts of speech, etymological notes, the date of appearance in American speech, and "usage labels" such as archaic, nonstandard, or informal. American regional speech is a priority, and a special section covers "New Words."

A for-fee online version is available at http://unabridged.merriam-webster .com/. Classification: LC PE1625; Dewey 423.

## Desk Dictionaries

Most dictionary users need only a guide to words in common use. While based on publishers' archives and unabridged dictionaries, desk dictionaries have fewer entries and are more portable; they allow users to proceed directly to words and definitions that are most likely to match up with words found in daily use.

3. *Merriam-Webster's Collegiate Dictionary*    6th ed 2018 ou-order
Publisher: Merriam-Webster, Springfield, MA (2003)
Price: $25.95
Review by Staff, Libraries Unlimited.

Some 25 years have passed since the last edition of *Merriam-Webster's Collegiate Dictionary* was published in 1993, and in that time the world and the English language have changed dramatically. The most obvious change has come in the form of the technological boom, but changes have also occurred in the areas of science, business, and slang and popular culture. The 11th edition provides more than 165,000 entries and 225,000 definitions, 10,000 of which are new to this edition. In all, the book boasts more than one hundred thousand changes since the last edition. The basic format of the dictionary remains much the same. The work begins with a preface, an explanatory note and chart, a guide to pronunciation, a list of abbreviations used in the work, and pronunciation symbols.

The work concludes with a 6-page list of foreign words and phrases; biographical names; geographical names; signs and symbols used in astronomy, biology, business, chemistry, computers, and mathematics; and a style guide. The most significant changes occur within the bulk of the volume—"The Dictionary of the English Language." Here users will find new words in the areas of technology (e.g., dot-commer, DSL), business and finance (e.g., identity theft, fast-track), science (e.g., Little Ice Age), health and medicine (e.g., LASIK), and slang (e.g., dead presidents, phat), just to name a few. The editors have taken care to update definitions as well and provide cross-references, etymology, and example phrases. The online edition of *Merriam-Webster's Collegiate Dictionary* allows users to research the meaning and etymology of words, find rhyming words and words of opposite meaning, or browse words beginning or ending with the word. The dictionary also provides a thesaurus, encyclopedic entries, a Spanish-English dictionary, a style guide, and a selection of word games. Users can bookmark, print, or e-mail selected word definitions. Two factors make this dictionary a valuable addition to any academic, public, or school library: the reputation of the publisher and the publication and the accessibility of the reference tool in print, CD-ROM, and Internet formats. Individuals buying this product are provided with a CD-ROM at the back of the volume as well as free access to the dictionary's website for one year. This work is highly recommended.

---

There is a free online version, including a thesaurus, at https://www.merriam-webster.com/. Classification: LC PE1628; Dewey 423.

---

4. *New Oxford American Dictionary*

Publisher: Oxford University Press, New York, NY (2010)

Price: $60.00

Review by Megan W. Lowe—Reference/Instruction Librarian, University Library, University of Louisiana at Monroe.

Five years after the 2nd edition, Oxford University Press has released a new edition of its *New Oxford American Dictionary* (NOAD). Boasting two thousand new words, senses, and phrases, the 3rd edition also highlights the availability of OUP's dictionaries as e-books, apps for iPhones and mobile devices, and on CD-ROM. It also features crisp illustrations—either black-and-white photographs or black pencil sketches. The NOAD includes several new and revised explanatory notes, redesigned pages, and claims to have the most comprehensive and up-to-date coverage of the English language. A new aspect of the 3rd edition is "Word Trends," which tracks changes in word meanings. OUP's in-depth language research program, including the Oxford English Corpus, fuels the comprehensive and up-to-date content. This particular edition also advertises six months of free access to Oxford Dictionaries Online. Despite these positive elements, there are a few negative points. Some of the entries provide additional inset information, which the dictionary identifies as being "encyclopedic information" or "additional information." Why separate this information and not include it in the definition? Moreover, the "Word Trends" do not seem remarkable and function more like slang *see also* entries. Finally, the cover advertises a subscription to Oxford Dictionaries Online; however, the subscription is only free for six months. Admittedly, the subscription allows for a much more interactive, current, and customizable experience, as well as specialized features for language experts and a puzzle solver section for word game and crossword puzzle enthusiasts. While these are certainly interesting extras, it makes one wonder about its usefulness to the average user who simply wants a dictionary, which can be found on the Internet quickly and for free. While the *New Oxford American Dictionary* is undeniably a reputable and useful resource, and the $60 price tag is not too dear, the release of an edition that adds just two thousand to the existent two-hundred-thousand-plus entries just five years after the 2nd edition seems unnecessary. If a library has the 2nd edition, purchasing the 3rd edition would not be necessary. If it is an academic library supporting a linguistics program, the 3rd edition is highly recommended.

Classification: LC PE1628; Dewey 423.

5. *The American Heritage Dictionary of the English Language*
Publisher: Houghton Mifflin Harcourt, New York, NY (2009)
Price: $60.00

Review by Martha Lawler—Associate Librarian, Louisiana State University, Shreveport.

This newest edition of *The American Heritage Dictionary of the English Language* has about ten thousand new words, many of which are from the sciences, social changes, sports, and cultural development, as well as several new biographical and geographical entries. A listing of entries, which include added notes, is provided at the beginning and divided into five types: notes on usage, regional aspects, modern variations of common terms, word histories, and synonyms. These added notes, which serve to enhance the text, are found throughout the overall listing. Immediately preceding the main body of the text are a series of extensive essays that discuss regional patterns of American speech, variation and changes in language, and the significance of Indo-European and Semitic roots, as well as guidelines on using the dictionary and a pronunciation key. The table of contents has a separate listing of charts and tables. An added feature is the use of color and black-and-white illustrations to enhance the definitions.

The 5th edition appeared in 2011. Classification: LC PE1628; Dewey 423.

6. *Cambridge Dictionary* [digital]
Publisher: Cambridge University Press, New York, NY
Price: Free online. Date reviewed: 2017.
URL: http://dictionary.cambridge.org/us/
Review by Staff, Libraries Unlimited.

The *Cambridge Dictionary* allows quick keyboard access to millions of words in addition to a variety of helpful tools that can facilitate the understanding and use of them. The dictionary is available in 11 languages, and addresses English usages in both the United Kingdom and the United States. Users can simply type a word into the prominent search bar to access its definition(s). The word will be displayed accompanied by the figure of speech, phonetic and syllabic transcription, definition(s), and sample sentence. Users can also click the red sound button to hear how the word is pronounced. If the word is incorrectly spelled in the search bar, the site will present a list of similarly spelled or pronounced words from which to choose. Users can also browse or search a large variety of focused dictionaries by clicking the Dictionary tab at the top of the page. These include several English dictionaries (Essential American, Essential British, Learners, etc.) and several translation dictionaries (e.g., English to Korean, etc.). Selecting a dictionary to search will bring up a list of popular searches, allow alphabetical browsing, and list key features of the particular dictionary. The Translate tab offers easy and free translations between languages of up to 160 characters in a field (up to 2,000 per day). The Grammar tab allows users to search, note popular searches, browse alphabetically, and scroll through a list of 7 topics such as Adjectives & Adverbs, Easily Confused Words, and Verbs. Other features on the site include a posted Word of the Day, New Words, and a link to the About Words Blog offering detailed breakdowns of word usage ("Peering and Gawking—Synonyms for the Word 'Look'"), tips on "Describing Landscapes," and much more. Registering (free) with the site allows users to create, save, and share word lists, quizzes, and other items. Advertisements do slightly affect the browsing experience, especially those using similar typefaces and interruptive placement on the page. Nonetheless, this site offers an important and easy-to-use resource for researchers and writers across a range of disciplines. Recommended for public, school, and academic libraries.

Classification: LC PE1628; Dewey 423.

## Etymological Dictionaries

The history of words, and past patterns of word usage, not only helps explain their original meaning in context but demonstrates how the meaning of words can change over time. While many dictionaries indicate the historic roots and early forms of words, etymological dictionaries emphasize this feature. While not listing as many words as an unabridged dictionary, an etymological dictionary may be longer because of the space devoted to presenting multiple examples of usage over time, often through dated quotations from specified sources.

7. *Oxford English Dictionary Online* [digital]
Publisher: Oxford University Press, New York, NY (2013)
Price: Price negotiated by site. Date reviewed: 2013.
URL: http://www.oed.com
Review by Staff, Libraries Unlimited.

The *Oxford English Dictionary* (*OED*) is widely regarded as the accepted authority on the English language, and this online version is keeping with this claim. This easily accessible database provides over 600,000 word meanings, histories, and pronunciations. Quarterly updates revise existing entries and add new words. Researchers will find fascinating commentaries, articles, and scholarly essays, all of which pertain to the English language in the context of use, time and place, the people who shaped the language, and word stories. The Historical Thesaurus contains 800,000 words and meanings in 235,000 entry categories. It is the first comprehensive historical thesaurus ever produced. Librarians will find a fully searchable resource section complete with ways of marketing the *OED* to patrons. The Resource section for teachers is sparse and lacks lesson plans, which would have truly enhanced the database. In spite of this, it is a great addition to both high school and public libraries.

> Many libraries retain the twenty-volume 1989 print-format edition of the *OED* on their shelves. Classification: LC PE1625; Dewey 423.

8. *Shorter Oxford English Dictionary*, by Angus Stevenson
Publisher: Oxford University Press, New York, NY (2007)
Price: $175.00
Review by Christine Rigda—Assistant Professor of Library Administration, University of Toledo, Toledo, OH.

The 6th edition of the *Shorter Oxford English Dictionary* is the 2-volume condensed version of the 20-volume *Oxford English Dictionary* (entry 7) and includes one-third of the coverage of the larger version. As in previous editions, the dictionary shows the etymology of words and their evolving use. It also includes over 80,000 quotations taken from literary works that are highlighted in gray to make them readable. Last edited in 2002, this edition has 25,000 new words and phrases, over 1,300 new illustrative quotations, and for the first time ever Internet sources have been consulted. This edition includes a companion CD-ROM, which, while not as inclusive as the print, has other helpful tools such as sound files and an advanced search function to search for specific authors' quotations, the earliest date of use, and geographical region. On the lighter side, the CD-ROM also has an "anagram solver" and a "crossword solver." The *Shorter Oxford English Dictionary* is an affordable and highly useful resource and continues to deliver the high quality one expects. The addition of the CD-ROM makes it very portable and convenient to use.

---

Classification: LC PE1625; Dewey 423.

---

9. *The Oxford Dictionary of Word Histories*, by Glynnis Chantrell, ed.
Publisher: Oxford University Press, New York, NY (2002)
Price: $25.00
Review by John B. Beston—(former) Professor of English, Santa Fe, NM.

The etymologies in standard dictionaries are usually curt, factual, and minimally informative, conveying little except to those with some knowledge of the history of the language and linguistics. The entries here either condense information in the *Oxford English Dictionary* (entry 7) or make it fuller for clarity, typically adding explanations of origin and supplying reasons for changes in meaning and in form. Chantrell intelligently selects from the bulky information in the *OED* about the word "water" to tell us that it comes from an Indo-European root shared by Russian *voda*, Latin *unda*, and Greek *hudor*, a piece of information that stays in the user's mind by reason of its simplicity. She is particularly good at indicating links that are not obvious between words, as between "charade" and "charlatan." She is not always consistent in that, however, overlooking some clear links: is not "leak" related to German *Loch*? And is not "cheek" related to Russian *shcheka*? Chantrell's love of words is obvious, and it gives a human touch, even a charm, to the book, a quality that dictionaries do not normally have. She assumes an educated audience that has some knowledge of European languages without being trained linguists, and so writes only a brief history of the English language. She does not explain linguistic phenomena like assimilation or *Ausdehnung*; when she uses a term like "metathesis," she immediately defines it. Her list of entries is of course selective, but much less arbitrary than one might expect; the entries are extremely well chosen.

Classification: LC PE1580; Dewey 422.

## Specialty Dictionaries

Fields of study often use their own vocabulary and terminology. Subject-specific dictionaries appear in relevant sections, such as entry 81 for the social sciences, entry 128 for law, entries 388–389 for the sciences, and entries 466–468 for the health sciences.

10. *Dictionary of American Regional English* [digital]
Publisher: Harvard University Press, Cambridge, MA
URL: http://www.daredictionary.com/. Price negotiated by site. Date reviewed: 2015.
Review by Staff, Libraries Unlimited.

The *Dictionary of American Regional English* (DARE), the epic compendium that traces word usage regionally and covers close to 400 years of U.S. speech and writing, is now available online in its entirety. In addition to easy navigation, the site offers several enhancements. Users have access to more than 5,000 audio clips gathered by fieldworkers, access to all the regional maps in one place, the responses to the DARE survey, 1965–1970, and a bibliography of more than 12,000 sources from the seventeenth through the twenty-first centuries. Other features, such as the word wheel, which allows users to browse nearby words (an important part of looking through dictionaries for some), and an ability to save and organize entries, will be welcomed by DARE users. This is a resource that can be used by students and scholars from many disciplines. For institutions, there is a cost of $5,500 for perpetual access; a fee of $1,200 per year for six consecutive years also guarantees perpetual access. For those contemplating purchase, there is a 30-day free trial. Individuals can pay an introductory rate of $150 per year. This website is highly recommended.

Classification: LC PE2843; Dewey 427.

11. *NTC's Dictionary of American Slang and Colloquial Expressions*, by Richard A. Spears

Publisher: National Textbook, Lincolnwood, IL (2000)

Price: $100.00

Review by Jeffrey E. Long—Editor of *SoutteReview Newsletter*, University of Massachusetts Medical School Library, Worcester.

Marking Spears's 1st revision of this work in 5 years, this edition, containing definitions to some 8,500 terms, contains several significant changes. Entries (words, phrases, and sentences) are now arranged alphabetically by letter rather than by word. Although each entry's headword remains in boldface type, the guideword atop each page of the dictionary is now set only in regular type. Also, the 2nd edition's helpful keyword markers have been removed from the phrase-finder index. Less noticeable alterations include the dropping of periods within acronyms and initialisms (e.g., FOB and AC-DC), the elimination of cross-referencing cues between entries in close proximity to each other, and the breaking out of nine sample numerical entries into a listing preceding the "A" entries. Also, within the guide of how to use this dictionary, Spears has regrettably removed more than 15 useful examples and has stricken 4 of the previous edition's 19 points of guidance. As usual, the entries themselves—informal, colorful, and (in some instances) offensive expressions—have been drawn from such diverse sources as college life, street life, medicine, securities markets, the military, and the computer industry. Helpful caveats accompany entries whose use has been objected to regionally or historically, or whose original sense has evolved into self-parody. Regional, cultural, and ethnic contributions along with juvenile lingo and baby talk are represented. A number of entries evoke particular historical times or contexts. For the first time, Spears has included a sizable number of obscene terms among his entries. Not surprisingly, the author has set aside space in this edition's introduction to discuss and defend the presence of such language. Besides this expansion of entries that are sexual or scatological in their subject matter, a substantial number of entries carried forward from the 2nd edition focus on drug abuse and states of intoxication. Several variants of included terms are unaccountably absent from this work. However, Spears does provide a sufficient number of variant spellings for entries. On the other hand, cross-referencing between related entries is spotty. For instance, there are no *see* or *see also* notes between many entries. Some tightening up of entries is also needed. Essentially, there are several redundant entries. Although etymological information is scant in this work, Spears does provide insight into some entries' derivations. Also, it is unfortunate that the pages of this volume are so lightly peppered with pronunciation aids. In summary, this volume is a serviceable and affordable reference work, though less comprehensive than its principal rivals—Green's *Cassell Dictionary of Slang* (Cassell, 1999) and Chapman's *Dictionary of American Slang* (HarperCollins, 1997). However, its value is enhanced when used in tandem with such companions as NTC's *American Idioms Dictionary* (National Textbook, 1993) and, to a lesser degree, NTC's *Dictionary of British Slang and Colloquial Expressions.*

---

Classification: LC PE2846; Dewey 427.

---

12. *The Concise New Partridge Dictionary of Slang and Unconventional English*, by Tom Dalzell and Terry Victor, eds.

Publisher: Routledge/Taylor & Francis Group, New York, NY (2015)

Price: $88.95

Review by Martha Lawler—Associate Librarian, Louisiana State University, Shreveport.

Every entry found in the new Partridge (an update of the 1984 edition) is included here, but without the original citations. The criteria for inclusion are words and expressions that lower the formality of language or express identity with a particular group and are used anywhere in the English speaking world after 1945. All senses of a word are combined in a single entry and some phrases that contain a similarity are combined under a shared concept (e.g., "roll the dice" and "roll on" are listed under "roll"). Entries are listed alphabetically and preceded with prefaces and an introductory essay, which describe the layout and intention of the entries and discuss the basic concept of unconventional English. Each entry is highlighted in bold print, as are any related terms. An indication of the part-of-speech (including if it is used as a nickname), brief definitions, an approximate date of first usage, a cultural or geographical place of origin, and any *see* references comprise the majority of each entry. The alphabetical listing is followed by a brief section of numeric slang. Many of the terms included are offensive, but offer a large cross-section of human expression. Not as thorough as previous editions, this version is a good source for quick reference or as a starting place for future research.

---

Based on the *New Partridge Dictionary of Slang and Unconventional English* of 2006, which is widely held. Another noteworthy recent work is Green's *Dictionary of Slang* (Chambers, 2010) with global coverage of English: full content requires a subscription, but https://greensdictofslang.com/ offers definitions. Classification: LC PE3721; Dewey 427.

---

13. *The Gallaudet Dictionary of American Sign Language*, by Clayton Valli, ed.

Publisher: Gallaudet University Press, Washington, DC (2005)

Price: $49.95

Review by Staff, Libraries Unlimited.

*The Gallaudet Dictionary of American Sign Language* is the most complete sign language dictionary on the market today. More than five years in the making, this dictionary illustrates more than three thousand words, along with finger spellings when appropriate. The full index at the back of the volume allows users to cross-reference words and signs throughout the entire volume. The book is arranged in alphabetic order with each word providing its own illustration. The illustrations are about 2-x-2 inches in size and show the motion of the sign with the use of arrows. The bold printed part of each illustration indicates the conclusion of each sign. The introduction to the work provides valuable information for those unfamiliar with sign language. The word order of sentences in American Sign Language can be very different from that of the spoken word. Often grammatical information is depicted with expression, body language, and surrounding space. The introduction to this volume describes how there are five parts to each sign that make it distinctive from the meaning of other words. These include the hand shape, the location of the hand in relation to the body, the movement of the hand (up and down, or side to side), orientation of the hand (palm up or palm down), and nonmanual signs (facial expressions, eye gaze, body position). The introduction is followed by a section on the importance and use of classifiers in American Sign Language. Classifiers are a critical element of sign language as they allow the signer to express whole phrases with a single sign. Following this is a list of words that are typically spelled out in sign language (e.g., air, ice, mud, nap, social security number). Because sign language cannot easily be learned through the use of a book alone, this volume also comes with a CD-ROM that provides ASL signers demonstrating each of the three thousand signs. The CD-ROM is fully searchable and allows users to quickly view a sign and go directly to its synonyms. This feature makes this book ideal for reference use, instructors, students, and those just learning the language. This volume will become the standard in sign language reference sources and should be made available in public, college and university, and many school libraries.

Classification: LC HV2475; Dewey 419.

14. *Oxford Rhyming Dictionary*, by Clive Upton and Eben Upton

Publisher: Oxford University Press, New York, NY (2004)

Price: $37.95

Review by Jeffrey E. Long—Editor of *SoutteReview Newsletter*, University of Massachusetts Medical School Library, Worcester.

Occupying a humble but useful niche in the pantheon of reference works, the rhyming dictionary is most often consulted by poets, lyricists, and writers of advertising copy and greeting cards. This title is skewed toward those who are conversant with the vocabulary, pronunciation, and spelling of present-day British English. It contains more entries than *Webster's New Explorer Rhyming Dictionary* and has about the same number of entries as *Words to Rhyme With: For Poets and Songwriters*. This volume is divided into two equal parts. The first is the dictionary proper, whose entries are displayed in bicolumnar fashion on each page. Each entry starts with a boldface numerical code heading, followed by English-language expressions that perfectly or imperfectly rhyme with one another. The entries are arranged by these codes in ascending order. Occasionally, an entry will end with a cross-referencing citation (in the form of another numerical code). The expressions listed within each coded cluster are arranged by pronunciation, rather than by spelling. The *Oxford Dictionary of Pronunciation for Current English* (Oxford University Press, 2001) serves as arbiter, in this regard. Expressions having more than one acceptable pronunciation appear in more than one entry. The second half of this book is the index, which consists of an alphabetic list of some ninety thousand entries. Each index entry references one or more of the numerical codes appearing in the dictionary half of the work. Although most of the index entries are standard English expressions, colloquialisms and vulgarisms are also in evidence. Many proper nouns have been included, such as personal names (e.g., Abigail, Jeff), surnames (e.g., Shatner, Spillane), and place-names. (Some of the included American place-names are Massachusetts, San Quentin, Des Moines, and Niagara.) Dozens of well-known trademark names are also sprinkled throughout. It is true that this resource does not boast 150 pages of ancillary features addressing the intricacies and nuances regarding varieties and methods of versification, such as appear in the magisterial *Wood's Unabridged Rhyming Dictionary* (World Publishing Company, 1943). Nevertheless, Oxford has issued a useful, more updated tool that should be considered for inclusion within liberal arts collections lacking comparable works.

An update appeared in 2012 as the *New Oxford Rhyming Dictionary*. Classification: LC PE1519; Dewey 423.

### Thesauri

Unlike other dictionaries, a thesaurus defines a word by setting it in a context of words with similar meanings (synonyms) or very dissimilar words (antonyms or opposite meanings). Peter Mark Roget introduced the concept to modern English usage. An online version of *Roget's 21st Century Thesaurus* at http://www.thesaurus.com/ is free and handy.

15. *Roget's International Thesaurus*, by Barbara Ann Kipfer, ed.

Publisher: HarperCollins, New York, NY (2010)

Price: $19.99

Review by Staff, Libraries Unlimited.

The 7th edition of this valuable reference contains over 464,000 words and phrases and begins with a biography of Peter Mark Roget (1779–1869). This is followed by a usage guide that explains, among other things, the cross-referencing policy and that bold type indicates a word or phrase is the one most commonly used for a topic or idea. There is also a usage guide before the index. The thesaurus can be employed in a variety of ways. A user can consult the "Synopsis of Categories" in the front matter, which groups terms and phrases into 15 categories according to meaning—Feelings, Natural Phenomenon, Behavior and the Will, Arts, and Science and Technology, to name a few. Users may prefer instead to flip to the comprehensive index to locate a term like "dupe," after which appears a list of like terms and where to find them in the thesaurus by category and paragraph number. In the case of dupe, "sycophant" (138.3) is number one in the list. On opening the book to 138.3, users will find sycophant and other like meanings under the main heading "Servility" (in the Feelings category). The index lists phrases by the first letter of the main word, leaving off articles, and does not include many adverbs if the adjectival form of the word is already included. The book has evolved edition to edition, and this one definitely includes terms and phrases useful in a twenty-first-century world. For instance, in the final category, Sciences and Technology, readers will find an extensive amount of information under entry 1073, "The Environment," including a list of related words under "environmental sciences" or specific "environmental pollutants" (carbon dioxide, lead, paint, smoke, etc.). Not just a source for handy synonyms, the thesaurus allows readers to see the nuances of a term or phrase and to find the one that best conveys a particular meaning. The thesaurus works best if used in conjunction with a reliable dictionary. Highly recommended for public, school, and academic libraries.

> One of many similar works and editions. Some versions provide word entries in alphabetical order, rather than by category. Classification: LC PE1591; Dewey 423.

16. *Oxford American Writer's Thesaurus*, by Christine A. Lindberg, comp.

Publisher: Oxford University Press, New York, NY (2008)

Price: $40.00

Review by Martha Lawler—Associate Librarian, Louisiana State University, Shreveport.

This newest edition draws on the expertise of various individuals and on resources produced by the Oxford University Press to present over fifteen thousand main entries, three hundred thousand synonyms, and ten thousand antonyms, along with notes on word associations and writing formats. A preface, foreword, and introduction explain the approach and organization of the information. An example entry is provided with explanations of the various parts of each entry. A list of the labels used to describe the origin and use of each term include a brief description of the label and how it is applied, such as formal, informal, vulgar slang, technical, literary, dated, historical, rare, humorous, archaic, derogatory, and euphemistic terms. A brief discussion of the use of trademarked terms is followed by a discussion of the various featured notes that are offered as aides to choosing the right work and by a listing of note authors. These featured notes are small sidebar items that are interspersed throughout the main listing of entries often with appropriate *see* references and with background discussion on common or historical usage. In the middle of the listing of entries is a separately paged "wordfinder" section that includes an index, thematic lists (such as words about "animals," subdivided by types of animals), a listing of archaic works with definitions, and a listing of literary works that are used in poetry and other elevated forms of writing. At the end of the main listing of entries is a language guide, which discusses grammar, spelling, capitalization, and pronunciation. A very thorough examination and interesting approach makes this thesaurus different and more useful than the usual simple listing of terms.

---

The 3rd edition appeared in 2012. Classification: LC PE1591; Dewey 423.

---

### Visual Dictionaries

Dictionaries confirm spellings and provide definitions for words, but what happens when the reader has an image in mind and needs to know the corresponding word? Visual dictionaries and dictionaries of symbols and signs are built around pictures, labeled to indicate the correct term. The same images may also be used for bilingual dictionaries. Merriam-Webster provides a *Visual Dictionary Online* at http://visual.merriam-webster.com/index.php.

17. *Oxford Picture Dictionary: Monolingual,* by Jayme Adelson-Goldstein and Norma Shapiro

Publisher: Oxford University Press, New York, NY (2016)

Price: $32.00

Review by Staff, Libraries Unlimited.

This is the go-to dictionary for English-language learners, now in its 3rd edition. Author Jayme Adelson-Goldstein organizes the content into twelve sections: Everyday Language, People, Housing, Food, Clothing, Health, Community, Transportation, Job Search, The Workplace, Academic Study, and Recreation. Based on the words people need to use most, as well as on real-life situations, users will find the necessary vocabulary for shopping, childcare and parenting, household repairs, eating out, a garage sale, a medical emergency, buying a car, looking for a job, sports and recreation, and much more. There are more than four thousand words and phrases in total. Pages contain several color illustrations. Sections also include practice activities to reinforce what has been learned. For example, in the third unit on words associated with the home, a two-page color picture of a home with numbers that correlate to fourteen vocabulary words from attic to basement begins the unit. The activities on these pages ask users to practice such things as pointing to different rooms and using phrases like "It's on the floor." For English-language learners, this is an easy-to-use, effective resource by an experienced English-for-Speakers-of-Other-Languages professional. This resource is also a good place for English-language teachers to find curriculum materials. Highly recommended for public, school, and academic libraries.

---

Classification: LC PE1629; Dewey 423.

---

18. *The Firefly Five Language Visual Dictionary*, by Jean-Claude Corbeil and Ariane Archambault

Publisher: Firefly Books, New York, NY (2004)

Price: $49.95

Review by Barbara M. Bibel—Reference Librarian, Science/Business/Sociology Department, Main Library, Oakland Public Library, Oakland, CA.

This beautiful dictionary is full of information in English, French, German, Italian, and Spanish. It contains more than six thousand color illustrations that demonstrate the meanings of thirty-five thousand words. The dictionary has seventeen color-coded chapters representing subject areas: astronomy, the animal kingdom, food and kitchen, society, and more. Each of these is divided into sections and subsections representing increasing degrees of detail. The animal kingdom section begins with a chart of evolution and a diagram of the cell and progresses to the primates. Each picture is clearly labeled in all five languages, including gender designation for non-English nouns. The entry for honeybee includes the morphology and anatomy, the types of bees, a beehive, and a honeycomb on three pages. The entry for lighting in the house section has pictures of every type of light bulb as well as the parts of a lamp socket. This is a wonderful tool for students learning languages because they can use it to find the word to express an idea or find the exact meaning of a word. Since this dictionary only contains nouns, they will need to use it in conjunction with more complete sources to construct full sentences. It is, however, extremely useful for anyone looking for the name of an object and as a communication tool when working with those who speak other languages. It is highly recommended for all reference collections.

Classification: LC P361; Dewey 413.

19. *1000 Symbols: What Shapes Mean in Art & Myth,* by Rowena Shepherd and Rupert Shepherd

Publisher: Thames and Hudson, New York, NY (2002)

Price: $29.95

Review by Amy K. Weiss—Coordinator of Cataloging, Belk Library, Appalachian State University, Boone, NC.

Contrary to its subtitle, this book does not focus on the meaning of shapes or graphic representations. The book uses a Jungian definition of symbols that covers anything with a meaning secondary to its obvious meaning. Symbols are divided into eight categories: "Heaven and Earth"; "Characters and People"; "The Body and Actions"; "Living Creatures"; "Mythical Beasts"; "Flowers, Plants and Trees"; "Objects and Artifacts"; and "Abstracts" (which does include a section on shapes). The purpose of the book is unclear, but it would be more useful to students of religion or mythology than students of art or graphics. Taken as a dictionary of mythology, the book is entertaining. Each short entry (usually two or three paragraphs) encompasses a wide span of religions and cultures. For example, the entry for "Well" discusses the symbolic meaning of wells in ancient Egypt, Cameroon, Japan, China, and in Christianity and Islam. Cross-references to other symbols discussed within each entry are given in bold typeface. Schematic drawings accompany each entry, but art reproductions would have given greater cultural context. There is an alphabetic list of symbols at the front of the book, and a short bibliography in the back. The book would have more scholarly value if there were a more in-depth bibliography or, even better, bibliographic references after each article. This book is suitable for a quick reference, but users in need of more substantial information will need to consult one of the many books on individual mythological or religious systems.

Classification: LC BF458; Dewey 302.

20. *The Complete Dictionary of Symbols,* by Jack Tresidder, ed.

Publisher: Chronicle Books, San Francisco, CA (2004)

Price: $22.95

Review by Terrie L. Wilson—Art Librarian, Michigan State University, East
    Lansing.

This new resource on symbols is set apart from earlier works in that it aims to
be more "worldwide" in its approach. The majority of entries, over two thousand, are related to Classical or Christian themes, but there are some examples
of symbolism from other areas, such as Africa, North and South America, and
Asia. The book is well constructed visually, with the main text offset by notes
and cross-references in the margin printed in a light purple font, making them
more noticeable and presumably more useful. Entries are alphabetical and range
in length from a couple of sentences to an entire page. A few illustrations are
included, perhaps fewer than other similar publications, but this allows the
author to include a larger number of entries. The limited number of illustrations
makes this book more useful to look up terms rather than pictorial symbols.
Two useful finding aids include an index of themes and an index of supplementary words, which highlight terms used in the texts that are not main entries
themselves. Some of the themes included in the index are "agriculture and food,"
"animals," and "hunters and hunting." A useful addition would have been themes
by country, continent, or culture (such as "Africa" or "Incan"). The bibliography,
however, does categorize books by region. The *Complete Dictionary of Symbols* is
easy to use, provides concise but relevant information, and even supplies alternate versions of popular myths. It will be useful as a reference across many disciplines and is highly recommended.

Classification: LC GR391; Dewey 302.

## Bilingual Dictionaries

Bilingual dictionaries can be as comprehensive as multivolume sets
and as limited as vest-pocket phrase books for international travelers. For
many languages, helpful visual dictionaries are on the market. There are
many high-quality bilingual dictionaries: the titles listed here are widely
held, but similar publications from Cassell, Langenscheidt, Duden, Collins, Oxford/Clarendon, Barron's, Hachette, Larousse, Vox, and other
presses also are widely owned and offer good value. Online translation
tools are another option, especially outside the library and on the road.
The languages selected here are commonly in demand, but a given
library will want to assist with other languages as well to meet local needs.

Unabridged and etymological dictionaries also exist for other languages: for example, the *Dictionnaire alphabétique et analogique de la langue français* and *Duden, das grosse Wörterbuch der deutschen Sprache in acht Bänden.* Bilingual visual dictionaries (such as entry 18) can assist language learners.

### Arabic

21. *Oxford Essential Arabic Dictionary*
Publisher: Oxford University Press, New York, NY (2010)
Price: $19.95
Review by Staff, Libraries Unlimited.

The book begins with a preface, followed by abbreviations, a guide to using the dictionary, the Arabic alphabet, Arabic diacritics used in the dictionary, and an English pronunciation guide. There are two main sections, English to Arabic and Arabic to English. Sandwiched in between is a section on Arabic numbers, Arabic verbs, English numbers, and English irregular verbs. This short section conveys the basics of numbers most likely to be needed by speakers and gives a very useful explanation of Arabic verbs, which are characterized as strong or weak rather than regular or irregular. Containing sixteen thousand words and phrases in total, this compact dictionary serves as a valuable resource to commonly used and contemporary vocabulary for learners of Arabic and English, travelers, and businesspersons. The focus is on frequently used words, and should meet the needs of users, except Arabic majors or those doing research in Arabic. Highly recommended for academic and public libraries.

---

The longer *Oxford Arabic Dictionary: Arabic-English, English-Arabic* (2014) includes fifty thousand words, lists of irregular verbs, tables of verb forms in Arabic, examples of idioms and common expressions, and a variety of labels to assist in accurate translation. Classification: LC PJ6640; Dewey 492.

---

### Chinese

22. *ABC Chinese-English Comprehensive Dictionary*, by John DeFrancis and others, eds.
Publisher: University of Hawaii Press, Honolulu, HI (2003)
Price: $59.00
Review by Karen T. Wei—Head, Asian Library, University of Illinois, Urbana.

*ABC Chinese-English Comprehensive Dictionary* is a much-enlarged edition of its earlier version, *ABC Chinese-English Dictionary*, published in 1996. Unlike the traditional Chinese lexicons that are exclusively based on written language and Chinese characters, the present work features entries in single-sort alphabetic order and pinyin romanization based on spoken language. Its editor, a renowned scholar of Chinese, John DeFrancis, has for years advocated this alphabetically based computerized (ABC) dictionary aiming toward the needs of the learner of spoken Chinese. In compiling the current volume, the editors consulted a wide range of works, drew on frequency data from China and Taiwan, and extended coverage quite comprehensively to 196,501 head entries or more than 233,000 total entries in the fields of humanities and social sciences. The book is divided into 4 sections: a brief introduction, a 12-page reader's guide, 1,340 pages of entries, and 10 appendixes. A Kangxi radical chart and a comprehensive radical chart are provided in case the pronunciation is not known. All entries also contain the corresponding characters in simplified and traditional forms. However, Chinese written in pinyin is far more complex; this entirely pinyin-dependent, letter-by-letter organized dictionary may be confusing to some users. Furthermore, despite the "Basic Rules for Hanyu Pinyin Orthography" adopted as the official standard in China in 1996, problems with standardization remain. DeFrancis' tireless effort in promoting and eventually achieving the goal of standardization of pinyin orthography should be beneficial to both Chinese and non-Chinese learning the language. In sum, the present work is a valuable reference tool for the learners of spoken Chinese and scholars of Chinese alike.

---

Classification: LC PL1455; Dewey 495.

---

23. *Oxford Chinese Dictionary*, by Julie Kleeman and Haijiang Yu
Publisher: Oxford University Press, New York, NY (2010)
Price: $75.00
Review by Karen T. Wei—Head, Asian Library, University of Illinois, Urbana.

Using a web-based electronic dictionary compilation system, the *Oxford Chinese Dictionary* is the product of an extensive collaboration between the Oxford University Press and the Foreign Language Teaching & Research Press in China, two of the world's leading dictionary publishers. Comprising more than 2,000 pages, over 300,000 words, 370,000 translations, and tens of thousands of examples, it is likely the largest one-volume bilingual English-Chinese, Chinese-English dictionary in print. The dictionary is derived from corpus research, with Oxford English Corpus as the base for English-Chinese and the Linguistic Variations in Chinese Speech Communities Corpus (from the City University of Hong Kong) for Chinese-English. Not only does the dictionary cover general Chinese and English, it also provides new words from specialized fields such as business, computing, media, medicine, and technology. The entries are in alphabetic order, with Chinese organized by the Pinyin Romanization system and simplified characters used throughout. The dictionary layout is clear and easy to use. An 80-page supplement in-between the English-Chinese and Chinese-English parts provides some useful tools, including model letters; using the telephone, e-mail, and the Internet; basic vocabulary for text messaging; brief chronology of U.S. history; chronology of Chinese dynasties; Chinese kinship terms; pinyin and radical indexes for Chinese; and more. It is accurate, authoritative, and up-to-date. An online version of the dictionary is available for subscription and is updated regularly. This dictionary is highly recommended.

---

Classification: LC PL1455; Dewey 495.

---

### French

24. *Barron's French-English Dictionary/Dictionnaire français anglais*, by Majka Dischler

Publisher: Barron's Educational Series, Hauppauge, NY (2006)

Price: $16.99

Review by Mary Ellen Snodgrass—Freelance Writer, Charlotte, NC.

A valuable addition to the home, classroom, office, and public and school library language shelf, Barron's new two-state English-French dictionary packs a wallop for a few bucks. The easy-on-the-eyes layout varies typefaces with slate-blue entry words, boldface idioms, and judicious use of accent, circumflex, and grave markings. Entries on words like coup, faire, and suite offer numbered idioms to explain uses in a variety of settings. Current terms (skateboarder, tattoo, and mugging in English; *SIDA, jeu video*, and *ours en peluche* in French) assist students and young travelers with common items, front-page news, and up-to-date conversation topics. Valuable additions include seven crayon-bright world maps; postal codes; places and people; acronyms; and a description of the White House, Indians, a king cake, prime minister, All Saints' Day, and the workings of NASA. Back matter summarizes grammar, prefixes and suffixes, geographical terms, symbols, and abbreviations. Colored thumb tabs simplify the search for answers. The sizeable text fits neatly into a plastic cover and comes with a free electronic version to download for PC and SmartPhone use. To the user's detriment is the arcane pronunciation system and the absence of pronunciation guides from each page.

---

Classification: LC PC2640; Dewey 443.

---

25. *Oxford Hachette French Dictionary*, by Marie-Helene Correard and Valerie Grundy, eds.

Publisher: Oxford University Press, New York, NY (2007)

Price: $55.00

Review by Gregory Curtis—Regional Federal Depository Librarian for Maine, New Hampshire, and Vermont, Fogler Library, University of Maine, Presque Isle.

The 4th edition of this work continues the tradition of a well-thought-out and executed bilingual dictionary. Easily accessible with colored, alphabetic markings, the entries provide a wealth of information and examples to the user. For example, codes are provided for varying degrees of formality of usage-standard, informal, very informal, vulgar, or taboo-to aid in word selection. Additional information on French spelling reform, effective French/English communication, living in France, model correspondence of a general and business nature, and French telephone etiquette is provided in the center of the volume. This information makes an easy visual divide between the French to English and the English to French sections of the dictionary. A CD ROM entitled "Speak French" is included with the dictionary to get one started in conversational French. The work is a worthwhile addition to any library or private reference collection, especially considering the price.

Classification: LC PC2640; Dewey 443.

### German

26. *Collins German-English, English-German Dictionary*, by Peter Terrell and Veronika Schnorr. Wendy V. A. Morris and Roland Breitsprecher, eds.

Publisher: HarperCollins, New York, NY (1997)

Price: $55.00

Review by Joseph W. Dauben—Professor of History and History of Science, City University of New York.

This is a new edition of the unabridged *HarperCollins German Dictionary*, which includes 280,000 entries with 460,000 translations. As the editors say, a dictionary is like a map, and this HarperCollins dictionary is a map of the German and English languages, including the language of everyday communication (e.g., newspapers, radio, television), of business, politics, science, technology, literature, and the arts. The previous edition of this dictionary (1990) was published before the demise of the Deutsche Demokratische Republik and the unification of Germany in 1990. However, vocabulary specific to the former East Germany, words like *Stasi* (*Staatssicherheitsdienst*), for example, are marked with DDR to indicate their former significance. Moreover, words whose orthography has changed due to the German Spelling Reform of 1996 are clearly noted with a special symbol. The new spelling forms are listed in a supplement that also gives the old spelling as well as a detailed explanation of the grammatical and linguistic rationale behind the reform. As for the entries themselves, the dictionary is consistently careful to provide straightforward, concise definitions, including idioms and commonly used expressions, along with illustrative phrases showing standard usage of given words. Explicit distinctions to be drawn between different meanings of the same word are clearly indicated, as are informal usages. Special labels indicate whether a word is formal, informal, literary, vulgar, dated, or euphemistic. As for grammatical information, phrasal verbs are clearly identified and genders of German words are clearly shown, as are all relevant grammatical labels. There is even a "Language in Use" section intended to aid users in their own writing of either English or German. Models given include different ways of expressing comparisons, opinions, preferences, and apologies. Examples of job applications, commercial correspondence, and general correspondence; ways to express best wishes, issue invitations or announcements, or construct a *Lebenslauf* or Curriculum Vitae; and even suggestions for basic phrases to use on the telephone are all provided. If there is any shortcoming in this dictionary, it is the lack of any indication of how to break words into their correct syllables, a feature that would be of considerable use to editors and anyone writing in English and German and having to know how to break a word at the end of a line when necessary. Apart from this one exception, the *HarperCollins German Dictionary* will offer users a complete guide to both languages, and should be a basic reference work in any school or public library.

Classification: LC PF3640; Dewey 433.

27. *Oxford-Duden German Dictionary: German-English, English-German*, edited by the Dudenredaktion and the German Section of the Oxford University Press Dictionary Department

Publisher: Oxford University Press, New York, NY (2005)

Price: $55.00

Review by Lawrence Olszewski—Director, OCLC Library and Information Center, Dublin, OH.

Though it has only been a few years since the publication of the 2nd edition of this work, the 3rd edition of the *Oxford-Duden German Dictionary* has implemented some noteworthy changes. It includes over three thousand new up-to-date words, especially from technology and pop culture, such as blogger and reality TV. Headwords are now in blue bold type. It incorporates both the old and the new 1996 reform spellings, cross-referencing the old to the new. A supplemental CD-ROM provides instruction on how to pronounce the language. The special correspondence guide includes traditional guidelines as well as a section on text messaging. A calendar of traditions, festivals, and holidays describes the German ones in English and vice versa; likewise call-outs on the respective cultures of the two countries are described using terminology of the opposite language. This policy makes sense in light of the bilingual nature of the work, but if Americans are looking for a counterpart definition of the Ku Klux Klan in English, they will not find it here. With a total of over 320,000 words, the *Oxford-Duden German Dictionary* is now one of the largest bilingual dictionaries on the market. In terms of size and comprehensiveness, its closest competitor is the *Collins German-English Dictionary* (entry 26). Its currency and readability make it a paragon of modern lexicography, and the Oxford-Duden publishing combination is simply tops.

---

Classification: LC PF3640; Dewey 433.

---

### Hebrew

28. *Modern English-Hebrew Dictionary*, by Avraham Zilkha

Publisher: Yale University Press, New Haven, CT (2002)

Price: $55.00

Review by Anthony Gottlieb—Assistant Clinical Professor, University of Colorado School of Medicine, Denver.

The author wrote this dictionary to address a common problem in most bilin-
gual dictionaries-translating words that have multiple meanings in a way that enables the user to make a distinction between them. As an example of the need for this dictionary, if a student had an assignment to translate "I am traveling home for the spring break" from English into Hebrew, he might accidentally write "I am traveling homeward on the path of the broken metal spring" in Hebrew. Zilkha's dictionary quickly shows the student that, while the word for bedspring or metal coil is *kafitz*, the season is *aviv*. This attractive volume should be quite user-friendly for English-speaking students who will find it handy for Hebrew courses and trips to Israel.

---

Classification: LC PJ4833; Dewey 423.

---

### Korean

29. *NTC's Compact Korean and English Dictionary*, by B. J. Jones and Gene S. Rhie
Publisher: NTC Publishing Group, Chicago, IL (1995)
Price: $40.00
Review by Staff, Libraries Unlimited.

The dictionary begins with the Korean alphabet, a listing of the Korean alphabet and its sounds (for vowels, compounds, consonants, and double letters), a chart of consonants and a chart for vowels for Hangul (the Korean alphabet), Hangul writing models, syllable writing models, and guidelines on the Romanization of Korean. In the main part of the dictionary, the English to Korean section comes first. Altogether, there are more than twenty thousand useful words and phrases (parts of speech are included for English words). The Korean to English section alphabetizes according to Romanized Korean. The Romanized word comes before the word in Korean characters. The dictionary is geared toward real-life situations encountered by tourists, businesspeople, teachers, tourists, and students. A sample of words from the English to Korean section, for example, includes accident, car, invest, power, sell, storm, and where. In the Korean to English section, users will find *ch'atchip* (tea [coffee] house), *hakkyo-e tanida* (attend [go to] school), and *shilmul* (real thing). The format is easy to follow; helpfully, the font is large, which makes it easier to read the Korean characters. The ease of use, combined with the content, makes this a highly recommended text for public and academic libraries.

Classification: LC PL937; Dewey 495.

### Latin

30. *Oxford Latin Desk Dictionary*, by James Morwood, ed.
Publisher: Oxford University Press, New York, NY (2005)
Price: $19.95
Review by Staff, Libraries Unlimited.

The 1st edition of this book (1994) was partially in answer to the need for a more accessible and affordable version of the larger *Oxford Latin Dictionary*. There are some notable changes to this 2nd edition, including an extension of the scope of the dictionary from the so-called Golden Age of Latin (100 B.C.E.—the death of Livy) to include Plautus and Terence, as well as Pliny the Younger and Tacitus. In addition, the dictionary now incorporates many words from late and medieval Latin. An appendix summarizes significant differences between

Classical Latin and later forms of the language. Of special interest are the more than one hundred textboxes in the Latin to English section that cover interesting points of grammar and culture. For example, one textbox explains that "*decuria*," defined as a group of ten, was generally a division of the cavalry. An additional change was the expansion and redesign of the grammar section; this dictionary uses the order of cases generally taught in the United Kingdom. The front matter includes "The Pronunciation of Classical Latin" (consonants, vowels, numbers of syllables, and stress), "Abbreviations," and "Using the Dictionary." The first, and, according to the editor, most important section, is Latin into English. Sandwiched between this section and the English into Latin part is the "Summary of Grammar." This section does not give guidance on the word order and constructions of Latin—this can be found in the Oxford companion *Latin Grammar* (1999). The dictionary's grammar section has information on nouns, adverbs, adjectives, and verbs. In this middle chunk of the dictionary, users will also find information on Roman dates and times, weights and measures, and money, as well as metres of Roman verse. Following the English into Latin portion, users will find "Historical and Mythological Names" (names are followed by a brief description); "Geographical Names" (with definitions—e.g., Mona is defined as (1) Isle of Man; (2) Isle of Anglesey). As an extra bonus, the dictionary contains nearly four pages of "The Latin Writers," including such luminaries as Augustine, Jerome, and Virgil. For each person, the dictionary provides life and death dates, the author's major work(s), and more. There is also a timeline of important dates in Roman history from 753 B.C.E. to the 1453 C.E. conquest of Constantinople and the aforementioned notes on "Late and Medieval Latin." Several black-and-white maps of the Roman world conclude the work. Highly recommended for public, school, and academic libraries.

Classification: LC PA2365; Dewey 473.

### Russian

31. *The Oxford Russian Dictionary*, by Marcus Wheeler, Boris Unbegaun, and Paul Falla, eds. Revised by Della Thompson

Publisher: Oxford University Press, New York, NY (2000)

Price: $60.00

Review by Koraljka Lockhart—Publications Editor, San Francisco Opera, San Francisco, CA.

Having encountered several sloppily put-together dictionaries in recent years, it is great to report on one that is practically perfect. This edition, completely revised, features over 185,000 words and phrases and 290,000 translations, all aimed at providing a reliable resource for definitions in contemporary Russian and English. Because the dictionary originated in the United Kingdom, some of the English terms, such as cash machine, are provided. The coverage of contemporary terms is extensive, and it includes words such as hyperinflation, multimedia, road rage, sound card, spacecraft, and proactive. Gay exists in both meanings of the word. Some of the selected phrases are quaint, such as "he drove smash through the shop window," "the gas is escaping," "what kind of box do you want?" or "he kissed away her tears," but they are all translated correctly. The layout is attractive and the typeface (both in Cyrillic and Latin) is user-friendly (yes, user-friendly is also in the dictionary). This dictionary is a superior achievement.

The 4th edition appeared in 2007. Classification: LC PG2640; Dewey 491.

### Spanish

32. *The American Heritage Spanish Dictionary: Spanish/English, Inglés/Español*
Publisher: Houghton Mifflin Harcourt, New York, NY (2001)
Price: $26.00
Review by Joseph W. Dauben—Professor of History and History of Science, City University of New York.

This dictionary differs from most Spanish/English-English/Spanish dictionaries in that it emphasizes American English and Latin American Spanish. It covers more than 120,000 words and phrases, including terms commonly used in technology and on the Internet, and includes such areas of language interest as medicine, sports, ecology, and popular culture. Various senses of a word are distinguished, numerous model sentences are given to illustrate meaning and usage, all entries are fully syllabicated with pronunciation guides for English words, and gender specifications are given for Spanish words. In terms of grammar, tables of English and Spanish irregular verbs are provided, and words presenting special grammatical difficulties are keyed to notes on grammar and usage in both parts of the dictionary. Also useful are tables for weights, measures, and common abbreviations in both Spanish and English.

Classification: LC PC4640; Dewey 463.

33. *Oxford Spanish Dictionary: Spanish-English, English-Spanish*, by Beatriz Galimberti Jarman and Roy Russell, eds.
Publisher: Oxford University Press, New York, NY (2008)

Price: $49.95

Review by Joanna M. Burkhardt—Head Librarian, College of Continuing Education Library, University of Rhode Island, Providence.

The *Oxford Spanish Dictionary*, now in its 4th edition, offers extensive assistance for both English and Spanish speakers by including a wide array of definitions and related information about words in both languages. The 1st edition was compiled to reflect Spanish and English as spoken or written in the 1990s. The 4th edition updates existing entries and adds new words and senses of words. A special section on practical problems in communication, especially for those living in a foreign country, has been updated and expanded. The differences between English and Spanish require a good deal of explanation when conveying both the definition of a word and the sense or senses in which it can be used. This dictionary provides an overwhelming amount of information to make those explanations available. Abbreviations used are spelled out inside the front and back covers. A ten-page section explains how entries are structured, including headword and definitions, grammatical information, labels, examples, translations, and cross-references in both languages. This is followed by a twenty-two-page explanation of how to use the dictionary, including the interpretation of all signs and symbols, explanation of regional and local usage, and how cross-references are constructed. The general rules of pronunciation for Spanish and English complete the introductory material. Approximately three hundred thousand words and phrases in English and Spanish are defined in the body of the work. Entries are in strict alphabetic order, including acronyms. Selected words are given extended explanation and/or put in context in box insets scattered throughout the dictionary. Separating the Spanish-English and English-Spanish sections is a sixty-eight-page section entitled "Guide to Effective Communication." This section provides advice on the effective use of the language, difficulties in each language, variations in each language, transitional words and phrases, living in a Spanish/English speaking country, correspondence on various topics with sample letters, using the telephone, electronic messaging, and using the Internet. The final section of this dictionary includes Spanish verb tables, giving the conjugation of the most common verbs, lists of irregular verbs for each language, a glossary of grammatical terms, and an index to inset boxes. The dictionary also comes with a CD-ROM. While a beginner could use this dictionary to find a definition, the complex nature of the entries makes really understanding all the possible uses for a word a matter for more advanced linguists. The numerous abbreviations, symbols, signs, and numbers might become more meaningful with constant use, but for a casual reader, finding out how to read an entry may take longer than is worthwhile. The section of practical advice on living and communication in a foreign country is useful, but the dictionary is not the first place this reviewer would look for that type of information. The size and weight of the volume indicate that this dictionary would be used in a personal or institutional library. It is not easily portable. This Spanish dictionary is recommended for advanced students and reference collections in public, language, and academic libraries.

---

Classification: LC PC4640; Dewey 463.

---

34. *The University of Chicago Spanish-English Dictionary. Diccionario Universidad de Chicago Inglés-Español*, by Carlos Castillo, Otto F. Bond, David A. Pharies, and María Irene Moyna

Publisher: University of Chicago Press, Chicago, IL (2012)

Price: $15.00

Review by Susan J. Freiband—Associate Professor, Graduate School of Librarianship, University of Puerto Rico, San Juan.

This new edition of a well-known, concise Spanish-English/English-Spanish dictionary has been substantially revised, updated, and expanded since the last edition ten years ago. It includes six thousand brand-new entries (bringing the total up to eighty-six thousand entries), divided into two sections, each with a list of abbreviations, guide to pronunciation, and notes on grammar. The brief definitions include pronunciation (English), grammatical category, and illustrative phrases. There is no systematic attempt to distinguish regional usage, in English or in Spanish. The dictionary is well organized and easy to read, using two columns and boldface for the headword and phrases. There is a short preface and helpful introduction (both in Spanish and English) on how to use the dictionary. It clearly describes the order of entries, spelling, omissions, and structure of entries. The dictionary is aimed for the American learner of Spanish and the Spanish-speaking learner of American English, at any level of fluency. It aims to provide a core, up-to-date vocabulary, one that is concise yet comprehensive enough to satisfy both beginners and advanced speakers. Its scope is broad, and this edition has an emphasis on including new terms in science, digital technology, medicine, business, politics, and popular culture. Among abridged Spanish-English/English-Spanish dictionaries, this new edition of a classic, authoritative work provides a useful tool for a large and growing audience in the United States as well as in other parts of the Spanish-speaking world. It is an important addition to reference collections, particularly in high school, community college, and public libraries.

---

Classification: LC PC4640; Dewey 463.

---

### Vietnamese

35. *NTC's Vietnamese-English Dictionary*, by Đình Hoà Nguyen

Publisher: National Textbook, Lincolnwood, IL (1995)

Price: $17.95

Review by Binh P. Le—Reference Librarian, Abington College, Pennsylvania State University, University Park.

This dictionary was first published in 1955 under the title *Vietnamese-English Vocabulary* with some nine thousand Vietnamese words. It was designed as a study aid for U.S. students of the Vietnamese language. By the mid-1960s, in response to the escalation of the United States' involvement in Vietnam, this dictionary was greatly expanded. The work under review is the updated version of this latter edition. By far, this is the most comprehensive and perhaps the best Vietnamese-English dictionary available. It contains approximately fifty thousand Vietnamese words, morphemes, compound words, and phrases. Also, unlike previous editions, this volume includes more sociopolitical, economic, literary, and Vietnamization of English and French terms (e.g., *ga-lo-ri* [gallery]). Entries are accompanied by their English equivalents and, where appropriate, synonyms, antonyms, and usage are provided. Also included are a guide to pronunciation and a fifty-page supplement of new Vietnamese words. Native Vietnamese speakers who have been living abroad for some time should find the supplement useful. The paper, printing, and binding of the dictionary are good, and the price is reasonable. Overall, this is an excellent resource. It should prove useful not only for students of the Vietnamese language, travelers, and businesspeople, but also for Vietnamese users.

Classification: LC PL4376; Dewey 495.

## Encyclopedias

An encyclopedia organizes and summarizes general knowledge or knowledge related to a particular topic, as understood at a particular time and place. Writing about encyclopedias in his own landmark *Encyclopédie* of 1755, Denis Diderot says that "the purpose of an encyclopedia is to collect knowledge disseminated around the globe; to set forth its general system to the men with whom we live, and transmit it to those who will come after us" (quotation from the online "Encyclopedia of Diderot & d'Alembert Collaborative Translation Project" hosted by Michigan Publishing and the University of Michigan Library). Because knowledge grows and advances, encyclopedias typically appear in a series of updated editions: today, online texts can be updated continuously. In a climate in which factual information may be disputed, the authorship and therefore the authority of an information source matters. Encyclopedias can claim authority through the reputation and credentials of their brands, editorial teams, and publishers.

36. *World Book Online* [digital]

Publisher: World Book, Chicago, IL

Price: Price negotiated by site. Date reviewed: 2016.

URL: http://worldbookonline.com/

Review by Peg Billing—District Librarian, Tomahawk School District, Tomahawk, WI.

*World Book Online* is a suite of digital tools that includes an encyclopedia, atlas, dictionary, digital learning tools, interactive activities, study aids, and curriculum guides. Information is offered on three levels: Kids, Student, and Advanced; each with grade-appropriate support and digital media that includes pictures, video, and maps, links to websites, and games. Kids presents interactive opportunities for learning and exploration geared to early and mid-elementary; Student focuses on middle-level learners with information organized into easy-to-locate areas. A well-defined research center guides students through the research process. Advanced features include primary sources, world newspapers, today in history, online book archive, and other tools. Pathfinders and research guides allow search and exploration to suit student needs. Searching is user-friendly and simplified for student success; illustrations and graphics within all levels are interactive. The range of materials offers easy integration into all learning environments and classroom activities, while engaging students through inquiry-based learning. Recommended.

> The updated 2018 print version in twenty-two volumes appeared in November 2017. *World Book* is the last major encyclopedia still sold in print format. Classification: LC AE5; Dewey 031.

37. *Britannica Online* [digital]

Publisher: Encyclopaedia Britannica, Chicago, IL

Price: Price negotiated by site. Date reviewed: 2012.

URL: http://www.britannica.com

Review by Charlotte Ford—Assistant Professor, School of Library and Information Science, San Jose State University, San Jose, CA.

*Britannica Online*, the Internet version of *Encyclopaedia Britannica*, made its first appearance in 1994. It includes the full text of the articles that were provided in the print *Britannica* (the print publication ceased in 2010), plus many additional features: videos, timelines, access to Merriam-Webster's dictionaries and thesauri, links to over three hundred thousand magazine and journal articles (as well as to selected websites), and news headlines. Basic and advanced search options are provided as well as an index and an "A-Z browsing" list of entries. Britannica products are offered to libraries in various subscription packages; the public library package, for instance, includes access to the content of *Encyclopaedia Britannica*, *Britannica Elementary Encyclopedia*, and *Compton's Encyclopedia*, along with many of the "extras" enumerated above. Free access to a much abbreviated version, *Britannica Concise Encyclopedia*, is available without a subscription at their website. *Britannica Online*'s strengths lie in the scope of its coverage and the level of its writing; many experts have contributed to it over the years, and it remains impressively authoritative. A box for suggesting changes to content has recently been added, reflecting a growing understanding of the ways in which public participation can add value to an encyclopedia.

---

A limited subset of online content is available without fees. The twenty-nine-volume 11th edition of 1910 is regarded as a landmark of reference: no longer subject to copyright, cheap reproductions (including e-books) are available, but of course the content is a snapshot of the knowledge (and ignorance) current in Europe and America a century ago. The 2010 edition was the last in print format. Classification: LC AE5; Dewey 031.

---

38. *Wikipedia* [digital]

Publisher: Wikimedia Foundation, San Francisco, CA

Price: Free online. Date reviewed: 2007.

URL: http://www.wikipedia.org/

Review by Charlotte Ford—Assistant Professor, School of Library and Information Science, San Jose State University, San Jose, CA.

*Wikipedia* was established by Jimmy Wales in 2001 as a free Web-based encyclopedia that is collaboratively written and open to editing by anyone with an Internet connection. A favorite source of general information for many Web-surfers, its strengths include the provision of up-to-date information on a tremendous range of topics: as of early 2007, over 5.5 million articles (1.6 million of them in English) written by 75,000 active contributors. *Wikipedia* is available in 10 major languages; it is extensively hyperlinked, easily searchable (and browsable), and articles from the site can also be retrieved through major search engines such as Google or Yahoo. Of course, there are disadvantages to having such an open source; as stated in *Wikipedia* itself, "articles and subject areas sometimes suffer from significant omissions, and whilst misinformation and vandalism are usually corrected quickly, this does not always happen." The writing style and level also varies greatly. On the other hand, a 2005 study published in *Nature* found that *Wikipedia* "comes close to *Britannica* [entry 37] in terms of the accuracy of its science entries"; reviewers of 42 articles appearing in each of the publications found 4 serious errors and 162 minor problems in *Wikipedia* entries, compared to 4 serious errors and 123 minor problems in *Encyclopaedia Britannica* entries. (*Encyclopaedia Britannica* has refuted the findings.) Despite its shortcomings, *Wikipedia* does provide a useful starting point for information on some topics, at no cost. However, patrons using this source should be made fully aware of its "grassroots" nature, and the problems that this can sometimes create.

> *Wikipedia* has grown to some forty million articles, with content in more than two hundred languages. While the accuracy of content has been regarded as acceptable, balance in the selection of topics and the depth of treatment is skewed by the demographics (largely young and male) of the volunteer contributor base. For *Wikipedia*, "authority" also resides in ongoing collective review and revision of articles by a mass user base. Classification: LC AE5; Dewey 031.

## Almanacs and Calendars

Classical and medieval almanacs recorded astronomical information. Modern almanacs also include calendars and "perpetual calendars," lists of important dates, tide tables, weather information, and planting advice. As mini-encyclopedias—because they also may feature maps, color plates for flags, and summaries of recent events—almanacs are handy, low-cost sources for current information about countries, election results, or sports championships.

39. *The World Almanac and Book of Facts*

Publisher: Infobase Publishing, New York, NY

Price: $14.99

Review by Gregory A. Crawford—Head of Public Services, Penn State Harrisburg, Middletown, PA.

Now in its 150th year, *The World Almanac and Book of Facts* remains a core resource for libraries and for researchers. The 2017 edition continues the excellence of the series and is a compendium of statistics from the memorable year of 2016. Of special interest are the results of the 2016 U.S. elections, as presented in the year in review section. The editors have provided a good narrative of the presidential election while also giving a breakdown of the 2016 and 2012 votes by state and county. In addition, the results of senatorial, representative, and gubernatorial races are reported. The remainder of the year in review gives a chronology of events (from November 1, 2015, to October 31, 2016), obituaries of significant individuals who died during the year, key congressional activities, U.S. Supreme Court decisions, notable quotes, and historical anniversaries. The bulk of the work provides updated statistics from nine realms: economy, business, and energy; health and vital statistics; personalities, arts, and awards; science and technology; consumer information; U.S. history, government, and population; world history and culture; nations of the world; and sports. The sports section includes special information from the 2016 Summer Olympic Games held in Brazil. This is an indispensable ready reference tool and should be on the reference shelves of every school, public, and academic library.

> Annual. There is an online for-fee version. Classification: LC AY64; Dewey 310.

40. *Information Please Almanac Online* [digital]

Publisher: FEN Learning, Boston, MA

Price: Free online. Date reviewed: 2013.

URL: http://www.infoplease.com

Review by Adrienne Antink, Medical Group Management Association, Lakewood, CO.

The *Information Please Almanac* online (http://www.infoplease.com) includes information from the *Time Almanac* and the *ESPN Sports Almanac*. The almanac information is integrated with the *Random House Webster's Unabridged Dictionary* (entry 2) and the *Columbia Encyclopedia* (6th edition) into a single reference source with a wealth of facts. The search page offers several ways to find information, including a keyword box, an index of topics, and a directory of information divided into the following categories: World and News, United States, History and Government, Biography, Sports, Arts and Entertainment, Business, Calendars and Holidays, Health and Science, Homework Center, and Fact Monster. One can click the Daily Almanac link near the top of the search page to access such features as "This Day in History," "Today's Word Quiz," "Today's Weather Fact," and "Today's Birthdays." The site is continuously updated, offering more recent information than can be found in the paper edition.

> Published in print as *Time Almanac* from 1999 to 2013; ceased in print in favor of this "Infoplease" online version. Classification: LC AY64; Dewey 310.

## 41. *The Old Farmer's Almanac*
Publisher: Yankee Publishing, Inc., Dublin, NH
Price: $7.95
Review by Staff, Libraries Unlimited.

*The Old Farmer's Almanac*, published in print since 1792, provides traditional almanac content, including astronomical information, weather forecasts, and gardening tips. It offers a freely available companion site that has been online since 1996 (http://www.almanac.com). The weather pages in the almanac offer detailed seven-day forecasts for thousands of cities and towns across the United States and Canada. A searchable weather history database contains weather conditions for two thousand locations in the United States and Canada for any date from 1946 to the present. The weather features page explains such phenomena as tornadoes and droughts. Gardening pages include frost charts, planting tables, and source lists for seeds and flowers. Astronomy pages offer charts and tables for various celestial events, including moon phases, comet and meteor appearances, and rise/set times for the sun, moon, and planets. Cook pages, household pages, and forums are also available.

> Annual. The online version at http://www.almanac.com/ has some free content. Classification: LC AY81; Dewey 310.

## 42. *Chase's Calendar of Events*
Publisher: Rowman & Littlefield, New York, NY
Price: $89.00
Review by Michael Levine-Clark—Collections Librarian, University of Denver, Denver, CO.

For 50 years *Chase's Calendar of Events* has been an indispensable source of information about events happening on a particular date. Although it is easy to find information in countless sources, including the free Internet, about the events recorded in *Chase's*, there is no other source that allows you to locate that information by date. Some 4,000 birthdays, 1,400 historical anniversaries, over

800 holidays, and various other important days, weeks, and months are recorded chronologically, each with a brief description. In addition to the chronology making up most of the book, there is a section at the beginning of the volume that spotlights people and historical events, as well as a range of almanac-like information in the back. This latter section includes such information as state and provincial abbreviations and the names of the current U.S. senators and governors-information that could easily be found elsewhere and for which some-one would likely not consider this source. . . . In most cases, events can easily be found using the print index. . . . This is still a valuable source, although some of the extra information at the rear of the volume is not necessary. All libraries will want to acquire *Chase's Calendar of Events*.

---

Annual. Prior to 1994, the title was *Chase's Annual Events*. Classification: LC GT4803; Dewey 394.

---

## Atlases and Geography

Basic questions about place—"Where is it?" "How big is it?" "How far away is it?" and "How do I get there?"—call for a variety of reference tools. A helpful reference collection can also include a world globe because spatial relationships on a round planet are not always clear when displayed on the flat surfaces of books or computer screens.

## Atlases

A typical atlas has one or more themes such as the geography of a region, the geography of an entire planet, historical events, geological infor-mation, travel assistance, economic facts, or social and cultural profiles. Statistics, tabular data, and commentaries often complement the maps.

### *Atlases of the World*

43. *The Times Comprehensive Atlas of the World*
Publisher: HarperCollins, New York, NY (2011)
Price: $200.00
Review by Staff, Libraries Unlimited.

The finest general world atlas available is *The Times Comprehensive Atlas of the World*. *The Times* is regarded as the highest-quality English-language world atlas, providing balanced geographical coverage. The scales of many maps are generally larger and show greater detail than the *Hammond World Atlas* or the *Oxford Atlas of the World* (entry 44). Its map pages, produced by the highly respected firm of Collins Bartholomew, provide excellent regional maps to answer all but the most specialized reference questions. This atlas is divided into three general sections: an introductory section including general physical information and thematic world maps, a series of regional maps showing political and physical features, and a final section that is a large index-gazetteer with more than two hundred thousand names. Locations are indexed by map page, a map-page grid system, and latitude and longitude.

---

The 14th edition appeared in 2014. Classification: LC G1021; Dewey 912.

---

44. *Oxford Atlas of the World*

Publisher: Oxford University Press, New York, NY (2011)

Price: $89.95

Review by Adrienne Antink, Medical Group Management Association, Lakewood, CO.

The *Oxford Atlas of the World* represents a more traditional atlas, similar to that of *The Times Comprehensive Atlas of the World* (entry 43). Its use of color tints to show relief results in large patches of purples and browns to show mountains. To its credit, it provides an encyclopedia of geographical information in its introductory pages, with color maps illustrating climate, the greenhouse effect, health, population and migration, global conflicts, and more, and also provides a glossary of geographical terms and a gazetteer of nations. This atlas has a large collection of world metropolitan maps and a separate index with more than eighty-three thousand place-names. There is something about a large atlas that is multicolored, comprehensive in its coverage, and exciting in the presentation of the content, that draws users to open the book and explore. This volume aptly fills that description.

---

Updated annually. The 23rd edition appeared in 2016. Classification: LC G1021; Dewey 912.

---

45. *National Geographic Atlas of the World*

Publisher: National Geographic Society, Washington, DC (2010)

Price: $175.00

Review by Benet Steven Exton, St. Gregory's University Library, Shawnee, OK.

The *National Geographic Atlas of the World* has a long tradition of publication. This latest edition, the 9th, brings the world up to date, including new regional maps for several areas such as Afghanistan and Pakistan, the Korean Peninsula, and Iraq and Iran. Maps include a large number of place names. Arrangement is by continent, including satellite, political, and physical maps, and a section with country summaries, with official flags and demographic and economic data for all independent nations arranged alphabetically. Political maps for regions and specific countries follow. New thematic maps treating environmental issues, natural resources, and human culture have been added as well as maps of space, the ocean floor, and Earth's poles. The index includes more than 150,000 entries for cities and natural features.

> The 10th edition appeared in 2014, with updated maps of England, Wales, Scotland, and Ireland; new regional maps of Australia; and additional coverage of Africa and regions near the Mediterranean Sea. Classification: LC G1021; Dewey 912.

46. *Google Maps* [digital]
Publisher: Google, Mountain View, CA
Price: Free online. Date reviewed: 2017.
URL: https://www.google.com/maps/
Review by Staff, Libraries Unlimited.

*Google Maps*, the go-to site for those in search of directions from point A to point B, has many useful tools that make navigation a snap. By simply typing in an address or the name of a place, *Google Maps* will produce directions for driving, walking, or using public transportation. Users can choose to view the maps in satellite or terrain mode. For some places, street views are available. As an online tool, *Google Maps* can be continuously updated (even showing current levels of road traffic for some places). Users can adjust the scale of coverage by zooming in and out. Drivers can get turn-by-turn instructions via cell phone or can print out maps prior to a trip. Google provides previews for some routes. *Google Maps* can also serve as an interactive online travel guide. Tourist attractions, restaurants, and other places of business may include links to handy information such as hours of operation, photographs, and reviews. Users can make their location publicly available, submit reviews and photographs, save a route or place in a personalized list, and more.

> Classification: LC G1021; Dewey 912.

47. *MapQuest—Maps, Driving Directions, Live Traffic* [digital]
Publisher: MapQuest, Denver, CO
Price: Free online. Date reviewed: 2017.
URL: https://www.mapquest.com/
Review by Staff, Libraries Unlimited.

This multifunctional website offers users an enhanced mapping experience for locations throughout the United States. Employing the open source Open-StreetMap platform as a foundation, *MapQuest* contains information on thousands of U.S. locations from the smallest park to the largest metropolis and provides a number of tools for use in studying routes, geography, local resources, etc. Users can select from a number of options on the drop-down menu on the left tool bar, or work directly from the large U.S. map graphic. The Map tab offers a search bar where users can enter their desired location. It is important to enter precise information (e.g., name, address, city, state, etc.) due to the commonality of many place-names throughout the country. The graphic will then show the pinned location alongside a number of details and options, such as street address, phone number, website link, and directions. The Get Directions tab on the main menu allows users to map routes as well. Users simply enter the location from which they are starting the trip with any potential stops, in addition to the location they have mapped. The site will display any available routes, estimate fuel costs, and more. The Route Planner tool allows users to incorporate up to 26 separate locations within a trip and estimate time and distance. The map graphic can be layered with a good variety of local services and attractions relating to things like food, gas, hotels, shopping, coffee, airports, hospitals, and parks. Users can manipulate the map by zooming in or out, expanding the view to fit the entire page, incorporating traffic information and/or employing a satellite view. Registered users may incorporate new locations into the map, and can Create a Custom My Map (printable and shareable) from the menu as well. The site also provides local travel tips and national park guides, and allows users to directly book hotels, flights, and rental cars with a partner business. It is important to note that *MapQuest* will highlight partner businesses (e.g., Hampton Hotels) in its search fields or layering function, and that a number of advertising banners will appear throughout the browsing experience. Nonetheless, *MapQuest* is an excellent, easy-to-use site.

In addition to online street maps, *MapQuest* provides a search feature to locate nearby businesses, directions for walking or driving, real-time traffic congestion reports, satellite imagery, and links to travel booking sites. Maps can be printed or viewed on a smart phone. Classification: LC G1021; Dewey 912.

48. *Perry-Castañeda Library Map Collection* [digital]

Publisher: University of Texas Libraries, Austin, TX

Price: Free online. Date reviewed: 2004.

URL: http://www.lib.utexas.edu/maps/

Review by Staff, Libraries Unlimited.

The *Perry-Castañeda Library Map Collection* at the University of Texas, Austin, is an invaluable site for teachers and students at all levels. The physical map collection has more than 250,000 maps, approximately 20 percent of this collection is currently available online, and the library intends to add more sources as time and money allow. Most of the maps are in the public domain, and those that are under copyright protection are clearly marked. There are 14 map categories: world, Africa, Americas, Asia, Australia/Pacific, Europe, Middle East, Polar/Oceans, Russia/Republics, U.S., Texas, Historical, Thematic, and Topographic. There is information here for geographers, historians, political scientists, anthropologists, and scholars in numerous other fields. Historians, for example, will delight in the 1919 map of Cuba and the 1893 map of St. Petersburg. In addition, the site has links to many other map-related sites.

> As a live virtual atlas, the library home page provides an evolving selection of topical maps keyed to current news events: some from the University of Texas collection and others from global Web sources. Classification: LC G1021; Dewey 912.

### Atlases of the United States

49. *Oxford Atlas of the United States*

Publisher: Oxford University Press, New York, NY (2006)

Price: $27.95

Review by Staff, Libraries Unlimited.

This atlas continues to be a valuable addition to public and academic libraries needing the most up-to-date geographical information. The work is organized into four sections. "North American Geography" provides statistical information on topics such as politics, energy, and minerals, climate and weather, indigenous people, immigration and population changes, urbanization and agricultural uses of land, and languages and religion in North America. Following this is a section entitled "United States," which provides detailed maps of the regions and each of the fifty states in the United States as well as Puerto Rico and the U.S. Pacific Territories. Next is a section of city maps that provides detailed maps of fifteen major cities. One of the most useful sections of the atlas is the gazetteer, which provides general information on the state (e.g., nickname, state bird, state flower), a brief history of the state, information on the state's capital, and a side bar with statistical information on the population, businesses, and geography. The index provides access to the thirty thousand place-names in the atlas, along with latitude/longitude and letter/figure grid references. The *Oxford Atlas of the United States* is well executed and accurate. It should be a useful addition in academic, public, and school libraries.

---

Classification: LC G1200; Dewey 912.

---

50. *Road Atlas: United States, Canada and Mexico*
Publisher: Rand McNally, Skokie, IL
Price: $14.95
Review by Staff, Libraries Unlimited.

The *Rand McNally Road Atlas* packs a large amount of information into a compact and affordable guide. The inside front cover contains a map legend, followed by a nice bonus, six suggested "best of" road trips to northern New England, the Blue Ridge Parkway, Miami and the Florida Keys, Lake Michigan, Canyon Country, and San Francisco and the California central coast. Following is the handy mileage chart that covers ninety North American cities and U.S. national parks. Readers can find more mileages at http://maps.randmcnally.com/mileage_calculator. Front matter also provides quick map references for states and provinces as well as selected cities and national parks, which allows readers to jump quickly to their desired location. Following is a two-page map of the United States. State maps appear in alphabetic order, with map insets of cities. The atlas concludes with maps of individual Canadian provinces and a map of Mexico. An index rounds out the work. Readers also can visit http://Rand McNally.com/index for an even more complete map index. The accuracy, reliability, detail, and affordability of the road atlas make this a highly recommended suggestion for public and academic libraries. Published annually, with special editions such as large-print.

---

The 2018 atlas appeared in 2017. Classification: LC G1201; Dewey 629.

---

## Gazetteers

Atlases, maps, and globes employ images and visual tools, while gazetteers rely on text to indicate locations (sometimes by longitude and latitude), the spelling of place names, alternative and historical place names, and basic facts such as population or elevation.

51. *The Cambridge Gazetteer of the United States and Canada: A Dictionary of Places*, by Archie Hobson, ed.

Publisher: Cambridge University Press, New York, NY (1995)

Price: $49.95

Review by Gary R. Cocozzoli—Director of the Library, Lawrence Technological University, Southfield, MI.

The geographic scope of this gazetteer is limited to places affiliated with the United States and Canada and their possessions. The listings are not limited to municipal features, but also include physical geography, national forests and monuments, historic and legendary places, and military sites. For example, Devils Tower (Wyoming), Mall of America (Minnesota), Route 66, and River City, Iowa, stand alongside traditional gazetteer listings. A typical entry includes the population, or size (in acres and hectares), and in many cases the distance and direction from a major city. There is no latitude or longitude given. The emphasis is on description and economic geography, but many entries include historical background or significance. Entries are linked together by highlighting with capital letters to signify additional or related information. There are also entry *see* references that are helpful. The quality of the entries is uneven. Some entries surprise with their completeness, while others are vague or include some inaccuracies or misinformation. It is unfortunate that the incorporation date/founding date is not noted for every city or municipality, as this is likely a key need for the user. The supplementary maps are suitable for quick reference and encompass several historical periods, and there are general maps of several cities most likely to receive tourists. In spot checking entries, recently popular Madison County, Iowa, is not mentioned, several colleges that have changed names five years ago have not been updated, and a number of entries have misleading statements. Yet there are numerous entries offering greater-than-expected depth and lengthy descriptions of lesser-known locations that may barely be mentioned in other gazetteers or geographic dictionaries. The gazetteer is suitable and recommended for any site with frequent North American place-name identification questions, whether actual or fictional. Sites with few of these requests may do just as well with a comprehensive world gazetteer and an additional one for regional (e.g., state, province) coverage.

Classification: LC E154; Dewey 917.

52. *The Columbia Gazetteer of the World*, by Saul B. Cohen, ed.

Publisher: Columbia University Press, New York, NY (2008)

Price: $595.00/set

Review by Michael Levine-Clark—Collections Librarian, University of Denver, Denver, CO.

Since its publication in 1998, *The Columbia Gazetteer of the World* has been the standard geographical reference source, continuing the tradition of its predecessor, *The Columbia-Lippincott Gazetteer of the World*. The new edition will remain in that spot. With over 170,000 entries, the *Gazetteer* is the most comprehensive A-Z listing of geographic locations and features available. There are 7,000 new entries, and numerous revisions reflecting changes to the physical environment, demographic shifts, and human conflict. Hurricane Katrina, the 2004 tsunami, the Three Gorges Dam, various wars, and numerous smaller events and decisions that have altered the geographic landscape are all reflected here. The online version has been updated continually and the changes have now been added to the new print edition. This is still an important source that almost all libraries will need to have in their reference collections, although some may opt for only the online version.

---

An online version requires a fee: *see* http://www.columbiagazetteer.org/. Classification: LC G103; Dewey 910.

---

53. *Historical Gazetteer of the United States*, by Paul T. Hellmann

Publisher: Routledge/Taylor & Francis Group, New York, NY (2005)

Price: $125.00

Review by Michael Levine-Clark—Collections Librarian, University of Denver, Denver, CO.

This gazetteer provides brief chronological overviews of thousands of cities and towns across the United States, gathering information on the founding and major events in the history of each municipality covered. Although most of the information included could be found fairly easily, it would require digging through multiple sources. Hellmann has created a valuable reference tool by pulling this information together into one volume. The book is arranged alphabetically by state, and then within each state by municipality. A lengthy index provides access by the name of each locale. Coverage varies from a few lines to two pages. A few major cities, such as New York City (six pages) and Washington, D.C. (five pages), get much more extensive coverage. All "major" and "secondary" cities and any other municipalities with significant history have been included. Unfortunately, due to space concerns, Hellmann has left out many towns not fitting these definitions, making this work ultimately less valuable than it could have been. It is a shame that this useful resource was not expanded to include every town in the United States. Despite this minor criticism, the *Historical Gazetteer of the United States* is a valuable addition to any reference collection.

> Classification: LC E154; Dewey 911.

54. *Geographic Names Information System/GNIS* [digital]
Publisher: United States Board on Geographic Names, Reston, VA
Price: Free online. Date reviewed: 2015.
URL: http://geonames.usgs.gov/
Review by Staff, Libraries Unlimited.

Created in 1890, the U.S. Board on Geographic Names is charged with maintaining uniform usage of geographic names throughout the federal government. The board serves as a central authority on place names, including inquiries, name changes, and proposals for new names. Search results for domestic names provide users with the federally recognized name, type of feature, exact coordinates, state and county, elevation, and variant names for populated places, bodies of water, and a variety of other features. Links to multiple mapping sites including the U.S. Geological Survey's *National Map*, Microsoft's *Virtual Earth*, and *MapQuest* (entry 47) are also provided. The site also supplies links to search for names of foreign, undersea, and Antarctic names. While most people will be content with searching *Google Maps* (entry 46), this site will be useful for those needing a topographic authority, those looking for variant place names, as well as those trying to answer such questions as "how many towns are called Glendale in the U.S.?"

> GNIS covers places in the domestic United States and its dependencies, and in Antarctica. For the rest of the world, the preferred tool is the *GEOnet Names Server* (entry 55)—the GNIS site provides an easy link to reach GEOnet. Classification: LC E154; Dewey 917.

55. *GEOnet Names Server* [digital]
Publisher: National Geospatial-Intelligence Agency, Springfield, VA
Price: Free online. Date reviewed: 2013.
URL: http://geonames.nga.mil/gns/html/
Review by Staff, Libraries Unlimited.

This is the U.S. National Imagery and Mapping Agency's (NIMA) database of foreign geographic feature names as approved by the U.S. Board on Geographic Names. This site provides latitude, longitude, area, and UTM and JOG number. The database also contains variant spellings (cross-references), which are useful for finding purposes, as well as non-Roman script spellings of many of these names. All the geographic features in the database contain information about location, administrative division, and quality. The database can be used for a variety of purposes, including establishing official spellings of foreign place names, cartography, GIS, GEOINT, and finding places. There are currently more than 3.5 million entries, and the scope is worldwide, including the United States and Antarctica. Note: You must know the country in which the feature is located in order to utilize this site efficiently.

The *GEOnet Names Server* covers places worldwide outside the United States, its dependencies, and Antarctica. It is "the official repository of standard spellings of all foreign geographic names." Sometimes called the *NGA GEOnet Names Server* (NGA is the acronym of the National Geospatial-Intelligence Agency). Formerly operated by the National Imagery and Mapping Agency. For U.S. place features and Antarctica, the correct tool is *GNIS*, the *Geographic Names Information System* (entry 54). Classification: LC G105; Dewey 910.

56. *Getty Thesaurus of Geographic Names* [digital]
Publisher: Getty Research Institute, Los Angeles, CA
Price: Free online. Date reviewed: 2013.
URL: http://www.getty.edu/research/tools/vocabularies/tgn/
Review by Staff, Libraries Unlimited.

Created by the Getty Research Institute, this site provides a structural vocabulary with an emphasis on art and architecture, covering continents, nations, historical places, and physical features. Each record includes geographic coordinates, notes, sources for the data, and the role of the place (e.g., inhabited place, state capital). Names can include vernacular, English, other languages, historical names, natural order, and inverted order. Currently there are around one million entries, which are current, historical, and international in scope.

Coverage is global and takes into account alternative names: for example, a search for the city of Skopje also retrieves notations for Skoplje, Üsküb, Üsküp, Shkup, and Scupi. Classification: LC G104; Dewey 910.

## Biography

Specialized biographical reference sources provide more details, cover a wider array of persons, and may offer indexes that identify persons with similar careers or from the same places, compared with biographical entries in general encyclopedias. Biography sources owned by libraries in the United States tend to emphasize American and British figures, but similar publications exist for many nationalities and countries. Many print sets have moved to online versions, which allow continuous updating to reflect recent accomplishments or deaths. See also works on historical biography such as entries 244, 250, 251, and 266 in chapter 3.

## United States

57. *American National Biography* [digital]

Publisher: Oxford University Press, New York, NY

Price: Price negotiated by site. Date reviewed: 2011.

URL: http://www.anb.org

Review by Staff, Libraries Unlimited.

The *American National Biography* (ANB), first published in 1999, was a landmark publication and winner of several prestigious awards, including the 1999 Dartmouth Medal Award. It has since been launched as a searchable Web database and has now been updated to feature more than 18,500 biographies of significant Americans in politics, scholarship, science, sports, business, and now actors and activists. Important people from all eras of American history are represented here, including the unexpected: Vikings, cowboys, and influential social workers. The biographies have been written by more than 2,000 contributors and provide an overview of each person's personal and career highlights. Often compared to the *Dictionary of American Biography* (DAB; Charles Scribner's Sons), this product differs in several ways: the most significant is that DAB only provides biographies of people who died up to 1980, while ANB provides updates twice a year. The site also includes some 900 articles from the *Oxford Companion to United States History* (entry 234), which provide historical and social context to the biographies. Users can jump-start their research on a specific person by browsing a complementary article and observing one of the 2,700 accompanying illustrations. The preselected list of articles includes the topics of American literature, Black history, civil rights, Westward expansion, Native American heritage, and many more. The online edition of this valuable resource offers several features useful in a reference library setting. New biographies are added quarterly and semi-annually, and many of those include illustrations or photographs. A typical update provides about 30–50 new biographies. Past biographies are updated with new information. Biographies online also often include hyperlinks to related biographies within the database as well as websites of interest outside of the site—more than eighty thousand in all. The site is searchable by subject name, occupation, gender, birth date, birth place, death date, contributor name, or full text keywords. Access to this site is highly recommended for large public and academic libraries. The fact that it is updated so regularly is a strong selling point, as is the fact that at 25 volumes the print version will take up quite a lot of space and become dated fairly quickly.

> The authoritative source for concise biographies of significant persons related to the United States. This for-fee online resource succeeds and complements the twenty-four-volume print edition of 1999, and the original *Dictionary of American Biography* of 1928. Classification: LC CT213; Dewey 920.

58. *Marquis Who's Who on the Web* [digital]
Publisher: Marquis Who's Who/Reed Reference Publishing, New Providence, NJ
Price: Price negotiated by site. Date reviewed: 2011.
URL: http://www.marquiswhoswho.com/online-database/product-description
Review by Staff, Libraries Unlimited.

The *Marquis Who's Who on the Web* database provides aggregate, searchable access to 23 Marquis Who's Who titles. More than 1.4 million individuals are included in the database, which may be searched by 15 fields, including name, occupation, gender, degrees, colleges or universities, year of graduation, hobbies, religion, and more. These fields may be searched individually or in combination to create specific search statements. Such access points, and particularly the ability to combine criteria, far surpass the access points available in the print format. Another advantage of the electronic format is the daily updating, both of biographical facts and of included figures.

> Marquis Biographies Online publishes several resources for contemporary coverage of significant figures in the United States. Marquis publishes familiar and important biographical sources such as *Who's Who in America* for living figures (published in print format since 1899), and *Who Was Who in America* for deceased figures dating back to 1607 (in print format since 1942). There are also regional editions. Classification: LC E176; Dewey 920.

## Great Britain

59. *Oxford Dictionary of National Biography*
Publisher: Oxford University Press, New York, NY (2004)
Price: $13,000.00/set
Review by Staff, Libraries Unlimited.

The long-awaited *Oxford Dictionary of National Biography* is a cooperative research project that has been 12 years in the making. This impressive 60-volume scholarly work is an update of the original *Dictionary of National Biography* that provides 50,000 biographical entries on influential English-speaking people from all over the world. For this new edition, the 36,000 biographies presented in the 1st edition have been rewritten and revised and 13,500 new entries have been included, with some 3,000 of them being women of influence. The people presented here represent a variety of backgrounds, including politics, the sciences, entertainment, the arts, business, and literature, just to name a few. What makes this work unique is the quantity and the quality of the biographies. The biographies typically run several pages in length and discuss the person's life in depth, including their personal life as well as their professional contributions. Although more than 10,000 specialists worldwide contributed to these volumes, the work has been well edited and the biographies are consistently well written and well researched. At the end of each entry the contributor has listed their sources of information and each biography is signed by the contributor. New to this edition are black-and-white photographs of many of the biographees— 10,000 in all. At $13,000 this 60-volume, 280-pound set is a monumental purchase for any library. It will be considered a standard and one of the first resources that many librarians and patrons will turn to because of the number of people featured and the reliability of the information. This work is also available online to individuals and to institutions by annual subscription. The online edition offers all of the information presented in the print volumes and is searchable by name, date, profession, place, religion, and more. The online edition also offers the original biographies that were provided in the 1st edition, which will be important for those doing historical research. The online edition is updated three times a year; supplemental volumes of the print edition can be expected as well. This work is a must-purchase for most large academic and public libraries, whether it be in the print or online edition, or both.

---

The authoritative source for concise biographies of importance for British history and society. Many libraries will prefer the for-fee online resource, which updates content in the sixty-volume print edition of 2004: see http://www.oxforddnb.com/. That massive print set updated the original print-format *Dictionary of National Biography* (DNB) of 1901. Classification: LC DA28; Dewey 920.

60. *Who's Who Online* [digital]

Publisher: Oxford University Press, New York, NY

Price: Price negotiated by site. Date reviewed: 2010.

URL: http://www.ukwhoswho.com/

Review by Martha Tarlton—Head, Reference and Information Services, University of North Texas Libraries, Denton.

Now in its 162nd annual edition, *Who's Who* continues to be a key reference source, especially for British figures. This directory provides biographical entries for more than thirty-two thousand notable living persons in government, academia, business, the arts, the clergy, and other fields. An anonymous editorial board is responsible for the selection of names for inclusion in the volume. The publisher states that approximately one thousand new entries have been added to this edition, and a substantial number of the previous year's entries have been updated. *Who's Who* has a decidedly British slant, with its principal focus on individuals residing within the United Kingdom, although it also contains selected entries for persons from Continental Europe, Ireland, the British Commonwealth, and throughout the world. New to this edition are several faces from the sporting world (e.g., Roger Federer), the entertainment world (e.g., Brad Pitt, Morgan Freeman, Ricky Gervais), and several from the business world (e.g., Matthew Brittin [managing director of Google UK]). Exclusively available from Oxford University Press since 2008, *Who's Who* is also available online. The online edition provides an additional one hundred thousand historical entries and is updated on a regular basis. The online edition is provided in the same platform as the *Oxford Dictionary of National Biography* (entry 59). With purchase of the print edition the online edition is free for twelve months in single-user access. As is the case with many biographical directories, entries vary somewhat in length and complexity. They typically list place and date of birth, family information, educational background, career history, publications or creative works, hobbies, and contact information. In some instances, e-mail addresses or telephone numbers are also provided. A number of cross-references appear throughout the volume. Preceding the biographies are several features, including an obituary section, a key to abbreviations, and a section on the British royal family. *Who's Who* is recommended as the principal source for current British biographical information and as a supplemental source for biographical information for individuals outside the United Kingdom.

---

A key source for contemporary coverage of figures significant to the United Kingdom. The successor and complement to the print serial *Who's Who*, published since 1849: the 169th print edition appeared in 2017. The same publisher produces *Who Was Who* for deceased figures. Classification: LC DA28; Dewey 920.

## Cultural and Social Norms

Shared norms, beliefs, and expectations about commonly held knowledge help to define communities. For a community of sports fans, that set of shared understandings could revolve around famous athletes; sharing in a community of musicians could involve a pantheon of songs; for a community of movie buffs, sharing could mean appreciation of landmark films. What are the expectations for shared points of reference for the communities served by American public or academic libraries—communities with rich diversity in ethnicity, age, gender, class, politics, and interests? The answers to such questions can be hotly contested: rather than endorse one set of answers and not another, libraries can offer a range of resources that represent different perspectives. This kind of curated collection can also help to answer frequently repeated questions. Additional resources about shared beliefs can be found in the Popular Culture section of chapter 2 (entries 163–177) and in the section on Religion and Beliefs in chapter 4 (entries 355–387).

61. *The New Dictionary of Cultural Literacy*, by E. D. Hirsch, Jr., Joseph F. Kett, and James Trefil

Publisher: Houghton Mifflin Harcourt, New York, NY (2002)

Price: $29.95

Review by John W. Storey—Professor of History, Lamar University, Beaumont, TX.

One could quarrel with the authors' subtle distinction between patriotism (a love of country that embraces diversity and harbors no fear of different cultures) and nationalism (a tribalistic presumption of cultural superiority that looks askance at things foreign), but their contention that a sense of community requires a shared body of knowledge is indisputable. Thus, this 3rd edition of a national bestseller, compiled by three Virginia professors whose respective disciplines are English, history, and physics, focuses on that common knowledge "every American needs to know." This common knowledge is what the authors call "cultural literacy," and it demands at least some familiarity with the Bible, American and world literature, history, geography, the social sciences, the fine arts, business and economics, the physical and life sciences, and technology. Regardless of one's religious persuasion, for instance, a culturally literate American must have some grounding in the Bible to understand references to a David and Goliath battle, the wisdom of Solomon, the patience of Job, extending an olive branch, a doubting Thomas, or the parables of Jesus. Likewise, how could any American participate in the national culture without knowing something of the Boston Tea Party, Benedict Arnold, the Bill of Rights, the Bronx, the Bible Belt, Cape Canaveral, Gallup polls, and DNA? Included herein are some seven thousand clearly written entries, of which numerous ones have been updated and about five hundred are new. Technology and science dominate the latter, reflecting the enormous changes in those fields since the second publication, when a Web page was unheard of. A sensible organization and an exhaustive index simplify access to this treasure trove of information. Beginning with "The Bible" and ending with "Technology," the work is divided into twenty-three sections, with relevant terms, events, and people alphabetically subsumed under each. A "Pronunciation Key" is also helpful. Since this is a work for a popular audience, it would be a suitable purchase for public libraries.

---

The original 1988 *Dictionary of Cultural Literacy* also is widely held. Classification: LC E169; Dewey 973.

---

62. *The Oxford Dictionary of Allusions*, by Andrew Delahunty, Sheila Dignen, and Penny Stock

Publisher: Oxford University Press, New York, NY (2001)

Price: $25.00

Review by Mark Y. Herring—Dean of Library Services, Winthrop University, Dacus Library, Rock Hill, SC.

Anyone who writes even only now and again will run into this problem: Editors consistently strike out anything that remotely smacks of an educated allusion for fear no one will understand and be offended. But the veil of Moses, if I might indulge a whim, has at long last been lifted. Now anyone can read with understanding. In *The Oxford Dictionary of Allusions*, listed alphabetically and thematically, are hundreds of allusions from all walks of literature. Although the vast majority come from classical mythology and the Bible, other sources abound, including Shakespeare, Dickens, Faust, Medieval fables, and the modern media of cinema and television. Under nearly two hundred subject headings are hundreds of allusions allusively used throughout literature that remained, until now, elusive to many. With this work, the sensitivities of our modern age may finally force intelligence to give way to the Procrustean bedstead.

---

The 3rd edition appeared in 2010 with a new title: *Adonis to Zorro: Oxford Dictionary of Reference and Allusion*. Classification: LC PN43; Dewey 422.

---

63. *Oxford Dictionary of Phrase and Fable*, by Elizabeth Knowles, ed.

Publisher: Oxford University Press, New York, NY (2005)

Price: $40.00

Review by Bradford Lee Eden—Dean of Library Services, Valparaiso University, Valparaiso, IN.


This 2nd edition, revised and updated from its first appearance in 2000, includes the origins of hundreds of phrases in the English language. Familiar and obscure names and sayings, from ancient times up to the present, are available in this book that draws from Oxford's bank of reference and language online resources. Areas such as popular culture, folk customs, science and technology, history, mythology, philosophy, religion, and superstitions are some of the topics from which word origins, sayings, maxims, proverbs, and adages are drawn. If a user wants to find out what "dark matter" is, what "elephant in the room" means, or what the origin of "women and children first" is, then this is where to find out. The *Oxford Dictionary of Phrase and Fable* will make a worthwhile addition to any library's reference collection.

---

Classification: LC PN43; Dewey 423.

---

64. *Brewer's Dictionary of Modern Phrase and Fable*, Adrian Room, comp.

Publisher: Sterling Publishing, New York, NY (2002)

Price: $39.95

Review by Jeffrey E. Long—Editor of *SoutteReview Newsletter*, University of Massachusetts Medical School Library, Worcester.


Like its forerunners that also bear the "Brewer's" imprimatur, this work consists of a single A-Z listing of about eight thousand defined entries that are names of persons, places, expressions, things, and ideas that are based in fact or fiction, and that largely define the cultural trappings and traditions most familiar to today's British and American citizenry. Specifically, Room focuses upon items that gained or regained appreciable cultural prominence during the twentieth century. This resource is essentially an updating of *Brewer's Dictionary of Twentieth Century Phrase & Fable*, edited by David Pickering, itself a descendent of generations of the venerable *Brewer's Dictionary of Phrase & Fable*. Further, the volume at hand updates its hardcover predecessor. Death dates for George Harrison and Ken Kesey are included here, as are entries for such 2001 films as *Bridget Jones's Diary* and *Tomb Raider*. In several entries, the terrorist attacks of September 11, 2001, are covered as well. While most entries consist of fewer than one hundred words, some extend to twice or thrice this length (e.g., Vietnam, Bandit Country, Peter Pan, Lawrence of Arabia). In addition, twenty-eight so-called "list entries" are lengthier yet (e.g., political correctness, medical abbreviations, string quartets). A significant number of foreign-language entry words and phrases are contained, as well. However, this book has a decided British slant in its selection and definition of entries. "Ants in one's pants" is accompanied by an aside informing the reader that "pants" means "trousers." Such skewing is evident in other instances as well. For instance, despite their formidable influence, it is arguable whether the Beatles and their music merit the thirty or so entries accorded them. The entry for the television game show *Price Is Right* states that the series aired only during the mid-1980s, without noting that the U.S. counterpart debuted in 1956, and has continued into the new millennium. On the other hand, Room accommodates interests from both sides of the Atlantic with his "Dennis the Menace" entry, which provides information on the two distinct cartoon characters created in 1951 by British cartoonist David Law and in the U.S. by Hank Ketcham. This compendium is particularly strong in its inclusion of entries of acronyms, names of obscure and semi-obscure personalities, and nicknames. Entries have not been devoted to such influential persons as Frank Sinatra, Billy Graham, Bob Dylan, H. G. Wells, Walt Disney, Fred Astaire, Gore Vidal, or Stephen King. It is sometimes only through serendipity that biographical information may be discovered in this book. For example, consult "Ol' Blue Eyes" or "Scooby-Doo" for information on Frank Sinatra or see "Blairism" for information on Tony Blair. Users may also be put off by the tabloid tone of many entries. Room's proclivity for chatty editorializing can become annoying. Do we need to know that he considers the Beatles' "All You Need Is Love" to be an "undistinguished" song, or that he believes Hillary Clinton to be a "long-suffering" wife? Unfortunately, in their degree of factuality, entries are occasionally incomplete, uneven, misleading, disputable, or incorrect. Why include sayings from Sam Goldwyn and Arthur Mizner, but not from Yogi Berra, Mae West, or Dorothy Parker? Why include one of London's airports (Heathrow) but exclude the other (Gatwick)? The entry on the film *Fail-Safe* fails to mention the award-winning film or book adaptation. Surprising omissions include marijuana, pot, joint, and acid; computer, microchip, and hacker; VCR and DVD; Stephen Spielberg, Bill Gates, and Jack Kilby (microchip inventor); O. J. Simpson; Philo T. Farnsworth (television inventor); Ted Bundy, the Zodiac Killer, and John Wayne Gacy; "right to die," euthanasia, and Karen Ann Quinlin; Osbert Sitwell; slinky; cloning; drive-by shooting; "go postal" (although "go ballistic" is included). Weaknesses and gaffes in this volume's format, layout, and copyediting crop up on occasion as well. Page numbers have been placed all but out of sight by the binding's crease. The name of Beavis' cohort is variously spelled "Butthead" (p. 12) and "Butthead" (p. 13). A spurious hyphen interrupts "paint-ing" (p. 25). Under Beatles, the reference to the Fab Four's first motion picture includes the unaccountable italicizing of a letter. For its breadth of coverage, this dictionary is of value to public and academic libraries. However, it should be used with some caution in light of its aforementioned shortcomings.

> An updated 2nd edition appeared in 2006. Editions of the original *Brewer's Dictionary of Phrase & Fable* have been reference standards for historical and classical content since 1870. Classification: LC PN43; Dewey 423.

65. *Letitia Baldrige's New Manners for New Times: A Complete Guide to Etiquette*, by Letitia Baldrige

Publisher: Simon & Schuster, New York, NY (2003)

Price: $35.00

Review by Staff, Libraries Unlimited.

As former social secretary at the U.S. embassies in Paris and Rome and as chief of staff for former first lady Jacqueline Kennedy, author Letitia Baldrige knows a thing or two about manners and the art of social grace. Her latest title, *New Manners for New Times* covers a large spectrum of questions that arise with our fast-moving, technologically advanced society. Baldrige's book is arranged into six parts and twenty-three chapters. The topics discussed here are wide ranging and cover the expected as well as the unexpected. Among those expected are relationship issues, including those with family (both close and distant), how to teach children manners, maintaining friendships, and business relationships. She also discusses table manners; appropriate dress; the etiquette of engagements, weddings, and funerals; the art of entertaining; the art of communication via telephone, letter writing, and e-mail; and addressing people properly. The new and unexpected topics covered include rules for when an elderly parent comes to live with their child; how to welcome gay and lesbian couples into the family; talking to children about drugs and alcohol; rules of tipping; and the new rules of dating and Internet dating. There is little unaddressed in this compact volume. The arrangement of this book makes it valuable for both reference and circulating collections. The table of contents is laid out so that users can find answers to their questions quickly; the index is valuable in that as well. However, users may also want to have time to browse through these pages on their own as there is a wealth of material here and everyone has something to learn from it. Whether added to the reference collection, circulating collection, or both, *New Manners for New Times* is a must for all public libraries.

> An alternative choice could be *Emily Post's Etiquette*: the 18th edition appeared in 2011. Classification: LC BJ1853; Dewey 395.

66. *Guinness World Records*, by Claire Folkard, ed.

Publisher: Random House, New York, NY

Price: $28.95

Review by Staff, Libraries Unlimited.

*Guinness World Records* continues to be a popular book among the general public. Focusing on feats of nature, human endurance, scientific achievement, entertainment, business, and sports, this latest edition will please readers as well. New additions include 15-year-old Seb Clover, the youngest person ever to sail the Atlantic; a fastest marathon time (2 hours, 15 minutes, and 25 seconds); and Marshall Mathers (betters known as rap performer M&M) who sold a record 1.76 million copies of his album titled The Marshall Mathers LP the first week in June. This work is organized into 9 main sections: Humans, Natural World, Modern World, Material World, Feats of Engineering, Science and Technology, Art and Media, Music and Entertainment, and Sports. Users can find their areas of interest by consulting the table of contents or the back-of-the-book index. Most people will prefer, however, just to browse the book for the strange and fascinating topics that pop out at them. Black-and-white photographs are featured on nearly every page. This popular book should be a standard in most types of libraries, particularly school and public libraries.

---

Also well known as the *Guinness Book of World Records*. Updated annually. Famously launched in 1955 to settle bar bets, hence the connection to Guinness as a beverage. Classification: LC AG243; Dewey 032.

---

67. *Hoyle's Rules of Games: Descriptions of Indoor Games of Skill and Chance, with Advice on Skillful Play,* by Albert Morehead, Geoffrey Mott-Smith, and Philip D. Morehead.

Publisher: Berkley/Penguin Group, New York, NY (2001)

Price: $16.00

Review by Staff, Libraries Unlimited.

This 3rd revised and updated edition is the book for anyone who has ever wanted to have the rules for Fish, various games of Rummy and Solitaire, or even Whist close at hand. The book's organization allows users to access the desired set of instructions in a variety of ways. The front matter includes an index of games and a gamefinder section that groups games (there are separate sections for adults and children and for card games and dice and board games) into lists for two, three, four, or five players. From Accordian and Aces High to Brazilian Canasta and Bridge, and from Hurricane to Napoleon at St. Helena, *Hoyle's* provides broad coverage of games, both familiar and less well known. The book concludes with a page of further resource suggestions and a glossary. Offered at a modest cost, this book is recommended for public, school, academic, and personal libraries.

Edmond Hoyle taught and sold rules for card games in eighteenth-century England. Since 1742, card games have been played "according to Hoyle" and the phrase has expanded to cover authoritative rules for other games as well. There are numerous editions and versions of "Hoyle's" on the market under various titles, and similar guides to rules of games can be found on the Web. Classification: LC GV1243; Dewey 795.

68. *Robert's Rules of Order: Newly Revised*, by Henry M. Robert and Sarah Corbin Robert

Publisher: Da Capo Press, Boston, MA (2011)

Price: $18.95

Review by Staff, Libraries Unlimited.

This edition (the 11th) supersedes all previous editions; it also adds to and clarifies material in the 10th edition. All changes are enumerated in the preface. In addition, the preface points out that though there is an abbreviated version of *Robert's Rules* available, this version is the most comprehensive reference available to answer questions on any parliamentary procedure. Further support is provided at www.robertsrules.com, and electronic versions of the full and abbreviated versions of the guide are available through collaboration with American Legal Publishing. The introduction outlines a useful history of the book (originally published in 1876) and how it became the leading source on parliamentary law for deliberative bodies. The meat of the book follows in chapters from "The Deliberative Assembly: Its Types and Their Rules" to "The Main Motion" to "Incidental Motions" to "Officers; Minutes and Officers' Reports" to "Disciplinary Procedures." Next follows a handy section of charts, tables, and list that includes: "Table of Rules Relating to Motions," "Motions and Parliamentary Steps," and "Table of Rules for Counting Election Ballots." An extensive index with *see* and *see also* references follows. The detail in the index allows users to find easily a desired topic. Highly recommended to public and academic libraries.

Based on legislative procedures, in 1876 the American Henry Martyn Robert produced a standard set of rules for managing meetings. Often referred to as "parliamentary procedure" but in fact intended for nonlegislative societies, the rules can be modified for local use. Several competing systems exist, but Robert's approach is the one most often seen in the United States. Similar content is published under various titles and in various editions, and similar content can be found online. Classification: LC JF515; Dewey 060.

## Quotations

Collections of quotations serve various purposes: to record significant statements, to attribute famous sayings to the correct source, to inspire readers (and offer texts for inspirational speakers), or to entertain. Some of our earliest books—including portions of the Bible—contain records of sayings, proverbs, and aphorisms. Books of quotations typically focus on short statements rather than citing a long text or speech in full.

69. *Bartlett's Familiar Quotations: A Collection of Passages, Phrases, and Proverbs Traced to Their Sources in Ancient and Modern Literature*, by John Bartlett and Geoffrey O'Brien, eds.

Publisher: Little, Brown, and Co., New York, NY (2012)

Price: $50.00

Review by Staff, Libraries Unlimited.

The core quotations source is *Bartlett's Familiar Quotations*, now in its 18th edition, published since 1855. With twenty-five thousand quotations from more than two thousand authors, Bartlett's covers a wide variety of subjects, time periods, and people, from the Bible and Shakespeare to such contemporary authors as Maya Angelou and Frank McCourt. It is arranged chronologically and includes an author index and a keyword index to provide and enhance access. Its moderate price puts it within the reach of many libraries' budgets, and for the content and history contained in *Bartlett's*, it should be part of every library's collection.

---

Editorial decisions have taken *Bartlett's* in different directions over the years, so it can be useful to keep older editions on hand: the selected content varies. In particular, controversial changes took place in the 1960s with the addition of contemporary material at the expense of classical or literary quotations. The 10th edition of 1919 is out of copyright, and available online at http://www.bartleby.com/100/. Classification: LC PN6081; Dewey 082.

---

70. *Oxford Dictionary of Quotations*, by Elizabeth Knowles, ed.

Publisher: Oxford University Press, New York, NY (2014)

Price: $50.00

Review by Mark Y. Herring—Dean of Library Services, Winthrop University, Dacus Library, Rock Hill, SC.

Surely with the Internet now so firmly ensconced in every inch and fiber of our lives, we no longer need bulky, tree-killing tomes like this one? Moreover, even this text is on the godalmighty Internet. Coming in at over five pounds and more than 1,100 pages, what could possibly possess any publisher, especially one as reputable as Oxford, to undertake such an expensive and laborious undertaking for what we might call a publishing paralipomenon? Accuracy of phrase, ease of use, and profound assurance of source are just three reasons that come to mind, any one of which justifies the existence of the volume but all three make it a fortiori, or QED, as the philosophers might say. Yet apart from these reasons, the inclusion in this edition of the history of the volume and the introduction to the 1st edition by Bernard Darwin should make the matter incontestable even for tree-huggers. Well, okay, for everyone but them. Begins Darwin, "Quotation brings to many people one of the intensest [sic] joys of living." He goes on to point out that some will be disappointed at what is both included and what is left out, and he even points out one of his favorites that did not make that 1st edition cut. To which he muses, "Can it be, I ask myself, that this is due to the fact an Oxford scholar put several of the Master's [William Hepworth Thompson] sayings into his Greek exercise book and attributed them to one Talirantes? Down, base thought! I only mention this momentary and unworthy suspicion to show other readers the sort of thing they should avoid as they would the very devil." Alas, no one writes like this anymore but it is so charming to be reminded once again that elocution and felicitous expression used to be not only taught and practiced, but also admired. The *Oxford Dictionary of Quotations* brings together thousands (and thousands) of quotations with their sources matched and their phrasing parsed as pluperfectly as possible. As with all other editions the arrangement is by author with birth and death dates, when applicable, in place. The author's nationality and occupation is noted and the original language of the quotation given. Cross-references, when appropriate, are given. A most expansive keyword index is included. What makes this edition so important is that many contemporaries, for better or for worse, are given their place in the sun. Thus, Frank Zappa, Joan Baez, Bob Marley, John Lennon, and Paul McCartney are all included as well as scores of others one has never heard of. While it may not always be true that the Internet will give you several million answers in a few nanoseconds but a librarian the right one, when it is true, it is because books such as this one are still published and still used. Lauditor temporis acti.

---

Classification: LC PN6081; Dewey 082.

---

71. *The Yale Book of Quotations*, by Fred R. Shapiro, ed.
Publisher: Yale University Press, New Haven, CT (2006)

Price: $50.00

Review by Martha E. Stone—Coordinator for Reference Services, Treadwell Library, Massachusetts General Hospital, Boston.

Editor Shapiro is a librarian and lecturer at the Yale Law School, and this well-conceived collection of quotations for the twenty-first century should fulfill the needs of most general users. Twelve research editors assisted in the compilation and verification of over 12,000 quotations from an eclectic array of writers and sources, including entries under the topics of "Film Lines" and "Modern Proverbs." This reviewer found one error: Christina, not Cristina, Crawford, wrote *Mommie Dearest* [p. 178]. There is also a production flaw: in this reviewer's finished book, pages 723–724 are illegible on both sides. Authors of quotations range from the expected representation of Greek and Roman thinkers (Pliny the Elder, Plautus, Plato) to the eighteenth century's Holy Roman Emperor Joseph II to the twenty-first century's William N. "Bill" Joy, a founder of Sun Microsystems. There are also a small number of black-and-white photographs (e.g., Dylan Thomas, who accounts for 22 quotations; Frederick Douglass, who accounts for 16 quotations). Due to the strictly alphabetic nature of the book, there are some unusual groupings: Page 174, for instance, includes rapper Coolio (with 2 quotations from his songs); James Fenimore Cooper and Copernicus (with 1 quotation each); and seventeenth-century French playwright Pierre Corneille with three quotations. It should be noted that there are a relatively small number of women represented throughout. There is a keyword index, and each entry includes the author's dates of birth, nationality, and profession, with sources of quotations very briefly stated. It should be remembered that the 10th edition (1919) of *Bartlett's Familiar Quotations* (entry 69) is freely available at http://www.bartleby .com/100/ but libraries lacking in such late-twentieth-century sources as the *Oxford Dictionary of Quotations* (6th ed.; entry 70), containing 17,500 quotations, could not go wrong with *The Yale Book of Quotations*.

---

Classification: LC PN6081; Dewey 082.

---

72. *Oxford Dictionary of Modern Quotations*, by Elizabeth Knowles

Publisher: Oxford University Press, New York, NY (2002)

Price: $35.00

Review by Glenn Masuchika—Senior Information Specialist, Rockwell Collins Information, Iowa City, IA.

The 2nd edition of the *Oxford Dictionary of Modern Quotations* is truly a joy to read, and I mean "read" as one reads a joke book. As one makes their way through this extremely eclectic collection of sayings from the modern world's politicians, artists, and pop celebrities, one cannot help but marvel at what an utterly creative time we are living in to produce this panoply of witticisms, malapropisms, and flights of humorous illogic. If one needs a clever, ice-breaking quote to begin an after-dinner speech before the Rotary Club, this is the book to seek out. Although there are legitimate, intellectual uses for this book beyond amusement, I cannot fathom any. It is too sporadic, too noncomprehensive for sociological research and analysis, which is no fault of the editor since quotes are mere snapshots in a historical narrative, a timeline that often is not immediately apparent to the reader. Yet, it is this haphazard, disjointedness of aphorisms, leaping in and out, that is the strength of this tome. It has the serendipitous nature to titillate the imagination, to trigger within the memory of the reader stages, scenes, and landscapes from the past that have gone dark. This reviewer read with startling laughter the quotations of Monty Python's Flying Circus, and the daffy world of English humor came flooding back from my youth, complete with "silly walks, dead parrots," and the Spanish Inquisition, who no one expects (p. 230). The book can also frighten. I reread the comment by the American physicist J. Robert Oppenheimer as he witnessed the first atomic bomb explosion: "I remember the line from the Hindu scripture, the *Bhagavad Gita* . . . 'I am become death, the destroyer of worlds'" (p. 246) and I remembered the fear of living a childhood under the threat of the "Bomb." Being one of the "The Oxford Dictionary of" series, this book is naturally heavily saturated with the sayings of English politicians and celebrities who are relatively unknown to Americans, but that is not a disadvantage. However, a distinct disadvantage is its Anglo-American emphasis. It could have been more international in scope and included much more quotations from people of other nations. The book ends with a keyword index and a selected thematic (e.g., administration, age, American, art) index. Both tools are helpful to the after-dinner speaker. I can strongly recommend this book to be included in the collection of any library.

---

The 3rd edition appeared in 2007. Classification: LC PN6081; Dewey 082.

---

## Usage and Style

Guides to usage and style deal with grammar, syntax, word choice, and format. Their audience includes journalists and other professional writers, editors, teachers, and students. Like dictionaries, usage guides can range between prescriptive and descriptive models: editors of modern usage guides rely on databases of current writing (often including newspapers) to follow trends but may or may not endorse or adopt what they see. Usage over time can be fluid: for example, there has been an evolution in gender neutral writing and the choice of pronouns. "Style" can mean one of two things: effective wording and phrasing or adherence to a set of rules. For Strunk & White (entry 75), a discussion of style means setting a tone—formal or informal, lively or dry—through the choice of words and adoption of tone. In works such as the *Associated Press Stylebook* or the *New York Times Manual of Style and Usage*, style refers to a "house style" that dictates publishing details for punctuation, hyphenization, capitalization, abbreviation, and the design of tables. House style may include conventions about footnoting and the composition of a bibliography. *The Chicago Manual of Style* (entry 76) is best known as a guide to this kind of "citation" style, but a great deal of that book is devoted to other aspects of house style.

## English-Language Style Guides

73. *Garner's Modern American Usage: The Authority on Grammar, Usage, and Style,* by Bryan A. Garner

Publisher: Oxford University Press, New York, NY (2009)

Price: $45.00

Review by Helen Margaret Bernard—Reference and Interlibrary Loan Librarian, Writing Center Director, Southwestern Baptist Theological Seminary, Fort Worth, TX.

It is unusual to pick up a handbook on modern American English usage and find oneself not only better informed, but also engaged, entertained, and unwilling to put the book down. This 3rd edition of Bryan Garner's handbook of grammar, usage, and style is a rare exception. From the acknowledgment to the glossary, this work adroitly illustrates Garner's love of the skillfully used and well-placed word. It is designed to be browsed through, not merely referred to when "a sticky issue of usage emerges" (p. xiii). To that end, substantial essays on Garner's approach to usage, which is prescriptive rather than descriptive, begin the work and shorter entries on usage and style appear in the alphabetized entries that form the majority of the volume. The entries on individual words, however, are the heart of the work. The 3rd edition contains nearly double the number of words in previous editions, with each entry presenting a clear explanation of the issues surrounding a particular word, word ending, or set of words. Current examples of both correct and incorrect usage are often included. In this edition, Garner has also provided a language change index, which has a five-point scale of usage acceptability. The scale is explained in length in the Key to the Language Change Index and in the introductory essay "The Ongoing Struggles of Garlic-Hangers." Many of the words he discusses are ranked on this scale. Other noteworthy features of the book include a glossary, a timeline of books published on usage, and a selected bibliography divided into categories such as style and etymology. Cross-references can be found within the entries themselves, and an index of writers quoted or mentioned is included at the end of the volume. As a handbook that provides an easily accessible wealth of knowledge and exemplifies brilliant usage, *Garner's Modern American Usage* will be an invaluable resource for anyone who values careful writing: professional writers, editors, educators, students, and all who, like Garner, love words.

---

The 4th edition appeared in 2016. Classification: LC PE2827; Dewey 423.

---

74. *The Cambridge Guide to English Usage,* by Pam Peters
Publisher: Cambridge University Press, New York, NY (2004)
Price: $35.00
Review by Lori D. Kranz—Freelance Editor, Chambersburg, PA.

*The Cambridge Guide to English Usage* is a comprehensive guide to style and usage intended for writers, editors, teachers, and students. In an alphabetic format, these entries address easily confused terms, alternate spellings, grammar, political correctness issues, diacritics, punctuation, commonly used foreign terms, and myriad other language questions. The "international" scope indicated on the cover means that the "English" here includes American, British, Canadian, and Australian conventions, based on corpus data as well as language reference books used in these countries. As noted in the front matter, this guide is "descriptive" rather than "prescriptive," and thus the user can make an informed choice. This reviewer found the explanations for that old bugbear "that or which?" both thorough and enlightening. With more than four thousand entries, *The Cambridge Guide to English Usage* offers a wealth of information for all English users.

---

Classification: LC PE1464; Dewey 428.

---

75. *The Elements of Style,* by William Strunk, Jr., and E. B. White
Publisher: Penguin Books, New York, NY (2005)
Price: $24.95
Review by Staff, Libraries Unlimited.

Strunk and White's *The Elements of Style* has long been a standard style guide in the hands of journalists, professional writers, and students. This edition is little changed from earlier editions except that this volume has been illustrated with fifty-seven charming illustrations and has been set in a hardbound edition. The work follows the same layout as previous editions. It begins with a chapter titled "Elementary Rules of Usage," which discusses such topics as comma placement and the proper use of pronouns. The work continues with chapters on the "Elementary Principles of Composition" (e.g., active voice, omitting needless words), "A Few Matters of Form," and "Words and Expressions Commonly Misused." The most useful chapter for those looking to improve their communication style through writing or to master the craft is "An Approach to Style," which discusses such topics as the importance of revision, steering clear of clichés and figures of speech, and how to avoid overwriting and overstating. The work concludes with some spelling tips, a glossary, and an index. *The Elements of Style* remains a useful and insightful guide to writing clearly and with a purpose. Unfortunately, it has not been updated to include tips for writing e-mail or modern-day business correspondence. This guide, with its hardbound cover and illustrations, would make a good gift for the graduate going into journalism or communications, or the aspiring writer. However, since it has not been updated since the last edition, this 2005 copy does not need to be added to the library collections of those that already own previous editions.

---

The 1st edition appeared in 1918: frequently reprinted, as recently as 2009, with minor changes. E. B. White is also famous as the author of *Charlotte's Web*. Classification: LC PE1408; Dewey 808.

---

## Citation Manuals

Accurate, complete, consistent recording of the elements in a bibliographical citation—such as author, title, date of publication, and pagination—is a foundation skill for the use of text resources for research, writing, and reporting. Several systems are in use, sometimes associated with different areas of knowledge. Several software packages also can capture and organize accurate citations for books, articles, websites, and other sources. These packages may include formatting choices to reflect the various standards, such as the Chicago or MLA systems. The best known of these software packages are EndNote, Mendeley, and Zotero. Some of these services are free or offer basic versions at no cost; others require individual payments or institutional subscriptions, especially for advanced features such as sharing with colleagues or unlimited storage space.

76. *The Chicago Manual of Style*

Publisher: University of Chicago Press, Chicago, IL (2010)

Price: $65.00

Review by Staff, Libraries Unlimited.


*The Chicago Manual of Style* has long been one of the most used and well-regarded writing style guides for writers, editors, and publishers. In the fall of 2006 the online edition of this popular resource was launched. Currently users of the online edition have access to both the new content from the 16th edition as well as older content from the 15th edition. The editors decided to take this unusual step of keeping material from the previous edition available to users due to the way that most editors and publishers work and their need for having continuity throughout ongoing projects. This 16th edition of the print version provides many new updates since the last edition. The majority of these updates have to do with the increase in electronic publications, electronic editing, and citing of electronic materials (e.g., blogs, podcasts, websites). Other new features include an updated section on using bias-free language, a new hyphenation guide that is presented in a tabular format, an introduction to Unicode (the international computing stand for letters and symbols required by the world's languages), and updated advice on citing legal and public documents. Also included are an updated glossary that includes more electronic publishing terms and some overall reformatting that brings closely related topics closer together in the print version. Although significant updates and changes have been made, those familiar with the print version of *The Chicago Manual of Style* will find it compatible to past editions and therefore easy to use. *The Chicago Manual of Style* remains one of the most highly used style guides in the country and therefore is a recommended purchase for most libraries, especially university and public libraries.


The 17th edition appeared in 2017. "Turabian" (entry 77) is a less-intensive presentation of the Chicago style rules. Classification: LC Z253; Dewey 808.


77. *A Manual for Writers of Research Papers, Theses, and Dissertations*, by Kate L. Turabian. Revised by Wayne C. Booth, Gregory G. Colomb, and Joseph M. Williams

Publisher: University of Chicago Press, Chicago, IL (2013)

Price: $18.00

Review by Martha Lawler—Associate Librarian, Louisiana State University, Shreveport.

This latest interpretation and implementation of the Chicago Style has been enhanced by a section on research and writing adapted from Booth, Colomb, and Williams' *Craft of Research*. This section focuses on the gathering, organizing, and presenting of information and ideas and serves as a separate supplement to the mechanics of the style guidelines. It includes an examination of the ethics of scholarly research, as well as the technical aspects. The style guidelines are based on the 16th edition of *The Chicago Manual of Style* (2010; entry 76). The guidelines are meant to be standard practice, but may be altered by the requirements of specific disciplines or departments, if needed. The text is further enhanced by the use of blue typeface to highlight headings and examples. A section of citation formats is followed by another on style. An appendix displaying paper formats and submission guidelines with sample pages is followed by a bibliography of additional sources; a short biography of Booth, Colomb, and Williams; and an index. The newest edition in over seven years accounts for changes in technological applications and revised guidelines for formatting research papers, theses, and dissertations.

---

Often referred to as "Turabian" for the name of the editor. Classification: LC LB2369; Dewey 808.

---

78. *MLA Handbook*, by Joseph Gibaldi, ed.

Publisher: Modern Language Association of America, New York, NY (2016)

Price: $12.00

Review by Staff, Libraries Unlimited.

This 8th edition of the Modern Language Association (MLA) handbook provides the updated guide to citing sources in scholarly writing. While seemingly simple in scope, the new edition offers valuable information that works well to adapt to the evolving landscape of research writing. Since first experimented with in 1951, the MLA style sheet has undergone vast change. No longer does the manual need to remind writers to type their work; instead, the guide must deal with the proliferation of diverse sources and potentially complex rules. With mind to changes in literary studies, the needs of the modern student and certainly the advent of modern media, this 8th edition emphasizes a level of flexibility when creating the necessary source documentation. The book is separated into two parts, dealing with Principles of MLA Style (covering such things as information gathering, organization, etc.) and Details of MLA Style (covering the nitty-gritty of quotations, numbering, abbreviations, punctuation, and much more). Information in this part is delivered in short, sectioned paragraphs with clear examples following. Aids such as highlighting, lists, cross-referencing, and a practice template help readers navigate the technical material. The book is a must have for any student embarking on a path of academic writing and belongs in libraries of all sorts—public, middle and high school, academic, and personal.

> The longer previous title was *MLA Handbook for Writers of Research Papers.* Classification: LC LB2369; Dewey 808.

79. *Publication Manual of the American Psychological Association*
Publisher: American Psychological Association, Washington, DC (2001)
Price: $34.95
Review by Staff, Libraries Unlimited.

The editors of the *Publication Manual of the American Psychological Association* acknowledge that much has changed in the field of publishing since the 4th edition of this resource was published in 1994. This edition updates such information as how to properly reference electronic and legal references, provides a new section dealing with the content of methodological and case study reports, expands on issues of data sharing and verification, and updates the chapter on statistics to reflect the new standards in the field. Perhaps most importantly from the publishing aspect is the new focus on preparing manuscripts electronically. Chapters in this manual address how to organize a manuscript, expressing ideas through language, describe APA editorial style, and show how to compile a reference list. Remaining chapters discuss subjects specific to publishing in psychological journals, for books, and for dissertations and theses. The work contains a bibliography for the history of the *Publication Manual* and suggested readings. Appendixes include a checklist for manuscript submission, a checklist for transmitting manuscripts for electronic production, ethical standards for reporting, references for legal materials, and a sample cover letter. This style guide from the American Psychological Association remains the standard in the industry and should be in all university libraries with graduate and doctoral programs in psychology.

> The 6th edition appeared in 2010. Classification: LC BF76; Dewey 808.

80. *Purdue Online Writing Lab (OWL)* [digital]
Publisher: Purdue Writing Lab, Purdue University, West Lafayette, IN

Price: Free online. Date reviewed: 2017.

URL: https://owl.english.purdue.edu/owl/

Review by Staff, Libraries Unlimited.

The Writing Lab at Purdue provides writing resources and instructional materials free of charge via the *Purdue Online Writing Lab* (OWL) database. Users can easily navigate using links on the left-hand side of the main page—General Writing, Research and Citation, Teacher and Tutor Resources, Subject-Specific Writing, Job Search Writing, English as a Second Language, Purdue OWL Vidcasts—each of which has its own series of sublinks. Under General Writing, for example, users can access information about how to write research papers, book reports, annotated bibliographies, and more. This section also provides access to spelling, numbering, sentence structure, and sentence style exercises as well as grammar-related exercises. There are also sections on the writing process in general, academic writing, punctuation, and undergraduate and graduate applications, among other things. The Research and Citation link not only outlines the basics of the research process but offers links to the major style guides used across various disciplines, *CMS, APA, AMA,* and *MLA.* There is a wealth of information on the Teacher and Tutor Resources tab as well. For instance, one sublink takes teachers to exercises on how to contextualize and avoid plagiarism. A sublink under subject-specific writing connects users to many things including literary theory and schools of criticism (new historicism, Marxist criticism, post-colonial criticism, etc.). The *OWL,* moreover, is not just for coursework but has much to offer the job seeker, first time or otherwise, under Job Search Writing, which outlines best practices for resumes, cover letters, and applications. For those who learn by watching, it is worthwhile to investigate the OWL Vidcasts, which cover such things as how to analyze ethos and the semicolon. The Site Map for the OWL is particularly helpful since it functions as an index. Using the site map, users can go straight to subject-verb agreement, how to cite electronic resources in *AMA* style, how to close a cover letter, or a spelling exercise on "ible" and "able" word endings. As many students, teachers, and parents/ guardians already realize, the *Purdue OWL* is a treasure trove of writing resources and instructional materials. This resource is highly recommended to school, public, and academic libraries.

Classification: LC PE1065; Dewey 651.

# CHAPTER TWO

# Social Sciences

Reference titles supporting the many fields of study in the social sciences are prominent in reference collections. Given that coverage of current information is a key goal for reference resources, and given that students and the reading public seek information on emerging topics and recent issues (crime and constitutional rights are perennial topics of interest), it is not surprising that publishers produce a high volume of social science materials. *Library and Book Trade Almanac* (formerly the *Bowker Annual*) for 2017 reported that over half of "college books" published in 2016 (including reference titles) dealt with the social and behavioral sciences, more than the combined total for general works, works in the humanities, and works in science and technology.

## Dictionaries and Encyclopedias

The social sciences have had a particularly rich history of summary encyclopedias, beginning with the 15-volume *Encyclopaedia of the Social Sciences* edited by Edwin Seligman in the 1930s. This was followed by the 19-volume *International Encyclopedia of the Social Sciences* edited by David Sills in the 1960s. The 2008 second edition of the *International Encyclopedia of the Social Sciences* (entry 82) and the *International Encyclopedia of the Social & Behavioral Sciences* (editions of 2001 and 2015; entry 83) are the latest works of this kind. Online versions of such titles can be updated on a continuous basis.

81. *Dictionary of the Social Sciences*, by Craig Calhoun, ed.

Publisher: Oxford University Press, New York, NY (2002)

Price: $75.00

Review by Graham R. Walden—Professor, University Libraries, Ohio State University, Columbus.

While there is an abundance of dictionaries on individual social sciences, surprisingly there are few works that attempt to cover the whole spectrum. Calhoun, along with several associate editors (Joseph Karaganis and Paul Price) and 11 others listed under "Editors and Contributors," has produced a volume that covers anthropology, sociology, political science, economics, human geography, cultural studies, Marxism, and "dozens of other important fields." Basic terms, concepts, theories, schools of thought, methodologies, techniques, topics, issues, and controversies are covered in 1,800-plus entries ranging from 50 to 500 words. The presentation is designed for general readers, the "educated lay person," students, and scholars. There are 275 biographical entries for major figures who had a "profound impact." Words appearing in an entry that are defined elsewhere in the dictionary appear in capital letters. The words defined are in English, except for cases in which the foreign word is used in English—mostly German and French words. A 37-page bibliography is provided, which also is perhaps the least useful resource in the volume. The entries do not state the sources used, nor do the items listed in the bibliography state with which word they are associated. The reader, therefore, has an interesting list of further reading with no guidance as to what any of it relates to. This is an unfortunate situation, which renders the value of this portion of the project somewhat in doubt. Individual entries read well and are certainly stated in a way in which the average reader would have little trouble comprehending. By the very nature of the undertaking, space limitations restrict depth. For example, the term "survey research" is included, with what amount to *see* references to "sampling," "census," and "validity." However, the word questionnaire does not appear in the dictionary, nor do a number of significant other terms from the area of survey research. For purposes of becoming familiar with the general language of a number of disciplines, this volume is useful. For beginning-level undergraduates this book is a good starting point. For upper-level undergraduates and for graduate students, this volume will be appropriate for reading in an area of the field of major concentration. Again, for scholars this would only be valuable when reading in unfamiliar territory. Overall, the contribution is a good current dictionary. A future volume would be rendered more valuable through the association of the works researched to the terms defined. This work is recommended for undergraduate social science programs, public libraries, and community colleges.

Classification: LC H41; Dewey 300.

82. *International Encyclopedia of the Social Sciences,* by William A. Darity Jr., ed.
Publisher: Macmillan Reference USA/Gale Group, New York, NY (2008)

Price: $975.00/set

Review by Michael Margolis—Reference Librarian, City University of New York.

This is an alphabetically arranged nine-volume reference work and the 2nd edition of this study. Despite the many volumes, each article is not long and serves to introduce the reader to the topic. Typical articles are Labor, Revolution, Macroeconomics, and Sex and Mating. Most of the entries provide a succinct definition, description of historical origin and development, and a hint of the different points of view surrounding the entry. Each item is signed and has a small but useful bibliography, and *see* and *see also* references. The writing is good and written at the college level. The editors have made sure that each paragraph advances the understanding of some aspect of the idea being discussed. Students of sociology, anthropology, political science, psychology, economics, and history will benefit from this comprehensive work. The work manages to be both humanistic and scientific throughout. There are a list of articles, a list of contributors, and an introduction. The *International Encyclopedia of the Social Sciences* is of great value for both graduate and undergraduate students as well as researchers.

Classification: LC H40; Dewey 300.

83. *International Encyclopedia of the Social & Behavioral Sciences*, by Neil J. Smelser and Paul B. Baltes, eds.

Publisher: Elsevier Science, San Diego, CA (2001)

Price: $9,995.00/set

Review by Staff, Libraries Unlimited.

This twenty-six-volume scholarly encyclopedia on the social and behavioral sciences is the result of close to ten years of work on the part of the publisher and editors. Two other all-encompassing encyclopedias on this topic were published in the twentieth century, the *Encyclopedia of the Social Sciences* (Seligman and Johnson, 1930–1935) and the *International Encyclopedia of the Social Sciences* (Sills, 1968), so an update on this topic is both timely and appreciated. This work provides entries on four thousand topics, which were arranged and edited by fifty-two contributing editors. Topics provided include overarching topics such as the history and ethics of the social sciences, biographies, and broad concepts; methodology, including statistics and logic and enquiry; definitions and descriptions of the various disciplines found within the social sciences, such as anthropology, archaeology, education, political science, psychology, and sociology; and intersecting fields, including health, gender studies, religious studies, and environmental studies. The text is truly broad and all-encompassing when one realizes how many fields of study social and behavioral sciences touch upon. The list of contributing editors can be found in the front matter of volume 1 and provides information on the editors' fields of study, affiliations, and what other publications they have been published in. Each article runs several pages in length and is signed by the contributor. The articles provide *see also* references to relevant topics as well as extensive bibliographies. According to the publisher there are more than ninety thousand bibliographic references cited. The work is also available in online format through ScienceDirect but was unavailable for review at the time of publication. Elsevier's website claims the site will "be enhanced by flexible search-and-retrieval facilities and by a rich variety of electronic reference links." It also claims that every article in the electronic edition will be supported by an abstract prepared specifically for the online publication.

> The 2nd edition appeared in 2015; the online version is regularly updated. Classification: LC H41; Dewey 300.

## Issues and Trends

### Gender Issues

84. *Routledge International Encyclopedia of Women: Global Women's Issues and Knowledge*, by Cheris Kramarae and Dale Spender, eds.
Publisher: Routledge/Taylor & Francis Group, New York, NY (2000)
Price: $695.00/set
Review by Staff, Libraries Unlimited.

Kramarae and Spender developed this work to preserve women's knowledge and experience for visibility and empowerment in the future. Through this work they hope to address the concerns of women and the theory and practice of feminism around the world. Overall, this is a reliable reference work for scholars, professionals, and general readers. Because of space limitations, this set does not include any entries for individual women. Instead, it focuses on ideas and actions. It also covers certain topics in various regions (e.g., art and literature, education, religion). The articles are written by authors from many disciplines, languages, and cultures. Each article concludes with *see also* references and a list of references and further reading. Each volume contains an alphabetic list of articles, while the first volume also contains a topical list of articles and a list of contributors. The last volume contains an extensive index.

Classification: LC HQ1115; Dewey 305.

85. *Encyclopedia of Women and Gender: Sex Similarities and Differences and the Impact of Society on Gender,* by Judith Worell, ed.

Publisher: Academic Press, San Diego, CA (2001)

Price: $300.00/set

Review by Mary Ellen Snodgrass—Freelance Writer, Charlotte, NC.

Academic Press's new encyclopedia fills in one of the chasms in women's studies with a well-conceived reference guide on gender issues. Beautifully laid out, the work coordinates the writings of 161 contributors from colleges and universities across the United States, plus specialists in Canada and South Africa. The list of 104 topics covers current and perennial subject matter: violence, prejudice, anatomy, emotional ills, aging, social identity, media influence, and family and gender roles. Each entry follows a paradigm of outline: a glossary of such terms as "presbycusis" and "menarche," text, and a list of suggested readings. Tables and charts are orderly and beneficial, but few in number. As is common with compilations of scholarly chapters, the style varies from clear prose to academic fuzziness compounded by a scarcity of concrete examples and the dropping of cumbrous insider terms. Hindering the two-volume set is the failure of cross-referencing and indexing to unite the chapters into a cohesive and usable reference source. Missing, according to the index, are adequate commentaries on patriarchy, female genital mutilation, and fundamentalist religions— all key concepts in feminist concerns in the late twentieth and early twenty-first centuries. Another serious consideration for small libraries is the price. For college and university use, this source is a beginning. Its strengths include attractive presentation, up-to-date sources, readable overviews, and academic input from a variety of points of view, such as the excellent entry on disabilities and women compiled by four writers. Serious deterrents are weak editorial control and an absence of regard for ordinary readers and researchers seeking guidance into thorny gender issues.

Classification: LC HQ1115; Dewey 305.

86. *Encyclopedia of Feminist Theories,* by Lorraine Code, ed.

Publisher: Routledge/Taylor & Francis Group, New York, NY (2000)

Price: $140.00

Review by Susan J. Freiband—Associate Professor, Graduate School of Librarianship, University of Puerto Rico, San Juan.

This work is the result of a long, complex, interactive process involving not only the general editor, but also a group of 11 consulting editors and 270 contributors, mostly from universities in Canada, the United States, and the United Kingdom. The project aims to produce a multidisciplinary resource for students and teachers, those already involved in feminist studies as well as those interested in learning about this field. The encyclopedia is selective in coverage and cross-disciplinary in scope, including mini-biographies of 60 feminist theorists. It concentrates on second-wave feminist theory since the 1960s, focusing primarily on the English-speaking world. It contains little historical material or theories initially written in languages other than English, with the exception of several entries dealing with French feminist theory. There is a useful introduction discussing the context of the encyclopedia, presenting a historical sketch of feminist theories and describing coverage and contributors. The contributors and editors are listed with their affiliated academic institutions; however, their positions and academic fields are not identified, something which would have been helpful. The index includes page numbers in bold typeface, indicating references to the main entry, which is a useful feature. The entries are signed and include references and further reading. They also indicate in boldface terms that are included elsewhere in the book. Cross-references and *see also* references help guide the reader to more information on related topics. The information is presented in two columns, using different type sizes and bold typeface, which helps improve readability. This is particularly useful because the type selected for the text itself is light and small, not as clear or easy to read as one would wish. The book does not include illustrations, which would have been useful for the biographical entries. The *Encyclopedia of Feminist Theories* represents an important contribution to feminist studies and scholarship and would be a valuable addition to reference collections in academic and research libraries, particularly those in institutions with women's studies programs. It also would be useful in large public libraries and special libraries in the humanities and social sciences.

---

Classification: LC HQ1190; Dewey 305.

---

87. *International Encyclopedia of Women and Sports*, by Karen Christensen, Allen Guttmann, and Gertrud Pfister, eds.

Publisher: Macmillan Reference USA/Gale Group, New York, NY (2001)

Price: $350.00/set

Review by Michele Tyrrell—Media Specialist, Arundel Senior High School, Gambrills, MD.

This three-volume set is a comprehensive, accessible, and attractive resource. The work presents a global and historical perspective, with articles on individual sports, physical aspects, cultural issues, sportswomen, political topics, and sport as a business. Coverage ranges from discussions of obvious topics, such as eating disorders, Title IX, sponsorship, and the Race for the Cure, to the more obscure, such as baton twirling and the Brighton Conference. Numerous photographs, graphs, and sidebars add to the text, and the appendixes offer additional useful information. The writing style is readable rather than scholarly, making the content appropriate for a wide audience. A list of contributors is provided at the beginning of volume 1, and each article ends with a bibliography. The index provides numerous cross-references as well as the standard referencing to main topics. The *International Encyclopedia of Women and Sports*, while pricey, will provide a valuable research tool to high school and public libraries. Many may find themselves browsing off the research topic due to the many interesting sidelights.

Classification: LC GV709; Dewey 796.

88. *LGBTQ America Today: An Encyclopedia*, by John C. Hawley and Emmanuel S. Nelson, eds.

Publisher: Greenwood Press/ABC-CLIO, Santa Barbara, CA (2009)

Price: $349.95/set

Review by G. Douglas Meyers—Chair, Department of English, University of Texas, El Paso.

Directed toward academics and students in high school and beyond, *LGBTQ America Today* is an impressive 3-volume encyclopedia that would make an excellent contribution to any academic reference collection. More than 700 entries authored by over 250 scholars collectively trace the role that homosexuality has played in defining American culture in the twentieth and twenty-first centuries. Entries focus on lesbian, gay, bisexual, transgendered, and queer (LGBTQ) individuals (with an emphasis on those still living); key concepts; historical events; sociopolitical issues; religion; and popular culture. Entries are organized alphabetically; all include topic-specific bibliographies and some are enhanced by black-and-white photographs and illustrations. The apparatus in the book is uncomplicated, relying on a list of entries at the beginning of the book, a general bibliography and index at its end, and massive cross-referencing in bold print throughout. Starting with Steve Abbott and ending with David Zamora Casas and including entries on matters as diverse as bisexuality, Chicana feminism, drag, Melissa Etheridge, fat acceptance, gay rodeos, HIV/AIDS, queer theory, Stonewall Riots, Kitty Tsui, Gore Vidal, Wicca, and youth groups, *LGBTQ America Today* provides encyclopedic coverage of many aspects of American LGBTQ life, its main figures and historical events, and its impact on the arts, medicine, and the law.

---

This is an area in which publishing is challenged to keep up with events, such as the 2015 Supreme Court decision in favor of gay marriage rights: *Obergefell v. Hodge*. A source like the *Supreme Court* website from the Legal Information Institute (entry 122) can fill in gaps. The *SAGE Encyclopedia of LGBTQ Studies* is new (2016) but less widely owned. Classification: LC HQ73; Dewey 306.

---

## Immigration

Immigration is another rapidly developing issue. Older reference sources offer a solid foundation in terms of history, vocabulary, and themes to be updated by online resources like *Congress.gov* (entry 116). Newer publications like *Encyclopedia of American Immigration* (Salem Press, 2010) are on the market but less widely owned than the works listed here.

89. *Encyclopedia of American Immigration*, by James Ciment, ed.

Publisher: M. E. Sharpe, Armonk, NY (2001)

Price: $399.00/set

Review by Philip G. Swan—Head Librarian, Hunter College, School of Social Work Library, New York, NY.

The *Encyclopedia of American Immigration* is a well-written, exhaustive, and abundantly illustrated reference resource. The encyclopedia consists of four volumes. Volume 1 concentrates on the history of immigration to the United States. It starts with a chronological overview of major immigration trends. While some of these articles seem a bit cursory, they are well written. As is the case throughout the encyclopedia, each article includes an author byline, a bibliography, and cross-references as well as black-and-white illustrations and the occasional table or chart. After exploring the chronological history of immigration to the United States, the encyclopedia looks at such specific historical issues as immigrant living conditions. More abstract concepts include "America's Image in the Global Imagination." Finally, factors motivating immigration are examined. Volume 2 considers immigrant issues, including such familiar topics as the impact of families of assimilated children. The encyclopedia also considers some issues that are often overlooked, including gay and lesbian immigration. Laws and legislation are examined in more detail, including political arguments for and against immigration that are both handled in a relatively fair and unbiased way. The economic costs and benefits of immigration are weighed, and the effects of immigration labor in both the United States and the home countries are examined. Unionization, health care issues, and education are also touched upon. Finally, the impact of immigration on American popular culture and society is explored. Volume 3 examines immigrant groups in America. It begins by considering the portrayal of immigrants in the media. Articles relating to a variety of fields influenced by immigration follow. Specific immigrant destinations in the United States are explored in detail. The effects of the global economy on immigration patterns are considered, as are immigration trends in other nations. The rest of volume 3 covers individual immigrant groups in the United States arranged by the region of origin. For major immigrant groups like the Irish or the Chinese, an individualized analysis is provided. Volume 4 concentrates on immigration-related documents. There is an extensive collection of legal texts. Political party platforms are included, as are government reports and rulings. Finally, there are several historical texts of note, including some fascinating letters relating the feelings of individual immigrants. Volume 4 closes with a glossary and an outstanding bibliography. All four volumes include a general index. There are also indexes relating to geography as well as legal and judicial topics.

A less widely owned four-volume set of 2010, edited by Carl L. Bankston, III, and published by Salem Press, has the same title. Classification: LC JV6465; Dewey 304.

90. *Undocumented Immigrants in the United States: An Encyclopedia of Their Experience*, by Anna Ochoa O'Leary, ed.

Publisher: Greenwood Press/ABC-CLIO, Santa Barbara, CA (2014)

Price: $189.00/set

Review by Adrienne Antink, Medical Group Management Association, Lakewood, CO.

This compendium provides a survey of the issues and policies that shape the current debate on the 11.1 million undocumented immigrants in the United States. Although the irregular immigration of other minority groups is addressed, the bulk of the entries focus on Latino populations. Topics include key laws and court cases; economic, social, and employment issues; and the identification card debate, the different types of visas, and more. In general, the entries are just a few pages, necessitating a broad brush coverage of each topic, but there are references at the end of every essay for further depth. The target audience is high school and undergraduate students and teachers. The reference is timely given the demographic changes occurring in America and helps the reader to better understand proposed policies and their consequences as they are discussed in the ongoing immigration reform debate. As an example of the material presented, we often assume that undocumented means the individual entered this country clandestinely. But it is estimated as many as 4.4 million undocumented immigrants have entered the country by legal means, such as a non-immigrant visa, and never left. Currently the government does not track exit information. Many of these "overstayers" are East Asians. There is also a chronology of immigration laws and policies from 1790 to 2013 to set the context for the entries and demonstrates that immigration and its impact on the fabric of the nation is not a new challenge for America.

Classification: LC JV6475; Dewey 305.

## Crime

91. *Encyclopedia of Crime and Justice,* by Joshua Dressler, ed.

Publisher: Macmillan Reference USA/Gale Group, New York, NY (2002)

Price: $475.00/set

Review by David O. Friedrichs—Professor, University of Scranton, Scranton, PA.

The publication of the 4-volume *Encyclopedia of Crime and Justice* in 1983 was an auspicious development within contemporary criminology because it was the first major encyclopedia in the field. More recently, however, several publishers have produced—or announced—the publication of major criminological encyclopedias. The most noteworthy of these to date is the 4-volume *Encyclopedia of Criminology and Deviant Behavior,* edited by Clifton D. Bryant (2001). Now, the 2nd edition of the *Encyclopedia of Crime and Justice* has been published by Macmillan Reference USA and edited by Dressler (the 1st edition was edited by Sanford H. Kadish). The new 4-volume edition has as its objective a broad coverage of the essence of what is now known about criminal behavior and its control. The editor also has attempted to produce an encyclopedia that is useful to specialists in the field but is also accessible to a literate general audience. This attempt is a challenging aspiration, but, on the whole, it has been met. Some other criminological encyclopedias (for example, *The Encyclopedia of American Crime*, edited by Carl Sifakis [2nd ed., 2001]) are specifically organized to provide numerous entertaining accounts of the careers of celebrated criminals and of famous criminal events. The present work, however, is certainly not geared toward entertainment, but has the more serious purpose of providing well-informed overviews of fundamental criminological and criminal law topics. Contributors were specifically instructed to provide balanced—as opposed to opinionated or polemical—interpretations of their assigned topics. The contributors seem to have adhered to this guideline. Altogether, this encyclopedia now includes some 250 essays of varying length (ranging from 800 to 12,000 words). Some of the essays in the original edition have been updated (often by a new co-author), but most of the essays are entirely new. Obviously, much has changed in the almost two decades since the publication of the original edition. In the case of key criminological and criminal law concepts, however, only some modest updating is required. New entries are included on such topics as feminist criminology, hate crime, human immunodeficiency virus (HIV), and an international criminal court. Entries are included on basic concepts, major types of crime, variables associated with crime or some general trends, criminal law concepts, components of the criminal justice system, and a wide range of other issues or concepts. Some comparative topics—such as "Comparative Criminal Law and Enforcement: Islam"—are included, which is certainly important in an increasingly globalized twenty-first century. On the whole, the selection of topics for coverage is persuasive. Each essay concludes with a bibliographic section of references— necessarily selective and, in at least some cases, weighted more toward well-established contributions on the topic rather than the latest research or scholarship. The editorial board for this encyclopedia includes some of the most distinguished active scholars in the field (e.g., Thomas Bernard, John Hagan), and the editor has certainly succeeded in persuading an impressive group of highly accomplished scholars to contribute essays. While most of the contributors have contributed a single essay, some have taken on two or more, and one contributor is responsible as author or co-author for 18 essays. As might be expected from scholars of this caliber, the quality of the essays is quite uniformly high. By any criteria, this publication is a distinguished and important reference work within the field of criminology. It differs from the *Encyclopedia of Criminology and Deviant Behavior* principally in terms of a somewhat different focus, with much more attention to basic concepts within criminal law, and much less to the many different forms of criminal and deviant behavior. It has about half as many entries, although many of these are lengthier, and address the topic at hand in greater depth. Indeed, in many respects these two valuable resources complement each other. If an academic library cannot acquire both encyclopedias and has to choose, then this encyclopedia is recommended for libraries serving principally graduate programs, and the *Encyclopedia of Criminology and Deviant Behavior* is recommended instead for undergraduate libraries since it is more accessible and organized in a manner more appealing to typical undergraduates.

Newer and similar in length but less widely held is the *Encyclopedia of Criminology and Criminal Justice*, edited by Jay S. Albanese (Wiley, 2014). Classification: LC HV6017; Dewey 364.

92. *Crime in the United States*, by Shana Hattis, ed.

Publisher: Bernan Press, Lanham, MD

Price: $115.00

Review by Staff, Libraries Unlimited.

Previously published by the FBI, *Crime in the United States* is now in its 10th edition and is available from Bernan Press. The volume begins with a short section that summarizes the Uniform Crime Reporting Program. Section two, Offenses Known to Police, is divided into violent crimes (murder, forcible rape, robbery, aggravated assault) and property crime (burglary, larceny theft, motor vehicle theft, arson). Offenses are reported nationally and by region in tables like Crime by Region, Geographic Division, and State, 2013–2014, and Offenses Known to Law Enforcement by State (broken down further by city or town). This allows users to determine quickly, for instance, that there were 932 burglaries in Berkeley, California, in contrast to 4,065 burglaries in Bakersfield, California, during the same time period. The third section, Offenses Cleared, is short in comparison and has data on the number and percentage of offenses cleared by arrest or exceptional means in 2014. Section four, Persons Arrested, has tables that estimate the number of arrests in 2014 by type of crime followed by "Number and Rate of Arrests, by Geographic Region, 2013," "Ten-Year Arrest Trends, 2005 and 2014," "Arrests by State, 2014," "Female Arrests, Distribution by Age, 2014," and many more. A quick glance at the latter table reveals that most arrests were of women aged 18 or older. The tables in Law Enforcement Personnel, the fifth section, provide data on numbers of law enforcement employees by state and region. The last section conveys information about hate crimes. This is followed by four appendixes: "Methodology," "Offense Definitions," "Geographic Area Definitions," and "The Nation's Two Crime Measures." An index rounds out the work; when it is used in conjunction with the detailed table of contents, users will have an easy time finding the statistics they seek. Recommended to public and academic libraries.

Issued in print by the Department of Justice until 2004. Annual texts of *Uniform Crime Reports* beginning with 1995 remain available online from the Federal Bureau of Investigation at https://ucr.fbi.gov/ucr-publications, along with related online compilations such as *Hate Crime Statistics* and *Law Enforcement Officers Killed and Assaulted.* Classification: LC HV6787; Dewey 364.

93. *Crime and Punishment around the World,* by Graeme R. Newman, ed.

Publisher: ABC-CLIO, Santa Barbara, CA (2010)

Price: $380.00/set

Review by Martha Lawler—Associate Librarian, Louisiana State University, Shreveport.

Since some nations can be hesitant to reveal the extent of crime in their area or their methods of punishment, it is difficult to get an accurate accumulation of information. This compilation examines the various systems and provides an overview of the development of civilization and human attempts to maintain order. An introduction gives background discussion of crime and punishment worldwide, a brief comparison of civil and common law, and a brief discussion of Islamic, customary, and social legal systems. The introduction is followed by maps that give a graphical representation of statistics. The four volumes examine Africa and the Middle East, the Americas, Asia and the Pacific, and Europe. The entries are alphabetical by name of the country and give a brief indication of the type of legal system and the prevalence of various crimes and punishments (e.g., murder, burglary, corruption, prison rate, death penalty). The main part of each entry provides background information about the legal system of each country, discussions of crime classification and statistics, the method of determining guilt, and a general discussion of methods and amounts of punishment. Sometimes included are sections on crime prevention and juvenile crime. Each volume has a general bibliography, a list of contributors, and an index that applies to the whole set. Black-and-white illustrations serve to enhance the text, although a few seem more sensational than informative. The entries are well written and very informative and concise.

Classification: LC HV6025; Dewey 364.

94. *Encyclopedia of Prisons & Correctional Facilities,* by Mary Bosworth, ed.

Publisher: SAGE, Thousand Oaks, CA (2005)

Price: $295.00/set

Review by David O. Friedrichs—Professor, University of Scranton, Scranton, PA.

The recent era in the United States has been characterized by an extraordinary increase in the number of inmates in correctional facilities, with over two million incarcerated by the end of the twentieth century. As the introduction to this encyclopedia reminds us, the United States has a higher per capita rate of incarceration than any other equivalent developed nation, with an especially large disproportion of people of color behind bars. This immense correctional population has generated some practical problems, such as overcrowding and budgetary pressures on states, as well as serious concern on the part of many interested parties about the implications and ultimate consequences of such reliance upon penal institutions. Accordingly, a comprehensive encyclopedia exploring all aspects of imprisonment and corrections would seem to be especially timely and welcome. The over four hundred entries in this two-volume encyclopedia are classified in a "Reader's Guide" at the beginning of the first volume into a number of different categories. First, there are entries on "authors," including classic contributors to the penal literature (e.g., Jeremy Bentham), celebrated inmate writers (e.g., Jack Henry Abbott), and contemporary academic scholars who have addressed correctional matters (e.g., David Rothman). A section on health includes entries on such matters as psychological services in prison, suicide, and HIV/AIDS. A significant number of entries are classified as historical in focus and include important reformers (e.g., Dorothea Dix), early models for prisons (e.g., the Auburn System), and specific reviews of the history of prisons, of religion in prison, of correctional officers, and the like. Some entries are devoted to especially celebrated inmates, during the course of the twentieth century, including Elizabeth Gurley Flynn, Ethel and Julius Rosenberg, and Leonard Peltier. Another set of entries is focused upon famous prisons or noteworthy contemporary penitentiaries, including on the one hand the Walnut Street Jail, Alcatraz, and Sing Sing, but also INS detention facilities, the Massachusetts Reformatory, and Pelican Bay State Prison. Juvenile justice is addressed by entries on such matters as Child Savers, the juvenile justice system, and status offenders. The category of labor includes boot camp, prisoner pay, and work release programs. A general category of penal systems has entries on some foreign systems (e.g., Australia, Canada), on military prisons, and on women's prisons. A number of entries address prison architecture, including entries on high-rise prisons, Panopticon, and supermax prisons. An especially large number of entries address aspects of prison life, ranging from argot to food to riots to visits. Prison population entries include the Aryan Blood, homosexual prisoners, lifers, and mothers in prison. Prison reform entries include abolition, reformers such as John Howard, and the National Prison Project. Privatization—a growing recent trend—is addressed by general entries, as well as more specific entries such as Corrections Corporation of America. Prison programs include entries on such matters as education, group therapy, and religion in prison. Race, class, and gender—themes addressed in many entries—include some specific entries on minority race advocates (e.g., Malcolm X) and on racism. Security and classification is addressed by entries on such matters as home arrest and minimum security. Sentencing policy, presently facing new challenges with a major U.S. Supreme Court decision, includes entries on cases such as *Estelle v. Gamble*, determinate sentence, and Three-Strikes legislation. A series of entries on Staff include celebrated wardens (e.g., Joseph E. Ragen), Correctional Officers Unions, and volunteers. Theories of Punishment entries address such matters as capital punishment, deterrence theory, and restorative justice. And types of punishments include entries on corporal punishment, fines, and probation. Of course there are any number of overlaps between these different categories of entries. Altogether, Mary Bosworth, the editor, has done a fine job of putting together such a comprehensive reference work on this topic. It is always possible to quibble about some topic choices (and neglected subjects), but on the whole the coverage here seems admirably thorough and balanced. Contributors include academics as well as correctional practitioners, and as an especially noteworthy feature, a series of sidebars on topics ranging from family visits to arriving in prison to inmate codes have been produced by current inmates. The entries themselves typically run to several pages and include lists of further reading. *See also* cross-reference lists at the end of entries are also useful, as is a chronology at the beginning of volume 1. These volumes are accessible to, and should prove useful to, a wide range of constituencies, from high school students to scholars in the field.

---

Classification: LC HV9471; Dewey 365.

---

95. *Encyclopedia of Juvenile Justice*, by Marilyn D. McShane and Frank P. Williams III, eds.

Publisher: SAGE, Thousand Oaks, CA (2003)

Price: $99.95

Review by David O. Friedrichs—Professor, University of Scranton, Scranton, PA.

The juvenile justice system in the United States has been in existence for over 100 years now. If the need for separate procedures and penal options for most juvenile offenders has been quite widely accepted, the specific policies and practices for addressing such offenders have been a topic of enduring controversy. The media coverage of juvenile justice cases tends to focus on especially sensational and atypical cases, which contributes to public misperceptions of the true nature of juvenile justice. Our society has much at stake in ensuring that the juvenile justice system operates as effectively and fairly as possible. The co-editors of this encyclopedia, Marilyn D. McShane and Frank P. Williams, III, are enterprising and well-known criminologists. In addition to their own scholarly work—including the highly regarded *Criminological Theory* (3rd ed.; Pearson Education, 1998)—they have served as editors of monograph series and the *Encyclopedia of American Prisons*. For the present work they commissioned over 200 entries from 140 contributors. The contributors include some of the best-known scholars in the field, including Frankie Bailey, Robert M. Bohm, Gilbert Geis, Don Gibbons, John Laub, Doris MacKenzie, Alida Merlo, Laura Moriarty, Frank Scarpitti, David Shichor, Austin Turk, and Neil Websdale. Of course, many other accomplished scholars, as well as some junior scholars, also contributed to this encyclopedia. The encyclopedia articles are divided into the following categories: Delinquency Theories and Theorists (e.g., cycles of violence, Albert Cohen); Historical References: People and Projects (e.g., Augusta Bronner, Chicago Area Project); Delinquent Behavior (e.g., race and delinquency, status offenders); Treatment and Interventions for Delinquency (e.g., boot camps, scared straight); Juvenile Law and Legislative Initiatives (e.g., Juvenile Justice and Delinquency Prevention Act, waivers to adult court); and Juvenile Issues and Public Policy (e.g., missing children, school responses to juvenile violence). Although anyone working in the field of juvenile justice is likely to find one or more favorite topics excluded, a good deal of thought seems to have gone into the selection of the topics covered, and certainly all of the key issues are addressed. The entries typically run two or more pages; a few are more brief. They are broken up by appropriate subheadings. Cross-references are noted at the end of each entry; for example, at the end of the Child-Saving Movement users will find a *see also* reference to Courts, Juvenile-History; Female Delinquency-History; Law, Juvenile; Parens Patriae Doctrine; Reformatories and Reform Schools; and Status Offenders. A bibliography of typically between 5 and 10 sources can also be found at the end of each entry. A small handful of appropriate illustrations are scattered throughout this volume (e.g., Judge Lindsey Presides in the Chambers of His Juvenile Court; Elmira Reformatory). Appendix 1 lists print and online resources for juvenile justice, while appendix 2 lists Internet resources for juvenile justice. A fairly detailed index is included as well. Altogether, the editors are to be commended for once again making a substantial contribution to criminological knowledge. This attractively produced encyclopedia, with many well-written and informative articles, will surely be a useful resource for any party seeking basic information on a range of topics related to juvenile delinquency and juvenile justice. It can be recommended for purchase by public libraries as well as college and university libraries and those serving a scholarly community with an interest in juvenile justice issues.

Classification: LC HV9104; Dewey 364.

96. *Forensic Science: An Encyclopedia of History, Methods, and Techniques*, by William J. Tilstone, Kathleen A. Savage, and Leigh A. Clark

Publisher: ABC-CLIO, Santa Barbara, CA (2006)

Price: $95.00

Review by David K. Frasier—Assistant Librarian, Reference Department, Indiana University, Bloomington.

Since the debut of the highly successful television program *CSI: Crime Scene Investigation* in November 2000, reference publishing in forensic science has become a boom industry. Selected titles varying in scope, size, and target audience include the 3-volume *Encyclopedia of Forensic Sciences*, *Encyclopedia of Forensic Science: A Compendium of Detective Fact and Fiction*, *Encyclopedia of Forensic Science*, and *The Facts on File Dictionary of Forensic Science*. Into this crowded field comes the work under review, a modest but serviceable encyclopedia aimed at the lay reader. Lead author Tilstone is the well-published executive director of the National Forensic Science Technology Center in Largo, Florida. Co-authors Savage and Clark have extensive experience in forensics and law enforcement. In an impressive, highly readable, and lengthy introduction the authors trace the evolving history of forensic science highlighting the discipline's noteworthy individuals, methods, and scientific breakthroughs. Expanded discussions of some are found in the work's 238 entries. These range in length from a few paragraphs to several pages for one of the bedrocks of forensic science, fingerprinting. This entry is further subdivided into "Detection," "Chemical Processing," "Forgeries," and more. Most entries include a select bibliography focusing largely on monographs and websites. Interestingly, entries on notorious individuals like serial killer Ted Bundy are included because their cases present and highlight particular forensic challenges or methods. Sparsely illustrated with photographs and including a general bibliography (again largely limited to books and websites), this book is suitable for high school and public libraries.

Classification: LC HV8073; Dewey 363.

97. *Encyclopedia of Women and Crime*, by Nicole Hahn Rafter, ed.

Publisher: Oryx Press/Greenwood Publishing Group, Westport, CT (2000)

Price: $65.00

Review by David O. Friedrichs—Professor, University of Scranton, Scranton, PA.

Historically, crime and its control have been a dominantly male enterprise. Beginning principally in the 1970s, a growing number of feminist criminologists began to direct attention to women as offenders, as justice system personnel, and as victims of crime. By the end of the twentieth century a formidable literature on women and crime had developed. This encyclopedia is further acknowledgment of the breadth and depth of recent scholarship on women as criminals, victims, and law enforcers or adjudicators. It claims to be the first comprehensive encyclopedia devoted to this topic. A useful topic finder at the beginning of this encyclopedia provides users with an efficient map of the terrain covered. One series of entries addresses offenders, offenses, and theories of offending. Forms of crimes where women are especially well represented—such as shoplifting and prostitution—are highlighted here. For other types of crimes, such as domestic violence and homicide, patterns of female involvement are addressed. While the crimes of females have been explained by some of the same theories applied to male crime, a feminist criminology imposes an alternative framework on the understanding of female crime. A series of entries on juvenile delinquency address the differential treatment of juvenile females relative to males. And some entries describe specific classes of offenders (e.g., call girls) or notorious offenders (e.g., Barbara Perry's informative and entertaining piece on Bonnie Parker of Bonnie and Clyde). Women have been especially vulnerable to certain forms of victimization, such as rape and domestic violence, and another series of entries covers many aspects of victim proneness among women as well as the increasingly influential victims' rights movement. Another series of entries addresses policing, courts, and case processing as they relate to women. Since the early 1970s women have become a significant presence on police forces. Women in court proceedings have all too often had negative experiences. An entry on rape shield laws addresses the legal device that has been widely adopted to diminish the likelihood of rape victims being humiliated as witnesses in rape trials. Entries relating to punishment and treatment address some of the particular issues that arise when women go to prison and when women gain employment in the correctional system. Entries here range from co-correctional prisons to sexual abuse of prisoners. Entries on the treatment of prisoners include one on incarcerated mothers. Finally, some entries specifically focus on patterns of crime, victimization, and criminal justice system responses in Australia, Britain, and Canada—most of the entries focus on the American situation. Altogether, this encyclopedia is sure to prove indispensable to the growing number of students of women as criminals, as criminal justice personnel, and as victims before the system of criminal justice. The contributors include many well-known women criminologists and feminist criminologists. A variety of figures and tables enhance the usefulness of this volume, as does a bibliography of sources cited.

Classification: LC HV6046; Dewey 364.

98. *The Encyclopedia of Child Abuse*, by Robin E. Clark and Judith Freeman Clark, with Christine Adamec

Publisher: Facts on File, New York, NY (2007)

Price: $75.00

Review by Marianne B. Eimer—Head of Reference and Instruction, Daniel A. Reed Library, State University of New York, Fredonia.

Directly informing the user about the identification, treatment, and prevention of child abuse, this 3rd edition of *The Encyclopedia of Child Abuse* retains the 2001 edition's format and publication quality. Scholarly in nature, the content can be understood by both the layperson and the specialist. The advantage of a reference tool such as this is that there are specific subject definitions, encyclopedic articles, historic timelines, and pertinent resources all devoted entirely to the topic of child abuse, located in a single volume. International information can be found under country entries, and statistics from such organizations as the Children's Bureau in the U.S. Department of Health and Human Services are quoted. Slightly longer than the 2nd edition, the user is now able to consult a list of references located at the conclusion of the introduction to the encyclopedia which, written by the renowned child abuse expert Richard J. Gelles, Ph.D., gives a detailed overview of the subject matter, including recent developments. New entries were added on such recently publicized topics as "adults abused as children, effects of" and "clergy abuse." Alphabetic entries ranging in length from short paragraphs to several pages often have cross-references of *see* or *see also* at the end of the article. Frequently for lengthier entries, there is a references list included to facilitate further research. The volume has an alphabetized subject index at the back, facilitating its use in ready-reference situations. The appendixes have changed, now having seven rather than fifteen categories. More importantly, two of the new categories include a listing of state-by-state laws on termination of parental rights and a listing of state-by-state definitions of child abuse. This is a reasonably priced update and, because of the usefulness of all areas of this reference title, is recommended for all libraries.

Classification: LC HV6626; Dewey 363.

99. *Encyclopedia of Street Crime in America*, by Jeffrey Ian Ross, ed.

Publisher: SAGE, Thousand Oaks, CA (2013)

Price: $125.00

Review by David K. Frasier—Assistant Librarian, Reference Department, Indiana University, Bloomington.

This single-volume encyclopedia will prove a valuable addition to any reference collection. There are more than 175 entries that are supported by photographs and illustrations. In addition, there is a readers' guide that groups all of the entries into general categories. The volume shows that due to the implementation of security cameras in many public places street crime has changed over the past several decades. The focus is on urban crime, and some of the topics addressed include burglary, drug peddling, murder, and street scams. Also covered are terms associated with the police, courts, and other criminal justice subdisciplines. Each entry concludes with references (if any) to any related entries and recommendations for further reading. A chronology provides readers with a historical perspective of street crime in America, while the appendixes provide data and statistics on street crime. This work is highly recommended.

---

Classification: LC HV6789; Dewey 364.

---

100. *Encyclopedia of Organized Crime in the United States: From Capone's Chicago to the New Urban Underworld,* by Robert J. Kelly

Publisher: Greenwood Press/ABC-CLIO, Santa Barbara, CA (2000)

Price: $59.95

Review by Robert B. Marks Ridinger—Head, Electronic Information Resources Management Department, University Libraries, Northern Illinois University, De Kalb.

One of a group of broad-based reference works in historical and analytic criminology (the voluminous 1989 *Encyclopedia of World Crime* and Carl Sifakas's 1999 *The Mafia Encyclopedia* among them), Robert Kelly's new tome takes a more focused approach emphasizing the developmental history of American organized criminal efforts, imported and homegrown, from 1860 to the 1990s. The author has written and edited four previous books on hate crimes and criminal social evolution, most relevantly the 1994 *Handbook of Organized Crime in the United States* (Greenwood Press), whose contributed essays on formally structured illegal operations outside the traditional mafiosi make it a precursor of the present volume. While the bulk of the entries are biographies of individuals, articles on Russian organized crime, Colombian drug cartels, tongs, organized crime and the media, and crime commissions provide updated background on newly visible groups and historic underworld precedents. Suggested readings of books and articles drawn from the literatures of biography, history, and criminology are appended for each essay. A bibliography of selected reference works, general treatments of organized crime, memoirs and biographies, feature films, and government reports provides a valuable resource for collection development.

This work is most useful for public libraries; college and university reference collections supporting undergraduate and graduate programs in criminal justice, history, and political science; and law libraries.

Classification: LC HV6446; Dewey 364.

101. *Encyclopedia of Rape*, by Merril D. Smith, ed.
Publisher: Greenwood Press/ABC-CLIO, Santa Barbara, CA (2004)
Price: $75.00
Review by Nancy L. Van Atta, Dayton, OH.

This history of rape, from antiquity to present, focuses on the United States but also describes notorious attacks in other countries, such as the raping of Chinese men and women by the Japanese during the Rape of Nanking. The encyclopedia is not an investigation into the causes, but the recording of acts of rape offers some insight into the reasons for this unusually brutal crime; for example, the greater incidence against smaller men in prisons or against the mentally disabled is noted. The reader will quickly see a pattern of the stronger victimizing the weaker, with the criminals at times clearly demonstrating this intent to humiliate (as was the case with the rape of Jews by the Nazis). Indeed, the entry for the Nazis illustrates the risk of writing about rape without careful analysis. The entry recounts the likelier fate of sexual humiliation, in concentration camps, for Jewish women, rather than actual rape, because of the Nazi law against sexual intercourse with "other races" and the soldiers' fear of punishment by officers' enforcement of this law. Yet another explanation for the low incidence of rape is dropped into the middle of this line of thought: "Women in the camps were also often physically unattractive to the Nazis." At no point is the distinction between the conflicting theories of sexual assault as sex and sexual assault as assault more apparent than when the author of this entry failed to recognize it. However, the overall quality of the research and presentation of this and other entries is very high, and the encyclopedia is an excellent source of facts about rape not easily found. Making the information even more accessible are a time line of rape-related events from the Code of Hammurabi to the modern-day rapes of Air Force servicewomen by Air Force servicemen, a topical index, and a bibliography. The more than seventy-five contributors to this work reflect the variety of source material: historians, of course, but also experts in art, literature, and films, as well as attorneys, anthropologists, and other scholars. For readers who are interested in the history of U.S. laws about rape, Greenwood Press has also published by the same editor *Sex without Consent: Rape and Sexual*

*Coercion in America* (2001). *The Encyclopedia of Rape* is recommended for public, high school, and undergraduate libraries.

---

Classification: LC HV6558; Dewey 362.

---

102. *The Encyclopedia of Serial Killers*, by Michael Newton

Publisher: Facts on File, New York, NY (2006)

Price: $85.00

Review by Joe Hardenbrook—Reference Librarian, Staley Library, Millikin University, Decatur, IL.

Newspaper headlines touting the capture of the "BTK Strangler," and movies such as *Monster*, depicting one of the most notorious female serial killers, are evidence of the public's appetite for serial killers. Now researchers and aficionados alike have an updated source to whet their appetite. Newton, a prolific crime writer, has carved a niche as the author of all things kooky and weird, including *The Encyclopedia of Conspiracies and Conspiracy Theories* and *The Encyclopedia of Kidnappings*. Inside this new edition readers will find over 250 entries ranging from specific serial killers (e.g., Ted Bundy, Jeffrey Dahmer) to more topical entries (e.g., cults and serial murder, insanity defense). Law enforcement terms are also identified for lay readers (e.g., spree murders, team killers). In addition, unsolved cases are also highlighted (e.g., I-45 Killer, Tylenol Murders). The most notorious individuals, cases, and events occupy multipage spreads (e.g., Jack the Ripper, Zodiac killer), and many include a bibliography. Although the U.S. accounts for a majority of serial killers, the book is international in scope, covering infamous serial killers in other countries. Likewise, it also includes historical serial murders as well. This 2nd edition comprises more recent serial killers such as the 2002 Washington, D.C., area snipers and updated information on the 2005 arrest of the Wichita, Kansas, "BTK Strangler." The latter third of the book is devoted to several appendixes covering solo killers, team killers, and unresolved cases. Lastly, a bibliography of nearly 700 sources leads the reader to further areas of interest. Despite covering a sensational topic, the book's tone is sober. *The Encyclopedia of Serial Killers* is recommended for both public and academic libraries with strong social science collections. This book will appeal to both researchers and lay readers alike.

---

Classification: LC HV6245; Dewey 364.

---

## Extremism

103. *Encyclopedia of Terrorism*, by Cindy C. Combs and Martin Slann

Publisher: Facts on File, New York, NY (2007)

Price: $95.00

Review by Mark Y. Herring—Dean of Library Services, Winthrop University, Dacus Library, Rock Hill, SC.

Every author strives to strike the right chord in the minds of readers at just the right time, to successfully achieve "urphanomen" (to use Goethe's word), where ideal and reality converge. With fiction, the task is both harder (from a literary point of view) and easier (from the human frailty point of view) than with nonfiction. Nonfiction authors must strike the right note at the right time when events and ideas converge, a task not always easily to fashion, or contrive. The best nonfiction books in the world can be easily missed because either events or the reality is out of synch for readers. The present work may best represent the most explicit achievement of urphanomen: terrorism and the world today. This is an updated version, but even so a timelier book could not easily be named. This revised work from the 2002 edition carries with it all the angst of 9/11: the wars, the rumors of war, and those who want anything but war. The introduction captures this sense well, although its quotes around the phrase "war on terrorism" are odd, as if to say there is no war or only a putative one. Anyone who thinks the war on terror a conjuring of any administration—the Clinton or the Bush one—lives in a virtual reality: one that does not take into account actual events. The volume offers descriptions, analyses, recitations of what the contributors believe are the most serious and influential terrorist personalities, and organizations in the world today. Osama bin Laden, Khmer Rouge, jihad, and Homeland Security are all here. Together, the writers also point to the motivations of terrorists and terrorism. The book appears even-handed on the whole, but there are more than slanted articles with a certain political line in view. A list of the major acts of terrorism over the last fifty-plus years makes up one appendix, while a day-to-day account of September 11 and beyond makes up another. This is an excellent volume that anyone interested in this sad topic will want to have near at hand.

Classification: LC HV6431; Dewey 363.

104. *Encyclopedia of Terrorism*, by Harvey W. Kushner

Publisher: SAGE, Thousand Oaks, CA (2003)

Price: $125.00

Review by Robert B. Marks Ridinger—Head, Electronic Information Resources
    Management Department, University Libraries, Northern Illinois Univer-
    sity, De Kalb.

The latest in a genre of reference works begun in 1987 with John Thackrah's
*Encyclopedia of Terrorism and Political Violence*, this well-constructed volume
(begun one year prior to September 11, 2001) provides detailed historical and
contemporary coverage of a complex and politically timely subject. The author
is both a professor of criminal justice at Long Island University specializing in
the analysis of terrorism as a criminal phenomenon and a widely heard media
commentator for MSNBC, CNN, and Fox News as well as international networks. Of particular value for librarians is the "Reader's Guide," which groups
the content articles into 32 topical categories centering on organizations promoting terrorist actions (such as Al Qaeda, Abu Nidal, and Hezbollah) and specific attacks (such as the events of September 11, 2001, and the earlier World
Trade Center bombing of 1993), types of terror activities, and concepts widely
used in the literature of terrorism (such as the ideas of Jihad). Entries focus on
both providing historical background on individuals and organizations and
assessing their roles in the overall picture of terrorist activity, with further readings indicated. Four appendixes present the locations of terrorist activity by
continent; websites of journals and reports; media, nongovernmental organizations, and federal and international agencies related to terrorist activity and its
suppression; a chronology of terrorist attacks within the United States and on
American interests abroad beginning in 1865; and a bibliography. This bibliography is subdivided into overviews; counter-terrorism; primary documents and
biography; September 11th; and technical literature on such topics as bomb
detection and chemical and biological warfare. The work is indexed by personal, organizational, and geographic names and by subject. The *Encyclopedia of
Terrorism* is best suited for high school, college, and university reference
collections.

---

Classification: LC HV6431; Dewey 363.

---

105. *Encyclopedia of Modern American Extremists and Extremist Groups*, by Stephen
    E. Atkins

Publisher: Greenwood Press/ABC-CLIO, Santa Barbara, CA (2002)

Price: $74.95

Review by Mark Y. Herring—Dean of Library Services, Winthrop University,
    Dacus Library, Rock Hill, SC.

Extremists have been in America as long as America has been around. "Nothing exceeds like excess," Oscar Wilde is reported to have said, and extremists have certainly been excessive in this country. The *Encyclopedia of Modern American Extremists and Extremist Groups* stands as a sad testament to this country's homegrown hotheads, lunatics, and guttersnipes. "What is objectionable, what is dangerous about extremists," the late Robert Kennedy once opined, "is not that they are extreme, but that they are intolerant. The evil is not what they say about their cause, but what they say about their opponents." It is also what they do to those perceived opponents. Consider Marshall Applewhite, resident kook of the kookier Heaven's Gate. The comet Hale-Bopp was a signal for something, causing Applewhite to renounce lust, embrace (if one can use that word in this context) castration, and send himself and just over three dozen members to a new age by mixing phenobarbital sleeping pills in applesauce, pudding, or vodka. Other groups are less easy to dismiss. ACT-UP has the cache of Hollywood and the politically correct crowd even though its tactics are no different from dozens of other routinely denounced groups. Atkins covers them all: offbeat "religious" groups, militia, the KKK, David Koresh, the Unabomber, and more. Entries range in length from a few hundred words to nearly a thousand. Cross-references and bibliographies ("Suggested Readings") enhance the volume's usefulness. This is an excellent reference tool and should place Atkins in line for a second Booklist Editor's Choice Award.

Classification: LC HN90; Dewey 350.

## Political Science and Law

### U.S. Government and Politics

There are numerous useful and well-prepared works on the U.S. political system. In this section are general overviews and works about the legislative and executive branches: the next section includes resources with more details about the judiciary and the Constitution.

106. *The United States Government Manual*, by the National Archives and Records Administration
Publisher: Bernan Press, Lanham, MD
Price: $34.00
ISSN: 0092-1904
Review by Staff, Libraries Unlimited.

The standard way to obtain information about the federal government is to consult its official handbook, *The United States Government Manual*, which has been published annually since 1935 and which is online. Normally, a new edition is released in late summer. The manual describes the federal government and provides mission statements, descriptive information, organizational charts, and director information for legislative, judicial, and executive agencies and offices, as well as for independent boards, commissions, committees, and quasi-official agencies. Entries cover dates of establishment, key personnel, major sub-agencies, and programs and services. It is a convenient source for locating contacts, including those for public information inquiries and regional offices.

> A free online version of this annual official federal government publication can be reached from the National Archives Web page at https://www.archives.gov/federal-register/publications/government-manual.html. Classification: LC JK421; Dewey 353.

107. *Washington Information Directory*

Publisher: CQ Press/SAGE, Thousand Oaks, CA

Price: $165.00

Review by Adrienne Antink, Medical Group Management Association, Lakewood, CO.

This directory is a handy roadmap to find the thousands of governmental and nongovernmental organizations operating in Washington, D.C. The information is categorized by public service and advocacy, agriculture, business, communications, culture, education, labor, energy, environment, governmental operations, health, housing, international affairs, justice, the military, national security, science, social services, transportation, and the U.S. Congress. Entries include a brief description of the organization's main activities, address, telephone number, key contact name, and, if available, fax number and e-mail address. So the question is: Why do users need a hard copy directory when there is Google? The editors have organized the information in a user-friendly format that lets the user get to the right place quickly without surfing through endless Web pages and confusing menus with no assurance of when the information was last updated. The directory's content is also available online, giving users the best of both worlds—current contact information in both print and online formats. Users can search the online version by keyword, public policy topic, or organization type. The contact information can be downloaded to electronic address books, and users can link directly from the directory to organization websites. The online version is part of the CQ Press Political Contact Suite. If one is looking for associations that support home schooling, or has a child with a physical disability, resources are listed under these subcategories in the chapter on education. Are you looking for an internship in Washington? Consult the training program pages in the labor and employment chapter. Key features are organization charts to understand how federal departments and Congress are structured and boxes highlighting agency hotlines and public relations contacts. Each edition of this resource focuses on a topic of new or renewed interest. This year the focus is on organizations that rate members of Congress, including the new Club for Growth that has significant influence on Tea Party legislators. Appendixes include contact information for all members of Congress and Congressional committees; governors and other state officials; and ambassadors, embassies, and foreign offices. There is also a list of U.S. government websites, plus the text of the Freedom of Information Act and a summary of recent privacy acts. All entries are indexed by name, subject, and organizational name.

---

Classification: LC JK421; Dewey 975.

---

108. *The Oxford Guide to the United States Government*, by John J. Patrick, Richard M. Pious, and Donald A. Ritchie

Publisher: Oxford University Press, New York, NY (2001)

Price: $35.00

Review by Christopher Brennan—Associate Director, Drake Memorial Library, State University of New York, Brockport.

Billing itself as the ultimate resource for authoritative information on the U.S. presidency, Congress, the Supreme Court, and other federal government agencies, *The Oxford Guide to the United States Government* is an alphabetic dictionary of the American state, its past and present. Articles include biographies of all American presidents, vice presidents, and Supreme Court justices; selected biographies of some first ladies and past and present members of Congress; and profiles of some groups that have played significant roles in American public life. Additional articles include those on executive departments and agencies of the federal government, important events, terms, issues, concepts, and presidential and Supreme Court decisions. Each article concludes with a short bibliography and cross-references to related articles. The work itself concludes with seven appendixes, an eight-page bibliography, and a thorough index. However authoritative the aim, the tome is not exhaustive. First Ladies Edith Wilson and Nancy Reagan, despite wielding considerable influence behind the scenes, are omitted. So too are several significant federal agencies, including the Federal Deposit Insurance Corporation (FDIC) and the Bureau of Alcohol, Tobacco, and Firearms

(ATF)—important omissions in light of news events involving these bodies (i.e., the savings and loan scandal and the raid on the Branch Davidian compound in Waco, Texas). Nowhere is the rationale behind such exclusions explained, so readers must assume they were made arbitrarily, solely to keep the book to a manageable size. Greater clarity of the editorial guidelines would have been helpful. Nevertheless, the guide is recommended for academic and public libraries.

---

Classification: LC JK9; Dewey 320.

---

109. *Safire's Political Dictionary*, by William Safire

Publisher: Oxford University Press, New York, NY (2008)

Price: $22.95

Review by George Thomas Kurian—President, Encyclopedia Society, Baldwin Place, NY.

A political commentator and man who invented the craft of journalistic lexicography, Safire combines elegance with erudition in this incisive and colorful guide to the language of politics and commentary on the political landscape. Safire was a speech writer to the Nixon White House and wrote an op-ed column in *The New York Times* for thirty years and continues to write the "On Language" column in *The New York Times Magazine*. He displays an extraordinary range of what Germans call *Sprachgefühl*, an infectious love of language that inspires his readers and illuminates the nooks and crannies of the English language. Politicians are generally not known—with a few exceptions—for their literary qualities, yet politics is the Comstock Lode of American speech. That is because politics is drama and conflict, praise and ridicule, persuasion and pleading, and thrust and parry. Language is a tool of politics used both of personal destruction and of vehement partisanship. If the current lexicon is not enough to provide the vocabulary for this purpose, politicians invent words. Thus, politics becomes a fertile ground for neologisms of all kinds. The 1st edition of Safire's dictionary was a treasure trove of such words, but the new edition has been thoroughly revised, from "stem to stern" as the editor puts it, and the result is a slew of works such as Chad, Axis of Evil, Fire in the Belly, Fishing Expedition, Earmark, Exit Strategy, Family Values, Irrational Exuberance, Fuzzy Math, is-is (this jewel is from Bill Clinton), Islamofascism, Regime Change, Red/Blue State, and Triangulation. In addition to politicians, media pundits and talking heads also added to the catchment basin. Some of the words are media-driven and come out of the cauldron of talk shows and Sunday morning interviews. There are also malapropisms to which President Bush has made large contributions (misunderestimate). Safire appends an anecdote to most of his entries with the result that the reviewer ends up reading every entry and every page. The work is extremely up to date. There are references even to Mitt Romney's comments as late as March 2008. This work is highly recommended to all public libraries, academic libraries, and school libraries and in fact to political junkies and lover of the English language.

---

Classification: LC JK9; Dewey 320.

---

110. *The Almanac of American Politics*, by Michael Barone and Chuck McCutcheon
Publisher: University of Chicago Press, Chicago, IL
Price: $90.00
Review by Rosalind Tedford—Assistant Head for Research and Instruction, Z. Smith Reynolds Library, Wake Forest University, Winston-Salem, NC.

For decades, National Journal's *Almanac of American Politics* has been a standard on the shelves of academic and public libraries. The subtitle perhaps provides the best description of what the Almanac contains—the Senators, the Representatives and the Governors: Their Records and Election Results, Their States and Districts. Arranged by state, the almanac provides not only detailed information about each representative and state chief executive, but also portraits of the states and districts they represent. Group ratings from the ADA, ACLU and more are presented for each person, along with National Journal ratings. Key votes and election results are also presented. The strength of the almanac is not in any unique content but rather in great amounts of important information presented all in one place. For researchers looking into particular districts, congress people or governors, this resource provides the perfect starting place for the background and context so important in understanding the larger workings of our governments.

---

Classification: LC JK1012; Dewey 328.

---

111. *CQ Press Library* [digital]
Publisher: CQ Press/SAGE, Thousand Oaks, CA
Price: Price negotiated by site. Date reviewed: 2017.
URL: http://library.cqpress.com/
Review by Steven W. Sowards—Associate Director for Collections, Michigan State University Libraries, East Lansing.

While historical context and discussion of recurring issues play roles in library research about Washington politics and activity in the United States Congress (including interaction with the executive and judicial branches), some questions can be answered only by having very recent information. *Congress.gov* (entry 116) publishes official texts as they appear but lacks independent analysis. The combination of current reporting with analysis is the mission of CQ Press. *CQ Press Library* is an omnibus online resource to keep track of proposals, debates, and voting, and also provides a rich archive of older and related materials. *CQ Press Library* has multiple parts each with a specific role. The weekly *CQ Magazine* (until 2016 known as *CQ Weekly*) covers recent issues and debates and the progress of legislation. In addition to articles about current Capitol Hill business, this is a source for a detailed record of roll call votes on the floor of the House of Representatives and the Senate. For October 2017, for example, the tally tracks 96 different votes ranging from confirmations of federal officials to procedural votes to final passage of bills into acts of law. *CQ Researcher* is another weekly, focusing on one major topic in each issue, such as abortion, climate change, or refugee policy. Recent issues looked at sexual harassment and cyber warfare. *CQ Almanac* is an annual summary of congressional business, extending back to the 79th Congress in 1945. Reports are grouped by topic, such as appropriations, defense, or science. Appendixes list new public laws and record the most important floor votes. *Politics in America* provides profiles for all members of Congress, with contact information. For each individual, there is a timeline of key votes and voting scores from interest groups such as Americans for Democratic Action (ADA: liberal), the Chamber of Commerce of the United States (CCUS: business interests), and the American Conservative Union (ACU: conservative). Appendixes identify members of caucuses and congressional committees. An archive extends back to the 106th Congress in 2000. *Supreme Court Yearbook* summarizes the work of the top court since 1989, with lists of cases, notes about key cases by topic, and biographies of recently serving justices. Texts of court opinions can be found using the Supreme Court web site at https://www.supremecourt.gov/; see also entries 120–125. The *Voting and Elections Collection* provides numerical election results for presidential, senatorial, congressional, and state gubernatorial elections, in some cases extending back to 1789. Interpretive maps include Electoral College results and results of House races by district in the states. *Political Handbook of the World* (entry 137) looks at overseas politics, with summaries for all world states (including the Palestinian Authority and China: Taiwan). The emphasis is on politics: identification of ruling figures or cabinet officers and summaries of recent political developments (for economic summaries consult the CIA *World Factbook*, entry 134; or *International Financial Statistics*, entry 205).

Classification: LC JK1; Dewey 328.

112. *The Presidency A to Z*, by Gerhard Peters and John T. Woolley

Publisher: CQ Press/SAGE, Thousand Oaks, CA (2012)

Price: $125.00

Review by Robert V. Labaree—Reference/Public Services Librarian, Von Klein-
    Smid Library, University of Southern California, Los Angeles.

This is the 5th edition of *The Presidency A to Z*, ready-reference encyclopedia
in the American Government A to Z Series from Congressional Quarterly. The
5th edition updates entries related to the Obama administration, including the
wars in Iraq in Afghanistan, new information on the budget process, presidential
relations with Congress, the Supreme Court, politics and the media, and campaign finance. The 5th edition also includes a number of new entries reflecting
the second half of President George W. Bush's first term in office. Given their
role in combating terrorism, the essays about the Federal Bureau of Investigation
and the Central Intelligence Agency have also been updated. Finally, the 5th edition includes new biographical profiles of key leaders who have emerged during
the last five years. These include John McCain, Joseph Biden, and Michelle
Obama. Unfortunately, presidential candidate Mitt Romney is only mentioned in
connection to campaign finance reform, the 2008 presidential election, and religion and the presidency, a reflection of the lack of timeliness that books have in
today's fast-moving information age. As with the previous volume, the entries
provide a brief but succinct description of key concepts and issues related to the
Executive Branch of government; profile the accomplishments and impact of
important political figures within the Office of the Presidency; and analyze relations with the other branches of government and the larger federal bureaucracy.
Numerous photographs and reproductions can be found throughout the book.
As with the 4th edition, only a selected number of essays include a list of additional readings that could lead the user to more substantial information about a
topic. However, this work continues to provide informative, introductory information on a broad spectrum of topics related to the American presidency and
remains a recommended addition to any library collection.

Classification: LC JK511; Dewey 973.

113. *Biographical Directory of the United States Congress, 1774–Present* [digital]

Publisher: United States Government Printing Office, Washington, DC

Price: Free online. Date reviewed: 2015.

URL: http://bioguide.congress.gov/biosearch/biosearch.asp

Review by Staff, Libraries Unlimited.

The *Biographical Directory of the United States Congress* does just as the name implies and provides short biographies of congressmembers since 1774. The main screen lets users search by name, position, state, party, and year or Congress. There are drop-down menus for position, date, and party, but researchers need to type in a first or last name, year, or Congress in the other two fields. Choosing the Greenback Party, for instance, returns a list of congressmembers, giving birthdates, position, party, state from which they were elected, and years served. A click on the member's name takes researchers to a brief biography.

---

The Web version is the successor to a series of print volumes, first appearing in 1928. The most recent edition in print covers "the Continental Congress, September 5, 1774, to October 21, 1788, and the Congress of the United States, from the First through the One Hundred Eighth Congresses, March 4, 1789, to January 3, 2005, inclusive." Sometimes called CLERKWEB: the Office of the Clerk, U.S. House of Representatives also maintains member profiles at http://clerk.house.gov/member_info/cong .aspx. Classification: LC JK1010; Dewey 920.

---

114. *Women in Congress, 1917–2017*, by Matthew A. Wasniewski [digital]
Publisher: U.S. Government Printing Office, Washington, DC (2017)
Price: Free online. Date reviewed: 2017.
URL: https://bookstore.gpo.gov/products/women-congress-1917-2017
Review by Staff, Libraries Unlimited.

This massive tome (more than 1,000 pages) is available via the Government Printing Office as a free download or for sale as a cloth-bound book. The material comprises four generations of women members of Congress starting with Jeannette Rankin in 1917. The 2006 (third) edition differs from the former two in scope, structure, and concept. These differences reflect the dramatic growth, changing characteristics, and increased influence of women House and Senate members. Another difference is the organization in chronological order of the material in part one. Moreover, individual profiles have been expanded, and more emphasis within profiles has been placed on congressional service. The profiles are typically 1,500 words; some exceed 2,000 words in cases where House and Senate service has been exceptional. The book includes shorter entries (approximately 550–750 words) for widows who served brief terms or for those congresswomen about whom there is only a small amount of information. Each entry has information on a woman's precongressional career and an analysis (where possible) of the first election campaign. Also covered are reelection efforts, major legislative initiatives, and brief summary comments on the member's postcongressional career. The first part is separated into four sections: "I'm No Lady, I'm a Member of Congress": Women Pioneers on Capitol Hill, 1917–1934, with a contextual essay and 20 profiles; Onto the National State: Congresswomen in an Age of Crisis, 1935–1954, with a contextual essay and 36 member profiles; A Changing of the Guard: Traditionalists, Feminists, and the New Face of Women in Congress, 1955–1976, with a contextual essay and 39 profiles; and Assembling, Amplifying, and Ascending: Recent Trends among Women in Congress, 1977–2006, with a contextual essay and 150 member profiles. An advantage of chronological order is that it allows readers to gain a fuller perspective of the era. In the print book, a much shorter part two covers current women members of the House and Senate. A series of appendixes follow the main content, and an index rounds out the work. The website and 2017 e-book edition are based on the 2006 book; however, the material is updated to 2017. Through the table of contents, users can link to a series of clickable portraits of all women members of Congress. Once an image is accessed, users will find further information (political party affiliation, links to external research collections, etc.). There are also a series of Historical Data links, including "Women Representatives and Senators by Congress, 1917–Present," "Women of Color in Congress," "Women in Party Leadership Positions, 1949–Present," and many others. A final section, Artifacts, links to paintings, photographs, election pins, and other items, all of which have annotated explanations. This is a highly recommended work (in either print or electronic format) for public, school, and academic libraries.

> The EPUB edition is compatible with various digital readers. Print copies of the 2006 edition, covering 1917–2006, were priced at $59.00. Classification: LC JK1030; Dewey 328.

115. *Major Acts of Congress*, by Brian K. Landsberg, ed.

Publisher: Macmillan Reference USA/Gale Group, New York, NY (2004)

Price: $290.00/set

Review by Steven W. Sowards—Associate Director for Collections, Michigan State University Libraries, East Lansing.

This 3-volume set has 262 signed entries in alphabetical order analyzing major pieces of U.S. federal legislation. Contributors include law professors, historians, economists, and political scientists. Entries range in length from 1 to 5 pages. Selected laws (acts) begin with the Northwest Ordinance of 1787 and end with the act creating the Department of Homeland Security in 2002. Each Congress enacts hundreds of legislative acts (even more if one considers private as well as public laws): this work highlights those with the greatest national and political significance. Examples include the Missouri Compromise of 1820, the Sherman Antitrust Act of 1890, the Family Medical Leave Act of 1993, the USA PATRIOT Act of 2001, and the No Child Left Behind Act of 2002. Each article provides a summary of the law with excerpts from the text and a discussion of context in terms of history, noting supporting and opposing interest groups, and mentions associated court challenges. A topical list allows browsing by subject, such as civil rights or education. Entries are supported by short bibliographies, illustrations such as photographs and political cartoons, a glossary, a timeline, and an index.

The set has citations to Public Law numbers and the *Statutes at Large*. For *Statutes at Large*, the Library of Congress provides links to full text at https://www.loc.gov/law/help/statutes-at-large/index.php for the period up to 1950; and *FDsys* (entry 117) covers from 1951 to 2011, the latest printed. For Public Laws, *Congress.gov* (entry 116) has a link for laws passed beginning with the 93rd Congress (1973–1974); and *FDsys* covers the 104th Congress (1995–1996) to the present. Classification: LC KF154; Dewey 348.

116. *Congress.gov: United States Legislative Information* [digital]
Publisher: Library of Congress, Washington, DC
Price: Free online. Date reviewed: 2016.
URL: https://www.congress.gov/
Review by Staff, Libraries Unlimited.

*Congress.gov* is a presentation of the Library of Congress and is the official website for U.S. federal legislative information. Its dignified look and abundance of useful links fit perfectly with its mission. Not only is *Congress.gov* a great place to see what's actually happening in the House and Senate on any given day, it's a very useful website for students—or others—who are interested in learning more about important issues like how a bill becomes law. The website includes some simple informational videos, a search engine that helps users find information among more than one million records, access to the entirety of the *Congressional Record*, and quick access to all bills being considered in the House and Senate. A glossary provides brief explanations of legislative terms used throughout the website. A link to the crowd-sourced "top-10 most-viewed bills" provides an easy entrée into the complicated world of reading legislation. A list of congressional committees links to the committee proceedings, recent activity, and websites of each committee. Information about each member of Congress (current and former) is easy to find along with important details like their contact information, remarks in the *Congressional Record*, and committee assignments. Content on the site is constantly being updated; for instance, a new video series called "Two-Minute Tips" teaches users how to get the most out of the website. A link to Law Library of Congress resources on Supreme Court Nominations ties into current news. Users can even stream live floor proceedings when the House and Senate are in session. Because people interested in the U.S. Congress might be recent immigrants or even users from other countries, a significant detriment is the paucity of Spanish-language (and other-language) resources. Overall, *Congress.gov* is an easy-to-navigate site that does a great job of making congressional legislation available and comprehensible to the average citizen. It's also an excellent starting place for links to other important websites like all those connected with the Library of Congress, information about visiting the Capitol, and a gallery of study resources about significant primary source documents from American history.

---

*Congress.gov* is the successor to the *THOMAS* web site. Full text of the *Congressional Record* extends back to 1995. Coverage of bills and resolutions begins with the 93rd Congress in 1973. The searchable list of members of Congress begins with the 93rd Congress in 1973 and is current. There are useful summaries about committees and a glossary. Classification: LC KF49; Dewey 348.

---

117. *FDsys, Federal Digital System: America's Authentic Government Information* [digital]

Publisher: U.S. Government Publishing Office, Washington, DC

Price: Free online. Date reviewed: 2017.

URL: https://www.gpo.gov/fdsys/

Review by Staff, Libraries Unlimited.

The U.S. Government Publishing Office hosts the *Federal Digital System* responsible for providing free online access to official publications from the Legislative, Judicial, and Executive branches of American government. The home page currently features 2 documents up front: the Fiscal Year 2018 Budget and the 2017 *Economic Report of the President*. It also features a Moments in History tab on the right sidebar which offers access to collections of historically significant documents, such as the *Warren Commission Report*, President Nixon's Watergate Grand Jury Testimony Transcripts, and the *9/11 Commission Report*. Each collection is introduced with a brief contextual essay. For other documents, users can conduct a basic or advanced search or can browse through the 13 categories of government documentation listed on the right sidebar. Categories include *U.S. Court Opinions, the Congressional Record, Economic Indicators, Congressional Hearings, Public & Private Laws, Compilation of Presidential Documents*, and much more. Also listed here is the extensive *Code of Federal Regulations* (CFR), which comprises all published rules established by each department, agency, commission, etc. of the federal government. Users are able to view and/or download each or all of the 50 annually updated "Titles" (or sections) in the *CFR* going back to 1996. Titles in this vast collection include, among others, The President, Domestic Security, Animals & Animal Products, Energy, Federal Elections, Aeronautics & Space, Customs Duties, Food & Drugs, Internal Revenue, Labor, National Defense, and Public Health. Each title in the code is further divided into chapters. For example, Title 22, Foreign Relations, lists 17 chapters related to publications from the Department of State, the Foreign Service Grievance Board, the Peace Corps, the Agency for International Development, and others. Chapters are further organized by part, subpart, and section. For clarification, the Department of State chapter alone consists of 199 parts, while the entire foreign relations title contains 1,799 parts. This page also provides a link to the e-CFR (Electronic Code of Regulations) which is the unofficial daily update for the standard legal CFR, compiling CFR material with Federal Register Amendments and a link to the List of CFR Sections Affected (LSA), which shows proposed, new, and amended regulations since date of the last full CFR title revision. The compiled *Federal Register* is here as well, and coverage for all 53 "Titles" (or sections) of the *United States Code*, with federal laws organized by subject. As a whole, the *Federal Digital System* site would definitely appeal to researchers in the broadly historical sense, particularly through its Moments in History collections. But the site's greatest appeal would be for users looking for the absolute fundamentals of government.

FDsys replaced the earlier *GPOAccess* website. In addition to *eCFR* (the online *Code of Federal Regulations*), the *Federal Register*, and the *U.S. Code*, *FDsys* content includes a wealth of congressional materials. Classification: LC JK468; Dewey 011.

118. *State and Local Government on the Net: The Official State, County, & City Government Website Locator* [digital]

Publisher: Piper Resources, Minneapolis, MN

Price: Free online. Date reviewed: 2011.

URL: http://www.statelocalgov.net/

Review by Susan C. Awe—Assistant Director, University of New Mexico, Albuquerque.

This site provides convenient access to all state and local government sites by listing the states alphabetically. Frequently updated, this directory of official state, county, and city government websites also provides a list of topics to choose from plus listings of government grants, with applications. Links are provided to even the smallest counties or state agencies in the nation if they have a Web presence. The directory lists 10,792 websites and can be searched by state, topic, or local government name.

Coverage includes the District of Columbia, and American territories such as Puerto Rico. The website leads to "official" local government Web pages but is not "official" in its own right. Classification: LC JK2408; Dewey 320.

## The Supreme Court and the U.S. Constitution

This section is devoted to topics in American constitutional law. See the following section for more general works about law and legal systems (entries 128–133).

119. *Encyclopedia of the American Constitution*, by Leonard W. Levy, Kenneth L. Karst, and Adam Winkler, eds.

Publisher: Macmillan Reference USA/Gale Group, New York, NY (2000)

Price: $500.00/set

Review by Daniel K. Blewett—Reference Librarian, College of DuPage Library, College of DuPage, Glen Ellyn, IL.

The 1st edition of this work won the 1987 Dartmouth Medal from ALA's Reference and Users Services Association. This work is a good introduction to the interesting and complicated subject of constitutional law. The time coverage of this edition ended in mid-1999 with the conclusion of the U.S. Supreme Court's 1998–1999 term. There is a list of articles and their authors at the beginning of volume 1, followed by lists of contributors. These lists, arranged by the year of publication of the edition, contain information as to where the person works and which articles they wrote. The contributors include political scientists, lawyers, judges, and historians. The over 2,750 signed entries (361 new ones) are arranged in alphabetic order and include suggestions for further reading. Some of the new topics covered in this edition include communitarianism, sex offender notification laws, and the Articles of Impeachment of President Clinton. To help readers judge the currency of the information, the year of publication of the article is added under the contributor's name. The over 180 updated articles are clearly marked and follow the original article. Cross-references are embedded in the text of the individual article, while *see also* references are at the end of the article. The entries on the relevant Supreme Court cases provide the legal bibliographic citation to the decision as printed in the official U.S. Reports series. There are also entries for many of the justices of the high court. The seven appendixes contain the texts of the Articles of Confederation, the U.S. Constitution, the resolution that transmitted the Constitution to Congress, and much more. The glossary can be found at the end of the last volume. There are separate subject, personal name, and court case name indexes. The most important document in American political history deserves a work such as this. It is not strictly legal or academic, but is intended for the general public as well as students at most levels. Librarians should be prepared to purchase the 3rd edition in another 15 years or so, since one can expect there to be enough new material and issues to justify such a publication. This title can be supplemented with works such as the *Encyclopedia of American Political History, The Constitutional Law Dictionary* and its supplements, and the *Encyclopedia of Constitutional Amendments, Proposed Amendments, and Amending Issues.* It is recommended for the government and political science sections of all academic and public library reference collections; the older edition can be placed in the circulating collection.

---

Classification: LC KF4548; Dewey 324.

---

120. *Encyclopedia of the U.S. Supreme Court,* by Thomas T. Lewis and Richard L. Wilson, eds.

Publisher: Salem Press, Hackensack, NJ (2001)

Price: $315.00/set

Review by Jack Ray—Assistant Director, Loyola/Notre Dame Library, Baltimore, MD.

From Abington to Zurcher, this comprehensive encyclopedia of some 1,075 topical essays will immediately take its place as a standard Supreme Court reference source for most high school, public, and academic libraries. The essays, which range from about 250 to 3,000 words, are signed by one of approximately 220 contributors, are clearly written for a general audience, and have specially formatted headers that describe or identify the topic in capsule form and briefly summarize its significance. The longer essays have bibliographic references, and most essays provide cross-references to other topics. There are numerous illustrations, including portraits with most biographical essays. Essay topics include specific cases (548); types of law, such as administrative (74); broad issues, such as abortion (131); and specific historic events and eras, such as the Civil War (38). Appendixes include a timeline, a list of justices in order of appointment, a glossary, a bibliography, and a grouping of essays by broad subject category (e.g., affirmative action). There is a general index, as well as an index of all cases referenced in the text. There is an unfortunate misstatement in the publisher's introduction that Supreme Court decisions can only be overturned when the Court reverses itself or by constitutional amendment (this is true only when the decision involves constitutional interpretation). But the essay on statutory interpretation makes clear that a significant volume of the Court's work involves interpreting Federal statutes. By and large, this encyclopedia does a superb job of clearly providing an enormous amount of information in an attractive format and is highly recommended.

> The second edition appeared in 2016 as *U.S. Supreme Court.* Classification: LC KF8742; Dewey 347.

121. *Encyclopedia of Supreme Court Quotations,* by Christopher A. Anzalone, ed.

Publisher: M. E. Sharpe, Armonk, NY (2000)

Price: $79.95

Review by Michael A. Foley—Honors Director, Marywood College, Scranton, PA.

The nine hundred quotations from Supreme Court justices in this collection range from the abolition of slavery to the protection of youth from exposure to images or ideas that a legislative body finds inappropriate. The basic criterion for quotation inclusion was readability, which includes clarity and coherence. Furthermore, the passages selected meet the additional criteria of "inherent beauty, literary quality, [and] profound philosophy" (p. xii). In addition, two goals contributed to passage selection, namely, the ability of a passage to stimulate thought or to foster disbelief. In short, the passages should make readers think and reflect on the nature, purpose, and function of the Constitution and the Supreme Court. The selection succeeds admirably. The quotations are grouped around thirteen chapters, including such chapter headings as "The Givers of Law," "The Least Dangerous Branch," "The Sacred Parchment," "Due Process and Equal Protection," "Liberty, Freedom, Happiness," and "The Arrest . . . The Trial . . . The Punishment." There are four useful and necessary appendixes: the Constitution, a table of cases with a brief summation of the case, a table of justices and their decisions, and a keyword index. The table of justices is arranged chronologically according to presidential appointment. For readers who seek quotations on specific topics, the keyword index is indispensable. Readers will not agree with all of the ideas expressed in these passages, but they will be moved to reflect more critically and carefully on the nature and purpose of law in general and constitutional law in particular. The passages selected avoid, for the most part, legalese (technical jargon) in favor of clarity, precision, profundity, and power. This book belongs in all reference collections. This volume is highly recommended.

Classification: LC KF8742; Dewey 347.

122. *Legal Information Institute. Supreme Court* [digital]
Publisher: Legal Information Institute, Cornell Law School, Ithaca, NY
Price: Free online. Date reviewed: 2017.
URL: https://www.law.cornell.edu/supremecourt/text/home
Review by Staff, Libraries Unlimited.

This site from Cornell Law School's Legal Information Institute (LII) offers free access to two collections of U.S. Supreme Court decisions: nearly three hundred decisions rendered 1990–present and over six hundred historic decisions focused on landmark cases going back to the early years of the court. The page is structured as a listing of Recent Decisions, followed by simple presentation of search or browse options relating to both collections. The Current Awareness category allows users to access current court Decisions, Orders, Case Updates, Cases Granted Certification, Cases Pending, Oral Arguments, Cases Argued This Term, and Oral Argument Calendars. Information within these categories varies between basic listings and substantial detail. Users can browse the Archive of Decisions for both 1990–Present and Historic Collections via a listing of alphabetized topics (e.g., antitrust law, capital punishment, Fifth Amendment, obstruction, etc.), author, or party. Depending on the case, users can access a syllabus, written decision, concurrence, notes, and dissent. Recent cases are generally downloadable in one or more formats. A Cites tab will link to a listing of relevant cases if the chosen case has been cited in later decisions. Supplementary information under LII Resources is generous and includes the excellent LII Bulletin, offering objective previews of each case on the docket, biographical information on seven of the nine current justices, current court rules, a glossary of legalese, and more. The Other Resources tab offers links to sites hosting oral argument recordings, briefs, and transcripts. Advertisements within the page may affect the browsing experience. In addition, some of the links may not be complete or functional (e.g., links to the biographies of past justices). Nonetheless, the site carries sufficient material that would appeal to students, educators, and other researchers interested in the U.S. Supreme Court.

*Westlaw* from Thomson Reuters and *LexisNexis* (recently rebranded as *Nexis Uni*) remain the leading comprehensive resources for legal texts but require paid subscriptions. Classification: LC KF242; Dewey 349.

123. *The Supreme Court Justices: Illustrated Biographies, 1789–2012*, by Clare Cushman, ed.

Publisher: CQ Press/SAGE, Thousand Oaks, CA (2013)

Price: $135.00

Review by Sara Anne Hook—Professor of Informatics and Associate Dean for Academic Affairs and Undergraduate Studies, IUPUI School of Informatics, Indiana University, Purdue University, Indianapolis.

The bulk of *The Supreme Court Justices* is devoted to biographical entries for the justices. The entries are arranged in chronological order by the date their service on the court began. Entries include birth and death dates, judicial title, beginning and ending dates of service, and the name of the president who appointed them. Each entry includes a handsome black-and-white portrait of the justice and a paragraph summarizing notable facts and achievements. The main text of each entry is two to three pages in length and gives a narrative of the justice's life and career, along with major highlights of their court service; their role in major cases; and the political, social, and religious philosophies that may have guided their decisions while on the bench. Each biographical entry provides valuable insight into their impact on American history and on the court. The entries are informative, concise, and easy and enjoyable to read, and will give the reader excellent background and insight into each of the justices and how they fit into the development of constitutional law and the American legal system. Each entry includes a brief reading list. A twenty-two-page bibliography follows the biographical entries and is organized by subject, including general sources, sources on individual justices, books about the Supreme Court and the Court justices for young readers. The index is extensive and detailed, adding to the usefulness of the volume. *Supreme Court Justices* is a useful and attractive volume that will be suitable for a wide range of audiences. The publisher indicates that it is intended for high school and college students and general readers. It would be an excellent addition to public, academic undergraduate, and school library collections, and the price is more than reasonable for the amount of information provided in the volume. It would also be a useful volume for law and government libraries to have on hand for ready-reference questions and to assist with questions from the lay public about the Supreme Court's history and function.

Classification: LC KF8744; Dewey 347.

124. *The Oxford Guide to United States Supreme Court Decisions*, by Kermit L. Hall and James W. Ely Jr., eds.

Publisher: Oxford University Press, New York, NY (2009)

Price: $35.00

Review by Alicia Brillon—Reference Librarian, James E. Faust Law Library, University of Utah, Salt Lake City.

*The Oxford Guide to United States Supreme Court Decisions* is a 2nd edition; however, somewhat strangely, it updates the 1st and 2nd editions of *The Oxford Companion to the Supreme Court of the United States*, which were additional products of Kermit L. Hall (recently deceased). Nearly four hundred pages are devoted to an alphabetic listing of the U.S. Supreme Court's most important decisions. From Abington *School District v. Schempp* (1963) to *Zurcher v. The Stanford Daily* (1978), each case is explained in under one page and includes a brief description of the facts, a summary of the majority and dissenting opinions, and a description of the case's possible impact on society and future laws. *The Oxford Guide to United States Supreme Court Decisions* includes more than fifty cases from 1992 through 2008 that were not included in the previous editions of *The Oxford Companion to the Supreme Court of the United States*. The Oxford guide also contains a glossary of terms as well as two appendixes. The eight-page glossary defines legal terms, such as comity, as well as many Latin terms, including quo warranto. The first appendix contains the Constitution of the United States, and the second appendix contains the nominations and succession of Supreme Court justices from 1789 through 2006. An alphabetic case index followed by a detailed sixty-four-page topical index completes the volume. The 2nd edition of *The Oxford Guide to United States Supreme Court Decisions* is a valuable and concise source for information on the most important Supreme Court decisions and is recommended for both law and public libraries.

Classification: LC KF4548; Dewey 342.

125. *Historic U.S. Court Cases: An Encyclopedia*, by John W. Johnson, ed.

Publisher: Routledge/Taylor & Francis Group, New York, NY (2001)

Price: $195.00/set

Review by Michael A. Foley—Honors Director, Marywood College, Scranton, PA.

This work is the 2nd edition of a nonencyclopedic encyclopedia containing 201 essays on "historic" court cases ranging in length from 1,000 to 5,000 words. There are no specific criteria to establish case inclusion. The selected cases range in scope from those that set an important precedent (*Marbury v. Madison*), constituted an historic event (*Roe v. Wade*), or presented a peculiarly American characteristic (*Liebeck v. McDonald's Restaurants*—the $2.9 million coffee spill), among others. While Supreme Court cases receive the most attention, they by no means overwhelm important lower court cases. The 2 volumes are divided into 5 sections: "Crime and Criminal Law"; "Governmental Organization, Power, and Procedure"; "Economics and Economic Regulation"; "Race, Gender, Sexual Orientation, and Disability"; and "Civil Liberties." Each case begins with a brief background statement containing information on the date, location, court, principal participants, and significance of the case. Each entry concludes with a brief, but useful, bibliography. The second volume contains an index of cases and an index of names and subjects, both of which are exceptionally helpful. The essays are written in an informative style and do not resort to ax grinding. In addition, as the editor notes, of the 85 contributors, legal experts wrote only 54 percent of the essays. The remaining essays were written by an assortment of scholars, including professors of history, social science, and the humanities. The essays will appeal to a broad audience, from lay to professional readers. This encyclopedia is highly recommended for all reference collections.

---

Classification: LC KF352; Dewey 349.

---

126. *First Amendment Rights: An Encyclopedia*, by Nancy S. Lind and Erik T. Rankin

Publisher: ABC-CLIO, Santa Barbara, CA (2013)

Price: $189.00/set

Review by Melinda F. Matthews—Interlibrary Loan/Reference Librarian, University of Louisiana at Monroe.

This is a dynamic two-volume written examination of the first amendment. Volume 1 includes chapters on First Amendment Approaches, Issues and Controversies, Freedom of Association, Freedom of Speech, The First Amendment and the SEC, Freedom of the Press, Twenty-First Century Issues, The Establishment Clause, and The Free Exercise Clause. This volume also provides an appendix of pre-2008 cases. Volume 2 consists of chapters on The Roberts Court; WikiLeaks; Social Media; "Sexting"; Student Speech; Student Free Speech and Free Exercise of Religion; Electronic Games; Markets, Free Speech, and Commercial Expression; The Right to Peaceable Assembly and Social Movements; The Intellectual Forebears of Citizens United; Corporate First Amendment Rights after Citizens United; Death, Grief, and Freedom of Speech; Muslims; and Contraception. The volume concludes with an appendix of post-2008 cases, a bibliography, and an index. Numerous examples of rights from the first amendment abound in the work. For example, in New Jersey, Freedom of Association kept homosexuals from being boy scouts according to *Boy Scouts of America v. Dale.* All researchers of the First Amendment will obtain knowledge after reading this resource. It will be a useful addition to academic and public libraries.

---

Classification: LC KF4770; Dewey 342.

---

127. *Encyclopedia of Gun Control and Gun Rights*, by Glenn H. Utter and Robert J. Spitzer

Publisher: Grey House Publishing, Amenia, NY (2011)

Price: $165.00

Review by John Howard Oxley—Faculty, American Intercontinental University, Atlanta, GA.

This ready-reference title provides a comprehensive updating of the original edition with a comprehensive coverage of recent developments in this arena. The scope of coverage is wide-ranging. In addition to legal cases in this arena, important events and individuals/organizations on all sides of the topic (specific major inventors and producers of firearms) have entries. While this volume's main focus is on issues in the United States, concise descriptions of developments in other major countries are also included. In a subject area characterized by an abundance of inflammatory rhetoric, the dispassionate, even-handed treatment throughout is particularly meritorious. The authors' writing style covers some complex legal issues in a clear, informative manner, with the monochrome illustrations restricted to major entries. The accuracy standard is high, with the only errors detected being "Hotguns" for "Shotguns" for the table header on pages xiv–xv and "Pitstol" for "Pistol" for the table header on page 132. In addition to standard finding aids (table of contents, running heads, an index, and internal references), a topical guide enables rapid thematic access. Suggestions for further reading follow each entry; many of these are quite current, and websites are included. The book is sturdily case-bound in a lay-flat binding and clearly printed on good-quality paper. It deserves consideration from any library serving a clientele where this subject matter may be of interest.

---

The 3rd edition appeared in 2016 as *The Gun Debate: An Encyclopedia of Gun Control and Gun Rights in the United States.* Gun rights of course revolve around the Second Amendment. Classification: LC KF3941; Dewey 363.

## Law

Law library collections encompass a wide range of advanced and specialized resources, some in print and others online such as the sweeping legal text databases *Westlaw* (from Thomson Reuters) and *LexisNexis* (now *Nexis Uni*) from Reed Elsevier. At the ready reference end of the spectrum, Nolo Press publishes numerous handy guides to specific topics, ranging from *How to Get a Green Card* to *Every Tenant's Legal Guide*. Of course, reference desks provide access to law-related texts, not legal advice. This section is devoted to general works about law and legal systems. See the previous section for topics in American constitutional law. Some resources in the section on crime (entries 91–102) may also be relevant.

128. *Black's Law Dictionary*, by Bryan A. Garner, ed.

Publisher: West Publishing, St. Paul, MN (2009)

Price: $74.00

Review by Staff, Libraries Unlimited.

The 9th edition of this venerable reference work begins with an impressive list of academic contributors followed by the prefaces to the 7th, 8th, and 9th editions. These three editions were all edited by Bryan Garner, who has overseen the complete rewriting of the dictionary. Terms have been removed and added with an eye to creating a resource in which all the entries are plausibly law-related terms and closely related to the law. New to this edition is the inclusion of a date in parentheses within the entry that indicates the term's earliest known use in the English language. Prior to the more than 45,000 A to Z terms, users will find a guide that explicates alphabetization, pronunciations, etymologies, tags, cross-references, typefaces, and more. Of special note are the quotations used throughout the dictionary. These are intended to help explain content. A series of appendixes follow: a "Table of Legal Abbreviations," "Legal Maxims," "The Constitution of the United States of America," the UN's "Universal Declaration of Human Rights," "Members of the United States Supreme Court" (with chief justices appearing first), a "Federal Circuits Map," "British Regnal Years," and a "Bibliography." Notably, the Latin maxims used to appear alphabetically within the main text of the dictionary. Starting in the seventh edition, Garner grouped them all in the appendix to facilitate searching. This scholarly and comprehensive work is an essential source for legal terminology. Highly recommended for public and academic libraries.

---

The 10th edition was published in 2014. There is a free online version based on the public domain 2nd edition text of 1910, but obviously much content will be out of date. Classification: LC KF156; Dewey 340.

129. *West's Encyclopedia of American Law*, by Jeffrey Lehman and Shirelle Phelps
Publisher: Gale/Cengage Learning, Farmington Hills, MI (2005)
Price: $1,195.00/set
Review by Staff, Libraries Unlimited.

In James Heller's review of the 1st edition of *West's Encyclopedia of American Law* he concluded by saying "both librarians and patrons will wear out the pages of this significant reference set." For those who have truly worn out the pages of their 1st edition, Gale has just published the 2nd edition of this noteworthy resource. Although how this edition has been added to and improved upon is not indicated in the preface, it is clear that more entries have been added (nearly 1,000 more, bringing the total to 5,000 in this edition) and the set has increased in size from 12 volumes to 13 volumes. The 5,000 entries included here provide terms, concepts, events, movements, cases, and people significant in U.S. legal history as well as today. Entries often run several paragraphs in length, with some running up to several pages. Most entries include cross-references to related terms as well as a concluding list of further resources. Terms that appear in small bold capital letters receive their own entry elsewhere in the set. The entries are well written and cover a variety of topics, both expected and unexpected. What makes this encyclopedia special, however, are the additional features that go beyond those of a typical encyclopedia. "In Focus" essays appear frequently throughout the book. These essays elaborate on topics that are highly controversial (e.g., gay rights, abortion), historical in nature, or involve highly detailed processes (e.g., the Food and Drug Administration's approval process for new drugs). Users will also find the sidebars full of informative facts, photographs, and biographical entries useful. Volumes 11–13 provide additional information beyond the encyclopedic entries, including an appendix titled "Milestone Cases in the Law," which presents the arguments of attorneys, reasoning of the judge, briefs presented by the parties to the U.S. Supreme Court, and the concurring and dissenting opinions of the Supreme Court judges of major cases. Volume 12 presents 60 primary documents, including presidential speeches, the Bill of Rights, and personal letters of Martin Luther King Jr. Volume 13 provides a dictionary of legal terms as well as indexes by case names and general terms. This is an all-encompassing encyclopedia of U.S. law that will be useful in both law libraries and undergraduate libraries. The writing is clear and easy to follow, making it understandable for a variety of students and professors.

The *American Law Yearbook* adds supplementary updated content. Classification: LC KF154; Dewey 349.

130. *Gale Encyclopedia of Everyday Law*, by Donna Batten

Publisher: Gale/Cengage Learning, Farmington Hills, MI (2013)

Price: $549.00/set

Review by Ladyjane Hickey—Reference Librarian, Austin College, Sherman, TX.

The *Gale Encyclopedia of Everyday Law* covers legal issues affecting everyday life for most Americans. It is designed for ready-reference use, not as a self-help or "do-it-yourself" legal resource. This 3rd edition contains 276 articles of varying length arranged under 26 broad subject areas, such as consumer issues, education, estate planning, health care, real estate, and retirement, presented in alphabetical order. The articles included in each subject area are named by topic and also arranged alphabetically. For example, the broad subject area of education has 23 articles, such as competency testing, discipline and punishment, homeschooling, student loans, and teachers' rights. An index and glossary are included. The table of contents assists patrons in finding these articles. A list of Web addresses for state and federal agencies and national organizations assist patrons who want further information. As in previous editions, each article includes a brief background of the issue, important cases or statutes or provisions, profiles of the various federal laws and regulations on the topic, and variations of the laws in the different states. Each article includes a bibliography and a list of national and state organizations and agencies. An Overview of the American Legal System explains the various components of the legal system in the United States. It is well written and can be easily understood by the average citizen. Also worth mention is the article The Patient Protection and Affordable Care Act, which attempts to provide real information about the act, popularly known as Obamacare. This work is highly recommended for all academic and public libraries.

Books from Nolo Press also address a wide range of "everyday law" situations, such as *Neighbor Law: Fences, Trees, Boundaries & Noise* or *Every Dog's Legal Guide: A Must-Have Book for Your Owner*. Classification: LC KF387; Dewey 349.

131. *The Oxford Companion to American Law*, by Kermit L. Hall, and David Scott Clark

Publisher: Oxford University Press, New York, NY (2002)

Price: $65.00

Review by Sandhya D. Srivastava—Assistant Professor, Serials Librarian, Hofstra University, Hempstead, NY.

*The Oxford Companion to American Law* is an excellent resource for the layperson as well as the professional. This volume provides biographical information of important lawyers, judges, and justices, including their personal lives to their professional careers. It also contains entries that focus on the concepts that concern American legal institutions and current controversial cases that have affected America's legal history. The volume is organized alphabetically with essays that offer a "historical and interpretive background . . . avoiding the use of arcane legal terminology" (p. ix). There are two indexes—one of case law and one of a topical nature that directs the user to the people, places, concepts, and institutions that are in the text. The text contains an integral system of cross-referencing that appears in each essay along with *see* and *see also* references after the piece. The true value in this text is that it is easy to use and functional for someone who does not understand law or for someone who wishes for a quick read on a legal topic or case law. I would recommend this volume for public libraries and college libraries.

---

Classification: LC KF154; Dewey 349.

---

132. *National Survey of State Laws*, by Richard A. Leiter, ed.
Publisher: William S. Hein, Getzville, NY
Price: $225.00
Review by Staff, Libraries Unlimited.

This smartly arranged book records the changes made to a wide variety of state laws since 2008. Covering eight general categories of law (Business and Consumer, Criminal, Education, Employment, Family, General Civil, Real Estate, and Tax), the book presents these changes in an easily referenced table format, wherein readers can compare each specific law from state to state. Each category is further broken down into more specific topics. For example, the Education Law section details legislation concerning compulsory education, corporal punishment in public schools, prayer in public schools, and privacy of school records. Specific topics are arranged alphabetically. Each topic includes an overview which examines the history of the particular laws, national and state outlooks, and any current issues or debate concerning the law. Specific topics are then examined in a table demarcated by state and applicable headings (so that headings will differ from topic to topic). For example, the topic of gun control within the Criminal Law section uses the headings of Code Section, Illegal Arms, Waiting Period, Who May Not Own, and Law Prohibiting Firearms on or near School Grounds. The Code Section heading is particularly useful to readers who would like to peruse the actual text of the law. The table structure makes it extremely easy to compare laws across states. Using the same example of gun control, we can see how California law mandates a ten-day waiting period after the purchase of a gun, while Colorado mandates none. The appendix of this recommended work references statutory compilations for each state and conveys abbreviations if applicable. This book would be put to great use by students of law, those just beginning their law careers, and more.

---

The 7th edition appeared in 2015. Classification: LC KF386; Dewey 348.

---

133. *Legal Systems of the World: A Political, Social, and Cultural Encyclopedia*, by Herbert M. Kritzer, ed.

Publisher: ABC-CLIO, Santa Barbara, CA (2002)

Price: $425.00/set

Review by Ladyjane Hickey—Reference Librarian, Austin College, Sherman, TX.

The scope of this work is very broad, encompassing 209 nations, 84 subnational areas of the world (both ancient and modern), and legal topics, for a total of 403 signed articles. Most articles are 3–6 pages in length and presented in alphabetic arrangement by topic heading. Geographic topics are placed in historic context with maps and a chart of the court structure. Subnational areas are listed separately for the United States, Canada, Australia, islands, and areas known to be diverse such as the Basque Region of France and Spain. Articles include references and lists for further reading to facilitate research. U.S. law is usually divided into 6 main categories: administrative, constitutional, statutory, judicial, civil, and criminal. Because of its international emphasis, this work is organized differently. It has articles titled administrative law, civil law, and criminal law, while constitutional law, statutory law, and judicial review are treated as subheadings under civil law. Entries on individual countries cover constitutional law, judicial review, statutory law, and court systems where appropriate. The topical entries explaining the civil law system and the common law system include the history of these 2 systems. The differences between the 2 systems and the characteristics necessary for each system are part of the articles, but the 2 systems are not contrasted in a chart or graph for ease in grasping the differences. In spite of this minor drawback, this work should be placed in collections that support pre-law, criminal justice, international law, and international commerce curriculums. Although in-depth works abound on individual topics, no other encyclopedia covers legal systems for the globe.

---

Classification: LC K48; Dewey 340.

---

## International Information

### *Handbooks*

Handbooks to the nations and states of the world can be quick sources to find recent information: election results, the names of top government officials, or economic figures. If all figures about a given economic condition are coming from a single handbook, one can rely on the editors' work for assurance that comparable figures have been compiled on a uniform basis (rather than reconciling figures from multiple sources).

134. *The World Factbook* [digital]

Publisher: Central Intelligence Agency, Washington, DC

Price: Free online. Date reviewed: 2015.

URL: https://www.cia.gov/library/publications/the-world-factbook/

Review by Staff, Libraries Unlimited.

*The World Factbook* is prepared by the Central Intelligence Agency for the United States government, but the information is available here, in an easily navigated site, as part of the public domain. *The World Factbook* provides users with data on the history, people, government, economy, geography, communications, transportation, military, and transnational issues for 267 world entities. The site's data is found by clicking on four reference tabs: regional and world maps, flags of the world, guide to country comparisons, and a user guide. For instance, under the Guide to Country Comparisons, researchers can find facts on myriad topics, such as life expectancy by country, the numbers of people living with HIV/AIDS by country, and national military expenditures as a percentage of gross domestic product.

Often known as the *CIA World Factbook*. Republished annually in print by commercial vendors as well. Classification: LC G122; Dewey 910.

135. *The Statesman's Yearbook: The Politics, Cultures and Economies of the World*, by Barry Turner, ed.

Publisher: Palgrave Macmillan, New York, NY

Price: $350.00

Review by Mark Schumacher—Art and Humanities Librarian, University of North Carolina, Greensboro.

This long-standing title, begun during the American Civil War, remains extremely useful today for its political, economic, and sociocultural information.

Its organization is straightforward, presenting information first on scores of international organizations (both worldwide like the United Nations and regional like the Organization of American States), then entries on the 194 countries of the world, with geographical subdivisions for the United Kingdom, India, Canada, and the United States, among others. From biographies of the current political leaders (e.g., the president and prime minister of France) to population tables by region within a country and summaries of social institutions, this volume provides concise but accurate details about many aspects of the world's nations. A brief "Further Reading" section provides other resources and occasionally Internet sites. Highly recommended to those libraries that can afford to purchase it. It is also available in an online format at http://www.statesmans yearbook.com/.

---

Classification: LC JA51; Dewey 320.

---

136. *The Europa World Year Book*

Publisher: Europa Publications/Taylor & Francis Group, Florence, KY

Price: $1,675.00/set

Review by Staff, Libraries Unlimited.

The 54th edition [2014] of the *Europa World Year Book* carries on the tradition of earlier editions by presenting timely, accurate information on political, economic, and commercial institutions around the world. Volume 1 begins by listing over 1,900 international organizations, including the United Nations and the European Union. It then provides an alphabetic survey of more than 250 countries and territories. For each country the following information is provided: an introductory survey on the country's history, government, defense, economic affairs, education, and holidays; statistical survey on area and population, health and welfare, agriculture, industry, external trade, transportation, tourism, and education; and directory information for government, legislature, diplomatic representation, religious centers, the press, finance, and trade and industry. The set concludes with a 3-page index of territories. New to this edition are information on the transfer of power to the next generation of leadership in the People's Republic of China, coverage of the 2012 U.S. presidential and legislative elections, an update on the conflict going on in Syria, and details of the election of Pope Francis in March 2013. The online version of this work is *Europa World Online*, which provides the same information but in an easy-to-search database format. The online edition also provides additional statistical surveys and is updated on a regular basis to ensure accuracy of information. Links to related sites are also made available with this database, saving the users much time in their research. Subscribers can now download archival content from the *Europa World Year Book*. The print and online editions of this valuable resource continue to be worthwhile investments for public and academic libraries, business and international organizations, and media and research organizations. It will be a boon especially to students, scholars, and journalists needing quick, up-to-date information.

> Despite the title, coverage is worldwide. The same publisher issues regional editions such as *Africa South of the Sahara* and *The Middle East and North Africa*. Classification: LC JN51; Dewey 320.

137. *Political Handbook of the World*, by Tom Landsford, ed.

Publisher: CQ Press/SAGE, Thousand Oaks, CA

Price: $365.00

Review by Linda D. Tietjen—Senior Instructor, Arts and Architecture Bibliographer, Auraria Library, Denver, CO.

This perennial reference work has been published more or less annually, under several publishing arrangements, since 1927. Beginning with the 2005–2006 edition, the publisher has been the respected CQ Press, with continued support from the Research Foundation of the State University of New York at Binghamton and scholars from other institutions. Such credentials insure the rigorous standards and continued reputation for comprehensive coverage and reliability that the *Political Handbook of the World* has enjoyed over the years. Essays comprising the 2012 and 2013 editions are arranged in a uniform style for ease of reading and for pinpointing facts about a country's governmental structure and political apparatus (e.g., political parties, leading politicians, legislatures, communication outlets), and intergovernmental representation. Each country receives between two and twenty-plus pages of information, including a small black-and-white inset map and short but very insightful background essay paragraphs that situate the countries in a recent historical and political context. The two-page preface is itself an excellent essay analyzing economic and political trends worldwide and their impact upon selected nations, particularly those currently experiencing political instability. In the 2013 edition users will find information on the growing violence in Syria, the death of the U.S. ambassador to Libya, the 2012 presidential election, and the parliamentary elections in Iran. In addition to country entries, the second section of the title, almost a publication within a publication, addresses over one hundred intergovernmental organizations such as the United Nations International Finance Corporation (IFC) and the World Trade Organization (WTO), bodies which become more important each year in our increasingly global world. Rounding out the title is a short back-of-the-book index. Perhaps due to the seismic political changes occurring worldwide, which necessitate constant monitoring and updating, this venerable reference work is now also offered in an online version. For those libraries who maintain print reference collections, it still makes good sense to keep a copy of this indispensable tome on the shelves. For academic and school libraries supporting large online and distance curricula, however, the online equivalent might better suit their users' needs.

---

Classification: LC JF37; Dewey 320.

---

138. *The Oxford Companion to Politics of the World*, by Joel Krieger and Margaret E. Crahan, eds.

Publisher: Oxford University Press, New York, NY (2001)

Price: $60.00

Review by David A. Timko—Head Reference Librarian at the U.S. Bureau of Census Library, Suitland, MD.

The 1st edition of *The Oxford Companion to Politics of the World* appeared in 1993 to generally favorable reviews. As the editor notes, much has changed in the world since the early 1990s and a new edition is much welcomed. Indeed, much in the world has changed, even since the 2nd edition went to press. The work consequently contains little on many individuals and entities of central interest in today's world, such as Al Qaeda and the Taliban. Even Hamas lacks its own entry. The work is equipped with an indispensably useful index, where Hamas and the Taliban, but not Al Qaeda, can be found. Useful bibliographies append most of the entries. This formidable, single-volume work contains 672 articles, written by more than 500 contributors, primarily academics but also a number of practitioners (policy analysts, politicians, and the like). The companion strives to be international in its scope (its contributors come from 40 different countries and each entry is signed), but, perhaps inevitably, it tends to be oriented toward the United States. In addition, the companion includes 23 extended interpretive essays that deal with larger themes, such as democracy, globalization, and modernity. A new feature of the 2nd edition is 6 pairs of essays on various critical themes, such as the future of entitlements and sustainable development. The 2nd edition claims that most of the articles from the 1st edition have been revised, but this is clearly not always the case. For instance, no items listed in the bibliography for the entry "Holocaust" are more recent than 1989, despite the large number of important works on the topic that have appeared over the last decade. Similarly, the entry for "Information Society," remarkably, fails to address the 1990s, and its most current bibliographic reference dates to 1990. To be fair, many of the essays in the companion have been revised and many of the bibliographies updated. Some will detect a liberal bent in the companion, despite the claim made on the dust jacket that "varying viewpoints" were deliberately sought out. These varying viewpoints are most clearly in evidence in the 6 pairs of essays on critical themes. But it is at least coincidental that liberal figures from the past such as Gramcsi, Trotsky, and Hugo Grotius are granted their own entries, while conservative thinkers who arguably have had a more direct impact on recent politics, such as Milton Friedman, Friedrich Hayek, and Ayn Rand, are to be found only in the index and receive only brief mentions in the text. In spite of, or perhaps because of, these qualities, the companion is generally a good read, very suitable for dipping. But it should be emphasized that the work is self-consciously not an encyclopedia— it is not the best place to go for actual facts. Yet, basic factual information is readily available elsewhere anyway. For brief interpretive essays and analysis on issues of topical importance, the 2nd edition of the companion is nearly as important as its predecessor.

Classification: LC JA61; Dewey 320.

## *The United Nations*

The Documents section of the official United Nations (UN) website, http://www.un.org/en/documents/index.html, provides online access to the Charter of the United Nations, the Universal Declaration of Human Rights, and other core texts. There are maps explaining UN operations and a registry of treaties and current information such as lists of programs.

139. *Encyclopedia of the United Nations*, by Jerry Pubantz and John Allphin Moore Jr.

Publisher: Facts on File, New York, NY (2008)

Price: $112.50/set

Review by Herbert W. Ockerman—Professor, Ohio State University, Columbus.

This book is a comprehensive guide to the United Nations' procedures, politics, specialized agencies, personalities, initiatives, and involvement in world affairs. It is organized in dictionary style, and entries range from a short paragraph to several pages in length. This book describes major world events and the role the United Nations played in them. Subsections include a preface, an introduction, a list of contributors, a list of acronyms, and A–Z entries. This is followed by appendixes that cover the Charter of the United Nations, universal declaration of human rights, United Nations member states, Secretary General of the United Nations, statue of the international court of justice, United Nations' resolutions (including uniting or peace resolutions), and declaration on the establishment of the new international economic order. Concluding the volume are lists of conventions, declarations, and other instruments contained in general assembly resolutions; a United Nations chronology; United Nations websites; a selected bibliography; and an index. The book has above-average paper and binding, and the font size is average. This encyclopedia should be in all major libraries and would be particularly useful for people interested in international politics and world peace.

Classification: LC KZ4968; Dewey 341.

140. *Encyclopedia of the United Nations and International Agreements,* by Edmund Jan Osmanczyk and Anthony Mango, eds.

Publisher: Routledge/Taylor & Francis Group, New York, NY (2003)

Price: $495.00/set

Review by Thomas A. Karel—Associate Director for Public Services, Shadek-Fackenthal Library, Franklin and Marshall College, Lancaster, PA.

The publication history of this encyclopedia is both interesting and unusual. The 1st edition was written by Osmanczyk in Polish in 1975. A year later a Spanish translation was published, and an English-language version finally appeared in 1985. A 2nd revised English edition was published in 1990, but by this time Osmanczyk had died. Anthony Mango and his editorial team have now released a long-overdue, and significantly expanded, new edition of this important work. Now filling four large volumes, the encyclopedia has not only been revised and updated, but has been refocused. There is more emphasis placed on the organization of the United Nations and the entire UN system, as well as major NGOs (nongovernmental organizations). Mango also emphasizes the United Nations' role in the codification of international law. He further explains this new focus in the introduction: "The focus in this third edition is on how the United Nations and its institutions work, and on the results of their work. The entries do not (in general) deal with the political disputes, bargaining, compromises, and quid pro quos that preceded the adoption of the various treaties, covenants, and declarations" (p. x). There are more than 5,700 entries in this edition—on countries, regions, conferences, and topics—arranged in one alphabetic sequence with many cross-references. The cut-off date for preparation of the entries was, in most cases, December 31, 2001. A list of all the entries is provided in the first volume, and a single comprehensive index is found in volume 4. Most of the entries contain a short list of references to other works. Also, the full text of over 50 General Assembly Declarations can be found scattered throughout the encyclopedia. A typical entry, such as "Aliens' Rights," will best illustrate the scope and arrangement of the encyclopedia. Two-and-a-half pages are devoted to this topic, with cross-references to "dual nationality," "asylum for aliens," "extradition of aliens," "the Bolivar Congress in Caracas," and the "Inter-American Convention on the Status of Aliens." Other conferences and treaties are discussed, and the complete text of the 1985 "Declaration on the Human Rights of Individuals Who Are Not Nationals of the Country in Which They Live" is provided. The entry concludes with references to five publications, including the *Yearbook of the United Nations*. In the index, "Aliens' Rights" directs the user to five additional entries. This is a very important reference source for all academic and most public libraries. Nothing comparable has been published on the United Nations recently that provides the same kind of thoroughness and level of detail. One minor complaint: this edition is classified in the fairly new KZ category of the Library of Congress classification system, which puts it far removed from most of the other United Nations resources in JX.

Classification: LC KZ4968; Dewey 341.

## Psychology

141. *APA Dictionary of Psychology*, by Gary R. VandenBos, ed.

Publisher: American Psychological Association, Washington, DC (2015)

Price: $49.95

Review by Amanda Izenstark—Assistant Professor, Reference and Instructional Design Librarian, University of Rhode Island, Kingston.

Functionally, the new edition of the *APA Dictionary of Psychology* is very similar to its 2007 predecessor. The vast majority of the volume is dedicated to providing definitions of terms, arranged alphabetically. A brief "Guide to the Dictionary" provides basic information on how to use the source. Users familiar with other dictionaries will not need most of this content, but the section on "Hidden Entries" explains the protocol for locating related words—similar to cross-references—but these are terms in bold face in the text of the definitions and used in context. Entries also frequently include standard cross-references and brief etymological information as appropriate. A significant change is in the biographical information. In the 2007 edition, biographical entries were included in the text of the dictionary, with an index of biographical entries at the end of the volume. In the 2014 edition, these have been placed in a separate section at the end, but they have also been greatly shortened; the entry for Carl Rogers, for example, has gone from approximately 250 words to under 40. The preface notes, however, that this has enabled the editors to include far more biographies than in the previous edition (p. vii). The remainder of the text has been updated to reflect current terminology and incorporate connections to the DSM-IV-TR and DSM-5 (entry 484). The volume concludes with lists of institutional entries, testing instrument entries, and techniques. Overall, this new edition is an excellent resource for students of all levels as well as practitioners. Recommended for high school, public, academic, and special libraries supporting researchers in mental health fields.

---

As a diagnostic tool, the entry for the *DSM-5* (the 5th edition of the *Diagnostic and Statistical Manual of Mental Disorders*) appears as entry 484 in chapter 6, for the Health Sciences. Classification: LC BF31; Dewey 150.

---

142. *A Dictionary of Psychology*, by Andrew M. Colman

Publisher: Oxford University Press, New York, NY (2009)

Price: $17.99

Review by Susan E. Thomas—Head of Collection Development/Associate Librarian, Indiana University, South Bend.

The 3rd edition of *A Dictionary of Psychology* provides thorough and comprehensible definitions to 11,000 terms primarily from the disciplines in psychology, with the inclusion of relevant terms from psychiatry, psychoanalysis, neuroscience, and statistics. There are a total of 160 new entries included in the 3rd edition. The intended goal of the entries is for the reader to be able to so clearly understand a term from its definition that it can immediately be applied in practice or research. Etymologies of terms are part of the entry and also include the name of the originator or discoverer of the term, where applicable. Some entries include notes about term usage, suggesting the preferred term when applicable. Cross-referencing has been increased with this edition, and black-and-white illustrations, while not overly abundant, are present to illustrate terms or visual phenomenon such as the Delboeuf illusion or the Corridor illusion. Three appendixes cover phobias, abbreviations, and symbols commonly used in psychology; and a new appendix provides a list of carefully selected and reviewed websites arranged by psychology subtopics such as personality and ethics. However the Web addresses are not included with the entries in the appendix. Instead, access is possible through the dictionary's Web page. A list of 140 reference titles, consulted in compiling this dictionary, is included at the very end. This very affordable and portable dictionary is intended for both students and practitioners.

---

The 4th edition appeared in 2015. Classification: LC BF31; Dewey 150.

---

143. *The Corsini Encyclopedia of Psychology*, by Irving B. Weiner and W. Edward Craighead, eds.

Publisher: Wiley-Blackwell, Hoboken, NJ (2010)

Price: $600.00/set

Review by Mark T. Bay—Electronic Resources, Serials, and Government Documents Librarian, Hagan Memorial Library, Cumberland College, Williamsburg, KY.

In the library community, there are a few reference resources that stand out. Whenever the updated version is published, librarians make a point to buy them without too much consideration because the reputation is so high and no library reference collection should be without it. Even in the age of electronic resources, certain reference sets need to be purchased by academic libraries in particular. Such is the case with *The Corsini Encyclopedia of Psychology*. Now in its 4th edition, *The Corsini Encyclopedia of Psychology* continues in the fine tradition of its predecessors as the premier psychology reference work. The entries are well written by eminent researchers in the field and have been updated to reflect the latest scholarship. Many new entries have been added to reflect the growth of the subject area. The volumes are arranged alphabetically, with an alphabetic list of all the entries at the front of each volume. The last volume contains a subject and an author index, along with brief biographies of notable personalities in the field of psychology. Nothing much has changed in the encyclopedia, which is actually a good thing in this case. The entries are authoritative, written and signed by prominent psychology scholars and practitioners. There are plenty of *see* and *see also* references to help users find useful information and to expand on topics. As always, Corsini could do with more illustrations and color, but the illustrations provided do a great job of explaining entries and the visually boring, conventionally laid-out books manage to give an impression of reassuring authority. Budgets are tight, so the price tag may place *The Corsini Encyclopedia of Psychology* out of reach of smaller libraries, but any academic library that supports programs in psychology, education, or other social sciences should definitely consider purchasing it.

---

Classification: LC BF31; Dewey 150.

---

144. *Encyclopedia of Psychology*, by Alan E. Kazdin, ed.

Publisher: Oxford University Press, New York, NY (2000)

Price: $995.00/set

Review by Jonathon Erlen—Curator, History of Medicine, University of Pittsburgh, PA.

The broad scope of the science of psychology presented a daunting challenge to the creators of this 8-volume encyclopedia. What should be included, how should these topics be handled, and how to present sufficient international coverage are only a few of the difficulties encountered by the senior editorial staff drawn from the American Psychological Association and Oxford University Press who labored jointly for 8 years on this project. Their final product fully justifies all their efforts. More than 1,400 contributors, many the leading scholars in their specialties, produced over 1,500 entries, including some 400 biographies of major figures in psychology's history. Entries vary in length from half a page to extensive, multipage coverage. Topics range in scope from narrowly defined subjects (e.g., deafness, cancer, xenophobia) to extremely broad conceptual entries (e.g., emotion, peace, creativity). Special attention is given to the historical aspects of the subjects covered, thus making this work an indispensable resource for the history of psychology. An additional useful feature is overview articles describing the development of psychology in specific countries or regions of the world. Partially annotated bibliographies are provided for every entry—a most helpful feature—with citations coming from both historical and current literature. The use of extensive cross-indexing in the text and a comprehensive master index in volume 8 provide easy access to this encyclopedia's treasury of information. As with any large-scale project the quality of the writing varies between entries, and some articles contain factual errors. For example, the famous Roman-era physician, Galen of Pergamon, is misdated, and the section on informed consent omits the key legal case that established this legal doctrine in 1957. However, taken as a whole this reference tool is a reliable source. The editors and contributors of this encyclopedia are to be congratulated for creating a reference work that will be of immeasurable assistance for anyone seeking information concerning both the history and current state of the science of psychology. These volumes are a valuable addition to the reference collection of all academic, healthcare, and large public libraries.

Classification: LC BF31; Dewey 150.

145. *Handbook of Psychology*, by Irving B. Weiner, Donald K. Freedheim, John A. Schinka, and Wayne F. Velicere, eds.

Publisher: Wiley-Blackwell, Hoboken, NJ (2003)

Price: $1,800.00/set

Review by Staff, Libraries Unlimited.

John Wiley is becoming well known for their advanced compilation of works in the area of psychology. In the past year alone, five handbooks in various areas of psychology have been released from this publisher, including *Handbook of Sport Psychology, Handbook of the Psychology of Women and Gender*, and *Handbook of Clinical Child Psychology*. This twelve-volume set provides an overview of the topics covered above as well as many others. Each volume is edited by a different scholar in the field and was compiled with the help of twenty-five contributing editors. The set begins with volumes 1 and 2 addressing the history and research methods of psychology. The "History of Psychology" volume gives an overview of each discipline, including abnormal psychology, counseling psychology, and school psychology. Volumes 3–7 provide comprehensive information on five broad areas of the study: biological psychology, experimental psychology, personality and social psychology, developmental psychology, and educational psychology. The final five volumes address the practice of five areas of study: clinical psychology, health psychology, assessment psychology, forensic psychology, and industrial and organizational psychology. The scholarly essays are well written, and all provide ample lists of references. Unfortunately, there are no cross-references, which would have served to interconnect the volumes. Each volume provides its own author index and subject index, but no cumulative index for the set is provided. This set will be worthwhile for graduate students of psychology, psychologists looking for the latest research in their field, and psychologists needing information outside of their own specialty. University libraries and health care libraries needing a comprehensive overview of both the history of psychology and new research in all fields should consider its purchase if budgets permit.

Classification: LC BF121; Dewey 150.

146. *The Oxford Companion to the Mind*, by Richard L. Gregory, ed.

Publisher: Oxford University Press, New York, NY (2004)

Price: $75.00

Review by Madeleine Nash—Reference/Instruction Librarian, Molloy College, Rockville Center, NY.

New developments in brain and mind research inspired this 2nd edition of the highly successful 1987 companion, according to Richard L. Gregory, Emeritus Professor of Neuropsychology, Bristol University, who again serves as editor.

Gregory, an expert in human perception and artificial intelligence, continues to emphasize scientific versus philosophical approaches to mind and mostly British research, but this edition has important changes. These include new and updated entries as well as elimination or sharp editing of worthwhile but less current content. Libraries buying this and owning the earlier edition should probably not discard it. This volume is about 20 percent longer and contains 900 articles by more than 90 contributors. There are over 160 illustrations including graphs, drawings and photographs, and a good index. New features are a glossary and three extensive "mini-symposia" on artificial intelligence, brain imaging, and consciousness, by specialists of different orientations. New and revised entries include attachment theory, autism and Asperger syndrome, compassion, cruelty, evolutionary psychology, and schizophrenia. The content of this edition, like the first, may evoke controversy. Much Freudian psychology has been omitted as well as an entire article on interpersonal processes by R. D. Laing. Familiar topics like homosexuality, post-traumatic stress, and meditation do not have entries or are not discussed at all. As in the earlier volume, article quality varies; clear strengths again are in scientific topics like perception and evolution. This is not an essential purchase for libraries that own the 1st edition; however, its unique flavor and educational value, which almost amounts to a first course in psychology, recommend it to academic and large public libraries that do not.

---

Classification: LC BF31; Dewey 150.

---

147. *Encyclopedia of the Mind*, by Harold Pashler, ed.
Publisher: SAGE, Thousand Oaks, CA (2013)
Price: $175.00/set
Review by Staff, Libraries Unlimited.

The *Encyclopedia of the Mind* is a multivolume set that brings together the work of experts from a range of fields. The volumes contain a table of contents, an alphabetic list of entries, and a reader's guide of topical entries. The first volume contains a list of contributors with names and affiliations. There are over three hundred signed entries covering topics ranging from consciousness, decision making, and attention to genetics, epistemology, and language and communication. The entries range in length from four hundred to five thousand words. All entries are followed by citations for further readings and references. Because of the broad coverage, the reader's guide is essential. The category names in the reader's guide are accessible to the general public. This is a cross-disciplinary tool that pulls from the fields of philosophy, psychology, neuroscience, anthropology, education, and molecular biology, just to name a few. The contributors have strived to cover the latest information from these fields to make the set as up to date as possible. Overall, this is a very good resource for the general public and undergraduate students. This work is recommended for public and academic libraries.

Classification: LC BF441; Dewey 150.

148. *The Encyclopedia of Phobias, Fears, and Anxieties,* by Ronald M. Doctor, Ada P. Kahn, and Christine Adamec

Publisher: Facts on File, New York, NY (2008)

Price: $67.50

Review by Cynthia Crosser—Social Sciences and Humanities Reference, Fogler Library, University of Maine, Orono.

The 3rd edition of *The Encyclopedia of Phobias, Fears, and Anxieties* does not differ significantly from the second (2000). The new edition adds an introduction that explains the difference between phobias and fears and provides a history of the understanding of phobias. The authors do not indicate what updates to the entries have been made in the preface, which is duplicated from the 2nd edition. The intended audience includes health professionals and the general public. The authors include over two thousand entries that range in coverage from a simple description (e.g., Ergophobia) to over ten pages with tables of statistics and references (e.g., Agoraphobia). Some theories (e.g., Double-Bind Theory) and therapies (e.g., Morita Therapy) are also included. The 2nd edition also included a few individuals, who have been dropped from the 3rd edition. Following the entries are a subject-specific list of helping organizations and a topically arranged bibliography. The references at the end of entries are not included in the topically arranged bibliography. Some of the entries have been updated (e.g., Post Traumatic Stress Disorder) or expanded (e.g., Abandonment, Fear of). In some cases (e.g., Zen Therapy) dated references have been removed but not replaced. The helping organizations' contact information has been updated, websites have been added where they did not exist in the previous edition, and URLs have been updated for those that have changed. Some topics (e.g., Addictions) have been updated with new resources in the bibliography. Others (e.g., Asthma) have pruned the oldest resources without making new additions. A few new topics (e.g., Workplace Violence) have been added. Despite its flaws this encyclopedia is still the only resource that combines resources on phobias, fears, and anxieties. Libraries that did not update to the

2nd edition will want to purchase this one. Libraries owning the 2nd edition will need to decide if having the updated URLs are worth purchasing a new edition.

---

Classification: LC RC535; Dewey 616.

---

## Sociology and Anthropology

### Dictionaries and Encyclopedias

149. *The Blackwell Dictionary of Sociology: A User's Guide to Sociological Language*, by Allan G. Johnson

Publisher: Blackwell, Malden, MA (2000)

Price: $29.95

Review by January Adams—Assistant Director/Head of Adult Services, Franklin Township Public Library, Somerset, NJ.

Rather than trying to create a comprehensive work on the language of sociology, Johnson has instead focused the definitions in this dictionary on what he considers the classic conceptual core of sociology. To this he has added representative samplings from the diverse areas of study within sociology, important concepts from related disciplines, and a section of brief biographical entries. Entries are approximately one hundred to two hundred words in length, although definitions for terms such as kinship, institution, and group are longer. Most of the entries include suggested titles for further reading. The index includes concepts and examples used to explain these concepts. The author has also chosen to write all of the entries himself, with the intention of giving the work continuity. The result is a dictionary that is clear and easy to read. Intended to serve as a guidebook, this dictionary is so well written that it could also be read cover to cover. Although the author states that the work is not comprehensive, it appears to include all of the terms found in other one-volume dictionaries of sociology. Additions to the 2nd edition include seventy-five new entries, revisions, updates, and expanded cross-references. All public and college libraries should have a copy of this work in their reference sections.

---

Classification: LC HM425; Dewey 301.

---

150. *The Cambridge Dictionary of Sociology*, by Bryan S. Turner, ed.

Publisher: Cambridge University Press, New York, NY (2006)

Price: $34.99

Review by Jonathan B. Stovall—Library Technology Coordinator, Radford Public Library, Radford, VA.

It is no surprise that initial reaction to *The Cambridge Dictionary of Sociology* should create speculation as to whether there is enough material to warrant such a work. Editor Bryan Turner relates a former colleague's own question to that effect when hearing that he was involved in this project. But Turner makes his case that sociology's success has been in effect its own undoing to its academic reputation. In the introduction we are reminded that sociology is a young discipline compared to the many academic studies of human nature and interaction and as such the many conclusions in the field of sociology have been absorbed and claimed by the more focused and particular disciplines of human interaction. Turner convincingly argues that sociology is a viable academic institution and is far from obsolete as a result of extensive borrowing from other related disciplines. Each article in this collection, and I should say article as extensive as many of the subjects and terms are covered, is thorough and complete as should be expected. Discussion of terms or names that are further included are bold and easily located in the alphabetic entries. The articles are clearly written, and I found myself again intrigued with the study of human interaction and how it is applied in the field of sociology. Just randomly opening to any place in the book one will find interesting and informative articles. This work will be an interesting reading for all and a must for any public library collection.

---

Classification: LC HM425; Dewey 301.

---

151. *Encyclopedia of Sociology*, by Edgar F. Borgatta and Rhonda J. V. Montgomery, eds.

Publisher: Macmillan Reference USA/Gale Group, New York, NY (2000)

Price: $500.00/set

Review by Staff, Libraries Unlimited.

This newly revised edition of the *Encyclopedia of Sociology* has been expanded to include the changes in society and the new terms associated with the broadening field of sociology in the new millennium. The 1st edition was well received by both experts in the field and interested laypersons researching the topic of sociology. This latest edition retains much of the same layout as the 1st edition but with more comprehensive entries and 66 new titles. The editors state in the introduction that contributors have diligently tried to explain how terms in the encyclopedia are relevant to the field of sociology, how the term or research method is used in the field, and what lies ahead in the future on that particular topic or area of research. This 5-volume set provides entries to 397 terms, each of which is given several pages of explanation. All of the entries are well written, although, as with most compilations, some are better written or more comprehensive than others. The contributors write in a nontechnical language to ensure that readers from all levels will be able to comprehend the subject matter. The articles cover studies of behavioral and social phenomena as well as research theory and methodology. Each entry concludes with *see also* references to other terms in the encyclopedia and a detailed list of references. The references will be especially useful for researchers on the topic because many of them are current and all provide complete bibliographic information. All articles are signed, and contributors are listed in the beginning of volume 1, with their areas of expertise noted. Although expensive, this set will be a must-have resource in academic libraries featuring programs in sociology and the behavioral sciences. Public libraries that can afford its steep price may also want to consider its purchase.

Classification: LC HM425; Dewey 301.

152. *Encyclopedia of Anthropology*, by H. James Birx, ed.

Publisher: SAGE, Thousand Oaks, CA (2006)

Price: $895.00/set

Review by Susan J. Gardner—Assistant Reference and Instructional Services Coordinator, USC Libraries Anthropology Liaison, University of Southern California, Los Angeles.

This new five-volume encyclopedia from SAGE purports to be the "first comprehensive international encyclopedia of anthropology" and, indeed, there is some truth in this statement. Anthropology, as the study of humankind, is arguably the broadest discipline in the social sciences and thus difficult to successfully capture. Until this new multivolume set there were only works that covered one facet (such as culture or archaeology) of the subject. Here there are over one thousand signed entries by scholars of varying length that touch upon the entire gamut of anthropology, including culture, archaeology, evolution, linguistics, paleontology, biology, and theoretical anthropology. In addition, cross-disciplinary entries related to philosophy, psychology, religion, and sociology are included. One-fifth of the entries are biographical and another one-fifth are cultural or social. Entries are alphabetically arranged and have a brief list of further readings at the end as well as *see also* cross-references where appropriate.

Entries are very readable, appropriate for undergraduates and above, and many are supplemented with color photographs. There is a chronology in the front of each volume with important events in the history of anthropology and a list of corresponding encyclopedia entries. Furthermore, the front of each volume contains an alphabetic list of entries and a list by subdiscipline (i.e., archaeology). Also included are a master bibliography and a comprehensive subject index; the latter lists only the page number and not the volume number, however. Obviously, an attempt at a broad encyclopedia in anthropology sacrifices more esoteric topics that can be found in specialized subdisciplinary resources. For example, the *Encyclopedia of Cultural Anthropology* includes an entry on teaching anthropology, and the *Encyclopedia of Human Evolution and Prehistory* includes an entry on the Laetoli Tanzania site—neither of which can be found in the *Encyclopedia of Anthropology*. Nonetheless, this resource is highly recommended for all academic libraries and any other library with patrons interested in anthropology. It is now available electronically through the Gale Virtual Reference Library.

Classification: LC GN11; Dewey 301.

153. *The Social Work Dictionary*, by Robert L. Barker

Publisher: NASW Press, Washington, DC (2003)

Price: $49.99

Review by Robert L. Turner Jr.—Librarian and Associate Professor, Radford University, Radford, VA.

The 5th edition of this dictionary adds over one thousand new entries and updates for over two thousand of the remaining entries, bringing the total number of definitions to over nine thousand. Each word was reevaluated and, as in past editions, reviewed by at least three experts and two editors. The definitions are remarkably concise, yet very clear. The author has tried to make each definition original to this work and thus has not quoted any definition from any other work. The terms defined in this work are taken from social work administration, research, practice, policy development and planning, health and mental health, macro and micro social work, and clinical practice. The author has included terms that describe the history, philosophies, organizations, values, and ethics of social work. Included are terms from social work as well as those borrowed from other fields, such as sociology, anthropology, medicine, law, psychology, and economics. All the symptoms and diagnostic labels for mental disorders are consistent with those in the *Diagnostic and Statistical Manual of Mental Disorders* (see entry 484), the *International Classification of Diseases* (10th edition), and the Person-in-Environment (PIE) System. Mini biographies of deceased individuals who have had a great impact in the field are also included. There are two additional sections. One is on acronyms that are frequently used by social workers. The second is a section detailing significant milestones in the development of social work. Both are very useful. The author removed two sections that were in the previous edition, namely the NASW Code of Ethics and a listing of state boards that regulate social work. I hope that they will be added in the next edition. This work is highly recommended for collections dealing in social work.

---

The 6th edition appeared in 2014. Classification: LC HV12; Dewey 361.

---

## Race and Ethnicity

154. *Gale Encyclopedia of Multicultural America*, by Thomas Riggs, ed.

Publisher: Gale/Cengage Learning, Farmington Hills, MI (2014)

Price: $555.00/set

Review by John R. Burch Jr.—Library Director, University of Tennessee at Martin, Martin, KY.

The 1st edition of the *Gale Encyclopedia of Multicultural America*, published in 1995, featured approximately 100 articles focusing on what the editors considered to be the most likely ethnic groups within the United States to be researched by high school and undergraduate students. Published five years later, the 2nd edition expanded the coverage to include more than 150 different groups. This latest edition features updates of all the articles contained in the previous edition and 23 new ones, bringing the total number of articles to 175. The articles in the respective groups range in length from 4,000 words to 20,000. Each entry includes 14 components: Overview; History of the People; Settlement in the United States; Language; Religion; Culture and Assimilation; Family and Community Life; Employment and Economic Conditions; Politics and Government; Notable Individuals; Media; Organizations and Associations; Museums and Research Centers; and Sources for Additional Study. Supplementing the articles are sidebars, maps, and full-color pictures. Since the publication of the previous editions the United States has become much more multiethnic. This is reflected in the nation's politics, especially in the polarizing immigration debates. Unfortunately, this work does not have the breadth to provide insights into the majority of the ethnic groups living within the United States. For example, although there are hundreds of Native American groups within the nation's borders, only 25 have an entry within this work's 4 volumes. Unfortunately the 25, which include groups such as the Cherokee, Hawaiians, and Sioux, are the ones that are easy to research as information about them is readily available in numerous reference works in print and online. Curiously, the Oneida are covered both in an individual article and in another focusing on the Iroquois Confederacy. This work is recommended for public and school libraries.

---

Classification: LC E184; Dewey 305.

---

155. *Race and Racism in the United States: An Encyclopedia of the American Mosaic*, by Charles A. Gallagher and Cameron D. Lippard, eds.

Publisher: Greenwood Press/ABC-CLIO, Santa Barbara, CA (2014)

Price: $399.00/set

Review by Anthony J. Adam—Director, Institutional Assessment, Blinn College, Brenham, TX.

Although numerous resources exist on race relations in the United States, including the volumes in Greenwood's American Mosaic series, this new set goes beyond examining the issues surrounding a particular race or ethnic group and instead brings attention to those groups which have experienced social or institutional discrimination in one form or another. The seven-hundred-plus alphabetically arranged entries cover the standard range of categories, including civil rights, education, politics and government, and slavery, from the passage of the Naturalization Act in 1790 through the re-election of President Obama in 2012. Particular topics focus on court cases, individuals, socio-economic theories and concepts (e.g., assimilation), and such hard-to-categorize topics as Archie Bunker Bigotry and Driving While Black. Each signed entry runs at least a page in length, with more significant entries running to multiple pages. *See also* references and a short list of further readings conclude most entries. Black-and-white photographs and sidebars are scattered throughout the four volumes. As they are written by a number of different scholars, the entries are of varied quality, but in general they are well written and cite recent findings. The language in most of the entries should be accessible to the average undergraduate students, although some of the more theoretical entries lean toward the graduate or professional level. All in all, however, because of its comprehensive overview of race and racism in the United States, this set would make a good addition to complement Pyong Gap Min's three-volume *Encyclopedia of Racism in the United States* and Angela Doolin's four-volume *Encyclopedia of Race and Racism* (2nd ed.) in all undergraduate collections.

---

Classification: LC E184; Dewey 305.

156. *The African American Almanac*, by Christopher Antonio Brooks and Benjamin Todd Jealous

Publisher: Gale/Cengage Learning, Farmington Hills, MI (2012)

Price: $312.00

Review by Anthony J. Adam—Director, Institutional Assessment, Blinn College, Brenham, TX.

The appearance of a new edition of *The African American Almanac* is always welcome. Now in its 11th edition, the present volume follows the same general format as previous versions, covering all topics related to the black experience in the United States, including history, politics, culture and the arts, the sciences and medicine, education, the military, religion, and much more. All material from the 10th edition was extensively reviewed by the editor, with several chapters substantially revised by subject experts. Over half of the biographies are updated, with nearly 50 new personalities added. Cross-references have also been added to the biographical section, as needed. The section titled "African American Firsts" has been updated to include nearly 100 new entries. Of the over 550 black-and-white photographs, illustrations, maps, and statistical charts, over half were not published in the 10th edition. The writing is excellent throughout, and all illustrations are clean and often striking. Appendixes of African American award winners (everything from the Olympics to Miss America), an extensive secondary bibliography, and an index complete the volume. Essential for all public, academic, and school libraries.

> Also widely owned is the single-volume *African American Almanac: 400 Years of Triumph, Courage and Excellence*, by Lean'tin L. Bracks (2012). Classification: LC E185; Dewey 973.

157. *Asian Americans: An Encyclopedia of Social, Cultural, Economic, and Political History*, by Xiaojian Zhao and Edward J. W. Park, eds.

Publisher: Greenwood Press/ABC-CLIO, Santa Barbara, CA (2014)

Price: $310.00/set

Review by Seiko Mieczkowski.

This comprehensive three-volume work provides historical information on the social, cultural, economic, and political lives of Asian and Pacific Islander American groups from 1848 up to the present day. This work will serve as a one-stop resource for those looking for accurate information on important policies, events, and notable individuals from this population. Special attention has been placed on ensuring that women are well represented here as well as some of the lesser-known ethnic groups. While many of the expected topics appear here, users will also find information on topics that will be difficult to find in other sources, such as transnationalism, gender and sexuality, and multiracial family units. Led by a professor of Asian American studies at the University of California, Santa Barbara, and a professor of Asian Pacific American studies at Loyola Marymount University, the volume has contributed entries by scholars, journalists, community activists, and other specialists of Asian American studies. The set is highly recommended.

Classification: LC E184; Dewey 973.

158. *Encyclopedia of American Indian Issues Today*, by Russell M. Lawson, ed.

Publisher: Greenwood Press/ABC-CLIO, Santa Barbara, CA (2013)

Price: $189.00/set

Review by Adrienne Antink, Medical Group Management Association, Lakewood, CO.

This reference gives the reader an array of essays on the legal, political, economic, educational, cultural, environmental, artistic, religious, demographic, medical, and social issues affecting contemporary American Indians. As an example, we see how gaming, the "new buffalo," has spread across Indian lands and its financial impact on tribes. We learn that American Indians and Alaska Natives have the highest high school dropout rate of any ethnic group—as high as 45 percent. The Native American Higher Education Movement is described including the creation in 1977 of the Navajo Community College (now the Dine College), which was the first college established and controlled by an Indian tribe. Today, there are 37 tribal colleges and universities in the United States and one in Canada. The authors tell us about the difficulties in preserving Native American cultures and identities and the intricacies of determining ownership and repatriation of Indian remains and artifacts. Given the breadth of the topic to be covered in only two volumes, the information is by necessity fairly superficial. The use of multiple authors provides diverse viewpoints but also results in redundancy in the information conveyed. Interestedly, a section is included on Canadian First Nations and their relationship to the Canadian government.

Classification: LC E76; Dewey 305.

159. *Encyclopedia of Latino Culture: From Calaveras to Quinceañeras*, by Charles M. Tatum, ed.

Publisher: Greenwood Press/ABC-CLIO, Santa Barbara, CA (2014)

Price: $294.00/set

Review by Kay Stebbins Slattery—Coordinator Librarian, Louisiana State University, Shreveport.

Charles M. Tatum provides a concise three-volume reference source on the Latino culture for the Cultures of the American Mosaic series. *Encyclopedia of Latino Culture* examines the various Latino cultures as there are many cultural differences among the various ethnicities. The work examines the historical, regional, and ethnic diversity within specific traditions. Topics covered include food, art, film, music, literature, religious and secular traditions, and beliefs and practices. Interspersed throughout the volumes are sidebars with biographies of influential Latin American personalities and leaders. This encyclopedia provides interesting facts that are not found in other Latin American cultural histories. Therefore it makes for a very interesting read. This current set is recommended for public, school, and academic libraries, especially in areas serving Hispanic students and patrons.

Classification: LC E184; Dewey 973.

## Modern Social Issues

160. *Encyclopedia of Drugs, Alcohol & Addictive Behavior*, by Henry R. Kranzler and Pamela Korsmeyer, eds.

Publisher: Macmillan Reference USA/Gale Group, New York, NY (2009)

Price: $620.00/set

Review by James C. Roberts—Assistant Professor of Sociology and Criminal Justice, University of Scranton, Scranton, PA.

Now in its 3rd edition, the *Encyclopedia of Drugs, Alcohol & Addictive Behavior* offers useful and timely information on a range of topics pertaining to substance use/abuse and addiction. While the primary focus of its entries is on the actions of drugs on the body, entries on social policy, history, politics, economics, international trafficking, law enforcement, scientific and medical research, treatment and prevention of drug use/abuse, and epidemiology are included to appeal to the wider interests of social science. The current edition of this encyclopedia boasts an impressive 545 entries written by some of the most prominent researchers and scholars in the fields of substance use/abuse and addiction. Each individual entry ends with a list of references used as well as cross-references directing readers to related entries found throughout the set. Many entries also contain black-and-white illustrations, figures, and tables, which help illuminate the material covered. The *Encyclopedia of Drugs, Alcohol & Addictive Behavior* is arranged alphabetically by topic. The first volume covers topics A–C and includes entries on adolescents and drug use, advertising and the pharmaceutical industry, aggression and drugs, alcohol and AIDS, anabolic steroids, anorexia nervosa, barbiturates, behavioral tolerance, blood alcohol concentration, brain structures and drugs, breathalyzers, caffeine, cannabis, child abuse and drugs, club drugs, codependence, and crime and alcohol/drugs. The second volume covers topics D–L and includes entries on designer drugs, dogs in drug detection, drug courts, drug interactions and the brain, drug interdiction, economic costs of alcohol/drug abuse, ED50, endorphins, epidemics of drug abuse in the United States, epidemiology of alcohol use disorders, families and drug use, foreign drug policies and laws, freebasing, Freud and cocaine, funding and service delivery of treatment, gambling, gangs and drugs, gender complications of substance abuse, gene regulation, ginseng, hair analysis as a test for drug use, hallucinogenic plants, harm reduction drug policies, hashish, heroin, impulsivity and addiction, inhalants, injecting drug users and HIV, international drug supply systems, intimate partner violence and alcohol/substance use, Jews and alcohol, jimsonweed, kava, khat, LD50, legal regulation of drugs and alcohol, legalization versus prohibition of drugs, and LSD. The third volume of the Encyclopedia of Drugs, Alcohol & Addictive Behavior covers topics M–R and includes entries on mandatory sentencing laws, methadone maintenance programs, minimum drinking age laws, models of alcoholism and drug abuse, morphine, myths about addiction and its treatment, Narcotics Anonymous (NA), needle exchange programs, neurotransmission, nicotine delivery systems for smoking cessation, opioid complications and withdrawal, drug overdoses, over-the-counter medications, OxyContin, personality disorders, pharmacokinetics of alcohol, physical dependence, substance abuse among physicians and medical workers, polydrug abuse, drug treatment in prisons and jails, racial profiling, raves, relapses, religion and drug use, and Rohypnol. The fourth and final volume covers topics S–Z and includes entries on schizophrenia, seizures and drugs, sexuality and drug abuse, sobriety, suicide and substance abuse, Students Against Destructive Decisions (SADD), tax laws and alcohol, terrorism and drugs, behavioral approaches to treatment, pharmacological approaches to treatment, specialty approaches to treatment, the organization of U.S. drug policy, agencies in drug law enforcement and supply control, agencies supporting substance abuse prevention and treatment, agencies supporting substance abuse research, existential models of addiction, the Vietnam War and drug use in the U.S. military, welfare policy and substance abuse in the United States, alcohol/drug withdrawal, women and substance abuse, and zero tolerance drug policies. Designed as a resource for the general public, the *Encyclopedia of Drugs, Alcohol & Addictive Behavior* provides accurate, research-supported information on a variety of complex and contro-versial issues pertaining to substance use/abuse and addiction. The thorough-ness and jargon-free style of its entries makes this encyclopedia a valuable guide for novice researchers and seasoned scholars alike. The editors in chief, both of whom are accomplished writers and researchers in the field, should be com-mended for their work on this thorough reference book. It is warmly recom-mended for anyone wishing to learn more about the very important issues of substance use/abuse and addiction.

Classification: LC HV5804; Dewey 362.

161. *Encyclopedia of Homelessness*, by David Levinson, ed.
Publisher: SAGE, Thousand Oaks, CA (2004)
Price: $299.00/set
Review by Rachael Cathcart—Assistant University Librarian, Florida Atlantic University, Boca Raton.

This 2-volume encyclopedia offers a broad look at the diverse and often mis-understood issue of homelessness, both in the United States and around the world. Covering a variety of issues and perspectives, Levinson aims to debunk the standard misconceptions of the homeless population as a mass of single, alcoholic adult men (think women, adolescents, and families, including many children) and offers the researcher a comprehensive place to begin any explora-tion of the topic. The general entries are thorough, ranging from 1 to 7 pages, and include references for additional reading; entry topics include countries (e.g., Australia, Japan, Nairobi), populations (e.g., families, older persons, women), legal issues, organizations, and service systems and settings. Included in this 928-page set are 5 appendixes that comprise nearly one-third of the book. One such appendix lists 23 primary source documents that give the reader a brief, yet wide-reaching history of homelessness, beginning with a list of rele-vant Bible passages. In another appendix one will find a nearly complete direc-tory of street newspapers throughout the world, listed alphabetically by country or state. However, page 638 is missing, and along with it the listings for papers in U.S. states such as Pennsylvania, Texas, and Washington—all of which carry such publications. Of particular note is the resulting absence of the Seattle-based paper entitled *Real Change*, which is mentioned elsewhere in the entry for street newspapers. Overall, this encyclopedia does an excellent job of accomplishing what Levinson set out to do and establishes itself as an engaging, definitive resource on homelessness. The extent to which the causes, history, and potential solutions of homelessness are explored makes this work a welcome contribution to the literature. The *Encyclopedia of Homelessness* is highly recommended for academic, public, school, and special libraries, as well as for the layperson.

---

Classification: LC HV4493; Dewey 362.

---

162. *International Encyclopedia of Marriage and Family*, by James J. Ponzetti Jr., ed. Publisher: Macmillan Reference USA/Gale Group, New York, NY (2003)

Price: $495.00/set

Review by Robert L. Turner Jr.—Librarian and Associate Professor, Radford University, Radford, VA.

This 4-volume set is a great expansion and revision of the 1st edition of the *Encyclopedia of Marriage and the Family*. There are 336 articles ranging from abortion to Zambia. Only 15 of those were transferred without a major rewrite from the 1st edition. The expanded size is due to the emphasis on the family internationally. Fifty countries from around the world were included, with articles about families and family life in those regions. Scholars from those countries, where possible, were selected to write the articles, giving an internal, rather than external, look at the subject. There are also 11 entries on specific religious or belief systems, such as Catholicism, Evangelical Christianity, Islam, and Mormonism, and their influence on family life and structure. There are 12 entries on unique ethnic groups, such as Yoruba families and Bedouin-Arab families, and how family life is affected by belonging to that group. A wide variety of topics are looked at in a cross-cultural approach, including such things as abstinence, academic achievement, birth control, divorce, family stories and myths, grandparenthood, housework, infidelity, later life families, nagging and complaining, orphans, parenting styles, peer influence, remarriage, and many more. The articles are well written by mostly academic practitioners. Each article has a good, current bibliography and also has cross-references to other articles in this set. High school students and above should be able to easily understand the writing. In the front of volume 1 is a list of all the articles and then there is a list of contributors. There is a good index in the fourth volume. This will be a great place to start for those interested in research on the family and it will be tremendously helpful to those looking at families in non-Western cultures and in lands other than North America.

---

Classification: LC HQ9; Dewey 306.

---

## Popular Culture

### Encyclopedias

163. *St. James Encyclopedia of Popular Culture*, by Thomas Riggs, ed.
Publisher: St. James Press/Gale Group, Farmington Hills, MI (2013)
Price: $767.00/set
Review by Josh Eugene Finnell—Reference Librarian, OH.

Since the inaugural publication of the *St. James Encyclopedia of Popular Culture* in 2000, the world has become enamored by the love affairs of teenage vampires and New York advertising executives. With a paucity of reference literature on the subject, the 2nd edition of this comprehensive popular culture encyclopedia is well received. Providing a broad historical overview to this five-volume set is Jim Cullen's introductory essay, underscoring the special case of American popular culture. With an additional decade included in the 2nd edition, ranging from 1900 to 2010, the topics expand to 3,034 items. Entries not only cover celebrities and television but also businesses (AT&T) and belief structures (Astrology). Entries are alphabetically arranged, cross-referenced, and complete with a brief bibliography for further reading. Volume 5 provides two indexes to facilitate discoverability: the time-frame index and subject index. Whereas the subject index is alphabetically arranged and useful in locating specific entries by volume and page number, the time-frame index is demarcated by decade and confusingly constructed. Without an explanation of the time-frame index organization, the reader is left to wonder why electric trains is indexed in the 2010s. Much like the 1st edition, the encyclopedia includes a general reading list on popular culture and a brief biographies on the advisers and contributors to the 2nd edition. Overall, there is much to applaud in the expanded 2nd edition, namely the update from black-and-white to color images. An invaluable resource to public and academic libraries, this encyclopedia will continue to be a foundational reference resource on the subject of popular culture.

Classification: LC E169; Dewey 973.

164. *Encyclopedia of Urban Legends*, by Jan Harold Brunvand
Publisher: ABC-CLIO, Santa Barbara, CA (2012)
Price: $173.00/set
Review by Alice Crosetto—Coordinator, Collection Development and Acquisitions Librarian, University of Toledo, Toledo, OH.

Urban legends, also known as contemporary or modern legends, continue to be passed along, whether true or not, through oral tradition and, more recently, the Internet. This two-volume set is an updated and expanded version of Jan Harold Brunvand's award-winning 2001 one-volume *Encyclopedia of Urban Legends*. Considered the world's foremost authority on urban legends, Brunvand has expanded most of the original entries as well as including almost one hundred new entries covering topics such as terrorism, current political events, and Hurricane Katrina. An introduction, which provides valuable background information regarding urban legends, precedes the five hundred entries. The entries, most containing a reference citation, are alphabetized by their conventional titles, specific topics and themes, or country names, and range from a single paragraph to several pages. The feature most needed and appreciated is the inclusion of the abundant *see also* and *see* references, particularly essential for urban legends with varying titles. Especially noteworthy is the section "Urban Legends in the Media, 2004–2011," that includes almost forty entries featuring examples of urban legends contained in television and email. An updated selected bibliography, a type index of urban legends, a paucity of black-and-white line drawings, and an index accompany the resource. This outstanding reference title represents Brunvand's professional commitment to the preservation and study of urban legends. Although mistakenly classified as folklore, urban legends and their influence on society continue to exist, with their popularity spreading even more rapidly via social networking. This comprehensive resource, which contains urban legends found in the United States, as well as numerous foreign ones, should be in the reference collection of all libraries.

Classification: LC GR105; Dewey 398.

## The Internet and Popular Culture

Recent events highlight the importance of understanding both the opportunities and the risks that go along with an Internet culture, social media, instantaneous transmission of text and image, and confusion about the sources and authorities behind information seen on the Web.

165. *Snopes.com* [digital]

Publisher: Snopes.com, San Diego, CA

Price: Free online. Date reviewed: 2017.

URL: http://www.snopes.com

Review by Staff, Libraries Unlimited.

Since its inception in 1994, Snopes.com has been a well-regarded and often-awarded place to fact-check urban legends and other news. The database generates most of its operating revenue from advertising and does not accept money from political parties, religious organizations, or other interest groups in order to stay free of bias. Further information about the site itself, including its funding sources and staff, can be accessed by clicking on the About link. The site is easy to navigate from a series of clickables on the left side of the page: What's New, Hot 50, Fact Check, News, Video, Archive, About, FAQ, Contact, and Random. Here the curious can discover the veracity of stories like whether or not President Donald Trump criticized President Barack Obama for lack of leadership during the 2013 federal government shutdown, if a man really had a five-foot-long intestinal parasite, and if the manufacturers of Tide decided to stop making detergent pods in response to reports of people ingesting them. Entries include sources of evidence and are signed by the fact checker.

> Fact-checking and coverage of political news has expanded in *Snopes*, with "top tags" for "Fake News" and prominent political figures across the spectrum. *Snopes* weathered a funding crisis in 2017. Classification: LC GR105; Dewey 398.

166. *Know Your Meme: Internet Meme Database* [digital]
Publisher: Literally Media, Ltd., Seattle, WA
Price: Free online. Date reviewed: 2016.
URL: http://knowyourmeme.com/
Review by Staff, Libraries Unlimited.

*Know Your Meme: The Internet Meme Database* launched in 2008 in order to research and document Internet memes and viral phenomena. By 2011 Know Your Meme (KYM) had more than 9.5 million monthly visitors when it was acquired by Cheezburger, the organization behind many other popular Internet sites. Registered members can submit memes and other viral phenomenon to KYM and/or can contribute to research. All material is evaluated by an editorial team that ultimately confirms or invalidates submissions. The research and reporting done by KYM has been used in such leading newspapers as *The New York Times* and *The Wall Street Journal*, as well as news magazines like *TIME* and such radio news outlets as NPR. In 2009, *TIME* selected KYM as one of the top 50 websites of the year. The American Folklife Center at the U.S. Library of Congress inducted KYM into its web archiving program in 2014. The site is free and easy to navigate via a series of tabs on the main screen. Featured memes and videos are discoverable under the Home tab. The Memes tab organizes memes according to their status: confirmed, researching, popular, submission, dead-pool (rejected), and all. There is also a place to submit a meme to the site. The Images and Videos tabs are further divided into Trending, Most Commented, Most Favorited, Most Liked, Least Liked, and Most Viewed. Like the Memes tab, there is a place for submission. The Forums tab offers a series of discussion threads (there is a link, for example, to serious discussions). Here users will also find links to places for such things as maintenance and suggestions. There are further connections to Interviewers, In the Media, White Papers, Episode Notes, Behind the Scene, and Meme Review under the Blog tab. The Episodes tab links to viral videos. Lastly, users can click on Memes of 2016 to find Outrages of 2016 as well as Election Memes of 2016, Music Memes of 2016, and Sports Memes of 2016. Although the site is riddled with advertising, it is nonetheless highly recommended.

---

Classification: LC GR105; Dewey 398.

---

167. *Factcheck.org: A Project of the Annenberg Public Policy Center* [digital]

Publisher: Annenberg Public Policy Center, University of Pennsylvania, Philadelphia, PA

Price: Free online. Date reviewed: 2017.

URL: http://www.factcheck.org/

Review by Staff, Libraries Unlimited.

The nonpartisan, not-for-profit FactCheck.org is a free website whose aim is to inform the general public of the accuracy of the information coming out of Washington, D.C., by key players in U.S. politics. The site was launched in 2003 by reporter Brooks Jackson and is a project run by the University of Pennsylvania's Annenberg Public Policy Center. The site is divided up between eight different tabs (Home, Articles, Ask a Question, Viral Spiral, Archives, About Us, Search, and More). The home page features a rotating banner comprising a handful of featured articles that check the accuracy of a range of policy-related topics. Below this banner is a list of recently published articles (with the most recently published article listed first). Users can access the full article by either clicking on the image associated with each article or the article title. The menu bar to the right-hand side of these articles contains an "Ask FactCheck" question-and-answer; includes an easy-to-find "Donate Now" button; and includes links (with useful visual graphics) to various other site features, like "SciCheck" and "Health Watch," among others. This bar is a permanent feature of the site and remains in place as the user navigates between pages. Some of the tabs offer pull-down menus to different pages related to that tab. For example, the Articles tab consists of links to the "Featured" articles page, "The Wire," and "SciCheck," which is related specifically to science policy. The Ask a Question tab is a Q&A forum that allows users to submit questions and which features answers to questions posed by users (with both a "FactCheck" and "SciCheck" option). Viral Spiral is a portion of the site dedicated to investigating and analyzing the credibility of widely disseminated—"viral"—stories. The Archives tab allows users to browse archived articles by month, section, people, location, and other tags. And the About tab gives information about the organization: its mission, process, funding, and staff. There's a search tab that allows for a custom Google search and a More section which features a pull-down menu of additional resources. The organization of the site isn't immediately intuitive and takes some scrolling around in order to get a good feel for its organization and breadth of content. Even then, it's not always clear what distinguishes some pages from others. While the writing is clear and informative, the site is probably best suited for an older audience already familiar with some of the material, as the nature of the content itself might be difficult for younger users. Nevertheless, this reliable site is recommended to school, public, and academic libraries.

---

Classification: LC JK275; Dewey 378.

---

## Customs and Cultures

168. *American Pop: Popular Culture Decade by Decade*, by Bob Batchelor, ed.

Publisher: Greenwood Press/ABC-CLIO, Santa Barbara, CA (2009)

Price: $375.00/set

Review by Sue Ellen Knowlton—Branch Manager, Hudson Regional Library, Pasco County Library System, Hudson, FL.

If you have ever wondered about the architectural styles of the 1920s, the origins of "Rosie the Riveter," or television entertainment in the 1970s, *American Pop: Popular Culture Decade by Decade* will provide information on these topics and a whole lot more. The four-volume set "examines the trends and events across decades and eras by shedding light on the experiences of Americans young and old, rich and poor, along with the influences of art, entertainment, sports, and other cultural forces" (p. xiii). The foreword offers an overview of events in American history that contributed to pop culture in the twentieth century. Each volume covers a range of decades: 1900–1929 in volume 1; 1930–1959 in volume 2; 1960–1989 in volume 3; and 1990–present in volume 4. The scope of the work is balanced between all decades. Each decade chapter begins with a timeline of significant events followed by an overview of the decade. Subsequent sections cover advertising; architecture; books, newspapers, magazines, and comics; entertainment; fashion; food; music; sports and leisure; travel; and visual arts. The set is enhanced by supplementary features. Sidebars and black-and-white photographs highlight significant people and trends of the times. Endnotes at the end of each chapter provide decade-specific resources for further study. Each volume also has a resource guide of print, Web, and video sources. The index is inclusive of all four volumes. There is also a general bibliography at the end of the fourth volume. This set is appropriate for anybody middle school age and up. The editors and contributors collaborated well, creating a work that is coherent and consistent throughout. One really nice addition to the set is an appendix of classroom resources providing ideas for the use of *American Pop* in the classroom. *American Pop* would make a great addition to any reference collection.

---

Classification: LC E169; Dewey 973.

---

169. *Countries and Their Cultures*, by Melvin Ember and Carol R. Ember, eds.

Publisher: Macmillan Reference USA/Gale Group, New York, NY (2001)

Price: $425.00/set

Review by Henry E. York—Head, Collection Management, Cleveland State University, Cleveland, OH.

There are many reference resources that focus on providing an overview of the government, politics, economy, and similar categories, along with basic statistics for the nations of the world. *The World Factbook* (entry 134) and the *Europa World Year Book* (entry 136) as well as many popular almanac titles contain much of this information. This new four-volume set from Macmillan Reference foregoes that familiar territory by turning its attention to the national cultures of 224 countries around the world, such as Scotland, Wales, Palestine, and Taiwan. The country portraits, which vary from about eight to eighteen pages, all contain the following major categories: name, demography, history, ethnic relations, urbanism, architecture, food and economy, social stratification, political life, nongovernmental organizations, gender roles, marriage, family, socialization, etiquette, religion, medicine, secular celebrations, arts, and the state of the physical and social sciences. The two hundred social scientists who contributed to this set made a special effort to comment on the distinctive national culture of each nation—the common culture, its diversity, and ethnic subcultures and conflicts. The goal of the editors was to provide an "integrated, holistic description of the countries, not just facts" (p. viii). This approach has produced a resource that is interesting to browse as well as to consult for specific information. It will be a useful reference work for those wanting cultural and social background information on the nations of the world. It will also be useful for those who are comparing cultures for research purposes, for teachers developing curriculum materials, and, of course, for travelers who want an introduction to the way of life in any country. The depth of coverage varies from profile to profile. For example, the article on Moldova provides a very useful orientation on the ethnic conflicts in that country. But the article on Ukraine offers no help in understanding the complex religious situation there that was highlighted by the recent visit of the Pope. The article on Mexico skillfully delineates the origins of Mexican culture and nationalism. In the article on Afghanistan, one sentence speaks volumes: "All scholars have left the country, and no higher education or scientific research is available" (volume 1, p. 11). The only supplementary materials are a list of contributors and an index. Each article concludes with a bibliography of source materials.

---

Classification: LC JK275; Dewey 378.

---

170. *Dictionary of Chicano Folklore*, by Rafaela G. Castro

Publisher: ABC-CLIO, Santa Barbara, CA (2000)

Price: $55.00

Review by Kennith Slagle—Collection Development Librarian, Northern Michigan University, Marquette.

The purpose of this book is to bring together from many sources both folklore and cultural information into one volume. To that end, the author has succeeded. Although the scope reaches back to the Conquest, the focus is on how all of Hispanic history and culture in the Americas has influenced the world of the modern Chicano. Given the history of this community, the book takes the proper tone. The audience is anyone interested in researching the subject; however, the information is directed at the undergraduate. Advanced study is pointed to and can be followed up from the extensive thirty-six-page bibliography. The index is quite detailed and specific. There is an interesting selection of black-and-white photographs and illustrations. Although the information is gleaned from many sources, the bulk naturally centers in the southwestern United States. There are entries on individual state folklore from Texas to California. Additionally, the many aspects of folklore and customs are traced to both rural beginnings and their urban evolution. The writing style is clear and straightforward. This dictionary is a good introduction to its subject in that the entries are cross-referenced to each other and to the bibliography at the end. Whether one is looking for a subject in either English or Spanish, one will either find it under its

Spanish heading or be redirected from English to the proper entry. This allows researchers from different levels of language expertise and cultural background to use this reference book.

---

Classification: LC GR111; Dewey 398.

---

171. *Encyclopedia of Jewish Folklore and Traditions*, by Raphael Patai and Haya Bar-Itzhak, eds.

Publisher: M. E. Sharpe, Armonk, NY (2013)

Price: $299.00/set

Review by Sara Marcus—Assistant Professor of Education, Touro University International, New York, NY.

This 2-volume set presents approximately 264 signed entries, ranging from half a page to several pages with subheadings in length on various aspects of Jewish folklore and traditions. Covering aspects including genres, authors, characters and people represented, themes, and ethnic and other groups, from biblical, historical, and contemporary times, this work will help any researcher who wants to know more about Jewish folklore. The traditions are addressed as found in the folklore; it is not a resource for in-depth information about the traditions as the title might mislead a user. The 100 contributors have performed research, and many entries include sources. The 18 color plates included, as well as the black-and-white illustrations throughout the set, lend visual interest, while the layout and use of white space make this book approachable for younger readers than scholars. The cross-references and index enable finding additional and desired information, although the location of the index only in the second volume necessitates both volumes being available when researching. Two appendixes offer a list of sources, definitions, and abbreviations in the Hebrew Bible, Rabbinic literature and medieval compilations, and a list of anthologies of Jewish folklore. This is of use to Jewish collections where users are interested in folklore, as well as any folklore collection where readers want to know more than the stories themselves.

---

Classification: LC GR98; Dewey 398.

---

172. *Encyclopedia of Christmas and New Year's Celebrations*, by Tanya Gulevich

Publisher: Omnigraphics, Detroit, MI (2003)

Price: $68.00

Review by Marlene M. Kuhl—Library Manager, Baltimore County Public
   Library, Reisterstown Branch, Reisterstown, MD.

One might wonder why a Christmas encyclopedia would need updating. After
all, Christmas has been around for a long time and its traditions are well established. In the case of this title, the reason for a revised edition just a few years
after the 1st edition is the addition of 60 new entries, making the total number of
entries 240. New to this edition are 21 articles on New Year's customs, obser-
vances, and symbols around the world. There are also 17 new entries about
Christmas in other countries, including Africa and several Middle Eastern countries. New articles related to Christmas in the United States shed light on how
slaves celebrated the holiday and White House Christmas celebrations. There are
also articles on Christmas as it is reflected in literature, music, art, and the popular media that did not appear in the earlier edition. The original entries on Christmas history and religious and secular symbols and traditions remain. Appendixes
include a bibliography, Webliography, and a list of holiday-related organizations.
Entries run from 100 to 2,500 words, and a brief bibliography follows each article. Bold type guides the user to related entries, as does the detailed index. Some
entries consist entirely of *see* references. This strategy works for some topics but
not all. The entry for "United States, Christmas in" consists of no less than 44
references to other entries, none of which provide an overview of the holiday as it
is celebrated in America. This is true for other countries as well. Yet for some
there is a nice summary article similar to those found in William D. Crump's
*Christmas Encyclopedia*. With 340 entries, Crump's title covers all of the same
information and more. He includes more historical and religious detail about
Christmas celebrations around the world. The illustrations, paintings, woodcuts,
commercial labels, Christmas stamps, and so on are far superior to the computer-
generated ones in this title. In fact, Christmas stamps are not included here at all.
Holiday books are always popular and, while this one is fun to browse, Crump's
is a more comprehensive and better organized choice.

---

An earlier edition was titled simply *Encyclopedia of Christmas*. This work is
more widely owned than Crump's *Christmas Encyclopedia*. Classification:
LC GT4985; Dewey 394.

---

173. *Death and the Afterlife: A Cultural Encyclopedia*, by Richard P. Taylor

Publisher: ABC-CLIO, Santa Barbara, CA (2000)

Price: $75.00

Review by Gregory A. Crawford—Head of Public Services, Penn State Harrisburg, Middletown, PA.

Taylor has written what is obviously a labor of love. As he states in the introduction, "The work attempts to draw out the underlying meaning of funeral and afterlife traditions" (p. ix). He fulfills this goal admirably. *Death and the Afterlife* is a well-written, fascinating compilation of information on the funeral practices and beliefs of cultures from around the world. The encyclopedia includes more than 280 topics, ranging from Aaru (one of the abodes of the righteous dead in ancient Egyptian belief) to Yizkor (the Jewish memorial service celebrated four times a year on the high holy days of Yom Kippur, Passover, Shavuot, and Succot). In between are 7 articles on burial and burial customs, 20 on funerary customs, 3 on heaven, 3 on hell, 3 on reincarnation, and 12 on the soul. Not only are ancient cultures, such as Egypt, Greece, and India, represented, but also modern cultures, such as China, Native North Americans, Christian, African, and Muslim. Each article provides an excellent summary of the topic and includes several current and historical references. Generally, Taylor gives passages from native authors as well as relevant stories or texts from the culture being discussed. Each article also lists several cross-references to other related topics. Of special note is the comprehensive index that aids in easily finding desired topics. The work includes a 14-page bibliography of all works cited in the individual articles. Although not a must-have purchase for many libraries, this encyclopedia is an excellent addition to the reference collections of colleges, seminaries, and most larger public libraries. Many of the topics are not included in other general encyclopedias, nor are they covered in as much depth in the various encyclopedias of religion or culture.

Classification: LC GT3150; Dewey 393.

## Food

Works emphasizing nutrition appear in chapter 6 for the health sciences (entries 495–498).

174. *The Oxford Companion to Food*, by Alan Davidson and Tom Jaine, eds.

Publisher: Oxford University Press, New York, NY (2006)

Price: $65.00

Review by Betsy J. Kraus—Librarian, Lovelace Respiratory Research Institute, National Environmental Respiratory Center, Albuquerque, NM.

This dictionary of foods and related topics is composed of four major categories and groups. These groups include food plants; animals, birds, fish, and more; cooked foods and beverages; and lastly culture, religion, meals, diet, and regional cuisine. This second edition has 72 new entries. The entries are arranged alphabetically; each has a definition; some have drawings of the item, a history of the item, its origin, how it is prepared, where it is grown and used, and a description of its flavor and texture. The entries are informative as well as fun to read. There are maps showing how foods traveled throughout the world, an extensive bibliography, and an index with cross-references. This is not a traditional stuffy dictionary; it is a history and geography book of food combined. The only drawback to the book is the very light green print for cross-references within the entries. It is a definite purchase for any library with a culinary program or public library with cooking schools in their towns or cities.

---

The 3rd edition appeared in 2014. Classification: LC TX349; Dewey 641.

---

175. *Cambridge World History of Food*, by Kenneth F. Kiple and Kriemhild Coneè Ornelas, eds.

Publisher: Cambridge University Press, New York, NY (2000)

Price: $175.00

Review by Staff, Libraries Unlimited.

The two-volume *Cambridge History of Food*, under the guidance of editors Kenneth F. Kiple and Kriemhild Coneè Ornelas, is a tour de force broken into eight parts in two volumes, starting with Determining What Our Ancestors Ate. This section re-creates the composition of human diets, including discussion of such things as malnutrition and what animals served as food sources. Part two, Staple Foods: Domesticated Plants and Animals, includes information on grains, starchy staples, vegetable supplements, nuts, oils, spices and sugars, and foods from animal sources (American bison, cattle, game, geese, rabbits, turkeys, etc.). Dietary liquids are the subject of part three. Beer and ale, coffee, kava, tea, water, wine, and more are all covered. In part four, different sections discuss vitamins; minerals; proteins, fats, and essential fatty acids; deficiency-related diseases like beriberi and scurvy; and such food-related disorders as anorexia nervosa, obesity, and food allergies. Volume 2 begins with part five, Food and Drink around the World, which contains separate sections for Asia, Europe, the Americas, and Sub-Saharan Africa and Oceania. This is followed by History, Nutrition, and Health, with a section on nutrition and the decline of mortality and including discussion of famine, adolescent nutrition, food fads, food taboos, medicinal foods, and much more. Part seven, Contemporary Food-Related Policy Issues, provides information about important topics in such sections as "Food Labeling," "Food Additives," and "Food Lobbies and U.S. Dietary Guidance Policy." A Dictionary of the World's Plant Foods comprises part eight. Sections conclude with lengthy bibliographies; shorter sections also include bibliographies. A list of sources consulted, an index of Latin names, a name index, and a subject index complete the volume. Highly recommended for public and academic libraries.

---

Classification: LC TX353; Dewey 641.

---

176. *Encyclopedia of Food and Culture*, by Solomon H. Katz and William Woys Weaver, eds.

Publisher: Charles Scribner's Sons/Gale Group, New York, NY (2003)

Price: $395.00/set

Review by Barbara M. Bibel—Reference Librarian, Science/Business/Sociology Department, Main Library, Oakland Public Library, Oakland, CA.

Since food is a necessity, it plays an integral role in all aspects of life and culture. The *Encyclopedia of Food and Culture* explorers this relationship with 600 alphabetic signed entries by an international group of scholars and food specialists. The interdisciplinary approach examines the significance of food from diverse points of view; historians, anthropologists, archaeologists, folklorists, economists, and food critics have contributed to this encyclopedia. The entries cover specific foods (chili peppers, soup); preparation methods (baking, roasting); distribution (farmers' markets, retailing of food); storage (packaging and canning, pantry and larder); and nutrition and health (vitamins, obesity). There are also articles about various cultures and cuisines, religions, food as a symbol, and writing about food. Readers will find everything from aphrodisiacs to "icon foods" (bagels, peanut butter) to the evolution of the chef de cuisine here. The contributors examine feasts, festivals and fasts, hunger, and how Betty Crocker's image has changed with the times as well as food as a weapon of war. They include biographies of people, such as Epicurus, Clarence Birdseye, Louis Pasteur, and Julia Child. All articles have bibliographies. Many have sidebars with interesting facts, such as one about Halloween in the article on candy and confections. Many color and black-and-white illustrations enliven the text. An appendix offers the revised Dietary and Reference Intakes from the National Academy of Sciences and a systematic outline of the contents as well as a list of contributors. A unique approach, accessible language, and fascinating content that covers gender and food and Rabelais's vivid food imagery as well as cannibalism, the noodle in Asia, and food in the Bible make the *Encyclopedia of Food and Culture* an outstanding resource for high school, academic, and large public libraries. Users will learn and be entertained in the process.

---

Classification: LC GT2850; Dewey 394.

---

177. *The Oxford Encyclopedia of Food and Drink in America*, by Andrew F. Smith, ed.

Publisher: Oxford University Press, New York, NY (2013)

Price: $450.00/set

Review by Barbara M. Bibel—Reference Librarian, Science/Business/Sociology Department, Main Library, Oakland Public Library, Oakland, CA.

Food plays a vital role in the daily life of all cultures. Until recent times, those who took food seriously did not feel that the United States was important. This updated edition captures the shifting attitude that Americans have concerning food. The 2nd edition of *The Oxford Encyclopedia of Food and Drink in America* is an update of the first major work to examine American food and drink in depth. Andrew F. Smith, who teaches culinary history at The New School University and writes widely on food topics, is the editor of this three-volume set. He and over 200 contributors who are academics and food writers have created 1,400 alphabetic signed entries with bibliographies that place American food in a historical and cultural context. The articles examine specific foods (fruit, mock foods), regional cookery (New England), ethnic influences (Southeast Asian American food), advertising (Elsie the Cow, the Jolly Green Giant), manufacturers (Betty Crocker, Nabisco), appliances and gadgets (can openers, bread machines), food personalities both fictional (Betty Crocker) and real (Orville Redenbacher, Clarence Birdseye). New entries look at the new foods created from ethnic food fusion recipes (e.g., Filipino hamburgers, southwestern sushi), a new health consciousness around food (e.g., transfat and calorie-count laws, obesity taxes), and trends in the food industry (e.g., locavorism). Entries have been added and updated on food science and nutrition, genetically modified foods, regional foods, food prices, and molecular gastronomy. The set includes separate food and drink bibliographies, lists of food periodicals and food websites, and directories of food museums, food-related organizations, biographies of famous chefs and food personalities, and food festivals. An alphabetic list of articles at the beginning of volume 1, a topical outline of entries, and an index make it easy for users to locate information. Black-and-white illustrations supplement the text. *The Oxford Encyclopedia of Food and Drink in America*, with a focus on the United States, is an excellent partner for M. E. Sharpe's *World Food: An Encyclopedia of History, Culture, and Social Influence from Hunter-Gatherers to the Age of Globalization* (2012). It is an informative and entertaining resource that will serve users in public and academic libraries well.

Classification: LC TX349; Dewey 641.

## Languages and Linguistics

178. *The Cambridge Encyclopedia of Language,* by David Crystal
Publisher: Cambridge University Press, New York, NY (1997)
Price: $69.95
Review by Paula Frosch—Associate Museum Librarian, Thomas J. Watson
   Library, Metropolitan Museum of Art, New York, NY.

The fascination with words, their meanings and implications, their origins and transformations is an integral part of an examination of the world, an effort to make sense of what is seen and heard. The development of language as a tool and the problems of communication—physical, psychological, and cultural—are of paramount importance in a world in which the transmission of information is almost instantaneous. *The Cambridge Encyclopedia of Language* is an ambitious but flawed work. Its aim is to describe the history of language and the scientific area of linguistics, but it is neither a simple examination of the myriad of human languages nor a technical investigation of linguistic origins and developments. The chapter descriptions promise valuable content, but the overall effect is a series of information bites. The format, somewhat like MTV in print, offers little ease to the eye, with many different colored insets, disruptive sidebars, and illustrations that do not always have labels or explanations for their inclusion. Perhaps the most interesting and potentially useful section is that dealing with the languages of the world, but the failure to include a reasonable number of samples of those languages discussed is a major deficit. It is not clear for whom this work is intended, but it is certainly not the beginning adventurer into the linguistic jungle or the highly sophisticated scientific researcher. One would imagine that the encyclopedia is aimed at the college and early graduate school level, including as it does an extensive glossary and bibliography. The cost of the book, particularly in paperback, would make it a useful purchase for libraries serving this population and for large public collections.

---

The 3rd edition appeared in 2010. Classification: LC P29; Dewey 403.

---

179. *The World's Major Languages,* by Bernard Comrie, ed.
Publisher: Routledge/Taylor & Francis Group, New York, NY (2009)
Price: $75.00
Review by Staff, Libraries Unlimited.

The 2nd edition of this well-received title provides information on more than fifty of the world's languages, two of which are new to this edition—Amharic and Javanese. The editor has chosen the languages based on their cultural and historical significance as well as on the number of speakers using it worldwide. The languages are looked at in depth, focusing on grammatical features, phonology and syntax, its role in history, and its role in culture. This is a book designed for specialists in linguistics and will serve as a research tool for those learning more about languages they are studying. A bibliography and an index are provided to aid research. This work will be useful in academic collections in larger universities.

Classification: LC P371; Dewey 400.

180. *Ethnologue: Languages of the World*, by M. Paul Lewis [digital]
Publisher: SIL International, Dallas, TX
Price: Free online. Date reviewed: 2013.
URL: http://www.ethnologue.com/
Review by Staff, Libraries Unlimited.

This site is an online version of M. Paul Lewis's *Ethnologue: Languages of the World* (16th ed.; SIL International, 2009). This encyclopedic work includes useful information on 6,909 known living languages. *Ethnologue: Languages of the World* is a comprehensive reference work cataloging all of the world's known living languages. Since 1951, the *Ethnologue* has been an active research project involving hundreds of linguists and other researchers around the world. It is widely regarded to be the most comprehensive source of information of its kind. The information in the *Ethnologue* will be valuable to anyone with an interest in cross-cultural communication, bilingualism, literacy rates, language planning and language policy, language development, language relationships, endangered languages, writing systems and to all with a general curiosity about languages.

Classification: LC P123; Dewey 409.

181. *International Encyclopedia of Linguistics*, by William J. Frawley, ed.
Publisher: Oxford University Press, New York, NY (2003)
Price: $495.00/set
Review by L. Zgusta—Professor of Linguistics and the Classics and Member of the Center for Advanced Study, University of Illinois, Urbana.

This 2nd edition of the 4-volume *International Encyclopedia of Linguistics* is one of the most recent works of this genre. Its main competitors on the market are, above all, *The Cambridge Encyclopedia of Language*, edited by David Crystal (Cambridge University Press, 1987), and the 2nd edition of *The Linguistics Encyclopedia*, edited by Kirsten Malmkjaer. The remarkable thing is that these three works, although titled similarly, are not real competitors as each of them has a unique profile. Crystal's encyclopedia covers a very broad area, using short articles that are ordered in thematically organized chapters rather than alphabetically. Each chapter and each article begins with an indication of their content. The encyclopedia, while giving the usual topics of such manuals their due, also finds a place for articles on topics such as various systems of shorthand, language, and other communication systems (e.g., chimpanzee communication). Also, the book offers not only maps and diagrams but also portraits of the authors and other interesting illustrations. Indeed, the book is useful not only for serious study, but also offers an opportunity for delightful browsing. The strength of the encyclopedia edited by Malmkjaer is what is frequently called "theoretical linguistics." Of course, there are good articles on topics such as aphasia and lexicography, but the subjects that seem to dominate the list of entries are behaviorist linguistics; Cognitive linguistics; Contrastive linguistics; Critical linguistics; Discourse analysis; Finite state (Markov process) grammar; Formal logic and modal logic; and Functionalist linguistics; Generative grammar; and Glossematics. The entries are written by outstanding scholars who are specialists in the respective topics. The value of a volume like this is self-evident. The 4 volumes of the 2nd edition of the International Encyclopedia of Linguistics comprise the total of 2,142 pages. Naturally, each article is signed by its author. In many cases, the subentries of an article are signed by different authors; for example, the entry parsing is divided into three subentries—Computational approaches, Semantic approaches, and Psycholinguistic approaches—each of which is signed by its author. The enormous wealth of information present in this encyclopedia is distributed into relatively short articles ordered alphabetically by title. At the end of the fourth volume, there are several indexes that help in the search for a subject. The most important is the topical index that lists the notions, terms, and names (also those of the scholars important in the history of linguistics). For instance, all remarks concerning the term parsing that are not mentioned in the article on parsing quoted above are listed in the topical index. The "Systematic Outline of Contents" (pp. 419–434) indicates in which articles one can find information relevant for a broader subject, and is also highly useful. For instance, "Historical Linguistics" has an index entry of its own; however, this entry plus the subentry "Culture History and Historical Linguistics" are also listed under "Anthropolinguistics" as pertinent to that topic. In addition to these dead entries and cross-references, in the introduction one can find detailed instructions on how to find a topic. The collection of the enormous wealth of information offered by this encyclopedia was made possible by locating several hundreds of authors willing to write the entries, not to mention about a dozen or so members of an advisory committee. The treatment of languages must be mentioned. The comprehensive list of the world's languages was prepared by B. Grimes, who also authored the list in the 1st edition. This improved version is, in most cases, organized by linguistic families, whose names are inserted into the alphabetic list of entries. Each subentry contains one language that belongs to the respective family and informs us about the area where the language is spoken, and by how many speakers, approximately. When the number of speakers is small (some numbers consist of one or two digits, alas), the author indicates, if possible, the number of people that still belong, at least partly, to the indigenous culture although they do not speak the language. Larger or better-known languages also have their own entry listed in the alphabetic sequence, authored by a specialist for that area. These language lists are accompanied by very good geographical sketches indicating the location of the individual languages. The sketches are reliable and indicate the respective names of the languages and indications of those geographical features that are necessary for the localization of the linguistic data. Naturally, there are points that could be improved in the next edition. For instance, I would think that terms such as lexicology and onomasiology deserve entries of their own. However, these instances are quite rare. As it is, this encyclopedia will be most useful.

---

Classification: LC P29; Dewey 410.

---

## Media and Communications

182. *Encyclopedia of New Media*, by Steve Jones, ed.

Publisher: SAGE, Thousand Oaks, CA (2003)

Price: $125.00

Review by John Maxymuk—Reference Librarian, Paul Robeson Library, Rutgers University, Camden, NJ.

In a two-page introduction to this work the editor struggles with limited success to define just what "new media" is. It is hardly surprising then that the entries, while generally fascinating, at times appear to be something of a grab-bag of loosely related topics. For example, under "D" we find Data Mining, DeCSS (related to DVDs and copyright), Desktop Publishing, Digital Art and Animation, Digital Cash, Digital Divide, Digital Millennium Copyright Act, Digital Subscriber Line, Digital Television, Disintermediation, Disposal of Computers, Distance Learning, and Distributed Computing. More broadly speaking, these entries cover art, entertainment, technology, research, and social, legal, and ethical issues. That is not to mention additional entries on such diversely prominent people as virtual reality and networking specialist Thomas DeFanti, management theorist Peter Drucker, and computer industry analyst Esther Dyson. In short, the *Encyclopedia of New Media* is an impossibly wide and steadily spreading connection of countless communications technologies. Entries represent all categories of the electronic tools of the information society—the Internet, the Web, entertainment multimedia, and e-business—as well as key movers and shakers and important organizations. Entries generally run from one to three pages and include a bibliography, a list of resources for further reading, and suggestions for related topics. Access points include a general index, a name index, and a thematic readers' guide to entry topics. This encyclopedia is engagingly written and full of interesting details. It should serve as a useful reference for a number of subjects and is recommended for all libraries.

> Classification: LC QA76; Dewey 302.

183. *The Museum of Broadcast Communications Encyclopedia of Radio*, by Christopher H. Sterling and Michael C. Keith, eds.

Publisher: Fitzroy Dearborn/Taylor & Francis Books, New York, NY (2004)

Price: $375.00/set

Review by Ralph Lee Scott—Professor, Assistant Head of Special Collections for Public Services, and Curator of Printed Books and Maps, East Carolina University Library, Greenville, NC.

*The Museum of Broadcast Communications Encyclopedia of Radio* is oriented toward radio broadcasting and its history. Entries cover a variety of radio topics including personalities (e.g., Wolfman Jack, Lord Haw-Haw), networks (e.g., Blue Network, National Public Radio), country-specific information (e.g., Cuba, Japan), specific programs (e.g., Adventures Is Good Music, Lone Ranger), stations (e.g., BBC-World Service, WQXR), pioneers (e.g., Edwin H. Armstrong, Edward R. Murrow), special topics (e.g., election coverage, female radio personalities, Native American radio, obscenity and indecency on radio), government use of radio (e.g., CONELRAD, Office of War Information), and technical terms (e.g., DXing, Digital Satellite Radio, Microradio). The work does not include any technical or electrical engineering information other than in a general discussion setting. A typical entry includes a brief overview of the topic, a chronology of important events, a biography, a list of important shows on radio and television dealing with the topic, an illustration, and further references. For example, for the entry on Wolfman Jack (1938–1995) the story begins with how Wolfman got into radio (skipping school and hanging out at local radio station WNJR); why Robert Weston Smith is called Wolfman Jack; his early career as a Fuller Brush salesman in Washington, D.C.; early gigs as "Daddy Jules" in Newport

News, Virginia; how his early career was frustrating. Next the article describes his continued early career at XERF, where he "played rock and blues, had an unconventional delivery, used strange language, and howled like a wolf." Wolfman's career as a "shock jock" is chronicled up to his death in 1995 at his home in Belvidere, North Carolina, of a heart attack after a twenty-city promotional tour for his autobiography. The article concludes with a short biography, a list of radio and television shows, films Wolfman was in (thirteen), a stage show, a reference to his autobiography, and suggested further reading. The article is illustrated with a black-and-white photograph of Wolfman Jack in a typical howling pose. This three-volume set is illustrated with a number of black-and-white photographs. The articles are well written and cover a wide range of topics on broadcast radio. The editors have included a list of entries, a general bibliography (called "A Radio Reference Shelf"), a list of the contributors and their affiliations, and an index. The hardbound volumes have a very attractively designed cover featuring a number of radio personalities, from Aimee Semple McPherson to Rush Limbaugh. The articles, written by a variety of contributors, have been molded into a seamless ethereal web by the editors of the encyclopedia. Old-time radio fans as well as more recent listeners will find something of interest in these volumes. Reference collections will want to include the set for mass communications majors as well as the general readers.

---

The *Concise Encyclopedia of American Radio* (2010) is an "updated excerpt" based on this work. Classification: LC TK6544; Dewey 384.

---

184. *Encyclopedia of Television*, by Horace Newcomb, ed.

Publisher: Fitzroy Dearborn/Taylor & Francis Books, New York, NY (1997)

Price: $250.00/set

Review by Walt Mundkowsky—Freelance Film and Music Critic, Beverly Hills, CA.

The Museum of Broadcast Communications was founded in 1987. It aims to document the moving target the television arena represents and to provide a forum for education and study of media issues. To that end, it makes its vast archive available to researchers and the general public alike. This admirable encyclopedia—1,948 elegant pages in 3 massive volumes—is an extension of that effort. Newcomb and his 14-member advisory board have employed both ends of the telescope to concoct a worthwhile portrait of the medium. Important shows and individuals (actors, writers, producers, journalists, network executives) rate their own entries, along with general topics and corporate entities. The English-speaking countries get most of the attention, but there are essays on television developments in many other places. However much one may quarrel with isolated choices (is The Outer Limits less significant than Honey West?), the thousand-subject format contains no glaring omissions. Contributors number in excess of 300, so a unified viewpoint (or singular prose) is out of the question. From My Little Margie to The Forsyte Saga to Beavis and Butt-Head, everything is viewed as equally deserving of one's time. No hierarchies or discouraging words need apply. Still, an enormous mass of material has been brought together, in a useful and attractive presentation. The alphabetic arrangement encourages browsing as much as serious endeavors; all names are indexed. This set is a must for reference libraries, but it also affords the casual reader much pleasure.

---

The 2nd edition appeared in 2004. The free online *Internet Movie Database (IMDb)* at http://www.imdb.com/ also covers television programs. For more information about motion pictures see entries 329–331. Classification: LC PN1992; Dewey 384.

---

185. *Encyclopedia of Social Media and Politics*, by Kerric Harvey, ed.

Publisher: SAGE, Thousand Oaks, CA (2014)

Price: $485.00/set

Review by Mark Schumacher—Art and Humanities Librarian, University of North Carolina, Greensboro.


This 1,500-page set explores the role, impact, and importance of social media in the realm of politics, both in the United States and the rest of the world. Entries such as Arab Spring, Middle East, China, and Latin America reflect the international scope of this work. Some of the entries will resonate more with younger readers of this work: Digg, Clicktivism, Vlogging, Ushahidi, etc. These articles, however, clearly present the importance of these "Web 2.0" sites and terms. Entries run from 1 to 8 pages, with suggestions for further readings provided. Additional resources for users include a chronology, a glossary, a resource guide (bibliography) of books, journals, and websites, a list of social media use by all 535 members of Congress, and an 80-page index. Organized along the same clean lines as a number of other SAGE encyclopedias published recently, the set (also available online) will be welcomed in public and academic libraries, as well as in many high school libraries, if they can afford it.

---

Classification: LC JF799; Dewey 320.

---

## Business and Economics

## Business

### *Dictionaries and Encyclopedias*

186. *The AMA Dictionary of Business and Management*, by George Thomas Kurian

Publisher: AMACOM/American Management Association, New York, NY (2013)

Price: $24.95

Review by William C. Struning—Professor, Seton Hall University, South Orange, NJ.

*The AMA Dictionary of Business and Management* provides concise and authoritative definitions for more than 6,000 currently used business and management terms and phrases. Definitions are clearly presented without resorting to excessive use of technical jargon. Where appropriate, terms are given fuller, more detailed treatment. Also included are brief biographies of those who have made notable contributions to, or have had significant influence on, the fields of business, management, or related fields such as economics. Cross-references are provided that are particularly useful in relating contributors to contributions. The dictionary serves not only as a comprehensive reference for deriving meanings, but also as a top-line overview of the modern business world. The book should be useful to students, instructors, and business practitioners as well as those in other fields who require understanding of business terminology.

Classification: LC HD30; Dewey 650.

187. *Encyclopedia of American Business*, by W. Davis Folsom and Stacia N. VanDyne

Publisher: Facts on File, New York, NY (2011)

Price: $125.00/set

Review by William C. Struning—Professor, Seton Hall University, South Orange, NJ.

The newly revised edition of *Encyclopedia of American Business*, under the general editorship of W. Davis Folsom, provides a comprehensive and user-friendly guide to the concepts and terms that characterize current business practices in the United States. The 2-volume set contains over 800 alphabetically arranged entries, prepared by more than 120 contributors, largely drawn from business faculties of American universities. The entries can be understood by nonprofessionals as well as by students, while yet retaining adequate rigor and embodying sufficient information to serve as references or refreshers for professionals. Many of the entries are followed by suggestions for further readings. Cross-references are used where appropriate, to provide useful relationships with other entries. A list of entries and an index facilitate searches for specific terms. The book also contains a list of contributors and a bibliography.

Classification: LC HF3021; Dewey 338.

188. *Encyclopedia of Business and Finance*, by Burton S. Kaliski
Publisher: Gale/Cengage Learning, Farmington Hills, MI (2014)
Price: $485.00/set
Review by Judith J. Field—Senior Lecturer, Program for Library and Information Science, Wayne State University, Detroit, MI.

This two-volume set provides general articles to the user who has little familiarity with business. Topical areas include accounting, finance, economics, marketing, management, and information systems. Some of the articles provide the reader with a historical perspective and data; other articles focus on current concepts with current quantitative data. Most of the bibliographies include citation to articles published in 2013 or 2014. Descriptions of relevant federal agencies have been included, as well as brief descriptions of important legislation. Two topics of general interest, careers and ethics, have been given special treatment and should be noted. There is an overview article provided for each of these two topics. Additional articles that focus on careers in accounting, finance, economics or additional articles dealing with the application of ethics in different fields of business follow the overview articles. This is a good title to enhance the business collection of a small- or medium-sized library by including current material and citations. The topics are easy to understand and provide clear definitions of the terms. Cross-references are plentiful.

Classification: LC HF1001; Dewey 650.

189. *Advertising Age Encyclopedia of Advertising*, by John McDonough and Karen Egolf, eds.
Publisher: Fitzroy Dearborn/Taylor & Francis Books, New York, NY (2002)
Price: $680.00/set
Review by Staff, Libraries Unlimited.

This three-volume set provides users with an authoritative look at the advertising industry worldwide. The text is arranged in an A to Z format and includes entries that vary in length from one page to as many as six to seven pages. Entries may include illustrations and contain suggestions for further readings. There are *see* references that facilitate use along with guide words. Entries are signed, and information about contributors can be found in the back matter. The book is incredibly comprehensive. One hundred twenty worldwide advertising agencies are included, forty of which are no longer in business. There are also topical entries on such subjects as ethics, women in advertising, sex in advertising, and advertising in particular countries or regions; important individuals like Henry R. Luce or Arthur C. Fatt; products and companies including Coca-Cola, FedEx, Levi Strauss, and American Tobacco; organizations like the Ad Council; and advertising concepts like account planning. Illustrations, including color, greatly enhance this work. There are a series of interesting appendixes: "Advertising Hall of Fame," "Notable U.S. Advertising Degree Programs," "Top U.S. Advertising Agencies," "Top U.S. Advertisers," "Top Worldwide Advertising Agencies," and "Top Worldwide Advertisers" as well as a detailed index. Highly recommended for academic and public libraries.

Classification: LC HF5803; Dewey 659.

190. *Encyclopedia of Leadership*, by George R. Goethals, Georgia J. Sorenson, and James MacGregor Burns, eds.

Publisher: SAGE, Thousand Oaks, CA (2004)

Price: $495.00/set

Review by G. Kim Dority, G. K. Dority & Associates, Centennial, CO.

"Leadership training" is consistently among the top priorities for corporate chief learning officers (CLOs), yet teaching someone just how to lead remains an ongoing challenge. The *Encyclopedia of Leadership* attempts to address our need for a broader understanding of leadership by bringing together nearly 400 articles that reflect our cumulative wisdom regarding leaders and their characteristics, leadership theory, and leadership studies. As noted in its preface, the encyclopedia's intended audience includes scholars and students of leadership, "citizens who want to put knowledge into action," leaders and managers in the workplace, and "practitioners in business, government, the military, nonprofits, and religious and lobbying organizations." Its scope is equally ambitious. The encyclopedia's interdisciplinary approach covers topics within broad categories including arts and intellectual leadership; biographies; case studies; cross-cultural and international topics; domains (for example, political leadership, leadership of nonprofits, and gender-based leadership issues); followership; leadership styles; military; personal characteristics of leaders; politics/government; power; religion; science and technology; situational factors; social movements and change; study of leadership; and women and gender. This work comes with some impressive credentials. Among the 400 scholarly contributors (drawn from 17 countries) are such notable names as Mihaly Csikszentmihalyi, author of the best-selling and highly regarded Flow (1990), a work on creativity. James MacGregor Burns, who arguably launched the discipline of leadership studies with his seminal work Leadership (1978), is the senior editor. Despite this assemblage of intellectual firepower, however, the encyclopedia does not quite achieve its goal of serving scholarly research. Instead, it will be perhaps most useful to high school or undergraduate students exploring aspects of leadership and, to a lesser extent, interested lay readers exploring leadership issues. The format and style of the articles follow a traditional encyclopedia approach; most entries are several pages in length, and all are signed and conclude with an unannotated list of materials for further reading. Current through 2002, these end-of-the-entry citations include some journal articles but often reflect popular books and general websites, neither of which are likely to be useful for scholarly research but could be of value to general readers or students just getting started on leadership topics. The selection criteria is somewhat vague; for example, the 150 leaders who merit biographical articles are "representative" rather than the greatest/best/most noteworthy, and some articles, such as one on e-commerce, seem to have little if any relevance to the topic at hand. Additionally, and surprisingly, there is no entry that defines leadership itself. On the other hand, the topics that have been included are generally written about in an accessible manner that is generally more engaging than scholarly. The articles within the categories of "Leadership Styles," "Personal Characteristics of Leaders," and "Theories" are especially interesting and informative. Surprisingly, the biographies are somewhat inconsistent—some do a good job of connecting the dots between an individual's life and its relevance to key leadership issues, while others do not. The articles are interspersed with numerous sidebars (key speeches, documents, or clarifying content), boxed quotes, occasional tables and charts, about 100 photographs and other illustrations, and occasional *see also* references. Four appendixes round out the encyclopedia: a bibliography of significant books on leadership (organized by topic and not annotated); a directory of leadership programs (often with mission statement, but surprisingly with no e-mail or website address); and two collections of "primary sources" (one presidential speech on foreign policy and war and the other on sacred texts). The *Encyclopedia of Leadership* is a useful overview of leadership topics and issues, especially for those new to this discipline. It will have most relevance for public, secondary school, and 2- and 4-year college libraries.

Classification: LC HD57; Dewey 658.

191. *Historical Encyclopedia of American Business*, by Richard L. Wilson, ed.

Publisher: Salem Press, Hackensack, NJ (2009)

Price: $364.00/set

Review by Judith J. Field—Senior Lecturer, Program for Library and Information Science, Wayne State University, Detroit, MI.

This 3-volume work should fill a niche for broad-based business information that smaller academic libraries, community colleges, middle-size public libraries, and large high school libraries might need. Its coverage includes business-related material from the early 1600s to the 2008 financial crisis. This work includes articles that provide an overview of such economic sectors as banking and agriculture; discussion of individual industries such as advertising, automobile manufacturing, and the computer industry; and general topics like bank failures, consumer boycotts, and labor strikes. The 477 articles range in length from 300 words to 3,000 words and provide a broad overview of the events that helped shaped our business economy. You will find brief profiles of 37 individuals who have played an important role in business and profiles of several companies that have had major influence in the business economy in the main section of this work. Additional individuals and companies are included in the appendixes. Other appendixes include a glossary, a timeline of notable events, a bibliography, federal laws, and notable court decisions that have impacted businesses. Most articles start with a definition of the term and its significance to business and conclude with some suggested readings. This is a good overview to many of the issues that have helped to shape our current business environment. These topics have been discussed in part in many books that discuss American history and economic history; here the material has been gathered together to create a good overview of business history. The articles are clear and not too technical.

---

Classification: LC HF3021; Dewey 338.

---

### *Company Information*

192. *Hoover's Handbook of American Business*, by Gary Hoover

Publisher: Mergent/Hoover's, Austin, TX

Price: $375.00

Review by Gordon J. Aamot—Head, Foster Business Library, University of Washington, Seattle.

Hoover's handbooks are well known to most librarians whose responsibilities include providing business reference services and purchasing business materials for reference collections. The 750 U.S. companies included in the volume are predominantly publicly owned, but about 40 private and nonprofit organizations are also included. The editors at Hoover's describe their criteria for inclusion in the *Handbook of American Business* as being based on four factors. The first is the size of the company based on sales and number of employees. Second, they consider the industry of which the company is part; traditional industries are represented, but preference is given to high-growth industries. Third, they consider the company's name recognition. Finally, they strive to include a broad representation of industries and economic activity in the volume. The 2010 edition of *Hoover's Handbook of American Business* follows a familiar pattern. Company listings are arranged alphabetically and each record shares a common format. These include a general company overview, history, list of top executives, location of headquarters and list of countries in which the company operates, sales by product line (if available), selected brand names, major competitors, a brief five-year table of historical financials, and selected 2008 year-end financials. Each entry is approximately a page and a half in length and is nearly identical to what one finds in *Hoover's Online*. The company entries are indexed by industry, location, and executive name. The volume also includes a "List Lover's Compendium." Some of the lists are drawn from Hoover's data, for example, Hoover's "300 Largest Employers" and "300 Most Profitable Companies." Other lists are reproduced from trade publications, for example, Forbes' "Largest Private Companies in the US" and Chain Store Age's "Top 20 US Retailers." The content and physical sturdiness of the Handbook are very good, but with so much public company information available online, changing user expectations, and tight collection budgets one should think long and hard about buying another company directory in print format. That said, libraries supporting general business information needs or wanting to maintain a print archive may find the volume a useful addition to their collections.

---

Now associated with Mergent, Inc., the online version at *D&B Hoovers* (http://www.hoovers.com) provides additional information about companies, while the print edition continues. Classification: LC HG4057; Dewey 338.

---

193. *Hoover's Handbook of World Business: Profiles of Major Global Enterprises*, by Gary Hoover

Publisher: Mergent/Hoover's, Austin, TX

Price: $375.00

Review by Lucy Heckman—Reference Librarian (Business-Economics), St. John's University Library, Jamaica, NY.

*Hoover's Handbook of World Business*, now in its 14th edition, profiles three hundred major companies based outside of the United States. This source is divided into four sections: "Using Hoovers Handbooks," which reviews the contents of the profiles and describes how data is gathered and compiled; "A List Lovers Compendium," which provides lists of largest, fastest-growing, and most valuable companies; the profiles of companies; and indexes by industry groups, headquarters location, and list of all executives found in the Executives Section of each profile. At the very beginning there is a list of companies profiled and pages where they are listed. Criteria used in selection of the companies by the editors was based on several points of interest: starting with the global giants, companies that dominate their industries, and companies with significant activity in the United States; companies that had a high profile with consumers; and the "Big Four" accounting firms. Each company listing includes history and overview; a list of key executives; locations (including address and telephone and website); competitors; historical financials; and end year financials. Each provides a summary and overview of the company plus key financials; this provides a starting point to further research on a company. *Hoover's Handbook of World Business* is one of the publisher's series of handbooks that also include *Hoovers Handbook of American Business* (entry 192), *Hoover's Handbook of Private Companies*, and *Hoover's Handbook of Emerging Companies*. Additionally, comprehensive coverage of over forty thousand companies is provided in their database, *Hoover's Online* (http://www.hoovers.com). *Hoover's Handbook of World Business* is an essential source that is, along with the other print volumes and the online database, a popular source for business researchers. This work is highly recommended for academic collections supporting a business program.

---

Now associated with Mergent, Inc., D&B Hoovers online (http://www .hoovers.com) provides additional information about companies, while the print edition continues. Classification: LC HG4009; Dewey 338.

---

194. *EDGAR—SEC.gov* [digital]

Publisher: Securities and Exchange Commission, Washington, DC

Price: Free online. Date reviewed: 2012.

URL: https://www.sec.gov/edgar/searchedgar/companysearch.html

Review by Staff, Libraries Unlimited.

The Securities and Exchange Commission (SEC) ensures that companies give the public basic facts about their business operations so that everyone has adequate information upon which to base investment decisions. Their website offers good educational material as well and provides a section specifically targeting librarians that is worth accessing. The SEC's Electronic Data Gathering, Analysis, and Retrieval System (*EDGAR*) can be used on this website to find most of the various company filings, each of which goes back about ten years. It should be noted, however, that many websites offer the ability to search SEC filings and then charge the user to access them. While *EDGAR* access is free, many patrons prefer the search functionality of another product when researching filings. Regardless, this is a good place to start company research when looking for detailed financial information.

The *EDGAR* "Company Filings" Web page provides coverage for twenty-one million publicly owned businesses. Privately held companies are exempt from filing some information with the SEC, but it may be possible to find 10-K forms and annual reports online. Other free and useful online tools include *Yahoo! Finance*. Classification: LC HG4910; Dewey 338.

## The Economy

### Encyclopedias

195. *The Princeton Encyclopedia of the World Economy*, by Kenneth A. Reinert, Ramkishen S. Rajan, Amy Jocelyn Glass, and Lewis S. Davis, eds.

Publisher: Princeton University Press, Princeton, NJ (2009)

Price: $250.00/set

Review by Staff, Libraries Unlimited.

This new two-volume encyclopedia on the world economy is well written for undergraduates in economics studies; the entries discuss many of the technical aspects of economics but in a way that will not overwhelm the novice. This book covers more than three hundred topics in international economics, including international trade, finance, production, economic development, offshore outsourcing, and trade agreements. Edited by Reinert, a professor of public policy at George Mason University, and Rajan, associate professor of public policy at George Mason University, this title has contributions by a team of international specialists. The entries cover concepts and principles, theories, policies, analysis and tools, and special issues in the area of international economics. Each entry concludes with cross-references to relevant entries and a list of further reading sources, many of which are annotated. A full index at the end of volume 2 will help users navigate the source, as will the topical list of entries found at the beginning of volume 1. This two-volume set will be a welcome addition in university libraries.

Classification: LC HF1371; Dewey 337.

196. *The Oxford Encyclopedia of Economic History*, by Joel Mokyr, ed.
Publisher: Oxford University Press, New York, NY (2003)
Price: $695.00/set
Review by Timothy E. Sullivan—Assistant Professor of Economics, Towson
    State University, Towson, MD.

This is a substantial and comprehensive reference work that will delight and inform both students and researchers alike. With more than 800 scholarly contributors, this distinctive 5-volume set has more than 875 signed articles that provide authoritative, useful information along with discerning interpretations of events, persons and places, institutions, abstract concepts, and processes over the full range of human history and across all regions of the world. As a reference work it is well organized and superbly edited, ensuring that novices and mature scholars will each be able to find sound and useful information. Entries vary in length from in-depth essays of up to 10,000 words to more concise entries of fewer than 1,000 words that are thoroughly cross-referenced in order to facilitate an awareness and understanding of the inter-relationships that exist between concepts, events, and ideas. There are a considerable number of expertly written entries and articles that contain a number of effective maps, illustrations, and tables. All entries include up-to-date bibliographies or annotated bibliographies. Another useful feature of this valuable and accessible reference work is the inclusion of a practical topical outline of the articles along with an extensive index. Among the many topics covered in this encyclopedia are histories of countries, regions, and cities, agriculture and tenure systems, industry surveys and industrial organization, business histories, institutional and technological change, demography, banking and finance, international economics, labor markets and working conditions, public finance and regulation, transportation, and natural resources and the environment, along with biographies of a number of inventors, business leaders, economists, and economic historians. This reference work also includes a practical and detailed outline of websites pertinent to the topics and concepts covered throughout its five volumes. The inclusion of these Internet sites will help to keep this significant reference work timely and practical. This is a reference set that deserves to be on the shelves of every library serving the needs of students and scholars. It provides not only useful information but also helps to organize a diverse array of significant topics and concepts in a sensible and logical manner.

Classification: LC HC15; Dewey 330.

197. *The Encyclopedia of Money*, by Larry Allen

Publisher: ABC-CLIO, Santa Barbara, CA (2009)

Price: $95.00

Review by Lucy Heckman—Reference Librarian (Business-Economics), St. John's University Library, Jamaica, NY.

*The Encyclopedia of Money* updates and expands the 1st edition published a decade ago. The author, Larry Allen, is a professor of economics of Lamar College's Department of Economics and has also written *The Global Financial System: 1750–2000* and *The Global Economic System Since 1945*. Entries focus on specific monetary terms (e.g., hot money, high powered money), types of currency, events, policies, and regulations, and coverage is from centuries-old events related to money and finance to the current U.S. financial crisis. Among entries are Federal Reserve System, U.S. Financial Crisis 2008–2009, Glass-Steagall Banking Act of 1933, Massachusetts Bay Colony Paper Issue, Medici Bank, Lombard Banks, Deutsche Bundesbank, Hyperinflation in Austria, legal tender, French Franc, check, and Coinage Act of 1792. Perhaps the most unusual entry is the Wizard of Oz, which "allegorically represented an important monetary debate in the United States in the 1890s." The entries include a description of the history of an event or when a term was first used and a definition. For instance, the entry for "check" defines what it is and the origin of the term and how they were first called "drawn notes" and how banks first issued "checks." After each entry bibliographic references are included. Illustrations are provided for selected entries. The *Encyclopedia of Money* also contains a bibliography, a glossary of basic terms (such as "assets," "barter," and "interest"), and an index. The author provides an overview of money, the functions of money, and a history/overview of money and finance. The *Encyclopedia of Money* is highly recommended to public and academic libraries. Students of business should find it especially useful.

---

Classification: LC HG216; Dewey 332.

---

### Economic Data

198. *Economy at a Glance* [digital]

Publisher: Bureau of Labor Statistics, U.S. Department of Labor, Washington, DC

Price: Free online. Date reviewed: 2013.

URL: https://www.bls.gov/eag/eag.us.htm

Review by Staff, Libraries Unlimited.

The Bureau of Labor Statistics compiles and publishes a number of prominent economic indicators, available from its Economy at a Glance website. Data on unemployment and consumer prices (usually called inflation) highlight BLS's data. Another popular indicator available from Economy at a Glance is productivity, a measure of the productive output of the nation's workers. Unlike many economic indicators, many of those available from the BLS, including unemployment and prices, include data at the state and metro levels.

The Bureau of Economic Analysis (U.S. Department of Commerce) produces a similar free online resource, U.S. Economy at a Glance, at https://www.bea.gov/index.htm. Classification: LC HC106; Dewey 330.

199. *Federal Reserve Economic Data | FRED* [digital]

Publisher: Federal Reserve Bank of St. Louis, St. Louis, MO

Price: Free online. Date reviewed: 2017.

URL: https://fred.stlouisfed.org/

Review by Staff, Libraries Unlimited.

This site from the Federal Reserve of St. Louis (eighth district of the United States Federal Reserve system) offers a wealth of economic data within the general areas of Money & Banking, Macroeconomics, and International & Regional Economics. Users can study over five hundred thousand U.S. and international series from eighty-seven diverse sources (such as Bank of England, Bank of America Merrill Lynch, U.S. Council of Economic Advisors, etc.) in addition to a vast research archive of working papers, essays, and more. For data, users can conduct a basic search from the prominent search bar, or browse data by Tag, Category, Release, Source, etc. Users can also select featured data from the At a Glance, Popular Series, and Latest Releases tabs near the bottom of the page. Selecting a data series will display the particular chart/graph identified with observation date, units, frequency, and source. Users can edit the graphic to display different time ranges. The graphic is accompanied by Notes (which may offer a narrative description, suggested Citation, etc.) and a listing of Related Content, which can be quite extensive and include such items as charts, blog posts, journal articles, and podcasts. Data series are downloadable, are constantly updated, and include Consumer Price Index, Civilian Unemployment Rate, Personal Consumption Expenditures, Real Median Household Income U.S., Corporate Profits After Tax, Lightweight Vehicle Sales, Existing Home Sales, GDP for Japan, and much, much more. A number of tools can help users manage their preferred data, including the Microsoft Excel Add-In and My Data Lists (with free site registration). Users can also access further research materials such as Regional Reports and Research Journals by clicking on the searchable Publications or Working Papers tabs on the menu bar. Highly recommended for public and academic libraries.

Classification: LC HC106; Dewey 330.

200. *Economic Indicators* [digital]
Publisher: U.S. Census Bureau, U.S. Department of Commerce, Washington, DC
Price: Free online. Date reviewed: 2017.
URL: https://www.census.gov/economic-indicators/
Review by Staff, Libraries Unlimited.

This page from the larger U.S. Census site provides a listing of fifteen economic indicators tracked by the census. Indicators include Advance Monthly Sales for Retail and Food Services; Advance Report on Durable Goods, Manufacturers' Shipments, Inventories and Orders; Advance U.S. International Trade in Goods; Homeownership Rate; Manufacturers' Shipments, Inventories and Orders, Manufacturing and Trade Inventories and Sales; Monthly Wholesale Trade; New Residential Construction; New Residential Sales; Quarterly Financial Report-Manufacturing, Mining, Wholesale Trade and Selected Service Industries; Quarterly Financial Report-Retail Trade; Quarterly Services Survey; Rental Vacancy Rate; U.S. International Trade in Goods and Services; and the Value of Construction Put in Place/Construction Spending. Each indicator is marked by an icon and listed with a general description, available viewing/downloading formats, release dates, and monthly comparisons. Clicking on an indicator will generally display an overview, links to the full report, tables, FAQs, related indicators, related information (such as historical data), and additional census resources, such as definitions. While the presentation of each indicator's information is different, users will generally find similar coverage. The green menu bar offers users the option to select the 2017 or 2016 Economic Indicator Calendar showing a listing (or calendar view) of release dates and times for all indicators. Business professionals, educators, and students of the American economy will appreciate the direct presentation and generous information on this focused site. Highly recommended for public, school, and academic libraries.

Classification: LC HC101; Dewey 330.

201. *Occupational Outlook Handbook* [digital]

Publisher: Bureau of Labor Statistics, U.S. Department of Labor, Washington, DC

Price: Free online. Date reviewed: 2009.

URL: https://www.bls.gov/ooh/

Review by Staff, Libraries Unlimited.

There are various ways to use the *Occupational Outlook Handbook* (OOH) depending on your interest (e.g., if you have a specific position in mind, you only want to browse a job category to get ideas). The "OOH Search/A-Z Index" is usually the quickest way to finding information on a specific line of work. If you are looking for a very specific job title, or the sorts of trendy titles that crop up in the tech industry (e.g., "chief creative officer"), you may not find an entry in the Handbook. But for a great many occupational titles, it will bring together an extremely useful package of information, including Nature of the Work; Working Conditions; Employment; Training, Other Qualifications, and Advancement; Job Outlook; Earnings; Related Occupations; and Sources of Additional Information. The only bad news is that this information is provided at the "nationwide" level only. Finding information on "job outlook" by state or city is, regrettably, beyond the entry-level scope of this text so more specialized sites or resources would be needed.

> The OOH repackages economic data around the practical business of job-seeking, with reports on median pay for specific occupations, and projections of the number of new positions to be filled. Also published each year in hard copy. Classification: LC HD8051; Dewey 331.

202. *Business Statistics of the United States: Patterns of Economic Change*, by Cornelia J. Strawser and Susan Ockert, eds.

Publisher: Bernan Press, Lanham, MD

Price: $165.00

Review by Lucy Heckman—Reference Librarian (Business-Economics), St. John's University Library, Jamaica, NY.

*Business Statistics of the United States* is "a basic desk reference for anyone requiring statistics on the US economy. It contains over 3,000 economic time series portraying the period from World War II to December 2013 in industry, product, and demographic detail." Also, in two hundred time series, the period from 1925 through 1948 is presented. New features for the 2014 edition are a comprehensive revision of data back to 1925 on private and government fixed assets; comprehensive revision of the International Transactions Accounts and the international investment position; and expanded producer price indexes covering services as well as goods. Business Statistics of the United States is arranged as follows: Preface; an essay on cycle and growth perspectives; an essay with graphs on the U.S. economy, 1929–1948; general notes, including a list of data sources; and the following chapters which contain tables of data, sources of data, and definitions: "National Income and Product," "Industrial Production and Capacity Utilization," "Income Distribution and Poverty," "Consumer Income and Spending," "Savings and Investment," "Government," "U.S. Foreign Trade and Finance," "Price," "Employment Costs, Productivity, and Profits," "Employment, Hours, and Earnings," "Energy," "Money, Interest, Assets, Liabilities and Asset Prices," "International Comparisons," "Product and Income by Industry," "Employment, Hours, and Earnings by NAICS Industry," "Key Sector Statistics," and "Index." In addition to the data, there are essays analyzing historical economic events (e.g., what was the Great Depression?) and URLs for U.S. government statistics sources. *Business Statistics of the United States* is a valuable, thorough source of data and recommended for researchers, as well as business school faculty and students. This is an essential source for research and larger academic library business and economics collections.

Classification: LC HC101; Dewey 338.

203. *The Value of a Dollar: Colonial Era to the Civil War, 1600–1865*, by Scott Derks and Tony Smith

Publisher: Grey House Publishing, Amenia, NY (2005)

Price: $145.00

Review by Patricia Rothermich—Reference/Business Librarian, Courtright Memorial Library, Otterbein College, Westerville, OH.

Grey House Publishing's motto is "We do the hard work of data collection so you don't have to." *The Value of a Dollar: Colonial Era to the Civil War 1600–1865* complements the earlier *The Value of a Dollar: Prices and Incomes in the United States, 1860–2009*, now in its 4th edition (entry 204). Scott Derks (South Carolina Commerce Department, with a background in journalism, marketing, and banking) has compiled an immense amount of data taken from primary public resources such as probate records and land sale documents. Each of the book's 6 chronological chapters contain Background (brief essay); Historical Snapshots (year-by-year timelines); Currency (essay); and tabular data in sections under the headings "Selected Incomes," "Services & Fees," "Financial Rates & Exchanges,"

"Commodities," and "Selected Prices" (24 to 50 pages). Slave trade prices are in the first four chapters up to the year 1807. The final section in each chapter is a 2- to 3-page Miscellany section presenting brief excerpts from books and articles that complement the data tables. Throughout the book there are simple currency conversion tables provided to help readers translate the historical prices to an approximate 2002 dollar value. After collecting all the data from a wide variety of sources, it is unfortunate that a number of editing problems exist. The 2-page index covers only broad terms, not specifics like the dollar, tea, coffee, or tobacco. The index also includes over 25 references to page numbers greater than the 436 pages actually in the book. The abbreviation N/R is used frequently in the commodities tables, but is never defined. Page numbers in the table of contents are transposed for the bibliography and the index. The bibliography is unsatisfactorily alphabetized by the authors' first names or initials. Websites are not identified with URLs. Libraries are listed as South Carolina State Library or the Library of Virginia, but nothing else is included to lead a researcher to the source of the data in those libraries. In the "Selected Incomes" tables, the U.S. Census (1976) is listed as the data source, but the closest connection in the bibliography is the *Historical Statistics of the United States, Colonial Times to 1970,* published by Basic Books in 1976 (see entry 222). Because this volume is targeted at students, teachers, writers, business historians, and reporters, it should provide complete bibliographic information for the sources used and the bibliography should be formatted in an acceptable citation style before it can be a creditable reference tool.

"MeasuringWorth.com" at https://www.measuringworth.com/ is a free online price converter that can address similar questions (formerly the website was "How Much is That?" from EH-Net). Classification: LC HB235; Dewey 338.

204. *The Value of a Dollar: Prices and Incomes in the United States, 1860–2009,* by Scott Derks

Publisher: Grey House Publishing, Amenia, NY (2009)

Price: $155.00

Review by Lucy Heckman—Reference Librarian (Business-Economics), St. John's University Library, Jamaica, NY.

Now in its 4th edition, *The Value of a Dollar,* according to the author, "is all about practical economy: what things cost and how much people have to buy them." Not only does the book contain prices of items but also provides information about investment options and income opportunities. This resource is divided into two sections. Section one breaks down into chapters several time periods, with each chapter describing the major social and economic influences of the time period, a historical snapshot of the time period and lists of jobs/income opportunities available, expenditures, investments, standard jobs, food pricing, and selected prices. Section two compares the prices of specific time period to today's prices. Features new to the 4th edition include more illustrations, new conversion charts, and an improved index. As an example of the content, in section one, the chapter covering 1925–1929 contains first the historical snapshot of the time with a year-by-year chronology of social and economic trends. Key events for 1925 included the introduction of Simmons Beautyrest mattress, the collapse of Florida land prices, and Chesterfield marketing cigarettes to women for the first time. Illustrations of selected advertisements from the time period are reprinted. By examining the statistical data for the time period, researchers can find out how much a carpenter could make an hour; how much consumers spent on utilities in 1927; annual dividend for General Electric; the average salary for street railway workers; how much coffee cost per pound in 1925; the cost of sending children to preschool; and medical costs. Section two, "Pricing Trends," includes charts and tables comparing costs over the years. Statistics are organized within various categories: Around the House (household products), Fashion; Help Wanted (comparing hourly wages); Items in the Refrigerator (food); the Outdoors (including sports equipment); the Sports Page (cost of sporting events); and Travel and Entertainment. Bibliographic footnotes listing specific sources of data and a bibliography are included. This source is recommended for academic libraries primarily and also to larger public libraries. It should prove to be of great use to students and faculty of business and history.

The 5th edition appeared in 2014. *The Value of a Dollar: Colonial Era to the Civil War, 1600–1865* is a companion volume (entry 203). Classification: LC HB235; Dewey 338.

205. *International Financial Statistics* [digital]
Publisher: International Monetary Fund, Washington, DC
Price: Free online. Date reviewed: 2011.
URL: http://data.imf.org/
Review by Staff, Libraries Unlimited.

The International Financial Statistics database, produced by the statistics department of the International Monetary Fund (IMF), contains time series data back to 1948 (annually) or 1957 (quarterly) on a wide variety of international financial statistics. The database contains approximately thirty-two thousand time series covering more than two hundred countries of the world including data on exchange rates, international liquidity, international banking, money and banking, interest rates, prices, production, international transactions, government accounts, and national accounts.

Beginning in 2015, the IMF opened its "free data portal" offering no-fee access to popular datasets with global information, data by country, and data by indicator. World Bank Open Data also provides free online data, at https://data.worldbank.org/. For world currencies, two widely used online tools are the XE Currency Converter at http://www.xe.com/currencycon verter/ and the OANDA Currency Converter at https://www.oanda.com/ currency/converter/. Classification: LC HG61; Dewey 332.

## Education

206. *The Greenwood Dictionary of Education*, by John W. Collins III and Nancy Patricia O'Brien, eds.

Publisher: Greenwood Press/ABC-CLIO, Santa Barbara, CA (2011)

Price: $95.00

Review by Joseph P. Hester, SRO-Learning, Claremont, NC.

This 2nd edition of is both a valuable and needed edition to the lexicon of educational terminology, programs, and trends that continue to evolve in the history of American education. Not unexpectedly, 850 new terms and revisions have been added by the editors and section editors to this revision. Like any professional field, education continues to change and develop as it serves an expanding diverse population of students. From students found to be autistic, developmentally delayed, gifted, or gender challenged, the over 300 contributors have provided clear and concise entries, along with 46 pages of references, that make this edition a valuable resource for teachers, administrators, and college professors involved in teacher education and research. Parents involved in the at-home education of their children, private school educators, and those in the media reporting on educational topics will benefit from this revised edition. The media and parents especially will appreciate the addition of some of the more esoteric terminology found in the education vocabulary, such as infusion, innumeracy, null curriculum, and quadrivium, to mention a few. Even the experienced teacher, not evolved in district and state decision making where such terminology is often used, will find this dictionary to be a valuable resource. Noticeably, some topics require more than one entry. An example is "creative" and its derivative, "creativity" which is found under "creative commons license," "creative discovery area," "creative expression," "creative thinking," and "creativity." For the common user, two changes could be made to this dictionary to make it more user friendly: cross-referencing of topics and listing resources with each entry. Otherwise, this dictionary remains a valuable resource in the education lexicon.

---

Classification: LC LB15; Dewey 370.

---

207. *Encyclopedia of Education*, by James W. Guthrie, ed.

Publisher: Macmillan Reference USA/Gale Group, New York, NY (2003)

Price: $850.00/set

Review by Stephen H. Aby—Education Bibliographer, Bierce Library, University of Akron, Akron, OH.

Some 30 years since the 1st edition of this resource was published (1971) users now have a completely new and updated edition of the classic *Encyclopedia of Education*. Included in this 8-volume set are 857 articles on key educational concepts, theories, people, institutions, and organizations, with entries ranging from 500 to 5,000 words in length. The signed essays are accompanied by an extensive number of *see also* references, as well as a bibliography and list of relevant Internet websites. The essays fall within a very wide range of subject areas in education, including the foundations of education (e.g., history, philosophy, sociology, comparative education), educational psychology, curriculum and instruction, higher education, educational technology, educational policy, and teacher preparation, among others. There are an extensive number of entries on important educational associations, such as the American Association of School Administrators, the American Association of University Professors, the International Reading Association, the National Council of Teachers of Mathematics, and more. Similarly, there are 121 biographical entries on such historically important individuals as John Dewey, Jane Addams, Aristotle, St. Augustine, Alfred Binet, W. E. B. Du Bois, Paulo Freire, Maria Montessori, Lawrence Kohlberg, Horace Mann, Jeanne Chall, Carter Woodson, Jean Piaget, and Mary Bethune. The last volume includes primary source documents (covering court cases, legislation, and international agreements), a thematic outline of the encyclopedia's entries, a list of widely used standardized tests (with addresses, telephone numbers, and Web addresses for the publishers), a list of state departments of education (with website addresses), a list of some education websites, and a bibliography of "classic works" in education. Finally, there is a substantial combined index to names, subjects, and titles. This is an important and much-needed addition to the reference literature in education. The list of contributing authors is sprinkled with distinguished experts, and the writing is good throughout. Overall, this set is an essential purchase for academic libraries supporting teacher education.

Classification: LC LB15; Dewey 370.

208. *Encyclopedia of American Education*, by Harlow G. Unger
Publisher: Facts on File, New York, NY (2007)
Price: $225.00/set
Review by Cynthia Crosser—Social Sciences and Humanities Reference, Fogler
   Library, University of Maine, Orono.

This is the 3rd edition of the *Encyclopedia of American Education* from Facts on File. This encyclopedia was first published in 1996 and last updated in 2001. The new edition contains updates of more than 750 articles and includes approximately 50 new articles. This book is structured like an encyclopedia with over 2,500 alphabetic entries on subjects ranging from recent topics like the No Child Left Behind Act to historical figures like John Dewey. However, it has a consistent point of view that makes it more engaging than the average encyclopedia. One reason for this is that there is no long list of contributors; like the previous editions, this is the work of Harlow Unger and a Board of Editorial Consultants. One new feature is an introduction that provides a short history of education in the United States. A change, not for the better, is the omission of the references after each entry. The encyclopedia retains its wonderful appendixes: a chronology of major events, an annotated list of significant federal education legislation, an annotated list of significant U.S. Supreme Court decisions on education, and a comprehensive list of undergraduate majors at U.S. colleges, supplemented with special material on undergraduate and graduate programs in education. Also retained is the extensive "Bibliography and References" section (pp. 1249–1293). The updating of this material is uneven. For example, in the large category of Elementary Education, the most recent reference for the subtopic of "Reading" is 1989, while "Science" has a 2004 citation. The entries overall are well written. Unger, a veteran journalist and formerly an associate professor of English, has written a number of books on education. This is a useful work that most general and academic libraries will consider essential.

Classification: LC LB17; Dewey 370.

209. *The Encyclopedia of Learning Disabilities*, by Carol Turkington and Joseph R. Harris

Publisher: Facts on File, New York, NY (2006)

Price: $75.00

Review by Stephen H. Aby—Education Bibliographer, Bierce Library, University of Akron, Akron, OH.

Now in its 2nd edition, this encyclopedia has been substantially revised and updated to include the most recent information on learning disabilities. Included here are approximately one thousand entries on key terms, legislation, drugs, diagnostic tests, and more. The entries can range from a short paragraph for basic terms to eight pages on substantial topics, such as attention deficit hyperactivity disorder (ADHD). Throughout, the entries are uniformly clear and well written. The authors are careful to address the wide range of issues that may relate to a particular entry, while still keeping the essays concise and comprehensible. For example, the entry on ADHD covers not only the symptoms, causes, and treatments for the condition, but also the social aspects of its possible over-diagnosis. Similarly, the clear overviews of intelligence tests and intelligence quotient also provide a succinct review of the controversies surrounding those topics. Within entries, terms that are defined elsewhere in the encyclopedia are capitalized. *See* references are used to refer the reader from unused to preferred terms. There are six appendixes that are directories to national organizations, government sources of help, assistive technology resources, hotlines, commercial technology resources, and books of interest to people with learning disabilities. A glossary and bibliography are also included. The detailed index includes keywords, names, legislation, court cases, standardized tests, and drugs. Overall, this is an excellent one-volume encyclopedia. Given the prevalence of learning disabilities in the population at large, and the importance of special education in teacher training, this encyclopedia is a recommended purchase for both public and academic libraries.

Classification: LC LC4704; Dewey 371.

210. *College Navigator* [digital]

Publisher: National Center for Education Statistics, Institute of Education Sciences, U.S. Department of Education, Washington, DC

Price: Free online. Date reviewed: 2015.

URL: https://nces.ed.gov/collegenavigator/

Review by Kristin Kay Leeman—Adjunct Faculty Instructor, University of Maryland, University College, Largo.

College Navigator provides a wide range of useful information on more than 7,500 postsecondary education institutions including public, private, vocational, and technical schools. The broad scope of information ranges from basic school contact information to size and composition of student body, tuition rates, type of campus setting (urban, rural, etc.), degrees offered, acceptance rates, average standardized test scores, amount of financial aid awarded, campus crime statistics, varsity sports programs, etc. Information is presented on a school-by-school basis, and College Navigator provides an excellent and user-friendly search/filter menu with over a dozen options to help users mine the information. Users can even search for a program with a certain distance from an indicated zip code and use the map to select a state or multiple states at one time. Schools can be saved to a favorites list, and up to four schools can be compared at one time. The lists and comparisons can be exported to a spreadsheet. This is a fantastic tool for beginning a college search. It allows users to systematically establish the major parameters important in the college search process. Despite its breadth, College Navigator could benefit from including information on two important points: acceptance of transfer credits and employment rates of alumni. As a tool provided by the National Center for Education Statistics (NCES), College Navigator relies on information reported on federally administered surveys. The data is gathered from mandatory surveys institutions complete as participants in federal student financial aid programs. Some surveys are not issued every year, creating an information lag on some data points. For example, the most recent year available for Campus Crime Statistics is three years old. However, the site is very transparent about the currency of information under the "About" tab. This is a highly recommended resource.

---

There are many published guides to universities and college admissions including the Peterson's Guides and Barron's Profiles. The National Center for Education Statistics (NCES) offers other resources at https://nces .ed.gov/datatools/. Classification: LC L901; Dewey 378.

---

## Statistics, Data, and Demography

### U.S. Statistics

Resources emphasizing economic data also appear in this chapter, in the Business and Economics section.

211. *Statistical Abstract of the United States: The National Data Book*
Publisher: Bernan Press, Lanham, MD

Price: $179.00

Review by Julienne L. Wood—Head, Research Services, Noel Memorial Library,
Louisiana State University, Shreveport.

Ignoring the protests of many librarians and citizens, the Census Bureau
recently decided to discontinue publication of this reference tool, the standard
source for accurate, comprehensive U.S. statistical information since 1878.
Issued in August 2011, the 2012 *Statistical Abstract of the United States* was the last
edition published by the U.S. Census Bureau. Beginning in 2012 ProQuest and
Bernan Press assumed responsibility for publishing "the most used statistical
reference tool in U.S. libraries" (p. v). This 2015 edition, issued in December
2014 with more than one thousand pages in a large 8.5 × 11-inch format, presents statistics current as of early September 2014. It contains forty-five new
tables listed on page xi and a deleted tables list on pages xii–xiii as well as
updated tables from the 2012 *Census of Agriculture* and the 2012 *Economic Census.* New or infrequent users will appreciate the "Guide to Tabular Presentation,"
pp. xiv–xv, and the third appendix, "Limitations of the Data," pp. 947–948.
Source notes below each table in this volume guide readers to other statistical
publications as does the first appendix, "Guide to Sources of Statistics, State Statistical Abstracts, and Foreign Statistical Abstracts." The extensive index yields
references to table numbers rather than page numbers. While Bernan Press produces the print version of the book, ProQuest offers an online version of this
title. Updated monthly, the online edition yields additional back year's data,
spreadsheets corresponding to each table in the print edition, and the option to
refine and manipulate data. It can be purchased alone or as a part of the publisher's ProQuest Statistical Insight package that includes "The Tables Collection," over one million tables published since 1999 on the basis of U.S. and
foreign statistical sources and "over 100,000 statistical reports in PDF," to enable
users to locate a specific table or number easily. This essential print resource
belongs at or near the reference center and/or government documents service
desk of all public and academic libraries as well as in many high school libraries.
Larger libraries with substantial government documents collections and a
research-oriented constituency or libraries with more expansive collection
development budgets may prefer the online Statistical Insight package.

---

Now known also as the *ProQuest Statistical Abstract of the United States.* The
Census Bureau posts an archive of annuals back to 1878 at https://www
.census.gov/library/publications/time-series/statistical_abstracts.html.
The U.S. government continues to offer two free online portals to find
statistics and data produced by federal agencies: FedStats at https://fed
stats.sites.usa.gov/ and its eventual successor Data.gov at https://www
.data.gov/. Classification: LC HA202; Dewey 317.

212. *State Rankings: A Statistical View of America,* by Kathleen O'Leary and Scott Morgan, eds.

Publisher: CQ Press/SAGE, Thousand Oaks, CA

Price: $100.00

Review by Lucy Heckman—Reference Librarian (Business-Economics), St. John's University Library, Jamaica, NY.

*State Rankings* 2015 "provides an easily accessible collection of data in a broad range of quality of life factors in the United States" and "compares data from the fifty states and the District of Columbia in 566 tables." Tables are arranged within the categories of agriculture; crime and law enforcement; defense; economy; education; employment and labor; energy and environment; geography; government finances: federal; government finances: state and local; health; households and housing; population; social welfare; and transportation. Sources for data were selected by the editors from various government and private sector sources. Subjects are designated as positive or negative (e.g., high state crime rates negatively affect a state's comparison ranking). In addition to the tables listed within the subject categories, this reference source contains 2015 state rankings; the date each state was admitted to statehood; state fast facts (e.g., state flower, name of capital); a list of names, addresses, phone numbers, and URLs; and an index. Each table's years of coverage vary; dates range from 2010 to 2015 (for instance, estimated new cancer cases is for 2014 and enrollment in institutions of higher education is from 2012). Each table includes title, national rates or totals, and states listed in alphabetical order. Sources are designated for each of the tables. Researchers can locate diverse data by state, such as Internal Revenue Service gross collections in 2013; unemployment rate in 2014; population per square mile in 2014; employees in leisure and hospitality in 2014; cattle on farms in 2015; and percent of population enrolled in Medicare in 2012. *State Rankings* 2015 is a valuable reference source that provides a wealth of data for researchers and also is a starting point for locating further information—the list of sources is especially helpful. Recommended for larger public libraries and academic library collections.

Annual. Classification: LC HA203; Dewey 317.

213. *Vital Statistics of the United States: Births, Life Expectancy, Deaths and Selected Health Data,* by Shana Hattis, ed.

Publisher: Bernan Press, Lanham, MD

Price: $121.00

Review by Julienne L. Wood—Head, Research Services, Noel Memorial Library, Louisiana State University, Shreveport.

Published by the federal government as a multivolume work until 1993, now published as a single volume by Bernan Press, this 7th edition, like its Bernan predecessors, yields essential demographic and health information, compiled by various government agencies, about the population of the United States. Part one, Birth, includes sixty tables ranging from birth rates for teenagers to Cesarean births together with two pages noting sources of the data, notes on the data, and concepts and definitions. Part two, Mortality, offers forty-four tables together with the sources, notes, concepts, and definitions on topics such as Life Expectancy and Death Rates from selected causes. Part three, Health, offers 78 tables on such subjects as Cancer Incidence Rates and Cigarette Smoking among Adults together with sources, concepts, and definitions. The relatively brief part four, Marriage, a new chapter in this edition, provides only three tables as well as sources, concepts, and definitions and could certainly be expanded in future editions. All tables are clearly identified first by part number and then in numerical sequence within each of the four parts of the book. The most recent statistics date from 2014, but many tables reflect government figures compiled in earlier years. For some users this volume's utility may be hampered by the puzzling idiosyncrasies of its index. In the index, capitalized boldface headings lead to subtopics or cross-references and numbers indicate pages, not tables. Under index letter A, ALASKA NATIVES, AMERICAN INDIANS OR ALASKA NATIVES, and ASIAN OR PACIFIC ISLANDERS boldface headings appear, but African Americans do not appear at all. Under B, the reader finds BLACK RACE in boldface, no subtopics, and a single cross-reference to RACE. Under RACE are a host of subtopics leading to tables where results are reported by race, including Black or African American statistics. In contrast, under H, boldface entry HISPANIC ORIGIN yields many subtopics complete with page references. Index limitations aside, this dense, compact volume is a rich source of research data for readers ranging from high school students to scholars in many disciplines and has value for all but the smallest libraries.

---

Biennial. For additional health statistics, see *Health, United States* (entry 500). Classification: LC HA203; Dewey 317.

---

214. *Black Stats: African Americans by the Numbers in the Twenty-First Century*, by Monique W. Morris

Publisher: New Press, New York, NY (2014)

Price: $14.95

Review by Staff, Libraries Unlimited.

In *Black Stats*, Monique W. Morris, Cofounder of the National Black Women's Justice Institute and 2012 Soros Justice Fellow, contextualizes extensive statistics on the condition of blacks in the twenty-first century, revealing both high points and bleak realities for this group of Americans. An introduction by Kahlil Gibran Muhammed discusses Morris's findings and the extreme need to address the problems associated with the color line, a need exposed more than a century earlier in a statistical study by W. E. B. Du Bois. This collection of statistics shows the diversity of black American identities presented in sets of basic facts, figures, and trends. This is not a dry rendering of facts, however, due to the book's format in which a question such as "how formally educated is Black America" is followed by a series of answers based on the data. In answer to the question "what subjects are Black teachers teaching," it is learned, among other things, that 7 percent of math teachers are black and that black teachers are least likely to teach a foreign language. The book's coverage is broad as indicated by the chapters: "The Basics," "Education," "Environment," "Entertainment and Sports," "Health," "Justice," "Lifestyle and Identity," "Military Service," "Money and Jobs," "Politics, Voting, and Civic Engagement," and "Science and Technology." Further analysis is provided in two appendixes "Black Females" and "Black Males." The book ends with extensive notes, suggestions for additional research, and an index. For someone writing a paper or a lecture, this book can be used as a quick reference; it can also be used, however, as a starting point for discussions and a basic way to learn about the general condition of blacks in America. This book, a value at under $15.00, is recommended for libraries of all sorts.

Classification: LC E185; Dewey 305.

215. *U.S. Religion Census 1952 to 2010* [digital]
Publisher: Association of Statisticians of American Religious Bodies, Lenexa, KS
Price: Free online. Date reviewed: 2017.
URL: http://www.rcms2010.org/
Review by Staff, Libraries Unlimited.

This website hosts the 2010 publication of U.S. religion data gathered in affiliation with the Association of Statisticians of American Religious Bodies (ASARB). Following studies done in 1952, 1971, 1980, 1990, and 2000, the census helps point to trends and changes across the great variety of denominations representing religion in the United States today. The report has expanded coverage since the 2000 study in significant ways, such as providing county-level statistics, incorporating counts of Buddhist and Hindu congregations, enhancing reporting on Muslim and Orthodox Christian faiths, and focusing on smaller, more exclusive traditions like the Amish. Notably, the 2010 release has nearly doubled the number of congregations and adherents reporting. From the introductory paragraph on the home page, users can select the A Quick Overview is Available Here link for access to the PDF *U.S. Religion Census 2010* Summary Findings published in May 2012. Otherwise, users can select from the links on the sidebar. While they could perhaps be better organized to emphasize the current report, they will nonetheless allow users to navigate through the census with general ease. It should also be noted that users must download data (free) to view. 2010 Maps & Charts allows users to search 236 entities by Religious Group, Series (Major Metro or Largest Group), or all groups in conjunction with their desired data. Datasets include Adherent 50%, Adherent Change, Adherent Quintile, Community Type Charts, Locations, and Penetration. From this page, users can also link to a PDF list of all religious groups (name only) used in the study, in addition to listings of counties with most adherents per religious group, largest ratio of adherents per group, largest number of congregations, and largest population penetration. Lists and Rankings is where users can download data sets for all years collected regarding Total Adherents and Congregations and Individual (religious) Groups. The former category includes 24 data sets ranking Groups, Metros, Counties, and States in regards to congregants, adherents, and more. Individual Groups provides related information on each particular religious group. 2010 Errata links to any corrected data made to the current census information after publication. Reports and Analyses offers links to some of the studies referencing the *U.S. Religion Census.* Methods presents links to the appendixes which follow the census data tables. The appendixes clarify general information regarding definitions, procedures, etc. for all groups, but also address the unique markers applicable to data collection methods for particular groups (e.g., Amish, Hindu). Other links on the sidebar include FAQs, 2000 Maps (good for comparison), Resources (noting where to purchase bound report, wall maps, etc.), and Religion and Congregational Research Links (e.g., Gallup: Religion Section, Congregational Resource Guide, etc.). The wealth of new and historical data would appeal to students, educators, social scientists, and many others. Highly recommended to public, school, and academic libraries.

---

The U.S. Census does not record religious affiliation. This free searchable database produces lists and downloadable maps. There is a corresponding print resource, *2010 U.S. Religion Census: Religious Congregations & Membership Study: An Enumeration by Nation, State, and County Based on Data Reported for 236 religious groups.* For more on religious groups in the United States, see entry 363. Classification: LC BL2525; Dewey 200.

---

## U.S. Census

216. *U.S. Census Bureau* [digital]

Publisher: U.S. Census Bureau, U.S. Department of Commerce, Washington, DC

Price: Free online. Date reviewed: 2011.

URL: http://www.census.gov/

Review by Susan C. Awe—Assistant Director, University of New Mexico, Albuquerque.

This Web page is the best place to start searching for the multitude of data produced by Census programs, publications, and statistics. The home page groups the data under People, Business, Geography, Newsroom, At the Bureau, and Special Topics. Under Business, you can click on the Economic Census, NAICS, Survey of Business Owners, E-Stats, and Foreign Trade. Under People, business owners will be interested in income statistics, housing data, and more. Analyzing the Demographic trends in the United States allows businesses to forecast future demands for their products or services. The "New to Using Census Bureau Data" page is very helpful in helping users locate what they need quickly. The Catalog, a Search feature, and links to related sites are also accessible on the left side of the home page. Users can check this site frequently to learn more about local demographics and even help start and grow a business.

---

Historical census records are available dating back to the first U.S. census in 1790: the census has grown more elaborate over time. Several genealogy tools also present census information, such as *Ancestry* (entry 296). Another source for finding and using recent census data is *American FactFinder* (entry 217). Classification: LC HA181; Dewey 317.

---

217. *American FactFinder* [digital]

Publisher: U.S. Census Bureau, U.S. Department of Commerce, Washington, DC

Price: Free online. Date reviewed: 2011.

URL: https://factfinder.census.gov/

Review by Susan C. Awe—Assistant Director, University of New Mexico, Albuquerque.

This federal government source for information on population, housing, economic, and geographic data is easy to use and well designed. You can get a "Fact Sheet" for your community by just entering town, county, or ZIP code. A quick link gets you to the Decennial Census of Housing and Population, American Community Survey, the Economic Census, or the Population Estimates program. A couple clicks under the Subjects A to Z will get you to County Business Patterns, information on the NAICS code, statistics about small business from the Census Bureau, the characteristics of business owners' database, and more. A glossary, list of FAQs, and search will also help you use this great, free resource.

American FactFinder emphasizes recent information, with "guided search" instructions to build data sets. *See also* entry 216 for the wider U.S. Census web site. Classification: LC HA181; Dewey 317.

218. *Encyclopedia of the U.S. Census: From the Constitution to the American Community Survey (ACS)*, by Margo J. Anderson, Constance F. Citro, and Joseph J. Salvo, eds.

Publisher: CQ Press/SAGE, Thousand Oaks, CA (2012)

Price: $175.00

Review by William C. Struning—Professor, Seton Hall University, South Orange, NJ.

The *Encyclopedia of the U.S. Census: From the Constitution to the American Community Survey (ACS)* represents the collective expertise and insights of 83 contributors—each knowledgeable in some aspect of population or census matters. The book is comprised of some 140 articles on a broad variety of topics related to census taking. Each article is presented alphabetically and is cross-referenced and followed by a bibliography to facilitate further investigation. A list of articles and an index enable readers to locate subjects of particular interest. The articles are rich in historical background, but treatment of recent innovations also provides an up-to-date look at census taking in the United States today. For example, considerable space is devoted to the recently introduced American Community Survey (ACS), which provides interim to the traditional decennial census. The text is complemented by tables and figures as well as a section of pictorial highlights. Complex topics, such as sampling, are discussed in understandable terms without sacrificing rigor, thus making the encyclopedia meaningful to a broad range of readers.

Classification: LC HA37; Dewey 304.

219. *State and Metropolitan Area Data Book 2013*, by Deirdre A. Gaquin and Gwenavere W. Dunn, eds.

Publisher: Bernan Press, Lanham, MD (2013)

Price: $89.00

Review by William C. Struning—Professor, Seton Hall University, South Orange, NJ.

This databook provides a summary of statistics on the social, political, and economic organization of the states and metropolitan areas in the United States, and it serves as a supplement to the *Statistical Abstract of the United States* (entry 211). Source citations allow it to act as a statistical reference and guide to other statistical publications and sources from the U.S. Bureau of the Census. Emphasis is, of course, on the states and metropolitan areas, but tables are also included that provide data for the counties that comprise the metropolitan area as well as its central city. This edition includes the 2010 census counts and even more recent population counts. There is expanded information on vital statistics, communication, and criminal justice data, as well as data on health insurance and housing and financials. Demographic and statistical data are provided for population, birth and death rates, school enrollment, crime rates, income and housing, employment, government, and transportation. Source notes now appear at the bottom of each page of tables and also in the source notes and explanations appendix. Also included is directory information for federal agencies with major statistical programs. Each agency's mailing address, telephone number, and Internet address is given. This inexpensive volume belongs in every library.

After this federal government publication ceased, Bernan Press undertook to publish similar content: a 2nd edition appeared in 2017. The related U.S. Census publication, *County and City Data Book*, ceased publication after the 2007 edition: Bernan now publishes similar content as *County and City Extra: Annual Metro, City, and County Data Book*. Classification: LC HA202; Dewey 317.

## World Statistics

220. *Statistical Yearbook/Annuaire Statistique*, by the United Nations Statistics Division (UNSD)

Publisher: Department of Economic and Social Affairs (UN DESA), United Nations, New York, NY

Price: $150.00

Review by Mihoko Hosoi—Public Services Librarian, Cornell University, Ithaca, NY.

Prepared by the Statistics Division, Department of Economic and Social Affairs of the United States Secretariat, *Statistical Yearbook* provides international statistics on various social and economic issues. It is complemented by the *Monthly Bulletin of Statistics* published by the same Division and is also available for purchase as a PDF file. This 2006 edition presents seventy-six tables, primarily for 1994–2003 or 1995–2004, and consists of four parts. Part one provides key world and regional statistics, and parts two through four present data concerning individual countries or areas. Part two, "Population and Social Statistics," includes Population and Human Settlement; Literacy; Health, Childbearing and Nutrition; and Culture and Communication. Part three, "Economic Activity," includes National Accounts and Industrial Production; Financial Statistics; Labour Force; Wages and Prices; Agriculture, Forestry and Fishing; Manufacturing; Transport; Energy; Environment; and Science and Technology and Intellectual Property. Part four, "International Economic Relations," includes International Merchandise Trade, International Tourism, Balance of Payments, International Finance, and Development Assistance. The emphasis seems to be on economic data. Each chapter includes a section titled "Technical Notes," which describes the data. The data sources are presented in the "Statistical Sources and References" at the end of the publication. Everything except for the index is in both English and French. Although the noncomparability of data due to currency conversion rate fluctuations, differences in sources, and variations in the institutional patterns of countries should not be ignored, this publication continues to be a core reference title for international statistics and is recommended for any serious reference collection.

Annual. Current and past editions (since 1948) are posted online at https://unstats.un.org/unsd/publications/statistical-yearbook. The same agency issues *Demographic Yearbook/Annuaire démographique*, emphasizing themes such as population, mortality and natality: also posted online at https://unstats.un.org/unsd/demographic/products/dyb/. Classification: LC HA202; Dewey 317.

221. *UNdata*, by the United Nations Statistics Division (UNSD) [digital]

Publisher: Department of Economic and Social Affairs (UN DESA), United Nations, New York, NY

Price: Free online. Date reviewed: 2017.

URL: http://data.un.org

Review by Staff, Libraries Unlimited.

This simply structured site allows free access to myriad statistics, estimates, and projections related to 20 general categories of current global topics such as tourism, crime, trade, human development, and finance. The material, gathered from 35 databases run through various United Nations agencies, is accessible via the Databases tab where users can scroll through the categories. Some categories offer access to more than one database. The Updates tab displays the UN Data Twitter feed noting database revisions as they happen in addition to other relevant news. The Country Data Services tab reroutes users to individual statistics center websites for nearly 150 countries and territories. Added features include an extensive glossary, information on the metadata or background on the various data collections, access to the Monthly Bulletin of Statistics and other data resources, and a listing of Popular Searches, such as Germany, population, and GDP. The abundant data would appeal to students, researchers, policy-makers, and many others. The site can also be accessed by the social media platforms Facebook and Twitter.

---

Content includes data sets from UNESCO, WHO, IMF, FAO, ILO, OECD, and other international agencies. Classification: LC HC59; Dewey 338.

---

## Historical Statistics

222. *Historical Statistics of the United States: Earliest Times to the Present*, by Richard Sutch and Susan B. Carter, eds.

Publisher: Cambridge University Press, New York, NY (2006)

Price: $1,095.00/set

Review by Staff, Libraries Unlimited.

This 4th-edition set includes five volumes on the following topics: Population, Work and Welfare, Economic Structure and Performance, Economic Sectors, and Governance and International Relations. Previous editions were published by the U.S. Census Bureau, which gave its approval to this publication. This is the first update to the series since 1975; the data contained herein represents the work of more than eighty scholars. Each volume has a guide to using this millennial edition, a summary table of contents for all five volumes, and a volume-specific detailed table of contents. Readers can find the names and affiliations of contributors and project support information in the first volume. The millennial edition guide addresses data selection and reliability, table documentation, dates, and more. Helpfully, each volume includes a cumulative index for the entire set, with terms followed by volume and page number. The index also has *see* and *see also* references. Within each volume, data is supported by scholarly essays. The data itself is incredibly comprehensive. In volume 1, Population, readers will find chapters on population statistics, vital statistics, international migration, family and household composition, cohorts, and American Indians. Welfare, volume 2, has chapters on labor, slavery, education, health, economic inequality and poverty, social insurance and public assistance, and nonprofit, voluntary, and religious entities. National income, business fluctuations, prices, geography and the environment, science and technology, financial markets and institutions, and more are covered in volume 3. Volume 4, Economic Sectors, provides data and interpretation for agriculture, natural resource industries, manufacturing, distribution, transportation, communications, and services and utilities. The last volume includes governance and international relations, elections and politics, crime, law enforcement, and justice, national defense, wars, armed forces, and veterans, international trade and exchange rates, outlying areas, colonial statistics, and the Confederate States of America. This volume also has three appendixes: "Weights, Measures, and Monetary Values," "States and Census Regions," and "Origin of Historical Statistics of the United States." This set of historical statistics is unparalleled in scope or content. For those who prefer online searching, there is an electronic version available from Cambridge University Press. Highly recommended for academic and public libraries.

This set updates *Historical Statistics of the United States, Colonial Times to 1970*, published by the U.S. Census Bureau in 1975, and posted online at https://www.census.gov/library/publications/1975/compendia/hist_stats_colonial-1970.html. Classification: LC HA202; Dewey 317.

223. *International Historical Statistics: The Americas 1750–2000*, by B. R. Mitchell

Publisher: Palgrave Macmillan, New York, NY (2003)

Price: $375.00

Review by Mihoko Hosoi—Public Services Librarian, Cornell University, Ithaca, NY.

The 5th edition of *International Historical Statistics: The Americas 1750–2000* provides key economic and social indicators for the last 250 years for countries on the American continent. There are two other companion volumes in the same series: Africa, Asia, and Oceania (4th ed.; entry 225) and Europe (5th ed.; entry 224). Each volume in the series provides statistical data for every country in easy-to-use tables and includes the following chapters: "Population and Vital Statistics," "Labour Force," "Agriculture," "Industry," "External Trade," "Transport and Communications," "Finance," "Prices," "Education," and "National Accounts." The statistics were taken mostly from the official publications of the various governments. This publication serves as an essential reference source for hard-to-find historical data. It is particularly recommended for college and research libraries.

The 6th edition of 2007 includes figures through 2005. There is an online version. Classification: LC HA175; Dewey 317.

224. *International Historical Statistics: Europe 1750–2000*, by B. R. Mitchell

Publisher: Palgrave Macmillan, New York, NY (2003)

Price: $375.00

Review by George Thomas Kurian—President, Encyclopedia Society, Baldwin Place, NY.

Historical statistics is a much neglected branch of statistics, but the field owes a debt of gratitude to Professor B. R. Mitchell for his yeoman work on *International Historical Statistics*, now in its 5th edition. The set consists of 3 volumes, of which the present one covers Europe for over 250 years, from 1750 to 2000 (actually 1998). Europe is the strongest of all the volumes because national statistics began to be compiled by major countries in that continent in the eighteenth century, whereas for most counties in Asia, Africa, and Latin America, national statistics in any field were not available until the middle of the twentieth century. Since the work first appeared over 30 years ago, the range and vintage of national and international statistical data have vastly improved, mainly as a result of the work of global statistical organizations. As a result many refinements have been made in enlarging not only the catchment basin but also the quality of data. The two primary users of historical statistics are economists and historians and for them, these improvements are not enough. Even published data need to be constantly revisited and updated to remove inconsistencies. Mitchell has successfully upgraded the quality of the data wherever possible, but there are a number of problems that simply cannot be overcome. Mitchell calls them traps. One is the definition of terms. The other is that national boundaries have varied over years, and some countries have disappeared while others were born. In the present volume as in the previous ones, Mitchell presents only raw data with little or no analysis or any effort to provide such value-added features as growth rates over time. This limits the usefulness of the compilation considerably. But, that having been said, *International Historical Statistics* remains the best published source of global comparative historical statistics in print and is worthy of purchase by all major academic libraries.

---

The 6th edition of 2007 includes figures through 2005. For the Americas, see entry 223. For Africa, Asia, and Oceania, see entry 225. There is an online version. Classification: LC HA1107; Dewey 314.

---

225. *International Historical Statistics: Africa, Asia & Oceania 1750–2000*, by B. R. Mitchell

Publisher: Palgrave Macmillan, New York, NY (2003)

Price: $375.00

Review by Robert B. Marks Ridinger—Head, Electronic Information Resources Management Department, University Libraries, Northern Illinois University, De Kalb.

This latest update of one of the most useful compilations of international statistics published outside the United Nations system of organizations fills a gap of some seven years since the appearance of the 3rd edition in 1998, extending coverage to the year 2000 for the nations of Africa, Asia, and Oceania. While the general format of older editions has been retained, librarians unfamiliar with this series will find the introductory essay and the "National Sources" page a valuable summary of international statistical publishing. Changes with this edition include the renaming of the first major section as "Population and Vital Statistics" to more accurately reflect its contents, while under the "Education" section, the second heading has been altered from "Number of Students at Universities" to "Students in Higher Education." A major difference in this edition from previous ones in the set is the separate listing under Asia of those former Soviet Republics that are now independent political units within the Commonwealth of Independent States. While some of the component data included within this work are available electronically from various international organizations and national statistical agencies (either online or in CD-ROM format), the continuing value of this source is the placement of data in a two-and-one-half-century perspective. Libraries owning the older volumes in this series will wish to add this to their collections despite its steep price. This volume is recommended for college, university, and large public libraries.

---

The 5th edition of 2007 includes figures through 2005. There is an online version. For the Americas, see entry 223. For Europe, see entry 224. Classification: LC HA4675; Dewey 310.

# CHAPTER THREE

# History and Area Studies

## Historical Atlases

Historical atlases record or reconstruct past conditions, instead of the most current information (the usual goal for reference works). As with the general atlases noted in Chapter 1, these works revolve around a theme, such as the history of a region or country, an era, or a type of historical activity (military, economic, etc.). The United States Military Academy at West Point maintains a rich collection of online atlases of military history, at https://www.usma.edu/history/SitePages/Our%20Atlases.aspx.

226. *Historical Atlas of the United States*, by Derek Hayes

Publisher: University of California Press, Oakland, CA (2007)

Price: $39.95

Review by Michael Margolis—Reference Librarian, City University of New York.

This reference work provides a geographic exploration of American history. The work is 273 pages and has about 500 historical maps telling the story of our nation. One of the first chapters is called "Conceptions of a Continent" and discusses European ideas about the unexplored world across the sea. The chapter discusses Columbus and his sponsors. There are maps reflecting their view of the sea and land at the time. In later chapters there are maps of the Eastern coast and discussion of their discovery and exploration. The prose is well written, and the written material is closely related to the information in the maps. Other chapters cover westward expansion, railroad surveys, and the Cold War, as well as space maps. The numerous maps are in color, and the quality of the images are very good. There is an index, map catalog, and bibliography. The book would be of interest to both graduate and undergraduate students of American history. The explanations accompanying the maps are of greater detail and more interest than in most similar reference books. This is certainly a useful and interesting addition to any academic library.

Classification: LC G1201; Dewey 911.

227. *Oxford Atlas of World History*, by Patrick K. O'Brien, ed.
Publisher: Oxford University Press, New York, NY (2002)
Price: $45.00
Review by Allen Reichert—Electronic Access Librarian, Courtright Memorial
    Library, Otterbein College, Westerville, OH.

This atlas covers the scope of human history. It is divided into five broad subject areas: ancient, medieval, early modern, age of revolutions, and twentieth century. Each section has an introductory essay. All entries are on a two-page spread with text, multiple maps, and usually a small picture. Sometimes the picture could be a little larger. Map types (political, topographical) and projections (Mercator, conical) vary as needed. Maps are crisp and often dense with information. A few are affected by the book gutter. A current, well-selected bibliography and thorough index round out this work. While valuable to a general audience, the editors obviously crafted this with the student in mind. Linkage between entries is ably provided within the descriptive text. Many entries detail political change, but there are also entries, particularly within the twentieth-century section, detailing social changes, such as the status of women, population, and human rights. Even within more traditional entries on empires there is often commentary or maps about trade, agriculture, or economy. The global inclusiveness is to be commended. Africa, Eastern Europe, Asia, and South America are well represented. It is clear from the editor's foreword to the end of the index that great care was taken to position this atlas within the current academic developments shaping the field of world history. Entries suggest possibilities and indicate scholarly debate rather than flatly stating one position. An excellent atlas, the *Oxford Atlas of World History* is highly recommended for all libraries.

The 2nd edition appeared in 2010 as *Atlas of World History*. Classification: LC D21; Dewey 909.

## Antiquity

228. *The Oxford Classical Dictionary*, by Simon Hornblower, Antony Spawforth, and Esther Eidinow, eds.
Publisher: Oxford University Press, New York, NY (2012)
Price: $175.00

Review by Jonathan F. Husband—Program Chair of the Library/Reader Services Librarian, Henry Whittemore Library, Framingham State College, Framingham, MA.

The 4th edition of *The Oxford Classical Dictionary* has been updated with hundreds of new entries and includes two new subject areas—Reception and Anthropology. In all, the title provides more than 6,000 entries in the areas of literature, art, philosophy, law, mythology, science, and cultural trends, just to name a few. Cross-references have been improved, and bibliographies have been updated. The revised edition has 150 more pages than the 2003 revised 3rd edition. *The Oxford Classical Dictionary* is the most extensive one-volume reference work to Classical history and culture available in English. No academic or public library reference section should be without a copy of the 4th edition. It provides profiles of all of the major figures of Classical Greece and Rome as well as legendary figures, mythological figures, famous architecture, landmarks, and literary and political terms. Libraries owning the 3rd edition will want to update their collection to include this 4th edition.

Classification: LC DE5; Dewey 938.

229. *Brill's New Pauly: Encyclopaedia of the Ancient World. Antiquity,* by Hubert Cancik, Helmuth Schneider, Christine F. Salazar, and David E. Orton

Publisher: Brill, Boston, MA (2002–2010)

Price: $7,711.00

Review by Steven W. Sowards—Associate Director for Collections, Michigan State University Libraries, East Lansing.

This fifteen-volume magnum opus is the most extensive and well-informed scholarly reference work on the classical world of the Greeks, Romans, and associated regions of the ancient Mediterranean during "Antiquity," the period from 2000 B.C.E. to 400 C.E. *Pauly* is a landmark of reference and a monument to German scholarship, in its origins and in the German original behind this translation. The set traces back to the *Realencyclopädie der classischen Altertumswissenschaft* edited by August Friedrich von Pauly in the early 19th century; the updated Pauly-Wissowa edition begun in the 1890s and completed a century later; the shorter 6-volume *Kleine Pauly* published in the 1960s; and now *Der Neue Pauly* (the *New Pauly*), launched in 1996 and completed in 2003 with sixteen volumes, followed by several supplements. The content identifies, documents, and discusses major and minor historical or mythological figures, both famous and obscure places, religious and literary works, social and cultural norms, legal practices, and aspects of science, medicine, architecture, and the arts, including drama, sculpture, and painting. Articles are signed with initials and range in length from a few sentences to multiple pages on important figures such as Aristophenes or topics like agriculture. Entries end with citations to original classic source texts and modern scholarly publications (often in European languages). The editors have embraced new techniques such as underwater archaeology and historical anthropology. The *New Pauly* reveals the richness of life in the ancient world. We can anticipate seeing a long article about Xenophon; we will not be surprised to read about marble and its uses; but we will not expect to learn about the place of ants in fables and rural life. Supporting features include genealogical tables; line drawings, maps, and architectural floorplans; cross-references; guides to transliteration from the ancient Greek, Hebrew, Turkish, Arabic, and Persian alphabets; and lists of abbreviations for common terms and frequently cited sources, ancient and modern. Volume 16 is an index with lists of persons by occupation such as Latin authors, or mythical persons; references to topics such as mosaics, or birds, or magic and sorcery; lists of maps and a geographic concordances matching up ancient and modern place names; chronological tables of treaties and rulers; and guides to systems of weights, measures, and coinage.

> A companion five-volume set, *The Classical Tradition*, traces the impact of classical ideas in medieval and modern times, in realms ranging from philosophy to politics to literature. A digital version, the New Pauly Online, covers both portions, and the original German text as well as the English translation. Classification: LC DE5; Dewey 938.

230. *Encyclopedia of Women in the Ancient World*, by Joyce E. Salisbury

Publisher: ABC-CLIO, Santa Barbara, CA (2001)

Price: $75.00

Review by Ken Middleton—User Services Librarian, Middle Tennessee State University, Murfreesboro.

Salisbury, a professor of history at the University of Wisconsin, Green Bay, focuses on women in ancient Western civilization in this attractive and engaging encyclopedia. Although some entries cover the prehistoric period, she emphasizes the period between 3,000 B.C.E. and 500 C.E. Biographical profiles of 150 ancient women form the heart of the encyclopedia. Although Marjorie and Benjamin Lightman's *Biographical Dictionary of Ancient Greek and Roman Women* covers many more women, Salisbury does a better job of placing ancient women in their historical context. For instance, she begins the entry for Clodia with a paragraph about the importance of family ties in ancient Rome, whereas the Lightmans simply recount Clodia's life. More than 30 topical entries (e.g., "Work," "Clothing," "Egyptian Women") further enhance the users' understanding of the world in which these and other ancient women lived. Finally, Salisbury includes over 30 entries covering mythological women and goddesses; she repeatedly emphasizes how these women reflected and influenced ancient ideas about women. Liberal use of cross-references enhances the usefulness of the encyclopedia. For example, the entry for the Roman empress Eudoxia, who died from complications of a miscarriage, refers readers to the "Gynecology" entry. All entries include a short list of suggested readings. Genealogical charts, maps of the regions covered, and 79 illustrations and photographs of artifacts round out the volume. Salisbury offers a well-written, accessible, and entertaining encyclopedia suitable for undergraduates and the general public.

---

Classification: LC HQ1127; Dewey 305.

---

231. *The Oxford Encyclopedia of Ancient Egypt*, by Donald B. Redford, ed.

Publisher: Oxford University Press, New York, NY (2001)

Price: $450.00/set

Review by Susan Tower Hollis—Associate Dean and Center Director, Central New York Center of the State University of New York, Saratoga Springs.

This three-volume set provides a welcome resource to the Egyptology-inclined researcher and layperson alike, particularly to the latter. Edited by a prominent Egyptologist and assisted by other well-known scholars in the field, it brings together discussions and commentary, some fairly extensive, some not so, on many of the different topics and issues present in the modern study of ancient Egypt. Most notably, it provides information aimed to modify and correct the many misconceptions and romantic ideas about the ancient culture as well as bringing up to date many of the shifts in understanding that have come about in recent decades. While the initial study of ancient Egypt was driven by treasure hunting and biblical prooftexting, along with searches for ever-expanding magical and occult practices, modern Egyptology has grown into a vastly multidisciplinary scholarship encompassing not just the obvious archaeology, but also including the new scientific archaeological tools of thermoluminescence, stratigraphic excavation, scientific epigraphy, and geomorphology along with economic history, art history, religion, literature, linguistics, sociology, and much more. Along with these expanded and newer approaches have come new discoveries, leading frequently to reinterpretation and expansion of earlier understanding. This set, which might well be consulted along with reading a good narrative history, provides much detail on topics written by international specialists. All articles are written in English and each has a solid bibliography, thus allowing the interested reader to pursue the topic further. It is clearly a set that belongs in every academic library and larger public libraries, though many mid-size libraries may wish to obtain it as well.

---

Classification: LC DT58; Dewey 932.

---

## The United States

The section "Military History" in this chapter (entries 284–292) notes works about the wars of the United States; multiple entries on political science and government in Chapter 2 (Social Sciences) look at U.S. historical developments.

## General Works

232. *Dictionary of American History*, by Stanley I. Kutler, ed.

Publisher: Charles Scribner's Sons/Gale Group, New York, NY (2003)

Price: $995.00/set

Review by Staff, Libraries Unlimited.

The *Dictionary of American History* has been a standard reference source for more than 60 years; the 1st edition was published in 1940 and the 2nd edition was published in 1976, with 2 supplemental volumes issued in 1996. Although history does not technically change, the interpretations and analysis of history are often changing. This 10-volume work reflects those changes within the last 25 years. This set provides 4,434 entries pertaining to American history. Some 1,785 articles have been retained from the original or 2nd edition; 448 articles have been revised significantly; 1,360 articles have replaced the original articles from the 1st and 2nd editions; and 841 articles are completely new to this edition. The set has also changed significantly with the inclusion of 1,200 photographs and 252 maps; the 1st and 2nd editions did not contain either. Cross-referencing has been enhanced as well with the use of internal highlighting (words in small uppercase lettering) and *see* and *see also* references. This work does not feature any biographies of key figures. Instead, the editor has chosen to focus on key events. The omission of biographies allows the editor to provide more thorough information on events and provide information on less-significant but still important events. Information about key historical figures can still be accessed through the set's index. Volumes 1–8 provide an alphabetic listing of key events, while volume 9 offers primary documents and archival maps and volume 10 offers a research guide and index to the set. Each article runs several paragraphs to several pages in length, and each has a bibliography and *see also* references. All articles are signed by the contributor. Because this set has been completely revised and updated, those libraries that own the 2nd edition will need to purchase this updated 3rd edition. The high price will make this set out of reach for some smaller libraries and many school libraries. Academic and larger public libraries should consider its purchase.

Classification: LC E174; Dewey 973.

233. *Encyclopedia of American History*, by Peter C. Mancall and Gary B. Nash, eds.
Publisher: Facts on File, New York, NY (2010)
Price: $1,150.00/set
Review by Staff, Libraries Unlimited.

This eleven-volume encyclopedia is designed with high school students in mind. The general editor, Gary B. Nash, was codirector of the National Standards for United States History Project, and has brought his experience with education to this multivolume set. The format remains the unchanged since the 1st edition (2003). Unlike other encyclopedic volumes it is not organized in the standard A-Z format. Instead, each volume covers a different era of American history, and the terms, events, and people relevant to that era are featured in that volume. Each volume provides a list of the entries and an introduction of the time period covered. New to this 2nd edition are hundreds of updated entries, several hundred new entries. Volume 10, covering the years 1969 to the present, has the most updated information since the editors have provided new entries for newsworthy historical topics. In other volumes fewer new entries have been added, but they included many new revisions that reflect recent scholarship in their respective time period. Entries are typically several pages in length and include biographies of important people and black-and-white photographs and maps. Each volume concludes with a chronology, a list of important documents, a bibliography, and an index to that specific volume. Along with biographies, entries cover topics on events, movements, political developments, the economy, literature, business, art and architecture, and science and technology of the time. Many of the entries provide lists of further reading so students can expand on their research and for this 2nd edition the further reading lists have been updated with new, useful resources. The use of illustrations and maps is extensive, and they successfully enhance the text. This 2nd edition features several new historical maps, many of which are in full color. Volume 11 provides a comprehensive index to the set, which serves to pull the 11 volumes together. This eleven-volume updated set would be a worthwhile addition of all middle school and high school libraries—its intended audience. Each library will need to decide for themselves if the updated information in one handy reference set is worth the hefty price tag.

---

Classification: LC E174; Dewey 973.

---

234. *Oxford Companion to United States History*, by Paul S. Boyer

Publisher: Oxford University Press, New York, NY (2001)

Price: $79.95

Review by Steven W. Sowards—Associate Director for Collections, Michigan State University Libraries, East Lansing.

This collection of 1,400 signed short essays in alphabetical order covers the full range of topics in American political, social, economic, and cultural history, from colonial times to the election of George W. Bush in 2000. There are entries for significant persons from all walks of life; key events, court decisions, legislative acts, and places; and influential publications, ideas, and movements. Articles vary in length from a few paragraphs to more than 10 pages. The longest essays deal with major topics such as slavery, the Civil War, American Indian history and culture, economic depressions, World War II, foreign relations, the federal government, music, literature, science, medicine, education, and agriculture. A sampling of entries indicates the range of coverage: circuses, the grain processing industry, mobility in American life, the Mayo Clinic, *The Grapes of Wrath*, the Battle of Midway, and Andy Warhol. This is a guide not only to historical facts but to the significance of figures and events, and the interpretation of trends by historians. Each article ends with suggested additional sources and reading. More than 500 entries are biographical, with citations to full-length biographies, autobiographies, and scholarly studies. The directory of 900 contributors indicates their credentials and the articles written by each scholar. There are numerous cross-references and a detailed index, and 25 black-and-white reproductions of historical maps (themselves primary sources) but no other illustrations.

---

Classification: LC E174; Dewey 973.

---

235. *Famous First Facts: A Record of First Happenings, Discoveries, and Inventions in American History*, by Joseph Nathan Kane

Publisher: H. W. Wilson, Bronx, NY (2015)

Price: $195.00

Review by Staff, Libraries Unlimited.

*Famous First Facts*, now in its seventh edition, was first published by editor Joseph Kane for H.W. Wilson in 1933. The sixth edition appeared in 2006. The current edition has almost eight thousand entries, more than one hundred illustrations, four indexes, and sixteen chapters covering firsts in several arenas—scientific, medical, technological, political, legal, social, and financial—from the colonial period to the present. Entries can be as short as a sentence, but most are several sentences in length. The book begins with a preface, notes on how to use the book, and "Expanded Contents." Chapters are organized into alphabetized subsections; "firsts" in these subsections are presented in chronological order. The chapters are as follows: Arts and Entertainment, Business and Industry, Daily Life, Education, Engineering, Media and Communications, Medicine and Health, Military and War, Nature and Environment, Population and Settlement, Religion, Science and Technology, Society, Sports and Recreation, and Transportation. Four indexes—subject, index by years, index to personal names, and a geographical index—facilitate searches. This book of first facts would be a welcome addition to a public or school library.

---

Classification: LC AG5; Dewey 031.

---

236. *The Encyclopedia of American Political History*, by Paul Finkelman and Peter Wallenstein, eds.

Publisher: CQ Press/SAGE, Thousand Oaks, CA (2001)

Price: $135.00

Review by Robert V. Labaree—Reference/Public Services Librarian, Von KleinSmid Library, University of Southern California, Los Angeles.

Readers would expect to find an encyclopedia survey of American political history to encompass multiple volumes covering thousands of events, people, and issues. However, that is not the intent of this work. *The Encyclopedia of American Political History* is a ready-reference book with more than 240 essays, written by academic and independent scholars, that provides speedy access to key topics in American political history. Coverage is broad and focuses on major events, key political leaders, concepts, and critical issues that have shaped the American political landscape. Most essays describe a historical issue, moment, or leader in terms of the lasting effect that person or topic has had, thereby establishing linkages between the past topic and the present condition of American politics.

Although limited in the amount of information they provide, each essay includes a bibliography of further readings, references to related entries, and selected reproductions and photographs. A comprehensive subject/name index is included. The encyclopedia has two useful quick-reference tools—a descriptive timeline of key political events subdivided under broad historical time periods (which could be enhanced in future editions by bolding those terms that correspond to entries in the encyclopedia) and an appendix of common acronyms and abbreviations associated with American political history. These items are an especially useful feature of this work. Reading the descriptive timeline gives clues to how many more entries could be added to this work, and several essays include references to persons, issues, or events that could easily form their own entries. For example, the two essays covering immigration and naturalization allude to issues of racism in American politics, a topic that likely deserves its own entry. Nevertheless, as stated by the editors, future editions will include updated and added entries. Currently, this work stands as a useful and well-written ready-reference tool for any library.

---

Classification: LC E183; Dewey 973.

---

237. *Encyclopedia of American Foreign Policy*, by Alexander DeConde, Richard Dean Burns, Fredrik Logevall, and Louise B. Ketz, eds.

Publisher: Charles Scribner's Sons/Gale Group, New York, NY (2002)

Price: $350.00/set

Henry E. York—Head, Collection Management, Cleveland State University, Cleveland, OH.

The editors of this core reference source have understandably determined that with the changes in the world since the 1st edition in 1978 a revised edition is in order. The end of the Cold War, the demise of the Soviet Union, the emergence of the European Union, NAFTA, China as a world power, and the explosion of ethnic conflicts in the Balkans and Near East are a few examples of the ways the world has changed dramatically in recent decades. In response, the new edition of the *Encyclopedia of American Foreign Policy* has been revised to include 48 new essays. The 120 essays in A to Z arrangement provide in-depth discussions on the principal figures, movements, events, and ideas in American diplomatic history, from the beginning of the nation to the present day. Some of the subjects covered are obvious choices—Superpower Diplomacy, Treaties, Nationalism, Cold War Origins, and so on. Others, perhaps less predictable, include such topics as African Americans, Gender, Ideology, and Religion. The essay approach provides for in-depth, interpretive coverage by scholars who are experts in their fields. This approach avoids "snippets of information" (p. xv) and the effort to provide a narrative of specific events. The emphasis is on the analysis of key concepts, themes, theories, doctrines, and the placing of events in a broad chronological and historical context. The essays average about 20 pages and end with 1 or 2 page bibliographies. The extensive index provides access to specific terms, concepts, and individuals. There is also a lengthy "Chronology of American Foreign Policy, 1607–2001," which provides the basic facts and dates some users may want from an encyclopedia. A list of contributors, mostly American historians, is provided. Since this three-volume set is scholarly but quite readable, it is suitable for a wide range of users, including faculty, students, government officials, journalists, and the general public.

Classification: LC E183; Dewey 327.

238. *Encyclopedia of American Cultural and Intellectual History*, by Mary Kupiec Cayton and Peter W. Williams, eds.

Publisher: Charles Scribner's Sons/Gale Group, New York, NY (2001)

Price: $325.00/set

Review by Mark Y. Herring—Dean of Library Services, Winthrop University, Dacus Library, Rock Hill, SC.

Only every once and again, and that very rarely, does a reference tool come along that excites the senses while informing sentience. The *Encyclopedia of American Cultural and Intellectual History* (EACIH) is one such tool. Each volume is an education in itself. Certainly home-school teachers will not want to be without this tool on the shelf. In fact, it is hard to think of any group (librarians, philosophers, and newspaper and magazine editors) who will want to be without these very fine volumes. Such topics as Puritan philosophy, Colonial womanhood, American religious transformation, slavery, Southern intellectual life, and American romanticism are covered. Transcendentalism, cultural modernism, art and the New Deal, the Cold War, feminism, Vietnam, postmodernism, and various American ethnic groups are also covered, as are numerous cultural groups. The volumes are broken into sections or themes as well as historical periods. Each of the more than two hundred essays run thousands of words each. Chronology pages help users locate both time and place in the volume, or even individual essays. Each essay contains a current bibliography and lists *see* and *see also* references. The writing is not only even throughout but also excellently edited. Moreover, interesting sidebars, graphs, photographs, and other illustrations to help the reader are scattered throughout each volume, making the reading as informative as it is entertaining. But what really makes

EACIH a marvel is its painstaking evenhandedness—especially in the essays where rancor and disagreement seem ever ready to explode. In the essays on liberalism and conservatism, for example, care has been taken to let both sides make their case. The effect is plain—readers are left to draw their own conclusions. For students interested in intellectual history and philosophy (many colleges or universities require at least one such course) these volumes will prove a godsend.

Classification: LC E169; Dewey 973.

239. *Colonial America: An Encyclopedia of Social, Political, Cultural, and Economic History*, by James Ciment, ed.

Publisher: M. E. Sharpe, Armonk, NY (2006)

Price: $499.00/set

Review by John A. Drobnicki—Acting Chief Librarian, City University of New York–York College, Jamaica.

This set contains 465 alphabetic entries written by 89 contributors on the Colonial Era (1607–1763), covering topics such as prominent individuals, groups (e.g., Free Blacks, Jews), events, places, institutions, and significant publications. Each article is signed and contains a brief bibliography as well as *see also* references. Other features include 17 maps, numerous black-and-white illustrations that enhance the text, 7 thematic essays (e.g., "Gender Issues," "Race and Ethnicity"), a glossary of 406 terms, and 24 chronologies, both thematic (which correspond to the essays) and geographic. A handy "Topic Finder" allows the user to quickly identify relevant articles by broad subjects (e.g., African Americans, Everyday Life). There are also three overall indexes— General, Biographical, and Geographical—which are helpfully printed in each volume. The final volume reprints 59 primary documents with full bibliographic information, and there is a well-chosen general bibliography of both primary and secondary sources. Although the military and political aspects of Colonial America are included in numerous reference sources, and there is much useful social information printed in *Colonial America to 1763* by Thomas L. Purvis, it is nevertheless very convenient and useful to have such a wide range of subjects available in one set in order to have a more complete understanding of overall life in the colonies.

Classification: LC E162; Dewey 973.

240. *Encyclopedia of the United States in the Nineteenth Century*, by Paul Finkelman, ed.

Publisher: Charles Scribner's Sons/Gale Group, New York, NY (2001)

Price: $325.00/set

Review by Paul A. Mogren—Head of Reference, Marriott Library, University of
Utah, Salt Lake City.

Following the fine tradition of the *Encyclopedia of the North American Colonies*
and *The Encyclopedia of the United States in the Twentieth Century*, this set, covering
the nineteenth century in U.S. history, is terrific. This 3-volume encyclopedia
provides articles about events, trends, movements, technologies, inventions, cultural and social changes, and intellectual trends in the United States in the nineteenth century. Each entry is followed by a bibliography and is signed by the
contributor. The bibliographies are thorough and the contributors/scholars are
identified at the end of the set. The 599 entries are on the average two to three
pages in length and quite often are accompanied by an illustration—usually a
drawing, photograph, or a reproduction of an art work—almost always provided
by the Library of Congress. The editor indicates that he has selected the topics to
cover major issues and ideas of the century. They include multiple entries reflecting the topics in the National Standards for United States History by the National
Center for History in the Schools, therefore focusing on one of the intended
audiences for this set—school students. The index is complete, and the synoptic
outline is an excellent overview of the conceptual framework of the set. The outline entries correspond to the index exactly. The entry topics are balanced
between specific events, places and individuals, and global topics like politics
and law. The topics on diverse groups in the population are excellent. *See* references are provided in the alphabetically arranged entries of the text. *See also*
references are provided at the end of virtually every entry as well. A spot check
of the veracity of entries by historians and scholars indicates that the history is
sound and the entries quite complete as encyclopedic articles go. The classics,
both old and new, are represented in the bibliographies, and the contributors are
indeed notable in their field. This work is highly recommended for schools, public libraries, and colleges. It would be great for home use as well, although the
$325 price tag might preclude that.

Classification: LC E169; Dewey 973.

241. *Encyclopedia of American Social Movements*, by Immanuel Ness, ed.

Publisher: M. E. Sharpe, Armonk, NY (2004)

Price: $359.00/set

Review by John W. Storey—Professor of History, Lamar University, Beaumont, TX.

This ambitious encyclopedia raises anew the question of consensus versus conflict in the nation's development from the 1700s to the present. Has American history been characterized by continuity and broad agreement on fundamental matters, or by vigorous social protests, sometimes violent, as disinherited elements struggled for justice? The emphasis here definitely is on conflict, as the numerous contributions recount the campaigns of the poor, the exploited, the disfranchised, and the excluded to secure for themselves justice, equality, and democracy. Although most social movements, defined herein as "the coming together of large numbers of people to pursue a goal they believe will improve society" (p. xix), have been progressive, or liberal, in their advocacy of greater human dignity, individual rights, and personal freedom, there have been notable exceptions. Some conservative, or right-wing, movements, for instance, have pursued censorship laws, sought to restrict if not halt the advancement of women and African Americans, and espoused a nativistic view that threatened the rights of ethnic minorities. But whether dealing with the left or right, the authors here strive for balance. The objective was to understand, not to glorify or vilify, particular movements or people. Sensibly organized, the encyclopedia consists of 16 major sections, covering everything from antislavery, civil rights, women's, environmental, and Native American movements to the labor, antiwar, student, group identity, and lesbian, gay, bisexual, and transgender movements. Subsumed under each section are articles on various aspects of the movement, brief biographies of significant figures, excerpts from primary documents, illustrations, and a bibliography. Many of these movements overlapped and numerous individuals engaged in several movements, and so to afford easy access to this wealth of material the editor has provided exhaustive general and biographical indexes. Scholars will find this reference useful, but it is intended for a broader audience. It is the best work of its kind, and high school and university libraries should consider it for their collections.

---

Classification: LC HN57; Dewey 303.

---

242. *Civil Rights in the United States*, by Waldo E. Martin Jr. and Patricia Sullivan, eds.
Publisher: Macmillan Reference USA/Gale Group, New York, NY (2000)
Price: $225.00/set
Review by Lucille Whalen—Dean of Graduate Programs, Immaculate Heart College Center, Los Angeles, CA.

Although it is not indicated in the title, the editors state in the preface that this two-volume work is an encyclopedia in both content and organization. Their purpose was to provide a highly accessible source of the latest scholarship on civil rights in the United States from a fresh historical perspective, beginning with the Naturalization Law of 1790. Stressing the multicultural reality of the American experience, the work includes both the theoretical and legal aspects of civil rights along with extensive material on the real struggles of individuals and groups to achieve these rights, especially for oppressed, marginalized, and excluded Americans. This work was produced in tandem with a series of Harvard summer institutes for college and university teachers who were in the process of developing a framework for understanding and teaching the civil rights movement. Following a lengthy preface are an introductory article on the Bill of Rights, an alphabetic list of articles with their authors, and a list of contributors with their affiliations and the articles they contributed. These precede the main text of alphabetically arranged subjects, which are followed by a single index. Although the majority of the articles are long and generally complete in themselves, most have references to other entries printed in bold typeface, making it convenient to pursue related topics. Each of the articles is signed and followed by a bibliography. The articles are clearly written, authoritative, and balanced in their presentation. Some weaknesses should be mentioned. The scope of the work is rather vaguely defined, but in the preface the editors state that it was intended to offer not only a fresh historical perspective but also a forward-looking vision of civil rights. While it is strong in the historical perspective, even up to the fairly recent past, it is curious that some subjects do not have separate articles, such as hate groups and privacy rights. The bibliographies and index present some problems also. It is surprising and disappointing to find almost no references to Internet sites. One or two carefully chosen websites would undoubtedly have provided the reader with much more current information. Other problems with the bibliographies include inconsistency in form and occasional incomplete citation. Some have only missing page numbers, but others, particularly for the papers of a prominent person, are too vague to be useful. The addition of a single, complete bibliography in the appendix would have enhanced the work and also could have helped to avoid such bibliographical problems. Furthermore, in the generally helpful index there is sometimes a lack of cross-referencing. Despite these mainly editorial problems, the work presents an excellent overall view of civil rights in the United States. The well-written articles, the pleasing format, and the ease of access to specific information make it a good choice for both public and academic libraries. Those who have *The Encyclopedia of Civil Rights in America*, however, may find that even though there are differences, much of the same material is covered in both.

---

Classification: LC E184; Dewey 323.

---

243. *The Oxford Encyclopedia of Latinos and Latinas in the United States*, by Suzanne Oboler and Deena J. González, eds.

Publisher: Oxford University Press, New York, NY (2005)

Price: $525.00/set

Review by Melvin Davis—Assistant Professor, Interlibrary Loan Librarian, Middle Tennessee University, Murfreesboro.

Oxford's four-volume encyclopedia dedicated to the Latino experience in the United States is a welcomed resource. Cross-disciplinary in nature, it examines not only important figures in Latino history but also Latino cultural, economic, social, and political achievements. Instead of casting Latinos as a homogeneous group, the editors cogently acknowledge the diverse cultural and social backgrounds of the peoples collectively referred to as Latino. As a result, this extensive undertaking encompasses a wide swath of peoples including Chicanos, Puerto Ricans, and Cubans. The encyclopedia contains more than 900 alphabetically arranged entries that are made up of four general types of essays—historical, thematic, issue, and biographies. Historical essays examine the social and cultural backgrounds of the various ethnic groups represented in the encyclopedia, while the thematic essays are interdisciplinary in nature and provide general information on these groups including discussions of important individuals and events. Issue essays elaborate on specific topics raised in the thematic essays, while biographies, naturally, focus on individuals who have contributed significantly to the Latino experience in the United States. These essays work well together, allowing the reader to transition from the general to the more specific with ease. They are clearly written, and most offer sufficient detail to spark further study. There are many tools to assist students and researchers in using the encyclopedia. Cross-references, bibliographies, a systematic outline, and an index make it accessible to a wide audience. Students, faculty, or general readers alike will find that this encyclopedia is a valuable tool for researching Latino history, culture, experiences, and contributions to the United States. Although no work is perfect, this one is well executed and is as close to comprehensive as possible given the breadth of its subject matter.

Classification: LC E184; Dewey 973.

244. *Notable American Women: A Biographical Dictionary Completing the Twentieth Century*, by Susan Ware and Stacy Braukman, eds.

Publisher: Harvard University Press, Cambridge, MA (2004)

Price: $45.00

Review by Ken Middleton—User Services Librarian, Middle Tennessee State University, Murfreesboro.

The appearance of the first three volumes of *Notable American Women* in 1971 was a truly groundbreaking publishing event because biographical information of any kind about notable women was otherwise very difficult to find. Volume 4, published as a supplement in 1980, profiled women who died between 1951 and 1975. This 5th volume includes biographical profiles of 483 women who died during the last quarter of the twentieth century. The five volumes in the set now include profiles of 2,284 women. Even today, with a plethora of print and online sources readily available, librarians should turn to this set first for information about notable American women. The new editorial team refined the already rigorous selection process of the previous volumes. They made a special effort to avoid a Northeastern bias, and roughly one-fourth of the entries are about nonwhite women. Although this reviewer expected considerable overlap with comparable sources, more than half of the women who are profiled in this volume are not covered in *American National Biography* (entry 57). The entries are well written and substantial enough to give readers a strong sense of why a woman is considered notable. Even the articles about women scientists convey complex topics in a manner that is accessible to a general audience. Fortunately, the bibliography that accompanies each entry includes both primary (if applicable) and secondary sources. The Index to Biographies by Field facilitates access to information about women who may not be known to many readers. Although Georgia O'Keeffe is of course listed among the artists covered, we are also directed to the entry for Estelle Ishigo, whose art captured the hardships that internment camp detainees faced during World War II. Readers impressed by Helen Taussig's determination to obtain a medical degree can quickly learn how Martha May Eliot, Edith Jackson, and others also overcame bias against women doctors. As Susan Ware notes in her fascinating introduction, this volume also provides multiple perspectives on the issues and events that marked the twentieth century, particularly during the period between 1920 and the mid-1970s. Thus, the volume stands on its own quite well. All academic and public libraries should purchase this very reasonably priced volume.

Classification: LC CT3260; Dewey 920.

## African American History

245. *Africana: The Encyclopedia of the African and African American Experience,* by Kwame Anthony Appiah and Henry Louis Gates Jr., eds.

Publisher: Oxford University Press, New York, NY (2005)

Price: $500/set

Review by Anthony J. Adam—Director, Institutional Assessment, Blinn College, Brenham, TX.

Librarians and scholars will want to invest in the 2nd edition of this title. Under the editorship of Appiah and Gates, two of the greatest names in contemporary black studies scholarship, the new 5-volume edition features over 4,400 articles, including over 1,200 brand-new entries and hundreds that have undergone extensive revision. Almost every article has been penned by a specialist in the field, and the advisory board is impressive. Articles range from a couple of paragraphs to 10 or more pages, depending on the topic, and most feature cross-references and secondary bibliographies. Material is presented for the most part matter-of-factly, without the one-sided commentary that has marred otherwise fine recent reference tools. Excellent full-color photographs, maps, and other illustrations complement the text, and charts and large graphs are scattered throughout. The new edition also includes a comprehensive index, missing from the 1st edition, along with a lengthy bibliography and topic list. The large type-face should attract browsers, although the slick pages also make for unusually heavy volumes. The only complaint one might have with this edition is that a portion of the articles are not original but rather are culled from other standard reference sources, such as the *Dictionary of American Negro Biography* (1982). Some of the subject headings also are a bit awkward (e.g., "Black Towns"), but that does not detract from the overall excellence of the work. This title is highly recommended for all libraries, to replace the 1st edition.

Classification: LC DT14; Dewey 960.

246. *Encyclopedia of African American History, 1619–1895: From the Colonial Period to the Age of Frederick Douglass,* by Paul Finkelman, ed.
Publisher: Oxford University Press, New York, NY (2006)
Price: $395.00/set
Review by Anthony J. Adam—Director, Institutional Assessment, Blinn College, Brenham, TX.

Finkelman (University of Tulsa College of Law) has a substantial history of producing fine works on African American history, and his steady hand shows through this latest endeavor. As the first half of a projected two-part series, these three volumes cover the period from the earliest colonial settlements through the death of Frederick Douglass in 1895. Although the focus of the nearly seven hundred entries and subentries (lengthy sections within long articles) is the United States, Finkelman wisely adds subjects that bring a more global scope to the work. All topics including biographies are featured, although space limitations preclude detailed coverage of lesser topics. Entries normally run from half a page to five pages in length, depending on the topic, and each article concludes with a brief secondary bibliography. Approximately three hundred black-and-white illustrations (sometimes a bit grainy), a good index, and a thematic outline conclude the set. Entries are generally well written, although quite a few "independent scholars" and Ph.D. candidates compose the team of scholars; the user will not find the African American Studies pantheon (e.g., Gates, Patterson) writing here. With the abundance of African American encyclopedias currently available, the librarian must wonder if one more is necessary. Finkelman's quality work makes that answer a strong "yes" for all academic libraries. This work compares favorably with Palmer's *The Encyclopedia of African-American Culture and History* (2nd ed.) and Appiah and Gates's *Africana: The Encyclopedia of the African and African-American Experience* (2nd ed.; entry 245).

See also entry 247 for the companion set, for events after 1895. Classification: LC E185; Dewey 973.

247. *Encyclopedia of African American History, 1896 to the Present: From the Age of Segregation to the Twenty-First Century,* by Paul Finkelman, ed.

Publisher: Oxford University Press, New York, NY (2009)

Price: $495.00/set

Review by Anthony J. Adam—Director, Institutional Assessment, Blinn College, Brenham, TX.

One of the monumental reference resources of the past few decades has finally reached completion with the publication of this new 5-volume set, which chronicles African American history from 1896, the year of *Plessy v. Ferguson*, through the present (fittingly, President Obama's face is central on each cover). The previous set (entry 246), published also by Oxford University Press in 2006, covered the period 1619–1895, and libraries therefore will need both sets for comprehensive coverage. This new work features 1,250 scholarly articles on nearly every topic relevant to the period, including politics, sports, entertainment, literature, and education, with separate articles on personalities, organizations, and movements. Articles vary in length, from a single column to around 10 pages, but all articles are well written and well researched, with secondary bibliographies (including websites) and *see also* at the end. Some black-and-white photographs are also included, but otherwise the set is not illustrated. Over one-half of the final volume is devoted to a chronology of African American history during the period, followed by a detailed index to the set. Undoubtedly some will discover missing topics, but in general the editors have done a fine job of inclusiveness and breadth. Considering the overall excellence of this work and its companion set, the *Encyclopedia of African American History* is an essential purchase for all academic and public libraries, along with Palmer's equally fine six-volume *Encyclopedia of African-American Culture and History* (2nd ed.), regardless of the degree of duplication of topics.

---

See entry 246 for the companion set, for events before 1896. Classification: LC E185; Dewey 973.

---

248. *Slavery in the United States: A Social, Political, and Historical Encyclopedia*, by Junius P. Rodriguez, ed.

Publisher: ABC-CLIO, Santa Barbara, CA (2007)

Price: $185.00/set

Review by Michael Margolis—Reference Librarian, City University of New York.

This is a 2-volume encyclopedia about slavery in America. The author first provides a 60-page chronology of events followed by 100 pages of chronological essays. After the essays a traditional alphabetic arrangement is used to present the major social political and historical events concerning slavery. The entries include important people, societies, movements, battles, court cases, important places, and legislation. Typical entries include such topics as Nat Turner, Confederate Congress, and the Dred Scott Decision. The work also contains a primary source document section. There are 150 primary sources that cover the period 1669 to 1883. These sources include a wide variety of sources and would be especially useful to scholars. The writing is both clear and interesting, and the entries range in size from a paragraph to 2 pages. There are maps, an index, and a table of contents. There are many reference books concerning African American history and slavery. This work is one of the better ones and would be of interest to both graduate and undergraduate students of American history.

---

Classification: LC E441; Dewey 306.

---

249. *Encyclopedia of the Underground Railroad*, by J. Blaine Hudson

Publisher: McFarland, Jefferson, NC (2006)

Price: $55.00

Review by Staff, Libraries Unlimited.

This encyclopedia focuses on the history behind the abolitionist movement that thrived up to the end of the Civil War and the freeing of slaves. It covers people, ideas, events, and places associated with the Underground Railroad. Also discussed is the struggle of African Americans for equality and the antislavery movement in general. Cross-references direct readers to related entries, and many entries provide suggestions for further reading. The terms have been drawn from primary documents, public records, slave autobiographies, and antebellum newspapers. Supplementary materials include appendixes (e.g., geographical listing of selected friends of the fugitive, noted underground railroad sites administered by the National Park Service, a bibliography of slave autobiographies, selected underground railroad songs) and a chronology of events. This inexpensive reference will be useful to the history collections of academic and high school libraries.

---

Classification: LC E450; Dewey 973.

---

250. *African American National Biography*, by Henry Louis Gates Jr. and Evelyn Brooks Higginbotham, eds.

Publisher: Oxford University Press, New York, NY (2013)

Price: $1,295.00/set

Review by Gregory A. Crawford—Head of Public Services, Penn State Harrisburg, Middletown, PA.

Containing nearly five thousand biographies of African Americans, the 2nd edition of *African American National Biography* (AANB) will be a long-lasting, regularly used addition to the reference collections of almost all public and academic libraries. In the 1st edition the editors claimed, "AANB is a work that tells the story, for the first time, of the broadest swath of the black people who, together, created our collective history" (p. xxxv). This assessment rings true with the 2nd edition as well. The original eight-volume set has now been expanded to twelve volumes, and many of the previously included biographies have now been updated to reflect achievements in the past five years. Designed as a complement to *American National Biography* (entry 57) and as an update to the *Dictionary of American Negro Biography* (Norton, 1982), the AANB increases dramatically the number of biographies of notable African Americans available to students and researchers. Biographies of African Americans included in *American National Biography* are reproduced in AANB, although photographs are often added and the bibliographies are usually abbreviated. In addition, many living individuals are included in the AANB, a significant difference from *American National Biography*. Thus, many prominent individuals, such as Colin Powell, Toni Morrison, Hank Aaron, Oprah Winfrey, and the editors themselves are included. Coverage has been expanded to include nearly nine hundred new influential African Americans, including Cory Booker, C. Vivian Stringer, and Michelle Obama. Coverage of women has also been increased. Over one thousand photographs are included, giving the AANB an added dimension. The final volume includes useful indexes such as by subject area and realm of renown and by birthplace. A listing of African American prizewinners, medalists, members of Congress, and judges concludes the work. The individual biographies are well written, placing the individual's life within the context of the time and stressing the person's contributions to American and specifically to African American history. The print is easy to read and the photographs are clear and crisp. The AANB is a required purchase. For those needing this type of information in electronic format the publisher offers all of the biographies in the Oxford African American Studies Center.

---

Classification: LC E185; Dewey 920.

---

251. *Black Women in America*, by Darlene Clark Hine
Publisher: Oxford University Press, New York, NY (2005)
Price: $520.00
Review by Steven W. Sowards—Associate Director for Collections, Michigan State University Libraries, East Lansing.

This 3-volume set updates the 1st edition of 1993, a pioneering effort to enrich the historical record concerning black women in the United States from colonial times to the twenty-first century. Some 500 signed entries in alphabetical order conclude with bibliographies for additional reading and often are accompanied by a black and white portrait or photograph. More than 300 of those entries are biographies, all for women: for example, while Martin Luther King, Jr., is mentioned there is an entry for Coretta Scott King. Many entries cover well-known persons, but others highlight significant women who are rarely acknowledged. Several "features" bring together multiple brief biographies by occupation such as "School Founders" or "Concert Musicians." Other articles discuss the status of women in a wide range of occupations such as education or literature. The longest articles deal with eras or overarching themes, such as the Civil War, Reconstruction, the Jim Crow Era, the Great Depression, or World Wars I and II; and Slavery, the Abolition Movement, Free Black Women in the Antebellum North, the Civil Rights Movement, Affirmative Action, Political Resistance, Legal Resistance, Marriage, or Race as a Social Construction. Perhaps half of the content deals with developments since the 1940s. The set concludes with a chronology from 1619 to 2004 with especially rich coverage from

1848 onwards; a bibliography of major monographs; a roster of personal papers held by archives and research centers; an outline of entries grouped by themes such as "Culture," "Gender," and "Politics, Laws & Government"; lists of biographical entries by occupation; a directory of some 250 contributors, with an indication of articles submitted by each scholar; and a detailed index of personal names, influential publications and organizations, topics, and places.

---

Classification: LC E185; Dewey 305.

---

## Native America

Information on the indigenous peoples of the New World, of course, also appears in works about the history of the United States, Canada, the Caribbean, and Latin America and in publications from the social sciences, including sociology and anthropology.

252. *Encyclopedia of American Indian History*, by Bruce E. Johansen and Barry M. Pritzker, eds.

Publisher: ABC-CLIO, Santa Barbara, CA (2007)

Price: $395.00/set

Review by John P. Stierman—Reference Librarian, Western Illinois University, Macomb.

The reference shelf is full of books on Native Americans. But there are not as many general encyclopedias on the subject as one might think. The Smithsonian Institution's twenty-volume *Handbook of North American Indians* is the standard of excellence in the field, but it is aimed at the scholar and the most curious students. Those who do not need such in-depth treatment may consider ABC-CLIO's latest Native American reference offering, *Encyclopedia of American Indian History*, edited by Bruce E. Johansen and Barry M. Pritzker. Experienced librarians will recall that ABC-CLIO published a similar title in the late 1990s titled *Native Americans: An Encyclopedia of History, Culture, and Peoples*, also edited by Pritzker. While both are aimed at a general audience and focus on the history and culture of Native Americans, the 2007 imprint is more ambitious. *The Encyclopedia of North American Indians* is a multifaceted four-volume reference tool that is mostly a collection of entries grouped around themes in American Indian history: chronology, events, culture, governments, people, and groups. Volume 1 includes six short articles signed by the editors or their contributing authors and includes references and suggestions for further reading. The bulk of this volume, however, is "Issues in American Indian History" and "Events in American Indian

History." As the reader might expect, the former is arranged alphabetically and the latter chronologically. Each entry is signed by an editor or contributor and includes a list of references. Volume 2 includes two broad themes, culture and governments, and follows much the same format as the previous volume with signed entries and suggestions for further reading. Students who are interested in how Native Americans have interacted with the U.S. government will find the second part of this volume especially useful. Two-thirds of volume 3 is dedicated to "People and Groups in American Indian History," from "Aboriginal Peoples Television Network" to "Wovoka." These entries are very similar in style and format to the earlier volumes. The last one-third of this volume is a collection of primary documents that is largely unnecessary due to the Internet. The majority of volume 4 is brief histories of Indian nations, arranged geographically and then alphabetically within region. These entries are not signed, but they are attributed to Barry Pritzker in the list of contributors. These histories, unfortunately, do not include references. The final pages of the set are "Resources," which include a variety of directory or handbook information. The set could benefit from a more descriptive introductory essay, discussing the encyclopedia's unique arrangement and contents. The list of contributors at the beginning of each volume is useful, but this reviewer would like to know each contributor's academic rank or position, not just affiliation. The user will not find the leading historians in American Indian history on this list. Bruce Johansen, the lead editor, wrote almost one hundred entries, while the average is three or fewer. The placement of a comprehensive index at the end of each volume is convenient. The *Encyclopedia of American Indian History* is an ideal acquisition for those libraries that lack good introductory material on North American Indians and that serve a general audience or junior college students.

---

Classification: LC E77; Dewey 970.

---

253. *Encyclopedia of Native Tribes of North America*, by Michael G. Johnson
Publisher: Firefly Books, New York, NY (2008)
Price: $49.95

Review by Karen D. Harvey—Associate Dean for Academic Affairs, University College, University of Denver, Denver, CO.

As users will expect of a new edition that has been updated and revised, there are some new and improved components to this volume. The most effective of these are the additions of excellent color photographs, maps, and a well-illustrated glossary. The author of the foreword states quite expansively that this is "a beginning student's book, a collector's book, a young person's book, a librarian's book, an artist's book, a general reader's book, a costume designer's book, and even a scholar's book." This excessive praise provides unrealistically high expectations for a topic so vast and so complex. The book is organized into the following parts: foreword, introduction, classification of Indian languages, distribution of cultures, the tribes (ten culture areas), the Indian today, glossary, select bibliography, museums, native populations, and index. Each of the sections/culture areas is replete with maps and charts, including language families, historical and cultural sites, and tribal locations. Historical and cultural information is given for each tribe. The entries are brief and provide only the most basic information. The reader will appreciate that the natives of both the United States and Canada are included. The author has taken exceptional care in explaining the population statistics that are complicated and difficult to understand. The last section, The Indian Today, is interesting and hopeful, summarized in the following sentence: "North American Indian life remains complex and dynamic today as it continues to adapt and adjust to an ever-changing world." It is obviously not written by an American Indian; it paints the picture in broad strokes and much of importance is absent. The photographs in this chapter tend to portray today's Indian people in tribal settings (e.g., the powwow, by a traditional clay oven). It would have been more realistic and authentic to include Indians in professional settings and urban environments also. A descriptive overview of significant issues in Indian America should have been added to the text as well. Some readers will suspect that the author is Canadian or British and that he does not bring academic credentials to the task. For Americans, the expansion of the author's perspective can be viewed as a positive feature. His lack of academic credentials will undoubtedly be a problem for many scholars. However, as an amateur, he has pursued knowledge about American Indians throughout his lifetime and his writing reflects this commitment. School librarians will appreciate this book, especially the colorful maps, charts, and photographs. It is quite easy to be dazzled by the photography.

---

The 2nd edition appeared in 2014. Classification: LC E76; Dewey 970.

---

254. *Encyclopedia of American Indian Contributions to the World: 15,000 Years of Inventions and Innovations,* by Emory Dean Keoke and Kay Marie Porterfield

Publisher: Facts on File, New York, NY (2002)

Price: $65.00

Review by Karen D. Harvey—Associate Dean for Academic Affairs, University College, University of Denver, Denver, CO.

While this first-of-a-kind encyclopedia was written to provide accurate, accessible information for students and scholars, it was also written to correct a historical wrong that has heavily influenced the general perception of American Indians. In an enlightening preface, the authors of this reference discuss the harm done when the indigenous people of South America, Mesoamerica, and North America were historically portrayed as savages or primitives who were incapable of complex ideas or inventions. The label of "primitive" or "savage" was conveniently used to justify conquest and colonization. It should be noted that one of the authors is an enrolled member of the Standing Rock Sioux Nation and the other has worked as a reporter for an Indian newspaper. To be included in this volume, contributions needed to have originated in North, Meso-, or South America; been used by Indian people; and been in use for some time. Some entries that were invented independently in more than one part of the world are also included. The many challenges in compiling this reference are discussed, including the difficulty of determining the date of origination and discovering which tribe came up with the idea first. While the authors acknowledge that to create a definitive catalog of American Indian contributions would take more than one lifetime to accomplish, this encyclopedia provides a wealth of little-known information and is certainly a welcome beginning. For those who want to delve further into a particular topic, each entry provides a list of sources for further reading. The appendixes have been thoughtfully created for the user's convenience and include tribes organized by culture areas; maps of culture areas; a glossary; a chronology; a bibliography and suggestions for further reading; lists of entries by tribe, group, linguistic group, geographical culture area, and subject; and a general index.

Classification: LC E54; Dewey 970.

255. *Oxford Encyclopedia of Mesoamerican Cultures: The Civilizations of Mexico and Central America*, by David Carrasco, ed.

Publisher: Oxford University Press, New York, NY (2001)

Price: $395.00/set

Review by John R. Burch Jr.—Library Director, University of Tennessee at Martin.

Carrasco, Professor of the History of Religions and Director of the Raphael and Fletcher Lee Moses Mesoamerican Archive at Princeton University, and 343 other specialists have produced a multidisciplinary reference tool that surveys 4,000 years of Mesoamerican history and culture. Encompassing the present-day countries of Belize, El Salvador, and Guatemala—plus portions of Costa Rica, Honduras, Mexico, and Nicaragua—Mesoamerica has seen the rise and fall of many great civilizations, including those of the Aztec, Maya, and Olmec. This work contains more than 600 alphabetically arranged entries that range in length from 500 to 7,000 words. The entries are signed and include an annotated bibliography for further research. Unlike many subject encyclopedias, the entries are not preceded by an overview of the subject matter or a chronology. Those particular features can be found in the entries entitled "Mesoamerica: An Overview" and "Mesoamerican Chronology." Particularly useful is the "Synoptic Outline of Contents" found in volume 3 that organizes the individual entries under subject headings. Also found in the 3rd volume is a cumulative index. While this will be the definitive reference work on the subject for the foreseeable future, it complements the recently published *Archaeology of Ancient Mexico and Central America*, edited by Susan Toby Evans and David L. Webster. In fact, both Carrasco and Susan Toby Evans are listed as contributors for both encyclopedias. Those wishing to supplement the subject encyclopedias should consider a recently published handbook entitled *The Cambridge History of the Native Peoples of the Americas, Volume II: Mesoamerica*, edited by Richard E. W. Adams and Murdo J. MacLeod. All three titles are highly recommended for academic libraries supporting programs in anthropology, archaeology, history, Mesoamerican studies, and Native American studies. Public libraries needing one book on this topic should opt for the title under review.

Classification: LC F1218; Dewey 972.

## Latin America

256. *Encyclopedia of Contemporary Latin American and Caribbean Cultures*, by Daniel Balderston, Mike Gonzalez, and Ana M. López, eds.

Publisher: Routledge/Taylor & Francis Group, New York, NY (2000)

Price: $399.00

Review by Staff, Libraries Unlimited.

The editors of the *Encyclopedia of Contemporary Latin American and Caribbean Cultures* have set as their goal to recognize and define cultural events, sites, and monuments of Latin America and the Caribbean while at the same time explaining how they contribute to the historical and social make-up of the region. The set is well laid out, which makes it easy for quick reference as well as browsing. The book begins with a brief introduction; a guide on how to use the volumes; and a forty-five-page thematic entry list, which is arranged by broad subject categories such as country name, the arts, and religions. The main entries begin with a list of the decades (e.g., 1920s, 1930s, 1940s) and then begin the alphabetic listings of terms. Entries range from one to two paragraphs in length to several pages. Words in bold typeface within entries indicate the word has its own entry elsewhere in the set. Many entries provide lists for further reading, although not as many as one might hope. All entries are signed by the author who contributed. A list of contributors can be found at the beginning of volume 1 along with their country of origin and sometimes university affiliation. The entries are well written, although some are a bit brief. The set concludes with a brief two-page bibliography and well-done index. This scholarly set will be useful in academic libraries. Public libraries with a large Latin American clientele may also want to consider its purchase.

Classification: LC F1406; Dewey 972.

257. *Encyclopedia of Latin American Politics*, by Diana Kapiszewski and Alexander Kazan, eds.

Publisher: Oryx Press/Greenwood Publishing Group, Westport, CT (2002)

Price: $74.95

Review by Adrienne Antink, Medical Group Management Association, Lakewood, CO.

Many Americans have misconceptions about Latin American politics. Rather than international conflict and resolution, the norm is democratically elected leadership and cooperation between states. This collaborative tradition is evident in the appendix that summarizes the numerous political pacts, trade groupings, and international cooperative efforts that are characteristic of the region. The editor profiles the 18 Spanish-speaking republics as well as Brazil, Haiti, and Puerto Rico. Each country's chapter gives demographics as to governmental structures, population, ethnic groups, religion, literacy rates, infant mortality and life expectancy averages, exchange rates, major exports and imports, Gross Domestic Product, and more. These statistical data are followed by a summary of the nation's history and political development plus entries on key leaders, treaties, and other major events with more emphasis on the twentieth century. Each section ends with a list of the heads of states and the dates they served, a bibliography specific to that country, and a list of electronic resources. It is interesting to note that spurred by the French Revolution, Haiti was the second colony in the Americas to gain independence and that Panama was a province of Colombia until 1902. Appendixes include information on multilateral agreements and wars, U.S. doctrines regarding Latin America, a glossary, and an index. This reference is useful to clarify and raise awareness of the diverse political histories of the countries that make up Latin America and who are now significant players in the global economy.

English-speaking Belize is not included. Classification: LC F1410; Dewey 320.

## World History

For summaries of the recent history of world states, including events taking place after the publication date for historical encyclopedias, one can turn to relevant sections of handbooks such as *Statesman's Yearbook* (entry 135), *Europa World* (entry 136), or *Political Handbook of the World* (entry 137). For world historical statistics, see entries 223–225 in Chapter 2.

258. *The Encyclopedia of World History: Ancient, Medieval, and Modern, Chronologically Arranged*, by Peter N. Stearns and William L. Langer, ed.

Publisher: Houghton Mifflin Harcourt, New York, NY (2001)

Price: $59.95

Review by Allen Reichert—Electronic Access Librarian, Courtright Memorial Library, Otterbein College, Westerville, OH.

This highly readable encyclopedia chronicling world history was last revised nearly thirty years ago. Naturally, it had become dated, in terms of both historical trends and strict chronology. The new editor, Stearns, has admirably balanced the need to reflect new trends while maintaining the integrity of the original encyclopedia. Entries have been extended through the year 2000. Major changes are an increase in social history and an expansion of coverage outside Western Europe and North America. Further, the format has been slightly altered, with an overview of historic and global trends included at the beginning of each section. Entries were changed only when needed. A fine entry on the 1857–1858 Indian Rebellion was kept verbatim, but the entry on the Sino-Japanese War eliminated the preponderance of references to European and U.S. involvement. Sections on social history include a look at multiple Olympic Games and the development of cinema throughout the world. As with any revision, a few entries are no longer included, particularly from the West. . . . This encyclopedia is highly recommended.

Classification: LC D21; Dewey 902.

259. *New Dictionary of the History of Ideas*, by Maryanne Cline Horowitz, ed.

Publisher: Charles Scribner's Sons/Gale Group, New York, NY (2005)

Price: $695.00/set

Review by Melissa M. Johnson—Reference Services, NOVA Southeastern University, Alvin Sherman Library, Ft. Lauderdale, FL.

The *New Dictionary of the History of Ideas* (NDHI), a six-volume work, updates and expands the landmark *Dictionary of the History of Ideas*, which studied selected pivotal ideas. The NDHI includes ideas in government, philosophy, social science, anthropology, cultural studies, education, religion, science, literature, and psychology. This work strives to cross academic disciplines to explore the oral, visual, participatory, and textual processes communities use to communicate and inculcate ideas. Ideas are broken into four types: oral, visual, exponential, and textual. Spread throughout the texts are four hundred visual examples of the topics covered. The first volume contains a list of entries and an excellent essay on the historiography of ideas, which readers should find informative and a great introduction to the main work. After the essay and in each subsequent volume there is a "Reader's Guide" that breaks down all entries into sections based on geographical areas, chronological periods, liberal arts disciplines, and professions. This guide serves to connect entries and place them in the contexts of time and place that greatly helped the editor's goal of contributing to global education. This thorough and superb work has extensive entries in alphabetic order. The entries range from one page to several pages and include subentries based on geographical area when applicable. When subentries appear they have their own cross-references and bibliography. The main entries also include cross-listings, when needed, and bibliographies. Entries that have a strong historical component include bibliographies with primary and secondary source sections. Each entry is signed; this includes subentries. Entries are, overall, clearly written at a college/university level. The index takes up nearly half of the sixth volume and is easy to use while being extensive and thorough. The sixth volume also contains the list of international contributors, where they are from, and which articles they wrote. Sure to become a standard in reference collections this set will be a great addition to all academic and large public libraries. Although there are a couple of curious exclusions, such as no subentry for North America under colonialism, the overall work is excellent.

Classification: LC CB9; Dewey 903.

260. *Encyclopedia of Historical Treaties and Alliances*, by Charles L. Phillips and Alan Axelrod

Publisher: Facts on File, New York, NY (2001)

Price: $165.00/set

Review by Daniel K. Blewett—Reference Librarian, College of DuPage Library,
    College of DuPage, Glen Ellyn, IL.

The approach of this book "is to look at treaties as seminal documents that
help to illuminate their times and to explicate their historical significance
through an understanding of the circumstances in which they were created and
an assessment of their impact" (p. xii). All types of agreements are covered in
this new reference book: peace treaties and truces, trade and commercial agreements, annexations and territorial agreements, diplomatic and defense treaties,
and proclamations and declarations. Not only will readers find the well-known
peace treaties that ended World War II, but also the U.S.-U.S.S.R. "Hot Line"
Memorandum. The time period covered stretches from 3100 B.C.E. to the
"Vienna Declaration on Human Rights" (June 25, 1994). The set's chapters are
arranged by broad chronological period ("Age of Reason," "The World at War,"
and so on). Each individual treaty starts off with the date completed/ratified, the
signatories, and a very brief overview. This information is followed by a longer
historical background section, the terms of the treaty, the text of the agreement,
and the consequences of the treaty. Some treaties may have a couple of suggested
readings at the end of the entry; otherwise, a reader will have to turn to the bibliography. More related bibliographic citations at the end of the entries, plus
perhaps some maps, tables, and photographs, would have been helpful. The
length for some entries may only be a couple of pages, while others go on for
several pages. A table of contents and an alphabetic list of all the treaties covered,
along with page numbers, can be found at the beginning of each volume. At the
end of volume 2 there is a chronological list of the treaties that are mentioned in
this title. Since there are far too many treaties in existence (most of them dealing
with routine bureaucratic matters) for all of them to be included, only the more
important ones are found here. Although international in scope, there is a definite American flavor to this work. This title supplements the earlier *Treaties and
Alliances of the World* (Gale, 1990); *The Encyclopedia of the United Nations and International Agreements* (Taylor & Francis, 1985); and *The Major International Treaties
of the Twentieth Century: A History and Guide with Texts* (Routledge, 2001). Since
many of the more recent publications focus on the last century, a strength of the
item under review is that it goes farther back in history. Its price is certainly
reasonable given the amount of information included in the set. It is recommended for the reference collections of academic and large public libraries.

Notes. The set includes two volumes, *From Ancient Times to World War I*
and *From the 1920s to the Present*. The updated edition of 2006 adds 15
significant treaties from the years 1997–2003. Classification: LC KZ1160;
Dewey 341.

261. *The Greenwood Encyclopedia of Daily Life: A Tour through History from Ancient Times to the Present*, by Joyce E. Salisbury and Gregory S. Aldrete, eds.

Publisher: Greenwood Press/ABC-CLIO, Santa Barbara, CA (2004)

Price: $599.95/set

Sandra E. Fuentes Riggs—Librarian, Montgomery Library, Campbellsville University, Campbellsville, KY.

*The Greenwood Encyclopedia of Daily Life: A Tour through History from Ancient Times to the Present* presents a worldwide picture of daily life, throughout six time periods: "Ancient," "Medieval," "15th and 16th Centuries," "17th and 18th Centuries," "19th Century," and "the Modern World." The encyclopedia is organized thematically, which makes it an unusual resource when compared to a typical alphabetic encyclopedia structure. Reading the six-page "Tour Guide," or preface, is highly recommended to make the best use of the work's organization and content. "Concept compass" icons in the margins at the start of sections help to orient the reader. These compasses contain text that look like a cross between a website navigation menu and a flowchart. Shaded boxes indicate the reader's location between broader and narrower concepts or geographic/civilization subdivisions. At the beginning of each volume, there is a "Historical Overview" chapter. The historical overview section can be an extremely important resource. Maps are included in this section for the major civilizations covered in the volume. Not all civilizations are covered, or could possibly be covered, so it is helpful to get an idea of each volume's scope through the overview section. The work has a clean layout, with several black-and-white illustrations. As in any decision to follow a particular organizational scheme, there are tradeoffs of convenience. While many users will enjoy the highly readable theme organization, which is good for serendipitous browsing and general research on a culture, it is highly likely that users who need a specific question answered will be frustrated by the thematic approach. These users will have to depend on the cumulative index. There are some difficulties with the index entries. For example, at this reviewer's library a frequently asked question from undergraduate communication students is: "How did people communicate news and ideas before modern technology?" Since communication is not included as a daily life theme, this question must be answered from the index. This would be difficult for some users. Communication is indexed with the majority of pages from the later (more recent time periods) volumes. Only one listing, for aboriginal smoke signals, is given from volume 1, "The Ancient World." There is a note in the index, "See specific methods (e.g., telephones)." However, only one example of a specific method (telephones) is given, assuming that the user has an idea of terms to select. A list of cross-references in the index would have been helpful. If a user were to try "news," they would find no entry. If the user tried "newspapers" they would find listings beginning with the sixteenth century. A student would have to think about the word "printing" to find entries from the medieval period. On the other hand, the user with deeper knowledge of terms would still not find any entries for "broadsides" or "pamphlets," important methods of communication of ideas in North American colonial life. One final consideration is the value of the encyclopedia in comparison to individual purchases from the Greenwood Press Daily Life through History series, or the online version of Greenwood Daily Life Online. Consideration may include investigation into the reviews of these resources and a check of the title list from Greenwood Press, available at http://www.greenwood.com/. Individual book titles are about $49.95, and online access to a single title is $70.00. The online version of *The Greenwood Encyclopedia of Daily Life* contains the contents of the print encyclopedia, plus the contents of twenty-seven volumes of the Daily Life through History series. Overall, *The Greenwood Encyclopedia of Daily Life* is a valuable resource and is highly recommended for school and public libraries as well as for academic libraries primarily supporting undergraduate research. Again, give consideration to the other Greenwood Press options before making a final decision.

---

As noted, related titles from the same publisher offer narrower geographic and chronological coverage, such as *Daily Life in Renaissance Italy*. Classification: LC GT31; Dewey 390.

---

262. *International Encyclopedia of Women's Suffrage*, by June Hannam, Mitzi Auchterlonie, and Katherine Holden

Publisher: ABC-CLIO, Santa Barbara, CA (2000)

Price: $75.00

Review by Courtney L. Young—Reference Librarian, Beaver Campus Library, Penn State Beaver, Monaca.

This encyclopedia focuses on the leaders and organizations of suffrage movements around the world, from 1893 to 1997. The table of contents lists all the entries in alphabetic order. Personal entries are by surname, geographic entries by country, and organizations by name. A geographic or regional arrangement (North America, South America, Asia, Africa, Europe, and Australia) might have been easier for the user. The index is extremely useful and becomes more important with this arrangement. The table of contents is less useful; for example, it points to an entry for "Race and Ethnicity" that is two and a half pages long but, unlike the index, cannot point to other related entries. At the end of each entry is a cross-reference for related information. Brief references for further reading also follow the entry, with the full citation in the extensive bibliography. The cross-references included in the index are slightly different than the ones included at the end of the encyclopedic entry. A sampling of Web resources in English is included. The authors provide brief annotations for some of the sites. The majority of these sites are from the United States. Also handy is the chronology, briefly noting the year in which noted countries granted women the right to vote. All libraries would benefit from adding this encyclopedia to their collection; however, those concerned with the price will be able to locate much of this information in other women's history sources. If access to non-U.S. and European information is of interest, this resource should be more strongly considered.

---

Classification: LC JF851; Dewey 324.

---

263. *Encyclopedia of Children and Childhood in History and Society*, by Paula S. Fass, ed.

Publisher: Macmillan Reference USA/Gale Group, New York, NY (2004)

Price: $360.00/set

Review by Lorraine Evans—Instruction and Reference Librarian, Auraria Library, University of Colorado, Denver.

If childhood seems to be a floating and ill-defined construct in our current society, history will at least give us a context for understanding why. This encyclopedia will serve as a reference tool for those interested in the historical, anthropological, or wide-ranging sociocultural study of children, childhood, and youth. The 3 volumes and 445 articles provide a wealth of interesting material for the student or professional looking for information on childhood. The encyclopedia should be of particular interest to those in education or professions that involve an interaction with young people. The historical scholarship inherent in the articles is an important feature of this work. In articles on toys, disease, work, war, education, and play, for example, the reader will see a treatment of the historical elements that we may take for granted as either a part of childhood or something to protect children against. Images of the social and historical context of children are further and powerfully represented by examples of art from the era. Many articles feature an important artwork or image, enhancing not only the aesthetic of the volumes but the information provided and its presentation. These images are typically annotated with a short comment on the significance or message conveyed in the work. The organization of the encyclopedia provides efficient access to the content. Articles are in alphabetic order and cross-reference other related articles. An "Outline of Contents" provided in the first volume groups articles by topic. This will be helpful for readers needing all articles that fit in a general category. A comprehensive and detailed index in volume 3 provides further access to the article content. Of particular note is a section of the encyclopedia devoted to primary sources. This is not simply a bibliography of important works, but lengthy excerpts or entire reproductions of the works. In this section one can read letters from Theodore Roosevelt; poetry from Robert Louis Stevenson; excerpts or reprinted case law; The United Nations Declarations of the Rights of the Child, 1959; and sections of important papers from Sigmund Freud, G. Stanley Hall, Emile Zola, and others. This encyclopedia is both engaging to read and an excellent source for the professional or student. It is appropriate for all academic and large public libraries.

Classification: LC HQ767; Dewey 305.

264. *Propaganda and Mass Persuasion: A Historical Encyclopedia, 1500 to the Present*, by Nicholas J. Cull, David Culbert, and David Welch

Publisher: ABC-CLIO, Santa Barbara, CA (2003)

Price: $85.00

Review by John A. Drobnicki—Acting Chief Librarian, City University of New York–York College, Jamaica.

Arranged in alphabetic order, each of the over 250 articles in this volume is signed and includes references. In addition to the fact that the contributors are from a wide range of countries, the scope is intended to be global. Articles range in length from a few sentences to several pages, and cover individual countries (for example, Israel) and regions (Africa), specialized topics (environmentalism), events (the Vietnam War), and persons both well known (Leni Riefenstahl) and obscure (Lord Northcliffe), from 1500 to the present. Up-to-date topics include "Gulf War (2003)" and Osama bin Laden. Although there are entries on Englishmen such as the anti-Catholic Titus Oates and minister of information Max Beaverbrook, the legendary American FBI director J. Edgar Hoover is only briefly mentioned in the entry on "Drugs." A few other notable omissions are Charlie Chaplin, Walter Duranty (and the Ukrainian famine), Lyndon LaRouche, and the animal rights movement (including PETA). The entry for "Protocols of the Elders of Zion" does not mention that Russian historian Mikhail Lepekhine determined in 1999 that Mathieu Golovinski was the author of that notorious forgery. Other features of this book include an informative introductory essay titled "Propaganda in Historical Perspective," *see* and *see also* references, numerous black-and-white photographs, and an index. There is no overall bibliography. Nearly half of the articles in this volume are also covered (frequently with more depth) in *The Encyclopedia of Propaganda*, edited by Robert Cole (M. E. Sharpe, 1998), which contains over 500 entries as well as a filmography and bibliography.

Classification: LC HM1231; Dewey 303.

265. *Antisemitism: A Historical Encyclopedia of Prejudice and Persecution*, by Richard S. Levy, ed.

Publisher: ABC-CLIO, Santa Barbara, CA (2005)

Price: $185.00/set

Review by John A. Drobnicki—Acting Chief Librarian, City University of New York–York College, Jamaica.

This two-volume set contains over six hundred articles on antisemitic incidents (e.g., the Kielce Pogrom), persons both historical (e.g., Vincente Ferrer, a fourteenth-century Spanish priest) and current (e.g., David Duke, Louis Farrakhan), political groups and organizations (e.g., American Nazi Party, Liberty Lobby), publications (e.g., Protocols of the Elders of Zion), and twenty-eight countries/regions. Each signed article contains a bibliography and *see also* references, and many of the entries were written by recognized authorities on the subjects, such as Geoffrey Cocks on Psychoanalysis, Peter Hayes on German Big Business, Jeremy Jones on Australia, John T. Pawlikowski on several Roman Catholic topics, and Roni Stauber on both Holocaust denial and David Irving. Articles range in length from a few paragraphs to several pages; other features include numerous black-and-white photographs and illustrations, and an index. While several topics can elicit strong opinions among the public (e.g., Poland, Jedwabne, Popes Pius IX and XII), they are treated here with balance and objectivity. Although many of this book's entries are treated in historical, Judaica, and religious reference books, it is convenient to have them discussed in depth in one set. This well-written and thoroughly researched encyclopedia should become the standard reference source in the field.

*See also* entries 273 and 274, for works on the Holocaust. Classification: LC DS146; Dewey 305.

## Europe

Needless to say, there are numerous specific works covering the history and culture of each of the European states, and libraries will select those of greatest local interest.

266. *The Rise of the Medieval World, 500–1300: A Biographical Dictionary*, by Jana K. Schulman, ed.

Publisher: Greenwood Press/ABC-CLIO, Santa Barbara, CA (2002)

Price: $99.95

Review by Jim Millhorn—Head of Acquisitions, Northern Illinois University
    Libraries, DeKalb, IL.

This useful work compresses eight hundred years of (largely) European history into biographical entries of four hundred figures of the medieval period. As
one might expect, the focus is on the privileged few, such as royalty, nobles,
churchmen, and intellectuals. Where sources allow, however, one also finds a
smattering of women, Muslims, and Jews. The book opens with a brief sketch of
the overall period and is followed by a chronology. Individual entries are rarely
over two pages in length and generally cite one or two items in the attached bibliography. In other words, this is more of a ready-reference work than a source
for detailed, scholarly information. However, for those with only a passing
knowledge of the medieval period it is a good launching point. The work concludes with a solid name index and general index. This work is recommended
for undergraduate libraries.

> There is a companion volume: *The Late Medieval Age of Crisis and Renewal,*
> *1300–1500.* Classification: LC CT114; Dewey 940.

267. *Women in the Middle Ages: An Encyclopedia*, by Katharina M. Wilson and
    Nadia Margolis, eds.
Publisher: Greenwood Press/ABC-CLIO, Santa Barbara, CA (2004)
Price: $199.95/set
Review by Benet Steven Exton, St. Gregory's University Library, Shawnee, OK.

*Women in the Middle Ages* is a very good tool for research into the study of
women during the Middle Ages. This two-volume set is mainly an encyclopedia
of biographies of various women by a number of scholars from around the world.
The set also covers items or issues connected to women like dowry and dress.
The set mainly covers European women, but there are several entries about
women from the other continents. The person or topic is covered in a variety of
lengths. Each entry has a bibliography that covers primary and secondary
sources in various languages. Most entries have cross-references as well. The
illustrations are black and white and are a good visual aid to the set. At the end
of volume 2 is a general bibliography, an index, and a list of the contributors. At
the front of volume 1 is a list of entries, a guide to related topics, and directions
on how to use this set. *Women in the Middle Ages* provides researchers and students with biographies of many little-known women of the Middle Ages and also

provides bibliographies for more sources on this topic. This set is a much-needed addition to libraries of all kinds because it is a great tool for the study of women.

Classification: LC HQ1143; Dewey 305.

268. *Encyclopedia of European Social History from 1350 to 2000,* by Peter N. Stearns, ed.

Publisher: Charles Scribner's Sons/Gale Group, New York, NY (2001)

Price: $595.00/set

Review by Terri Tickle Miller—Slavic Bibliographer, Michigan State University Libraries, East Lansing.

This monumental work draws together contributions of nearly 170 scholars from all over the world to create a fascinating and long-overdue reference source for European social history. The encyclopedia is divided into broad topics of social history, including "Gender," "Social Protest," "Rural Life," and even "Methods and Theoretical Approaches." Within each topic are lengthy articles on related subjects by prominent scholars in the field; for example, within the topic of "Deviance, Crime and Social Control" are articles on crime, prostitution, witchcraft, banditry, juvenile delinquency and hooliganism, police, punishment, and madness and asylums. Many articles discuss historiography and sources related to the subject and frequently cover the subject itself over the period from about 1300 to the current time. Each article concludes with *see also* references to other articles in the encyclopedia as well as lengthy bibliographies on the topic. The first 5 volumes contain the historical essays along with numerous illustrations and occasional maps. Sidebars often contain translations of primary documents related to the subject or shorter articles that illustrate the historical concept being discussed. The beginning of each volume contains a general table of contents of each volume, plus an alphabetic table of contents that serves as a quick index. Volume 6 contains the very lengthy main index as well as biographical sketches pulled from various Gale publications, including *Contemporary Authors, Encyclopedia of World Biography,* and *Historical World Leaders.* The final volume also lists the contributors along with a short summary of their academic credentials. Bringing together articles from so many different scholars must have been a challenge for the editor, and some of the articles are not as thorough in their coverage as others, but the overall quality of the encyclopedia is superb. Each article is accessible to students and scholars alike. What is most impressive about the encyclopedia is that it brings together in reference form much of the incredible research done in the past 50 to 70 years by social historians seeking to discover and analyze the roles that ordinary people played in history—not necessarily the deeds of individuals but how everyday social behavior shaped the course of history. In presenting this, the encyclopedia goes beyond the role of mere reference book and acts as an essential guide to the field of social (and cultural) history as a whole. Most disappointing, however, is the biography section in volume 6. The content of this section seems to be a tacked-on addition that does not meld with the intent and scope of the first five volumes. Many of the biographical entries are of rulers, major thinkers, or important writers; more appropriate would be biographies of the leaders of popular movements or of reform movements about which social history is more concerned. While the biographical section includes some such leaders and reformers, the inclusion of a biography of Walt Disney, much less biographies of Ivan IV or Otto van Bismarck, seems strange choices in a reference book on European social history. This caveat aside, the *Encyclopedia of European Social History* is a superb guide to both the study of social history and the field of social history as a whole. It provides an excellent starting point for anyone studying or doing research in European history.

---

Classification: LC HN373; Dewey 306.

---

269. *The Oxford Dictionary of the Renaissance*, by Gordon Campbell

Publisher: Oxford University Press, New York, NY (2003)

Price: $150.00

Review by Christopher Baker—Professor of English, Armstrong Atlantic State University, Savannah, GA.

For libraries not wishing to purchase Grendler's six-volume *Encyclopedia of the Renaissance*, this dictionary is the best single-volume work on its subject. It supplants Thomas G. Bergin's *Encyclopedia of the Renaissance* (1987) by offering a wider variety of non-English listings and more extensive recommendations for further reading. Campbell defines his work as covering "a long Renaissance" (p. vii), generally extending from 1618 backwards to 1415, but varying according to national culture or topic (e.g., entries on "Dante in the Renaissance" and "Lope de Vega" who died in 1635). No one born after 1595 is included. Campbell, who wrote most of the four thousand entries himself with the aid of specialists, diminishes the space given to English topics (these are addressed in other Oxford University Press volumes), favoring the relatively neglected Spanish, Scandinavian, and Dutch and Central European cultures. Most entries contain a brief reference for further reading, either to a larger biographical resource such as the *Dictionary of National Biography* or to recent secondary scholarship. Frequent black-and-white illustrations enliven the text. Entries are introduced by a thematic index. Four appendixes include "Tables of Ruling Houses"; "Place Names in Imprints"; "Dates at which Cities, States and Territories in Europe Adopted the Gregorian Calendar"; and "Ligatures and Contractions in Renaissance Greek." Until such time as a single-volume reference work on the Renaissance with the scope of the *Oxford Dictionary of the Christian Church* is produced, Campbell's book will provide the most authoritative one-volume coverage of the period.

---

Classification: LC CB361; Dewey 940.

---

270. *Encyclopedia of the Enlightenment,* by Alan Charles Kors, ed.

Publisher: Oxford University Press, New York, NY (2003)

Price: $495.00/set

Review by Philip G. Swan—Head Librarian, Hunter College, School of Social Work Library, New York, NY.

The *Encyclopedia of the Enlightenment* is a new offering from Oxford University Press that will surely be the definitive reference source for this enormously important epoch for years to come. Divided into four volumes of approximately five hundred pages each, the encyclopedia consists of more than seven hundred articles, which examine Western society from the rise of Rene Descartes in the late seventeenth century to the fall of Napoleon in 1815. The first volume opens with an alphabetic list of articles, as well as a list of maps and a preface outlining the rationale of the encyclopedia by the editor. This is followed by an outstanding topical outline of articles that should be extremely helpful to researchers. Subsequent volumes include articles listed alphabetically, with the fourth volume concluding with an alphabetic subject index and a repeat of the topical outline of articles. Based on the topical outline, the encyclopedia is organized under four conceptual blocks: "Definitions and Interpretations of the Enlightenment"; "The Political Geography of the Enlightenment," which encompasses nations, states, cities, towns, demographics, linguistics, and European contact with other cultures; "The Agencies and Spaces of the Enlightenment," which encompasses books, journals, academies, salons, and social exchange; and "Enlightenment Thought and 18th Century Culture," which encompasses philosophy, the arts, economics, religion, politics, and biographies. Many articles include illustrations, ranging from portraits and engravings to illustrations of events and maps. All articles are signed by their author, with a directory of contributors in volume four providing further information on their academic affiliation as well as a list of articles for which they are responsible. Each article includes a comprehensive bibliography, many of which are annotated, as well as cross-references. The text is scholarly in tone and seems to assume some prior familiarity with the topic in question given the amount of references to terminology and individuals not found elsewhere within the encyclopedia. The text is printed on acid-free paper and the binding is high quality. This reviewer's only criticism of the encyclopedia lies in its relatively small number of maps. Given the amount of geopolitical turmoil covered in these volumes, six maps, most of them small and not printed in color, do not offer the reader as much information on this score as one would expect. Nevertheless, the *Encyclopedia of the Enlightenment* will be a valuable addition to any reference collection in public or academic libraries.

Classification: LC B802; Dewey 940.

271. *The Encyclopedia of Eastern Europe: From the Congress of Vienna to the Fall of Communism*, by Richard Frucht, ed.

Publisher: Garland, Hamden, CT (2000)

Price: $95.00

Review by John A. Drobnicki—Acting Chief Librarian, City University of New York–York College, Jamaica.

More than two hundred contributors have lent their expertise to this excellent reference volume. Each of the over one thousand alphabetically arranged articles, which range in length from several sentences to many pages, is signed and includes suggestions for further reading. Topics covered include major cities and geographic territories, historical events and concepts, political leaders, authors, literary works, political parties, trade unions, and prominent universities. Social and cultural subjects are also included, such as art, music, cinema, and women. Users are guided by *see* and *see also* references as well as a thorough index, and there are 16 black-and-white maps. As with any work of this size and scope, questions will be raised about omissions of both fact and content. For example, the Baltic countries, which have historic ties to the region, are not included, and the article on Slovak nationalist leader Andrej Hlinka fails to mention anything about either his or his party's anti-Semitism. Although there are long articles on each country, it would have been more convenient if all the relevant articles were grouped together. For example, to use Poland as an illustration, both "Polish Culture" and "Polish Literature" appear under "P," but "Communist Party of Poland" and "Economic Development in Poland" appear, respectively, in "C" and "E," which does not facilitate browsing. This volume provides much more information (for a longer time period) than Joseph Held's *Dictionary of East European History Since 1945* and belongs in all reference collections.

Classification: LC DJK6; Dewey 947.

272. *Encyclopedia of Russian History*, by James R. Millar, ed.

Publisher: Macmillan Reference USA/Gale Group, New York, NY (2004)

Price: $475.00/set

Review by D. Barton Johnson—Professor Emeritus of Russian, University of California, Santa Barbara.

This four-volume encyclopedia meets the need for a thorough, up-to-date reference work on Russian history. None of the existing works brings together such breadth, currency, and depth of expertise. This durable, handsome, well-illustrated set provides nearly 1,600 entries written by over 500 scholars. The 250 to 5,000 word articles range from the Caucasian ethnic group "Abkhazians" to "Zyuganov," head of the revived Communist Party. The set is aimed at the general reader rather than the specialist. The prefatory material includes a "List of Articles" and an "Outline of Contents." The former is useful for the casual reader who may be uncertain as to what heading he or she should consult; for example, while there is no entry for "Anti-Semitism," the articles on "Jews" or "Cosmopolitanism" may be helpful, as will the former's cross-references to "Tsarist Pale" and "Pogrom." The contents outline provides a broad listing of articles broken down 21 subject categories, some further subdivided by time periods. The reader can thus conveniently locate nearly all articles in a given subject area, such as Agriculture or Political Policy, although not all relevant entries are included (i.e., the writers Bunin and Bulgakov are not listed in the category "Literature," although they are the subjects of articles). Apart from "Historical Events and People," the largest subject categories are "Economics," "Military," and "Regions, Nations, and Nationalities," while cultural subjects receive less attention. Both the historical role and cultural achievements of the Russian emigration are underrepresented. Some of the gaps are offset by the final index, which directs the readers to topics scattered within other articles. The otherwise satisfactory index cites only page numbers, without volume numbers, leaving the reader to guess which of the consecutively page numbered volumes to consult. The encyclopedia's greatest strength is the quality and timeliness of the articles, which include information as recent as 2003. Readers of the daily press will find succinct descriptions of the small ethnic groups and nationalities that have come into the news with the breakup of the Soviet Union. Up-to-date bibliographies are attached to each entry, although they are restricted to English-language publications. Concern for nonspecialist readers is also shown in the transliteration of Russian names and terms as found in publications such as *The New York Times* rather than in arcane academic systems. Also useful is the short guide to Russian abbreviations and acronyms. The numerous illustrations are supplemented by sections of colored photographs in each volume devoted to "Architecture and Landscape," "Arts," "Peoples," and "Power and Technology."

---

Classification: LC DK14; Dewey 947.

---

273. *The Columbia Guide to the Holocaust*, by Donald Niewyk and Francis Nicosia

Publisher: Columbia University Press, New York, NY (2000)

Price: 45.00

Review by John A. Drobnicki—Acting Chief Librarian, City University of New York–York College, Jamaica.

With so many new books on the Holocaust published every year, authors and editors are attempting to distinguish their works by offering features different from the rest. Such is the case with this volume by historians Niewyk and Nicosia, which consists of several valuable books in one. The authors begin by offering a well-written historical overview of the Holocaust, before moving into a balanced discussion of controversies and interpretations on topics such as intentionalists and functionalists, Jewish resistance, and bystanders and perpetrators. The 3rd section is a chronology covering 1918 to 1993, while the 4th is an encyclopedia providing information on 54 people, 41 places, 59 terms, and 29 organizations, which (due to obvious space constraints) is much too small to cover all the requisite persons and terminology. For example, there are no entries for either Martin Bormann or Rudolf Hess. The volume's 5th section is a valuable 150-page guide to resources (subdivided by subject headings), consisting of annotated bibliographies of both print and electronic materials (including primary and secondary sources, selected music recordings, and websites); an annotated filmography; and a list of Holocaust-related organizations, museums, and memorials, which provides addresses, telephone and fax numbers, and e-mail and URL addresses. Finally, there are 2 appendixes containing tables of statistics and 11 black-and-white maps, as well as an overall index. Because this book is a combination of monograph, dictionary, encyclopedia, and handbook, it is not fair to compare it with other books, since it obviously will not cover as many persons and events as Jack R. Fischel's *Historical Dictionary of the Holocaust*, or contain as many entries as Israel Gutman's *Encyclopedia of the Holocaust* or the *Dictionary of the Holocaust: Biography, Geography, and Terminology* by Eric Joseph Epstein and Philip Rosen. Nevertheless, it is an impressive volume, and the authors have succeeded in providing a handy 1-volume, multipurpose guide to the Holocaust.

Classification: LC D804; Dewey 940.

274. *The Holocaust Encyclopedia*, by Walter Laqueur and Judith Tydor Baumel, eds.

Publisher: Yale University Press, New Haven, CT (2001)

Price: $60.00

Review by John A. Drobnicki—Acting Chief Librarian, City University of New York—York College, Jamaica.

Of the approximately 310 articles in this massive volume, 193 are unsigned, giving brief factual information in a few sentences, usually on persons or places. The remaining articles (117) are long (often several pages in length) and scholarly, providing both historical overviews and current interpretations. The editors have assembled a truly distinguished group of 95 contributors who are recognized authorities, including Raul Hilberg on Auschwitz, Gerhart M. Riegner on the Riegner Telegram, Michael Burleigh on racism, Richard Breitman on American policy, James E. Young on Holocaust literature, and Henry Friedlander on euthanasia. Articles that frequently elicit controversy (e.g., Red Cross, Catholic Church, Polish-Jewish relations) are presented in a fair and balanced way, and entries on current topics (e.g., restitution, Holocaust denial) are up-to-date. Numerous archival photographs and maps enhance the text, and readers are guided by *see* references. Although individual articles do not contain references or suggested readings, there is a valuable bibliographic essay by Robert Rozett, and other features include a chronology (1933–1945) and an index. Except for the article on Hitler, many of the biographical entries are surprisingly short, such as Himmler (only 5 sentences). Omissions are expected in any work of this size but do not mar its value. This is a worthy 1-volume successor to Israel Gutman's 4-volume *Encyclopedia of the Holocaust*.

Classification: LC D804; Dewey 940.

## Africa

275. *Encyclopedia of African History*, by Kevin Shillington, ed.

Publisher: Routledge/Taylor & Francis Group, New York, NY (2005)

Price: $495.00/set

Review by Benet Steven Exton, St. Gregory's University Library, Shawnee, OK.

The *Encyclopedia of African History*, a three-volume set, is full of historical information about Africa. It covers the earliest days of Africa to the present. The editor, Kevin Shillington, has brought together many international scholars on African history to create this encyclopedia. There are articles about countries, the past and present, peoples, cities, places, and many other topics connected with Africa. The articles vary in length. Topics of importance have more than two articles on it. The writing styles of the articles make them easy to read. There are many cross-references and further reading references, which are not only in English. There are a lot of black-and-white illustrations. There are also several shaded maps. The maps of countries could have used a symbol to designate the capital. Each volume starts off with the thematic list of entries. The index to the set is in volume 3. This set is an excellent addition to any library's African collection. Do not get this set mixed up with the revised edition of the *Encyclopedia of African History and Culture* from Facts on File [2005].

*Africana* (entry 245) covers the history of both Africa and African Americans. Classification: LC DT20; Dewey 960.

276. *Encyclopedia of African Peoples*, by the Diagram Group

Publisher: Facts on File, New York, NY (2000)

Price: $55.00

Review by Georgia Briscoe—Associate Director and Head of Technical Services, Law Library, University of Colorado, Boulder.

This eye-catching resource on African cultures, history, and geography offers users information on more than one thousand ethnic groups and all fifty-three countries in Africa. The arrangement of the text is somewhat confusing because it is not one large alphabetic listing but has four main sections, some alphabetic and some not. Preceding these sections are ten pages of maps and explanations dividing Africa into five geographic areas: North, East, West, Central, and Southern. Section one, "The Peoples of Africa," comprises most of the book, with two hundred pages of alphabetically arranged descriptions of the continent's ethnic groups. According to the foreword, "ethnic group" is used to refer to people who are linked by a common language, history, religion, and cultural and artistic legacy. The coverage is often detailed. For example, the four-page entry for Maasai includes two maps, a timeline, and paragraphs on history, language, ways of life, industry, tourism, housing, diet, clothing, social structure, religion, and dancing. There are excellent illustrations: shield designs, cattle branding, cattle breeding, implements, children and adults in traditional costume, and battle dress of the Maasai. Cross-references are well supplied. When ethnic groups in this book are compared to the *Encyclopedia Britannica*, some offer more detail but some offer less, and sometimes with differing information. Section two, "Culture and History," offers a more "almanac" approach, with a hodgepodge of interesting and fun details including pictorial histories and chronologies for each of the five African geographic areas. A historical area spotlights entries like "Birthplace of Humanity," "Christianity in Ethiopia," and four pages on "Apartheid." Section three, "The Nations," is a fact sheet for each of the fifty-three countries. Section four, "Biographies," gives short paragraphs (alphabetically arranged) on three hundred famous Africans. An improved glossary and index would make this handsome book even handier.

Classification: LC DT15; Dewey 305.

## The Middle East

Chapter 4 "Humanities" includes additional resources about the development of the Middle East and Israel, including associated religious traditions.

277. *Encyclopedia of the Modern Middle East and North Africa*, by Philip Mattar

Publisher: Macmillan Reference, Detroit, MI (2004)

Price: $425.00

Review by Steven W. Sowards—Associate Director for Collections, Michigan State University Libraries, East Lansing.

In its 2nd edition, this four-volume set covers politics, history, geography, languages, economics, religion, society, culture and literature in twenty-three countries from Mauritania in the west to Iran and Afghanistan in the east, and from Turkey in the north to Yemen and the Sudan in the south; as well as aspects of regional ethnic groups without separate states of their own, such as the Druze, the Kurds, and the Palestinians. Expanded and updated since the 1996 edition, the set has more than three thousand articles, including some seven hundred short biographies. Revisions since the 1st edition of 1996 pay attention to the status of women as well as recent events, such as the U.S. military interventions in Afghanistan and Iraq. The editor is not shy about sensitive topics such as the behavior of terrorist groups, anti-Semitism, the Armenian genocide, female genital mutilation, the arms trade, and the slave trade. Written for an American audience, the set emphasizes developments in high-profile states such as Israel and Palestine, Lebanon, Egypt, Iran, Iraq, Syria, and Turkey (including the later periods of the Ottoman Empire outside Europe). Articles also discuss the involvement of major powers from outside the region such as the United States, the Soviet Union/Russia, Pakistan, and the United Nations. Napoleon's invasion of Egypt in 1798 arguably began the modern era in the Middle East: this work covers events in the nineteenth and twentieth centuries, and up to 2004. Notable attention is paid to gender issues; regional and local organizations; the Arab-Israeli conflict; and culture and society, with articles on camels, food, films, newspapers and print media, and radio and television. The articles are supported by suggested readings; cross-references; a detailed three-hundred-page index; a glossary of Arabic, Persian, and Turkish terms; outline lists of entries by topic and alphabetically; forty maps and some black-and-white illustrations; a list of some four hundred scholarly contributors; and genealogies of key families and dynasties in Morocco, Kuwait, Saudi Arabia, Yemen, Bahrain, Egypt, Persia/Iran, and the Ottoman Empire.

---

For coverage of earlier periods and traditions, the *Encyclopaedia of Islam* (Brill, 1954–1993) remains a crucial source. Classification: LC DS43; Dewey 956.

---

278. *The Oxford Encyclopedia of the Islamic World*, by John L. Esposito, ed.

Publisher: Oxford University Press, New York, NY (2009)

Price: $635.00/set

Review by Muhammed Hassanali—Independent Consultant, Shaker Heights, OH.

*The Oxford Encyclopedia of the Islamic World* (OEIW) is meant to expand on the coverage that its predecessor, *The Oxford Encyclopedia of the Modern Islamic World* (OEMIW), provided. The preface states that "OEIW represents a substantial expansion of OEMIW. . . . It includes not only OEMIW's coverage of Muslim societies and communities in the modern world (from the eighteenth century to the present), but also extensive coverage of religious and historical background extending back to the beginnings of Islam" (xxi). The five major categories—Islamic thought and practice, Islam and politics, Muslim communities and societies, Islam and society, and Islamic studies—which are the focus of OEMIW, have expanded to thirteen distinct categories listed in the preface. Before the alphabetized entries is a chronology that starts with the birth of the Prophet Muhammad in 570 C.E. and ends with terrorists taking over luxury hotels in Mumbai in November 2008. Following the alphabetized entries is a topical outline of entries that lists the alphabetized entries in the thirteen categories outlined in the preface. The thirteen main categories are further subdivided into additional categories for ease of reference. Next is a directory of contributors followed by an index. OEIW maintains the contemporary bias characteristic of OEMIW by laying greater emphasis on context as opposed to texts. Its approach is of exploring how Muslims live their faith with the pressures of local culture, beliefs, and practices. Most articles follow a general two-part structure: a short historical summary followed by a more extensive analysis of the contemporary situation. While the encyclopedia intends to provide worldwide geographical coverage, the coverage is uneven. Like other such reference works, OEIW has its share of entries that are less than satisfactory; however, most entries are well written and insightful. Surprisingly, most of the references listed are in English. The strongest aspect of OEIW is its extensive treatment of Islamic movements, parties, and brotherhoods. However, as the encyclopedia is not designed to be as detailed as *The Oxford Encyclopedia of the Modern Islamic World*, it will serve well to orient serious scholars looking up subjects outside their range of expertise. Overall, it is a valuable resource for both the specialist and the general reader. I would recommend it to not only libraries, but also individuals engaged in serious research on contemporary Islam and Muslims.

---

Classification: LC DS35; Dewey 909.

---

279. *Historical Dictionary of Iraq*, by Beth K. Dougherty and Edmund A. Ghareeb
Publisher: Scarecrow, Lanham, MD (2014)
Price: $150.00
Review by Joe P. Dunn—Charles A. Dana Professor of History and Politics, Converse College, Spartanburg, SC.

I have reviewed several of the historical dictionaries in this series, and they are outstanding works. This timely volume is no exception. The scope covers the long span of history from ancient Mesopotamia through 2013, with attention to ethnic, religious, political, and ideological groups; individuals; cultural elements; and much more. Besides the hundreds of well-crafted entries, the volume includes a lengthy chronology, maps (including a tribal area breakdown), a fine historical essay, and several useful appendixes. The appendixes include the structures and individuals of political leadership since 1920 and the important Iraqi individuals, organizations, and election results from 2005 to 2013. The general bibliography and an extensive topical bibliography are both quite good. This edition has considerably more entries than the last edition published in 2004, and the bibliography has also been significantly expanded. The compiler, Edmund Ghareeb, is a leading scholar of Kurdish Studies and a prolific author on many aspects of the region. Beth Dougherty specializes in ethnic conflict and human rights. Iraq will continue to be in the forefront for many years to come, and this source will be a valuable one for libraries to have available.

As noted, Scarecrow Press (now part of the Rowman & Littlefield Publishing Group) produces a long list of historical dictionaries for countries of the world: this example is widely owned. Classification: LC DS70; Dewey 956.

## Asia and Australia

Relative to size, population, economic power, and growing global significance, reference works on the history and culture of this region seem underrepresented in American libraries. Interest in Japan—and associated reference publishing—was greatest prior to 2000, through works such as the *Cambridge Encyclopedia of Japan* (1993).

280. *Encyclopedia of Modern Asia*, by David Levinson and Karen Christensen, eds.

Publisher: Charles Scribner's Sons/Gale Group, New York, NY (2002)

Price: $695.00/set

Review by Kay Stebbins Slattery—Coordinator Librarian, Louisiana State University, Shreveport.

The *Encyclopedia of Modern Asia* began in 1998 with a goal to become the standard reference on modern Asia, and with the September 11th attack on the World Trade Center igniting world interest in Asia, the publication is very timely. The six-volume set is alphabetically arranged by topic. Volume 6 provides the index for the set. Maps for the region described are grouped in the front of the volume. Unique to the set is a "Reader's Guide" arranged by topic. The topics cover the thirty-three Asian countries' geography, economics, politics, human rights, cultures and languages, and biographies. Sidebars derived from primary source materials and black-and-white illustrations are interspersed throughout the text. This new encyclopedia has been published at an important time in world history. This is a must-purchase for academic and public libraries' Asian collections.

Classification: LC DS4; Dewey 950.

281. *Encyclopedia of Modern China*, by David Pong, ed.
Publisher: Gale/Cengage Learning, Farmington Hills, MI (2009)

Price: $495.00/set

Review by Ma Lei Hsieh—Librarian, Rider University, Lawrenceville, NJ.

The *Encyclopedia of Modern China* encompasses a scholarly assessment of China from the late nineteenth century to the present on a wide variety of topics. This encyclopedia includes biographies of prominent people who have shaped China's political, social, economic, artistic, literary, and cultural history. The authors re-examine the historical and cultural impacts of these significant figures in relation to modern China and the world. Major philosophies, geographies, social and foreign relationships, and topics on daily life such as family, marriage, friendship, medicine, education, and cultural trends are interpreted from both traditional and modern perspectives. The entries in the four volumes provide a comprehensive overview and new insight that allows readers to shape their own understanding and opinions about contemporary China. The essays are well written with references for each entry. Valuable features include a section of primary sources, some of which are being translated to English for the first time. A brief introduction accompanies each primary source referencing the historical context. Many maps, charts, and valuable historical and current photographs further enhance the volumes. Other helpful features include a detailed index, a chronology of Chinese history since 1800 paralleled to world events, and a glossary of transliteration of Chinese and the Romanized names, places, and special terms. As China has rapidly developed into a major global force since the 1980s, the *Encyclopedia of Modern China* is an essential reference on contemporary China. This set is highly recommended for all libraries.

> The *ALA Guide to Researching Modern China* by Yunshan Ye (2014) can open the door to additional resources on a wide range of subjects. Classification: LC DS755; Dewey 951.

282. *India Today: An Encyclopedia of Life in the Republic*, by Arnold P. Kaminsky and Roger D. Long, eds.

Publisher: ABC-CLIO, Santa Barbara, CA (2011)

Price: $189.00/set

Review by Ravindra Nath Sharma—Dean of Library, Monmouth University Library, West Long Branch, NJ.

India is the birth place of four major religions of the world—Hinduism, Buddhism, Jainism, and Sikhism. Over 1 billion people live in this secular country, and it is the most successful parliamentary democracy in the world. India became an independent and free country in 1947 and has made good progress in many aspects of life since independence from the British. The book under review is a 2-volume encyclopedia that deals with the progress since 1947. It includes 250 articles written by 80 scholars arranged alphabetically A to Z. They are all signed articles from 300 words to 5,000 words and include many cross-references as well as lists of further reading. Both volumes have many black-and-white photographs, illustrations, and maps. Volume 2 has an extensive bibliography for further research. The entries cover many good topics including politics, religion, cities, states, biographies of many politicians and other prominent leaders, and social and economic aspects of modern India since 1947. The encyclopedia also has a selected chronology of events in the country since independence and a topic finder. According to the editors India is one of the most remarkable, diverse, and fascinating countries in the world, and they have proved it by including very selective entries to educate readers. They have provided a very good research tool for scholars. This encyclopedia is recommended very highly for all types of library collections that serve students, researchers, and scholars.

---

Classification: LC DS428; Dewey 954.

---

283. *The Australian People: An Encyclopedia of the Nation, Its People and Their Origins*, by James Jupp

Publisher: Cambridge University Press, New York, NY (2001)

Price: $234.00

Review by Steven W. Sowards—Associate Director for Collections, Michigan State University Libraries, East Lansing.

As an encyclopedia of Australian history, culture, and society, this work adopts the peopling of the continent as an organizing principle. From the origins of the indigenous Aboriginal population through the settlement of Europeans in the eighteenth and nineteenth centuries to today's phenomenon of global migration, there have been issues of immigration, multiculturalism, national identity, and ethnic diversity that are central to Australia's development. This revised edition is based on a work published in 1988 for the Australian bicentennial, updated with information from the 1996 census, and relies on contributions from some 250 experts. Part I summarizes "the Peopling of Australia" during the last 50,000 years, including evidence about the Aboriginal presence, the notorious transportation of convicts from Great Britain, subsequent settlement by both Europeans and non-Europeans, and the reception of refugee populations from World War II to the present. Part II is a lengthy section on the history, society, culture, and legal status of the Aboriginal population. Part III is the longest: a series of entries in alphabetical order on the origins, experiences and contributions of more than 120 immigrant nationalities. Some segments are quite long (particularly those about the English and the Irish), while others have a few paragraphs (for example, on Bengalis, Brazilians, and Tibetans). Part IV is a final section on nation building, citizenship, concepts of assimilation and integration, and the role of race. Seven graphs, 44 maps, and 51 tables support the text, as do many black-and-white or color illustrations, often illustrating aspects of ethnic culture. Appendixes offer figures from the 1996 census about overseas origins, languages spoken, and religious affiliation. There is a chronology from prehistoric times to 2001 (and especially since 1788), and a bibliography of works on relevant issues and various specific ethnic groups. There is a short index of selected terms that might be overlooked while browsing.

---

Classification: LC DU120; Dewey 994.

---

## Military History

Publishers have responded to reader interest with numerous publications, often on very specific topics. An ABC-CLIO series edited by Spencer C. Tucker covers essentially all of America's wars (not all titles are listed here): these works are prominent in the market and are found on many library shelves. Their quality is high, so this "monopoly" should not be a concern.

284. *The Oxford Companion to Military History*, by Richard Holmes, ed.
Publisher: Oxford University Press, New York, NY (2001)
Price: $60.00
Review by Staff, Libraries Unlimited.

This companion to military history provides basic background information for the social, political, technological, and economical history of world wars from Classical times to the present. This is an ambitious project and one that has been well done. There are more than 1,300 entries prepared by some 150 contributors, most of whom are professors at European universities. The entries generally run a half page to one page in length. Some topics, however, are given more in-depth treatment (8 to 10 pages) and are highlighted. These include the topics of air power, guerrilla warfare, peacekeeping, siege warfare, naval power, and uniforms, to name a few. The more than 70 black-and-white maps that illustrate famous battles and campaigns add significantly to the text. A few illustrations of weapons can be found scattered throughout the text as well. Missing from this work that would have improved its usefulness as a reference source are cross-references and lists for further reading. An index concludes the volume. This will be a useful work in undergraduate university libraries.

Classification: LC D25; Dewey 355.

285. *Encyclopedia of the American Civil War: A Political, Social, and Military History*, by David S. Heidler, Jeanne T. Heidler, and David J. Coles, eds.

Publisher: ABC-CLIO, Santa Barbara, CA (2000)

Price: $425.00/set

Review Donald E. Collins—Associate Professor, History Department, East Carolina University, Greenville, NC.

This impressive new encyclopedia should become a standard source for students, specialists, and others in the general public who either specialize in or are simply fascinated by the American Civil War. Some 300 historians cover political, social, and military aspects of the war in 1,600-plus signed articles. These are enhanced by *see also* references to other pertinent articles and lists of further reading. Primary source documents, maps, photographs, and other illustrations are abundant and well chosen. A lengthy bibliography adds to the value, while an extensive subject index ensures easy access to the massive contents. The editors and their editorial board are all nationally known historians, while experts in their particular areas write the signed articles. The alphabetically organized essays cover a surprisingly broad and inclusive range of subjects. Pertinent pre- and postwar articles provide users with information on such far-ranging topics as the Lost Cause Movement, national elections, the Ostend Manifesto, the Sand Creek Massacre, the Medal of Honor, foreign governments and their relationship to the war, state histories, women and women soldiers, medicine, specific weapon types and battles, German Americans and other immigrant groups, and a large number of biographical articles. Volume 5 operates independently of the four-volume alphabetic encyclopedia. Approximately one-half is devoted to separate Union and Confederate lists of officials of the respective governments and members of their congresses; addresses and telephone numbers of Civil War sites administered by the National Park Service; state-by-state battlefield location maps; a chronology of the war; a glossary of terms; an extensive bibliography of Civil War books; and a detailed subject index to the entire set. The first one-half of the volume is comprised of an excellently chosen collection of original source documents related to all aspects of the Confederate and Union governments, armies, military engagements, and to such miscellaneous topics as medicine, music, religion, prisoners of war, civil liberties, emancipation, and guerilla warfare. As a single example, the surgeon's report on the emaciated condition of former Confederate President Jefferson Davis following a year in virtual solitary confinement is important and fascinating. As a Civil War historian, this reviewer is both impressed and pleased with this new work. Few things are without criticism, however, and this is no exception. In any work with 300 authors, the quality of the articles varies with the writers. Two articles, "Southern Unionism" and "Unionists, Southern," by the same historian, are too similar not to have been merged into one. Had their titles not been transposed, thus separating them, this would have been glaringly evident. And while it is laudable to include relatively small engagements as individual articles, one wonders why others were ignored. The Confederate siege of Washington, North Carolina, which made national headlines for three weeks is a single example. A more serious omission is the total exclusion of articles or even minor references to the total or any one of the 85 Union army regiments recruited from among the white population of the Confederacy. Such units were formed in every Confederate state but South Carolina. A much lesser point is that the article on the Battle of Fort Anderson on the Cape Fear River is omitted from the battle map of North Carolina, while a different Fort Anderson on the Neuse River, which had only minor skirmishing, is shown. Such problems are to be expected, however, in a project of this scale and should be considered minor. This is an important work that is highly recommended for any and all libraries and individuals with an interest in the American Civil War.

Classification: LC E468; Dewey 973.

286. *Women during the Civil War: An Encyclopedia*, by Judith E. Harper

Publisher: Routledge/Taylor & Francis Group, New York, NY (2007)

Price: $135.00

Review by Helene Androski—Reference Librarian, University of Wisconsin-Madison.

This 1-volume encyclopedia by Judith E. Harper (credentials not given) claims to offer a panoramic view of the lives and contributions of women regarding all aspects of the American Civil War. The 128 entries bear up the claim. The usual major names—Clara Barton, Dorothea Dix, Julia Ward Howe, and Harriet Jacobs—are represented, but there are also entries for relatively unknown but significant and interesting women, such as Elizabeth Van Lew, who ran an operation of women and African American spies for the Union behind enemy lines in the Richmond area, and Fanny Fern, who was the first salaried newspaperwoman to write a regularly published opinion column (in the *New York Ledger*). There are also entries on categories of women (e.g., military women, Catholic nuns, prostitutes, immigrants), organizations (e.g., Contraband Relief Association), events (e.g., draft riots), and issues (e.g., courtship and marriage, guerilla war) to give a wide-ranging view on how the war affected women's lives and how they affected the war. The A-Z entries are supplemented by a glossary; an extensive but unfortunately unannotated, uncategorized bibliography; and an index. Each entry also has cross-references to other entries and a short list of suggested readings. The writing is accessible and lively, making this a good research tool for the general reader and college student as well as a contribution to an area of scholarship that still needs much more research.

Classification: LC E628; Dewey 973.

287. *World War I: Encyclopedia*, by Spencer C. Tucker and Priscilla Mary Roberts, eds.
Publisher: ABC-CLIO, Santa Barbara, CA (2005)
Price: $485.00/set
Review by Helene Androski—Reference Librarian, University of Wisconsin-Madison.

This is another in a series of encyclopedias on major wars published by ABC-CLIO and edited by Spencer Tucker, and a fine addition it is. It is rich in features: four volumes of A-Z entries covering both battlefronts and homefronts as well as individual biographies and art and literature; several sidebars examining historical controversies, such as the performance of African American troops; a fifth volume of the texts of nearly two hundred documents; a set of general maps included in each volume plus maps within entries for easy reference; numerous photographs; overview essays on the origins, conduct, and legacy of the war; an extensive general bibliography; a month-by-month chronology; a glossary; an index; a historiography on recent trends in research and interpretation; and an annotated selective list of Victoria Cross and Medal of Honor recipients. The list of contributors and the entries reflect a comprehensive scope. There are entries on subjects not well covered in more traditional surveys, such as the role of and impact on children and women and the war in Asia and Africa. Although, of necessity, the entries are short (three pages on the homefront in Britain hardly do justice to the topic), they are supplemented by *see also* references and suggestions for further reading. This encyclopedia is not only an excellent reference source for secondary and undergraduate students and the general reader, but its many special features make it a useful starting point for advanced researchers. It is highly recommended for public and academic libraries.

The same five-volume set sometimes appears as *Encyclopedia of World War I: A Political, Social, and Military History*. The 2nd edition appeared in 2014, under the title *World War I: The Definitive Encyclopedia and Document Collection*. The same editor and publisher produced the multivolume set *World War I: A Student Encyclopedia* in 2005 and the single-volume *World War I: The Essential Reference Guide* in 2016. Classification: LC D510; Dewey 940.

288. *World War II: The Definitive Encyclopedia and Document Collection*, by Spencer C. Tucker, ed.

Publisher: ABC-CLIO, Santa Barbara, CA (2016)

Price: $520.00/set

Review by Bradford Lee Eden—Dean of Library Services, Valparaiso University, Valparaiso, IN.

This five-volume tome is a revision of the five-volume 2004 title—*Encyclopedia of World War II: A Political, Social, and Military History*—by the same editor. This revised edition has added over two hundred new entries, and most of the 2004 entries have been revised and their bibliographies updated. Besides the excellent essays, there are a number of additional features detailed in the foreword and preface. Volume 1 includes some general maps, along with overview essays on the origins of World War II, a summary of World War II, and the legacy of World War II. Volume 4 includes information on medals and decorations, military organization, selected belligerents, chronology, glossary, overall bibliography, and a list of editors and contributors. Finally, volume 5 contains numerous important primary source documents related to World War II. There are numerous maps, black-and-white photos, charts, and tables interspersed throughout. This reference work is the definitive work on the subject of World War II; it should be included in any reference collection from high school up through university libraries.

The 2004 first edition was published as *Encyclopedia of World War II: A Political, Social, and Military History*. Also worth noting are the *Simon & Schuster Encyclopedia of World War II* (1978) and the *Oxford Companion to World War II* (1995). Classification: LC D740; Dewey 940.

289. *World War II in Numbers: An Infographic Guide to the Conflict, Its Conduct, and Its Casualties*, by Peter Doyle

Publisher: Firefly Books, New York, NY (2013)

Price: $29.95

Review by Scott R. DiMarco—Director of Library Services and Information Resources, Mansfield University, Mansfield, PA.

The numbers of sources that simply quantify historical facts are few and far between. Peter Doyle provides in this unique book a resource that is not only useful, but attractive to the reader. Designed "as a perfect companion for serious enthusiasts . . . a fact-filled visual exploration for general readers," it tells the story of World War II in an original way by using infographics to convey the mass of data that can be derived from all aspects of the conflict. In this effort the author is successful. Divided into six chapters, many aspects of the conflict are covered from the origins to the post-conflict. Covered are Preparation for War; Land Campaigns; Weapons and Innovation; In the Air; At Sea; and Costs. A well-done selected sources and further reading section is provided too, as is an index and appropriate credits. The range of entries is broad, and examples of topics covered include Lend-Lease to the Military Strength of the Axis; The Doolittle Raid to the Top Five Aces; The Battle of the Atlantic to the Hunting of the Bismarck; and Prisoners of War to the Polish Ghettos. Narration, graphs, and pictures are almost always included in each. This work is highly recommended.

---

Classification: LC D743; Dewey 940.

---

290. *Encyclopedia of the Korean War: A Political, Social, and Military History*, by Spencer C. Tucker and Jinwung Kim, eds.

Publisher: ABC-CLIO, Santa Barbara, CA (2010)

Price: $295.00/set

Review by Joe P. Dunn—Charles A. Dana Professor of History and Politics, Converse College, Spartanburg, SC.

The original of this encyclopedia in 2000 was an excellent contribution, and the updated version is even better. The new edition, with 125 academic and military contributors, includes 150 new entries (expanding the total to more than 750), 149 documents in a separate volume, updated and expanded bibliography, 350 illustrations, and 22 detailed maps. The new entries increase the coverage of cultural and popular culture topics, and Allan Millett's expanded historiographical bibliography includes the work of the last decade. The outstanding appendixes, which include the Order of Battle for all participant nations, Medal of Honor recipients, chronology, glossary, and index, remain. The single best addition is the large number of new photographs, which enhance the volumes immeasurably. Libraries that have the original edition are still well served, but institutions with collections in military history that do not have the original edition will find these volumes a very valuable addition.

---

Classification: LC DS918; Dewey 951.

---

291. *The Encyclopedia of the Vietnam War: A Political, Social, and Military History,* by Spencer C. Tucker, Paul G. Pierpaoli Jr., Merle L. Pribbenow II, James H. Willbanks, and David T. Zabecki, eds.

Publisher: ABC-CLIO, Santa Barbara, CA (2011)

Price: $395.00/set

Review by Scott R. DiMarco—Director of Library Services and Information Resources, Mansfield University, Mansfield, PA.

The American War in Vietnam involved every aspect of the American experience from the 1960s to the present. It defined a generation. The superlative military encyclopedia editor of over twenty-five works, Spencer C. Tucker, again does an impressive job of addressing U.S. involvement in this war with the 2nd edition of *The Encyclopedia of the Vietnam War.* He selects topics that go well beyond the actual battlefield and Southeast Asia to, as the subtitle suggests "A Political, Social, and Military History." Truly a scholar, this work is comprehensive and multidimensional in the event from its origins to its long-term consequences. This work is divided into four volumes arranged in alphabetic format. The first three volumes contain a list of entries; a list of maps; photographs; general maps; the actual entries; and an index. Volume 4 has numerous documents; unit designations; a list of military ranks; an order of battle; a glossary; a chronology; and a selected entry bibliography. A typical example is in volume 1 on pages 157–161: The Cambodian Incursion. It has solid and helpful information, a useful map, and a black-and-white photograph. This entry was written by a named scholar. Several associated entries are listed as are seven sources. This work is highly recommended.

---

Classification: LC DS557; Dewey 959.

---

292. *The Encyclopedia of Middle East Wars: The United States in the Persian Gulf, Afghanistan, and Iraq Conflicts,* by Spencer C. Tucker, Priscilla Mary Roberts, and Anthony C. Zinni, eds.

Publisher: ABC-CLIO, Santa Barbara, CA (2010)

Price: $495.00/set

Review by Scott R. DiMarco—Director of Library Services and Information Resources, Mansfield University, Mansfield, PA.

Rising up like an impending storm on the horizon, the wars of the Middle East came directly to attention of American foreign policy in the late 1970s and took center stage after the September 11, 2001, attack. The preeminent military encyclopedia editor of over twenty-five works, Spencer C. Tucker does a phenomenal job of addressing the United States' involvement in wars from the 1979 Soviet invasion of Afghanistan to the present War on Terrorism. The scope of this subject matter is immense, but especially vital and relevant today. This work is divided into five volumes in an alphabetic format. The first three volumes contain a list of entries; a list of maps; general maps; the actual entries; and an index. Volume 4 has all the same items as volumes 1–3 plus a list of military ranks and decorations/awards, a glossary, a chronology, and a selected list of hundreds of bibliographic entries. Volume 5 is a chronologically arranged volume of primary source documents with introductions to place each in context. Typical examples of entries are one to three pages in length. Several have black-and-white photographs and are authored by a subject expert. A list of cross-references is provided, as is a short bibliography for each. Some examples are The Special Air Service, United Kingdom; Tariq Aziz; The Central Command Air Tasking Order; Gold Star Families for Peace; Charles R. Holland; Iraqi-Soviet relations; General Peter Pace; and The Royal Marines. This work is highly recommended.

---

Classification: LC DS63; Dewey 355.

---

## Genealogy

While dedicated genealogists will still seek out rare and unique sources, there has been an explosion of online tools that provide research opportunities for even the casual investigator. Some digital sources require payment of fees (either by libraries or by individuals); others are free on the Web.

293. *The Researcher's Guide to American Genealogy*, by Val D. Greenwood

Publisher: Genealogical Publishing, Baltimore, MD (2000)

Price: $29.95

Review by Robert L. Turner Jr.—Librarian and Associate Professor, Radford University, Radford, VA.

It is good to have a new edition of this work. Greenwood manages to make research in American genealogy understandable. The book is divided into two parts, one covering background to research and the other covering records and their use. The first part includes discussions on understanding genealogical research, understanding the evolution of handwriting, the calendar, symbols used in records, and the evaluation of evidence. Greenwood then introduces research tools, giving a chapter discussion on the library and reference materials. The work deals successfully with organizing the research, corresponding with others, and discussing the purposes of family history beyond genealogy. Greenwood has greatly expanded the chapter on computers in genealogy. In fact, it was the great changes in computer technology that motivated him to bring out this edition since the other basics he discusses have not changed much. The second part has chapters on compiled sources and newspapers, vital records, census returns, probate records and basic legal terminology, wills, land records, governmental as well as local records, court records, property rights of women (a new chapter), church records, military records, and cemetery and burial records. This is a wonderful resource; however, Greenwood should have taken the time to update his references since some of the publications cited are no longer published. This will be useful in any collection needing information on basic genealogical research.

---

This 3rd edition has been frequently republished. Obviously, later works supply more current information about online sources. Classification: LC CS47; Dewey 929.

---

294. *The Source: A Guidebook to American Genealogy*, by Loretto Dennis Szucs and Sandra Hargreaves Luebking, eds.

Publisher: Ancestry, Orem, UT (2006)

Price: $79.95

Review Robert L. Turner Jr.—Librarian and Associate Professor, Radford University, Radford, VA.

The 3rd edition of this work has been heavily revised. There are four new chapters as well as massive rewrites of several others. All chapters were independently peer reviewed. Each of the authors has years of professional experience in doing genealogical research. This work is divided into four main sections, going from the simple to complex areas of research. The sections are "The Basics," "Records," "People and Places," and "Appendixes." The first discusses the basics with three chapters that deal with the methods of family research, computers and technology, and general reference guides. This section should be well studied before going on to the next sections. The second section has ten chapters devoted to business records, census records, church records, court records, directories, immigration records, land records, military records, newspapers, and vital records. The third deals with more specialized research and includes chapters on African American research; Colonial English research; Colonial Spanish borderland research; Hispanic research; Jewish American research; Native American research; and urban research. The fourth contains various appendixes, including abbreviations, family associations, and genealogical societies; hereditary and lineage organizations; historical societies; the LDS family history library; and state archives. This is a tremendous resource for anyone interested in American genealogical research. It will be useful in most libraries.

Classification: LC CS49; Dewey 929.

295. *Dictionary of American Family Names*, by Patrick Hanks, ed.

Publisher: Oxford University Press, New York, NY (2003)

Price: $295.00/set

Review by Philip G. Swan—Head Librarian, Hunter College, School of Social Work Library, New York, NY.

The *Dictionary of American Family Names* is an extremely comprehensive 3-volume collection of 70,000 surnames that should be especially helpful to genealogists as well as to those with a more casual interest in the history of their family moniker. Highlighting the most common names in the United States in alphabetic order, each name is analyzed in a variety of ways. The relative frequency of the name is expressed numerically, based on the number of people with the name in a sample of 89 million Americans. Thus, Smith is listed as 831,783 and Smulski, on the next page, as 72. The language of origin is then listed, along with variant spellings, regional predominance, as well as typological and etymological histories. Cross-references to related names are given, along with statistical information on the most common given names associated with the surname. If a name is connected in some way to a significant figure in U.S. history, a brief explanation is provided. The first volume begins with introductory texts. There is an excellent general introduction that covers a variety of topics, from the inconsistencies of spelling to a general history of the origins of family names. This is followed by a section that gives an explanation for the statistical methods used in selecting the surnames and their relation to particular given names. A final section consists of articles written by regional experts on the relation of surnames to particular languages and cultures, including those of European, Jewish, Middle Eastern, and Asian origins.

Classification: LC CS2485; Dewey 929.

296. *Ancestry Library Edition* [digital]
Publisher: Ancestry.com LLC, Lehi, UT
Price: Price negotiated by site. Date reviewed: 2009.
URL: https://www.ancestrylibrary.com
Review by Staff, Libraries Unlimited.

Ancestry has long been the dominant product in the genealogy market, both for home subscribers and for libraries. Ancestry is run by the Generations Network, a for-profit company that markets a subscription product for home users and offers a subscription product, Ancestry Library Edition, to libraries. The library product is distributed by ProQuest. Ancestry's market strength is due to its aggressive program of digitizing primary sources. It was the first company to completely digitize and index the population schedules of the U.S. census, which has long been the core of its content. But it continues to add more material daily. It now has a large collection of digitized military records, biographical indexes, passenger lists, and more. Overall, it includes over four thousand databases. One of the difficulties in using Ancestry is simply finding your way through the mass of information on the site. There are several ways to navigate. The most common way patrons navigate Ancestry is by entering an ancestor's name on the federated search on Ancestry's front page. This search will check all of the databases on the site for a specific name. This is a good way to begin research—it might find information in databases the researcher would not have checked otherwise. However, there are drawbacks to this broad search. First, it often returns too many results for common names, giving researchers too much data to sort through. Second, the broad federated search does not allow researchers advanced search options that might narrow the search effectively. So it makes sense for researchers to search some of the databases individually. Ancestry offers several other options for browsing its database holdings. First, it gives the option "see all databases" from the front page, which leads to a long alphabetic list of the databases. If you know the title of the database you are looking for, this is useful, but otherwise the list is too long for browsing purposes. So, Ancestry offers a "card catalog" search of the databases on the same page. Users can search for a database by title, keyword, or category. Another useful option is to browse the databases by location. By selecting the "search" tab, users can view database holdings by location. Currently, Ancestry Library Edition is a must-have for libraries that want to provide their patrons with in-depth genealogy research options. Ancestry provides content that is a basic starting point for many researchers, such as the digitized U.S. census and passenger lists. Having access to these resources can make the difference between helping your patrons in your library and sending them elsewhere.

Generations Network became Ancestry.com in 2009. In 2015, ProQuest also began managing HeritageQuest, a similar product for libraries, and the two databases now share some features. HeritageQuest has tended to have less content. Classification: LC CS68; Dewey 929.

297. *FamilySearch* [digital]
Publisher: Church of Jesus Christ of Latter-Day Saints, Salt Lake City, UT
Price: Free online. Date reviewed: 2014.
URL: http://www.familysearch.org
Review by Staff, Libraries Unlimited.

Affiliated with the Church of Jesus Christ of Latter-day Saints, FamilySearch claims to have the "largest collection of genealogical and historical records in the world." The site offers access to a treasure trove of more than 1,800 record collections including the U.S. Census as well as death, tax, probate, and other records, many of which are available as digital page scans. In some cases, users may search the records but must visit a partner subscription site such as ancestry.com or fold3 to view the actual text. Nonindexed records can be browsed while volunteer indexing is in progress. User-submitted genealogies, the International Genealogical Index, and the catalog for the Family History Library in Salt Lake City, Utah, can also be searched. The site also offers family tree software and other useful tools. This site is a key resource for both beginning and experienced genealogists.

Classification: LC CS16; Dewey 929.

298. *RootsWeb* [digital]
Publisher: Ancestry.com LLC, Provo, UT
Price: Free online. Date reviewed: 2009.
URL: http://www.rootsweb.com/
Review by Staff, Libraries Unlimited.

RootsWeb grew out of several early Internet message boards and was an early place for genealogists to exchange information online. Today, RootsWeb continues to offer a number of ways for researchers to exchange information online: message boards, mailing lists, and user-contributed databases. These include a collaborative database of pedigrees called WorldConnect, a website registry called Rootslink, and a set of user-contributed databases. There are two resources on RootsWeb that I find particularly useful. The first is the RootsWeb Surname List (RSL). The RSL is a registry of researchers investigating particular names. For common names, RSL is searchable by surname location. E-mail lists or list-servs are another useful RootsWeb resource. Like the surname list, the Roots-Web mailing lists are a popular and useful way to interact with other researchers. RootsWeb has several types of lists: surnames, localities, and topical. An index of these lists is linked from the main page of RootsWeb. Researchers can subscribe to a particular list and will then receive e-mail from any other subscriber who contacts the list. Belonging to such a community of researchers can be extremely helpful. For librarians, the archives of these lists are a useful resource of very specific local genealogy information.

USGenWeb and WorldGenWeb are additional online resource portals, leading to a variety of regional or specialized resources sites. Classification: LC CS9; Dewey 929.

# Humanities

## Art

### Fine Arts

299. *The Dictionary of Art*, by Jane Turner, ed.

Publisher: Grove's Dictionaries, New York, NY (1996)

Price: $8,800.00/set

Review by Lamia Doumato—Head of Reader Services, National Gallery of Art, Washington, DC.

The 34 volumes of *The Dictionary of Art* contain much of the knowledge of art compiled over the centuries. Approximately 6,700 scholars contributed essays on their areas of expertise, which comprise the 41,000 articles illustrated with 15,000 reproductions and documented with 300,000 bibliographic citations. The dictionary includes biographical essays on artists, architects, designers, craftspeople, collectors, dealers, art historians, critics, and art museum professionals. The entries on sites are impressive because of the comprehensive manner in which they are handled and because of the numerous cross-references furnished for related subjects. It is a delight for the reference librarian to have a single source to consult that provides terms and techniques, mythological subjects, institutions, art movements, and archaeological sites. The dictionary must be consulted through its index volume; otherwise, one would miss such esoteric topics as "Syriac manuscripts," which is part of a larger entry on early Christian and Byzantine art. The index is somewhat cumbersome when dealing with institutions, which are listed by city—a tedious and outdated research method. The dictionary does have some minor flaws; however, these are far outweighed by the comprehensive nature of the work as a whole, which makes it the most important art source published in the past few decades. Although there is room for improvement in the index and in the number of illustrations included, all university libraries, major public libraries, and art libraries must have this reference source in their collection.

Often referred to as the *Grove Dictionary of Art*. The complete set has a high price, but single-volume excerpts are available on topics of strong interest, such as the *Grove Dictionary of Art: From Monet to Cézanne, Late 19th-Century French Artists* or the *Encyclopedia of American Art before 1914* (entry 307). Available in online form as Grove Art Online. Classification: LC N31; Dewey 703.

300. *The Oxford Dictionary of Art*, by Ian Chilvers, ed.

Publisher: Oxford University Press, New York, NY (2004)

Price: $45.00

Review by Philip G. Swan—Head Librarian, Hunter College, School of Social Work Library, New York, NY.

The *Oxford Dictionary of Art* is an excellent resource for any casual researcher exploring the world of Western art. Chronologically, the dictionary covers art ranging from Ice Age cave paintings to the work of contemporary artists born before 1965. There are over three thousand articles, two hundred of which are new to the 3rd edition. The vast majority of the entries focus on the biographical details of individual artists, but there are a great many that discuss prominent critics, museums, collectors, schools, movements, and even artists' materials. Photographers and architects are not included among the biographical articles, with the focus being on painters and sculptors as well as the work of contemporary artists working with video and installation. Articles are generally short (usually no longer than a paragraph) and feature a novel system of cross-referencing using asterisks embedded in the article's text, along with a more traditional *see also* format located at the end of articles. The 3rd edition features a new classified list of entries, which arranges article titles under broader headings, including Ancient and Medieval art, artists' biographies, biographies of non-artists, and nonbiographical articles. After the main text of the dictionary, there is a chronology of Western art listing milestones from 530 B.C.E. to 2003. There are no illustrations of any kind, which is understandable given the amount of material covered. The text closes with an index of galleries and museums around the world, including contact information and the URLs of museum websites. The *Oxford Dictionary of Art* is recommended as a comprehensive, but purely introductory, source.

The 4th edition appeared in 2009 as the *Oxford Dictionary of Art and Artists*. Classification: LC N33; Dewey 703.

301. *Encyclopedia of Artists*, by William Vaughan, ed.
Publisher: Oxford University Press, New York, NY (2000)
Price: $180.00/set
Review by Staff, Libraries Unlimited.

This encyclopedia of artists from the Middle Ages to today is presented in six attractive, slim volumes. The set begins with an introduction to artists throughout this time period, explaining their cultural and societal influences. A timeline at the bottom of the introduction pages indicates the different art movements from 1100 to 2000. The first five volumes consist of biographies of more than two hundred painters, sculptors, and printmakers. Each artist is given a two-page spread featuring an article about the life and work of the artist; a sidebar with information on the artist's full name, nationality, style, dates of birth and death (if applicable), key works, "things to look for," people they have been compared to, and terms to look for in the glossary that refer to their work; and one photograph of a famous piece of their art with a description. Each entry is well written and will lead researchers to similar artists. Volume 6 in the set provides one-page definitions of the various art movements covered, a glossary, and an index. This set is beautifully written and illustrated. It will not only provide reliable information for researchers but also entertain the interested browser. It is most appropriate for high school, public, and undergraduate libraries.

Classification: LC N31; Dewey 709.

302. *The Yale Dictionary of Art and Artists*, by Erika Langmuir and Norbert Lynton
Publisher: Yale University Press, New Haven, CT (2000)
Price: $30.00
Review by John T. Gillespie—College Professor and Writer, New York, NY.

In approximately three thousand alphabetically arranged entries, salient aspects of the history of Western art from 1300 to the present are covered in this excellent single-volume work. About 90 percent of the entries are for individual painters, sculptors, and printmakers, with the remainder devoted to art terms, techniques, movements, concepts, and theories. There are no entries for architecture, museums, galleries, or specific art works, and only limited coverage on famous collectors and collections. Entries vary from a few lines to three or four double-column pages depending on the importance of the subject (e.g., the longest articles are for terms like abstract art and artists like Pablo Picasso and Michelangelo). The biographical entries are concise and readable and, in addition to personal information, often give details on style, influences, the nature and historical importance of the subject's work, and a current assessment. In many cases specific landmark works are cited with their present gallery locations. The many *see* references direct the reader to variant spellings of artist's names or pseudonyms. There is also a copious use of asterisks within articles to indicate entries on related subjects. There are no bibliographies or lists for further reading. Both of the editors are British (one a former administrator at the National Gallery in London and the other a professor emeritus at the University of Sussex). This national bias is revealed in the outstanding coverage on postwar British artists (particularly contemporary figures) over the more limited entries on their American counterparts (e.g., no entries for Alice Neel or Lee Krasner are noted). This is a small reservation for what is otherwise a fine, easy-to-use work that will be particularly valuable in libraries for quick reference. Its closest counterpart is *The Oxford Dictionary of Art* (Oxford University Press, 1997; entry 300), which contains roughly the same number of entries. It, too, is an excellent one-volume work, but it is not as up-to-date as *The Yale Dictionary of Art and Artists*, nor has it as extensive coverage on art terms and movements.

---

Classification: LC N33; Dewey 703.

---

303. *The Oxford Companion to Western Art*, by Hugh Brigstocke, ed.
Publisher: Oxford University Press, New York, NY (2001)
Price: $75.00
Review by Staff, Libraries Unlimited.

The editor of this volume, Hugh Brigstocke, who was extensively involved in the preparation of the Grove *Dictionary of Art* (entry 299), has put together a well-written and comprehensive volume on Western art. Originally planned as a revised edition of Harold Osborne's *Oxford Companion to Art*, which combines entries on both Western and non-Western art, Brigstocke decided it would be in the user's best interest to focus solely on painting, sculpture, and graphic arts in the Western world in order to provide the most complete coverage. He states in the introduction that the primary readership of this volume is people who travel and study Western art and will be, therefore, concerned primarily with biographical information on artists, contextual information on art pieces, and the changing aspects of art collecting. Brigstocke states that the main difference between this work and Osborne's work is "the radical changes in taste and the range of investigative scholarship that have taken place over the last 30 years" (p. ix). The book provides A to Z entries on all aspects of Western art, from individual artists and their pieces to different styles of art and their eras. Entries range from one paragraph to a full page. Some of the more interesting and complex entries are formatted within a box to catch the eye of the user. Almost all entries have a short list of references at the bottom, which users can use for further study. All entries are signed and the list of contributors is listed in the beginning of the book. (Some entries are from the original *Oxford Companion to Art* and state Osborne as the author.) The index lists only artists and writers that are mentioned in the entries but that do not have an entry of their own. The color plates included in the volume are impressive and give the reader a taste of Western art as a whole. This impressive scholarly work should be a standard in academic reference collections. Public libraries may also want to consider its purchase.

Classification: LC N33; Dewey 703.

304. *The Grove Encyclopedia of Classical Art and Architecture*, by Gordon Campbell, ed.

Publisher: Oxford University Press, New York, NY (2007)

Price: $250.00/set

Review by Robert L. Wick—Professor Emeritus, Auraria Library, University of Colorado, Denver.

Gordon Campbell has created *The Grove Encyclopedia of Classical Art and Architecture* as a distillation of the 34-volume Grove *Dictionary of Art* (entry 299) and Grove Dictionary of Art Online. More than one thousand entries were taken from the Grove *Dictionary of Art* to which over one hundred new entries were added to create the new work. In addition, more than six hundred halftone illustrations and thirty-two pages of full-color illustrations are included. Material taken from the larger work is limited to the Classical period of art and architecture. The two-volume encyclopedia begins with a section on abbreviations and a thematic index and continues with the A-Z entries, a list of contributors, and an index, which is particularly detailed and useful. The entries follow the well-established form of the other Grove encyclopedias. Each entry includes the name or term followed by dates and an article ranging from a few hundred words to several pages. At the end of each entry is a brief bibliography. Useful cross-references of terms are also included. The *Grove Encyclopedia of Classical Art and Architecture* is, no doubt, destined to take its place as an important reference source along with the other Grove dictionaries. Selection of only the most important articles from the larger Grove works makes this two-volume encyclopedia especially important as a reference source for smaller academic and public libraries, and as a reference source for individuals. The size and cost of the larger Grove *Dictionary of Art* limits its acquisition to larger academic and public library collections, but the two-volume distillation of Classical art and architecture will find its way into branch public libraries and many other collections. The *Grove Encyclopedia of Classical Art and Architecture* should be considered a must-purchase for all libraries and is highly recommended for personal collections.

Classification: LC N5610; Dewey 722.

305. *Art in the Modern Era: A Guide to Styles, Schools & Movements, 1860 to the Present*, by Amy Dempsey
Publisher: Harry N. Abrams, New York, NY (2002)
Price: $55.00
Review by Staff, Libraries Unlimited.

This glossy, hardbound volume clearly explains the dynamics of painting, sculpture, and architecture in the twentieth century. It begins the exploration of twentieth-century art by first looking at the rise of the Avant-Gardes in the late nineteenth century and finishes by discussing the latest trends of body art, installation art, and sound and Internet art. The work is arranged in five chronological chapters: "1860–1900: The Rise of the Avant-Gardes," "1900–1918: Modernisms for a Modern World," "1918–1945: Search for a New Order," "1945–1965: A New Disorder," and "1965-Today: Beyond the Avant-Gardes." The book provides in-depth definitions and discussion of one hundred art movements, including neo-impressionism, art nouveau, art deco, social realism, beat art, pop art, postmodernism, and conceptual art. Each entry runs several pages in length and provides discussion on the key artists, the reception from the critics and the public, and the presentation of the exhibits. Sidebars list key collections and books for further reading. The black-and-white and color photographs of the art are plentiful and serve to enhance the text. The work concludes with a list of two hundred "key terms" with one- to four-sentence definitions, a list of illustrations, and an index. This work will be useful in both reference collections in public and academic libraries as well in the personal reference collections of art historians and students of art. *Art in the Modern Era* is highly recommended.

Classification: LC N6490; Dewey 709.

306. *The Encyclopedia of Sculpture*, by Antonia Boström, ed.
Publisher: Fitzroy Dearborn, New York, NY (2004)
Price: $375.00/set
Review by Terrie L. Wilson—Art Librarian, Michigan State University Libraries,
  East Lansing.

Filling a gap in art reference sources, *The Encyclopedia of Sculpture* is the first major encyclopedia devoted solely to the medium. The three-volume set is a compilation of essay-style entries contributed by experts in the field, including art historians, curators, and independent scholars. Finding aids included in the set are an index, an alphabetic list of entries, and a thematic list of entries. Categories in the thematic list include, but are not limited to, artist biographies, styles and periods, and materials, forms, and techniques. Entries reflect sculpture of all time periods in Europe, the Americas, Asia, and Africa. *The Encyclopedia of Sculpture* is illustrated with small (quarter page or less) black-and-white reproductions. There are 763 essays included in the set. Essays are no less than a page in length, with many consisting of numerous pages of text; for example, the essay on African sculpture is approximately 10 pages long. All have a "Further Reading" list at the end that points the reader toward additional information on the topic. Entries for individual artists include the artist's name, birth and death dates, the essay, a separate biography, and a list of selected works. Entries on well-known artists often are followed by entries on one or more of their major works; for example, the entry on Rodin is followed by entries on The Gates of Hell and the Monument to Honoré de Balzac. Entries for individual works and monuments include the artist, birth and death dates, date of execution of the piece, medium, dimensions (height only), and present location. Entries that are more thematic, such as "Academies and Associations," consist of the essay, *see also* references, and the list of further readings. Overall, *The Encyclopedia of Sculpture* is an excellent resource for basic information and a springboard for further research in the subject. Most essays cover topics sufficiently, but for certain subject areas (e.g., Romanesque sculpture), other resources will offer good if not better coverage of the topic. This reviewer compared the entry on Romanesque sculpture with the one found in the Grove *Dictionary of Art* (entry 299) and found the Grove entry not only longer (53 pages compared to 4 pages) but, not surprisingly, more comprehensive. That said, it is often more convenient and timesaving for the librarian or the patron to go directly to a resource specifically geared toward the subject of their inquiry. Academic, museum, and larger public libraries will want to include *The Encyclopedia of Sculpture* in their art reference collections.

Classification: LC NB198; Dewey 735.

307. *Encyclopedia of American Art before 1914*, by Jane Turner, ed.

Publisher: Grove's Dictionaries, New York, NY (2000)

Price: $250.00

Review Robert L. Wick—Professor Emeritus, Auraria Library, University of Colorado, Denver.

The *Encyclopedia of American Art before 1914* is another of the scholarly and well-received Grove's Dictionaries of both music and art. This single-volume work begins with Colonial times and concludes its coverage at the time of the Armory Show in 1913. The entries for this work have been drawn from the thirty-four-volume *Dictionary of Art* (entry 299) and have been updated prior to publication. The editors point out that many of the most popular entries from the larger *Dictionary of Art* have been included in this volume. In addition, a number of new biographies of late-nineteenth- and early-twentieth-century artists not included in the larger work have been included. Some of the subjects updated in this volume are Thomas Cole, Currier & Ives, Isabella Steward Gardner, Luminism, McKim, Mead & White, and Shakers. There are more than eight hundred alphabetically arranged entries covering all major artistic developments. In addition, there are more than four hundred black-and-white and ninety color illustrations. (One criticism of the larger thirty-four-volume work has been that there are few color illustrations.) Each entry includes the topic or name of the artist, with birth and death dates, the article, and a brief bibliography at the end. In some cases a bibliography for further reading is included. For the most part the illustrations are of high quality. Black-and-white illustrations are included with the text, but the color plates are grouped together in several areas, making it necessary to look them up specifically. Appendixes include a list of locations, a list of periodical titles, a list of standard reference books and series, and a list of contributors. A complete index is also provided. This single-volume version of the larger *Dictionary of Art* is well done and will make a convenient reference work for artists, critics, and scholars. It is highly recommended for all libraries, especially smaller public and academic collections, and for branch libraries not in possession of the larger *Dictionary of Art*. It is also an obvious choice for school libraries.

Classification: LC N6507; Dewey 709.

308. *Encyclopedia of American Folk Art*, by Gerard C. Wertkin and Lee Kogan, eds., with the American Folk Art Museum

Publisher: Routledge/Taylor & Francis Group, New York, NY (2004)

Price: $125.00

Review by Simon J. Bronner—Distinguished Professor of Folklore and American Studies, Capitol College, Pennsylvania State University, Middletown.

Folk art is a difficult field to cover in an encyclopedia because there is fundamental disagreement on its very definition. The split is usually between an emphasis on the folk, or traditional, part of the combination and the art, or aesthetic, component. The editors of this volume lean toward the latter, while offering to "represent" other views and approaches. In editing their entry list, they ultimately rely on the practice of collecting objects, including the work of museums and programs tending to emphasize the "nature of the artist's training" (i.e., self-taught rather than through community tradition) to use the words of Holger Cahill—an obvious inspiration to the editors. The result is a reference heavy on exhibited artists, art institutions, and collectors. The genres featured are those that fit into usual distinctions of art, rather than folklife, such as sculpture, painting, and decoration. In its institutional connection, artistic approach, and biographical content, the volume is a complement to Chuck and Jan Rosenak's *Museum of American Folk Art Encyclopedia of Twentieth-Century American Folk Art and Artists*, but the scope of the present volume covers earlier centuries. I note, too, more attention in this latest reference to ethnic traditions (e.g., Jewish folk art, Scandinavian American folk art, Asian American folk art, Native American folk art). It may appear strange that there is no entry for English American, Irish American, or British American folk art generally, but one realizes after perusing the reference that this set of "mainstream" heritages is the norm by which ethnicity, at least in this scope of folk art, is judged. The structure and length of the entries are fairly consistent, with some notable exceptions such as long essays on "Painted and Decorated Furniture," "German American Folk Art," "Quilts," and "Religious Folk Art." Some notable entries, perhaps because they are exceptional in the scope, that treat often underappreciated material in the folk art canon appear, such as "Freemasonry," "Hmong arts," "Yard Show," and "Santeria." The quality of color reproductions, inserted in a sixteen-page signature and arranged chronologically, suggesting a periodization of folk art history, is more inconsistent. The reference will be especially useful for documenting artists' biographies, genres, and institutional profiles. It is well indexed to help users.

Classification: LC NK805; Dewey 745.

## Applied Arts

309. *A Dictionary of Modern Design*, by Jonathan M. Woodham
Publisher: Oxford University Press, New York, NY (2004)
Price: $45.00
Review by Neal Wyatt—Collection Management Librarian, Chesterfield County
   Public Library, Midlothian, VA.

This dictionary covers the last 150 years of international modern designing lexicon. By design, the author does not just mean fashion (although that is included), but instead the whole panoply of design from cars to buildings and furniture to brands. Within these pages are references to Volkswagen, Coco Chanel, Coca-Cola, Frank Lloyd Wright, Charles Rennie Mackintosh, Apple Computer Macintosh, Laura Ashley, Ikea, Mercedes-Benz, and Olivetti. The dictionary includes brief articles that focus on the major movements and key concepts of the age (such as the differences between Moderne and Modernism) as well as entries on key figures, events, and companies. The dictionary includes selected iconic black-and-white illustrations of modern zeitgeist designs such as Lego people, Mary Quant clothes, and Fiskars scissors, along with an index, timelines, and a bibliography. While much of this information is available scattered elsewhere, this new dictionary makes a useful selection for academic libraries and larger public libraries.

Classification: LC NK1165; Dewey 745.

310. *The Grove Encyclopedia of Decorative Arts*, by Gordon Campbell, ed.
Publisher: Oxford University Press, New York, NY (2006)
Price: $250.00/set
Review by Bradford Lee Eden—Dean of Library Services, Valparaiso University,
   Valparaiso, IN.

This two-volume reference work contains over three thousand articles on all aspects of the decorative arts. This topic has grown in interest and research in the last few years due to an increasing number of exhibitions and its focus in most core art history curricula in higher education. These diverse art historical materials were originally separated from the fine arts, which were intended to provide pleasure, and the mechanical arts (as the decorative arts were known). Decorative arts include things like weaving, interior decoration, glassware, furniture making, metalwork, and ceramics, among others. These "crafts" were considered lesser than the five fine arts: music, poetry, painting, sculpture, and architecture. Museums such as the Victoria and Albert Museum in London (initially known as the Museum of Manufactures) have become more prominent as the decorative arts have become more popular and worthy of study. Everything from artists, manufacturers, brand names, places, and families of importance are included in this encyclopedia. An abundance of illustrations and pictures can be found throughout the two volumes, along with a list of contributors and an extensive index. This work will be an important addition to any art reference collection.

Classification: LC NK28; Dewey 745.

311. *Dictionary of Furniture*, by Charles Boyce

Publisher: Facts on File, New York, NY (2001)

Price: $50.00

Review by Paula Frosch—Associate Museum Librarian, Thomas J. Watson Library, Metropolitan Museum of Art, New York, NY.

The 2nd edition of this excellent reference work offers additional entries and illustrations that feature the innovations during the past decade and the expanding interest in worldwide forms and styles. The inclusion of sections on Australian design, African furniture, and new timber uses has made this edition as current as possible. The work deals with details of construction, cultural influences, terminology, and materials as well as recent developments in the scientific study of furniture making. The introduction provides a brief history of world furniture, which serves as a reminder that the objects with which we live our everyday life have evolved and adapted as we have. The alphabetic entries are clear and well written, and the accompanying line drawings are simple and instructive. Perhaps the most important addition is the section on buying furniture, particularly the antique, which emphasizes the two salient points in any purchase: know the field and deal only with reputable dealers. The inclusion of a gazetteer of public collections of fine furniture is very useful to the reader who wishes to see authentic examples and informative guides in the pursuit of self-education. The bibliography, also a new addition, is a useful starting point and offers works both general and specific. The book is well produced and easy to read and, at the relatively low price, worthy of being a part of any decorative arts library—public or private.

The 3rd edition appeared in 2014. Classification: LC NK2205; Dewey 749.

312. *Encyclopedia of Clothing and Fashion*, by Valerie Steele, ed.
Publisher: Charles Scribner's Sons/Gale Group, New York, NY (2005)
Price: $395.00/set
Review by Lori D. Kranz—Freelance Editor, Chambersburg, PA.


This three-volume set is remarkable for its broad reach: unlike most sources on the subject, it has a multicultural focus and covers more than just haute couture. Here one can also find fabrics, textile making, garment construction, production and marketing, the theory and literature of fashion, the fashion media, fashion in art, body adornment, and class, social, gender, and sexual identity, from ancient times to the present. More than 300 scholars have contributed signed entries, and captioned black-and-white photographs of good quality support the well-written text. For such a visually oriented subject as this, more illustrations are desirable, but would undoubtedly drive up the cost. Occasional sidebars feature quotations from literature and fashion media or interesting details pertaining to the entries. Each of the three volumes contains a central section of color plates, cross-referenced to specific entries, although the plates are not mentioned in the entries themselves. Browsing through these 1,400-odd pages soon reveals the Encyclopedia's large and multidisciplinary scope. The general history of clothing of different cultures falls under country or region, as in "Japanese Traditional Dress and Ornament" or "Africa, Sub-Saharan: History of Dress." Under the category of body modification one can find "Body Piercing" and "Scarification." On the manufacturing and marketing side, there's "Sweatshops," "Department Store," "Spinning Machinery," and "Window Displays." Old and new trends and styles like the flappers of the 1920s, the Youthquake of the 1960s, and the hip-hop clothing of today are here. Of course, the most established fashion designers and houses receive their own entries, as do such icons as Princess Diana and Barbie and fashion photographers Richard Avedon and Cecil Beaton. Clothing worn for particular events or places falls under headings like "Wedding Costume," "Uniforms, School," or "Suit, Business." Writers and theorists such as Jean Baudrillard, Thorstein Veblen, Oscar Wilde, and Doris Langley Moore are included for what they have said about fashion. Although this encyclopedia follows the standard A to Z format, users should first consult the index or the listing of entries by subject, as the topic they are seeking may fall under a more general name—nylon stockings, for example, are treated under "Stockings, Women's," and "Nylon." The index and subject listing are found only in the back of the third volume, however, which users may find inconvenient. A few omissions were noted; handbags and purses have an entry, but not wallets. Although there are many entries on fibers and fabrics, there is no mention of patent leather or nubuck in the "Leather and Suede" entry; fake fur receives one sentence under "Fur" and "Outerwear" (although the index cites only the former entry); and fleece, a very popular outerwear fabric, is mentioned just once in a sidebar under "Polyester" and not listed in the index at all. Nor will one find discussion of more than just a few types of woolen fabric. These are minor quibbles, though, and the vast majority of users should find this reference work of great interest and utility.

Classification: LC GT507; Dewey 391.

313. *Oxford Companion to the Garden*, by Patrick Taylor
Publisher: Oxford University Press, New York, NY (2006)
Price: $65.00
Review by Staff, Libraries Unlimited.

Under the guidance of an expert editorial team with contributions from worldwide scholars, this edition updates the original 1986 volume, paying special attention to countries in which gardens have been a significant part of the culture and those in which gardens have not had such a prominent cultural role. This edition emphasizes the gardens themselves (most of those included in the companion are open to the public). The book now includes more entries on certain countries formerly underrepresented and more material on garden designers, the history of gardening, the influence of scientific development, the conservation and restoration of gardens, and more. Gardens of all sorts are covered, from the humble kitchen garden to those of Europe's grand palaces. Readers will also find information on such topics as the history of garden visiting and the design of hospital grounds. Much of the material in this new companion is original, though some content from the first edition has been retained. Altogether, there are more than 1,750 A to Z entries; more than 1,000 of these pertain to private and public gardens around the world. Entries vary in length from one to several paragraphs. These are signed by contributors, and some include bibliographies. There is also a select bibliography at the end of the book and a select index that lists gardens, people, themes, and features that do not have an entry of their own. The select bibliography has both a general section and sections divided by country. Before delving into the heart of the book, readers will find a thematic index and a list of color plates used generously throughout the book. The thematic index groups entries under the following headings: Biographies (which includes biographies separated by group—landscape and garden designers, botanists, and sculptors, among many others); Plants; Countries and Regions; Gardens (by name, grouped into region); Features and Terms; and Garden Issues. This section does not include page numbers, though page numbers appear next to the names of color plates. This well-curated and comprehensive book is highly recommended for public and academic libraries.

See entries 421–427 for works with a more botanical focus. Classification: LC SB450; Dewey 712.

## Literature

### American Literature

314. *The Oxford Companion to American Literature*, by James D. Hart. Revised by Phillip W. Leininger

Publisher: Oxford University Press, New York, NY (1995)

Price: $49.95

Review by Jeffrey E. Long—Editor of *SoutteReview Newsletter*, University of Massachusetts Medical School Library, Worcester.

Recently an editor of the rival *Benet's Reader's Encyclopedia of American Literature*, Leininger has revised the late Hart's work to produce the first revision of this well-known title in a dozen years. Nearly two hundred new entries are incorporated in this edition; fewer than half of these were derived from notes left by Hart in 1990. The chronological index has been enlarged as well, appending the major literary and social events from 1983 to 1994. Notable newcomers debuting in this volume include contemporary writers Amy Tan, Jim Harrison, Gloria Steinem, Larry McMurtry, and Amy Clampitt. Redressing previous editions' oversights, Leininger has written entries for Charlotte Perkins Gilman and Henry Roth. An unspecified number of 5th edition entries have been condensed, truncated, or dropped. Many deleted items are on obscure subjects (e.g., Hiram Chittenden, Moses Coit Tyler). Some writers' statures, however, would seem to warrant longer entries than they are accorded. A few omissions are questionable, such as those of entries treating the literary associations of certain U.S. cities and presidents. Significant twentieth-century writers remain underrepresented in *The Oxford Companion*. For example, only 4 percent of personal entries for names beginning with A through D are of women born since 1900. Modern male authors who are missing include Harlan Ellison, Andre Dubus, and Lowell Thomas. Coverage is generally superior, however, in terms of the updated entries carried forward from the 5th edition. The revised article on William Gaddis has been tripled in length, and the Philip Levine entry lists no fewer than five works that appeared since Oxford's previous edition. Several comparisons with *Benet's* yield telling results. The entry in *Benet's* for each of the following literary icons is more than twice the length of its Oxford counterpart: Herman Melville, Edgar Allan Poe, Mark Twain, James Fenimore Cooper, and William Faulkner. Yet, the breadth of the work under review is creditable in terms of embracing expatriates, explorers, colonists, and foreign discoursers on American matters (e.g., Kay Boyle, Richard Hakluyt, Samuel Sewell, and Charles Dickens). However, more could be written on Latin American and Canadian literature. Besides offering substantive overview essays on these literatures, *Benet's* offers entries on internationally acclaimed writers whose works are readily available in English translation, such as Jorge Luis Borges, Pablo Neruda, and Octavio Paz. Also, unlike Oxford, *Benet's* treats such Canadian luminaries as Margaret Atwood, Robertson Davies, and Michael Ondaatje. For such giants as these, it is unfortunate that the researcher using Oxford has to consult a supplementary source, whether it be *Benet's* or the Canadian or Spanish volumes in the Oxford Companion series. Finally, the reduction of typeface size since the 5th edition may prove irritating to librarians using this book on a regular basis. While the praises to be sung for *The Oxford Companion to American Literature* are considerable, one would be better served by employing *Benet's*, except involving more obscure areas of U.S. literature.

---

The 6th edition appeared in 2006. The most recent edition of *Benet's* under that name appeared in 1991: an updated revision was published in 2002 as the *HarperCollins Reader's Encyclopedia of American Literature*. The *Oxford Companion* is more widely owned. Classification: LC PS21; Dewey 810.

---

315. *The Oxford Encyclopedia of American Literature*, by Jay Parini, ed.

Publisher: Oxford University Press, New York, NY (2004)

Price: $495.00/set

Review by David Isaacson—Assistant Head of Reference and Humanities Librarian, Waldo Library, Western Michigan University, Kalamazoo.

This encyclopedia covers American literature from precolonial times to the present in over 350 essays written by 190 scholars. Major classic authors like Ralph Waldo Emerson as well as contemporary authors like Maya Angelou are covered in substantial articles, but somewhat less canonical writers, like Jones Very and Emma Lazarus, are covered in shorter articles. All genres are represented, with a rather equitable representation among fiction writers, poets, dramatists, literary critics, and essayists. The author entries review the author's whole career, often include an interesting photograph (the photograph of W. H. Auden smoking a pipe rather than his usual cigarette is delightful), provide a brief primary and annotated secondary bibliography, and provide cross-references to other articles where the author is discussed. In addition to the single author essays, other entries cover major novels (e.g., *The Adventures of Huckleberry Finn*), short stories (e.g., "The Lottery"), plays (e.g., "Our Town"), and poetry collections (e.g., "The Pisan Cantos"). Still other essays are devoted to genres (e.g., autobiography, science fiction) and various themes, such as the beat movement, transcendentalism, and writing as a woman in the twentieth century. The essays sampled by this reviewer live up to the editor's assertion that the contributors write for a general audience; we are thankfully spared the obscurities of literary critical jargon. Although there are some fine examples of what is now considered old-fashioned "close reading" of seminal individual literary works, this set as a whole reflects an intellectually stimulating multidisciplinary American studies approach that invites the reader to see literature in a larger historical, sociological, and sometimes psychological as well as an aesthetic context. Because the set is so broad any particular reader will question why certain authors or themes are included and others excluded. This reviewer, for one, wonders why fiction writer and poet Stuart Dybek is not included even in passing while Erica Jong rates a whole essay. On the other hand, it is hard to fault the authority of the writing in the essays that are included; for instance, David Ryan very perceptively says that prose style often becomes the subject of Stanley Elkin's often difficult novels, and Sheldon W. Liebman correctly identifies Robert D. Richardson's *Emerson: The Mind on Fire* as the definitive biography of Ralph Waldo Emerson. Besides the essays—many of which are meant for consecutive reading—the reference value of this set is enhanced by an alphabetic list of the author entries, a separate list of the thematic essays, a chronology, and a detailed name and title index. These authors and subjects are covered in greater depth by the hundreds of volumes in the *Dictionary of Literary Biography* series, and the factual data are more easily accessible in numerous shorter encyclopedias, dictionaries, and handbooks of American literature, but this handsomely printed and intellectually vigorous and ambitious encyclopedia has no contemporary competitor.

Classification: LC PS21; Dewey 810.

316. *The Facts on File Companion to the American Short Story*, by Abby H. P. Werlock

Publisher: Facts on File, New York, NY (2010)

Price: $150.00/set

Review by Staff, Libraries Unlimited.

Arranged alphabetically, this sturdily bound work should find its way into the reference collection of most academic, public, and high school libraries. Included here are author biographies and bibliographies; synopses and analyses of major short stories; summary descriptions of well-known characters; historical events that have influenced short story writers; notable awards for short fiction; and definitions of literary terms, themes, and motifs. In addition, overview articles dealing with various cultural, literary schools or techniques are provided. Valuable cross-references enhance the entries. This 2nd edition includes many new and updated entries, including those of up-and-coming authors such as David Foster Wallace, Dave Eggers, and Junot Díaz. Entries are for the most part terse and succinct, providing a capsule summary of the topic treated. Where appropriate, brief bibliographies are attached for further reading. Appendixes include winners of selected short story prizes (through 2009), such as the O. Henry Memorial Awards, Pushcart Prize, and so on. There is also a listing of short stories arranged by theme and topic such as "Ghosts and the Supernatural," "Love, Courtship, Romance," and "Prejudice," and a three-page selected general bibliography. A list of contributors followed by a full analytic index concludes the volume. Breadth of treatment is impressive, as is the execution of this volume. Contributors tend to be college and university faculty specializing in literature. Careful editing and consistency of approach create a valuable reference tool that will be celebrated by librarians, students, faculty, and writers. This work is quite readable and highly recommended.

Classification: LC PS374; Dewey 813.

317. *Encyclopedia of American Poetry: The Twentieth Century*, by Eric L. Haralson, ed.

Publisher: Fitzroy Dearborn/Taylor & Francis Books, New York, NY (2001)

Price: $125.00

Review by Mark Y. Herring—Dean of Library Services, Winthrop University, Dacus Library, Rock Hill, SC.

The *Encyclopedia of American Poetry: The Twentieth Century* is a very hefty volume. It covers everything from the first acatalectic foot to the last zeugma. Included here are entries on individual poets along with critical treatments of their work. The entries, hardly snapshots, list works, bibliographies, and achievements. These entries also position the poet in the pantheon of other twentieth-century poets. Coupled with this feature are entries on well-known poems, such as "The Road Not Taken" or Marianne Moore's Pangolin. Add to this information the volume's major topic entries, in-depth analyses of formal developments in twentieth-century poetry (such as free verse, light verse, and beat poetry), and readers have in hand everything anyone, layperson or scholar, needs to begin their study of twentieth-century poets, poetry, and poetic forms. All too often in works of this magnitude and form, the index is either skimpy or ignored altogether. Not so with the *Encyclopedia of American Poetry*—access is guaranteed throughout the work. No other work comes to mind that is so rich in detail or so exhaustive in coverage with respect to the subject matter. The *New Princeton Encyclopedia of Poetry and Poetics* has an entirely different focus and prospectus.

---

A companion volume covers the nineteenth century. Classification: LC PS323; Dewey 811.

---

318. *The Companion to Southern Literature: Themes, Genres, Places, People, Movements, and Motifs*, by Joseph M. Flora, Lucinda H. Mackethan, and Todd Taylor, eds.

Publisher: Louisiana State University Press, Baton Rouge, LA (2002)

Price: $69.95

Review by Charlotte Lindgren—Professor Emerita of English, Emerson College, Boston, MA.

This companion is more cultural than literary. Only 14 authors, 1 of whom is Shakespeare, and eight works, including films and the Declaration of Independence, receive a full essay. By contrast, there are twenty-six historical figures among the more than five hundred alphabetically listed entries. While writers such as Maya Angelou and Alice Walker appear only under the general heading of women writers, Elvis is accorded a full discussion. The wide coverage embraces literary terms, genres, motifs, types and stereotypes, schools, and theories. Each entry is followed by a *see also* list of related entries and a bibliography of useful sources. Words such as "Nigger," "Redneck," "Yellow Dog Democrat," and "Y'all" are explained along with their use in Southern literature. Historical figures range from Pocahontas to Martin Luther King Jr. Religion is broken into many separate entries from main stream to "Whoopin," "Snake Handling," and "Voodoo." The introduction discusses the principles governing selection and is followed by a list of general reference works. Although the choices of topic are rather idiosyncratic, the volume is well designed for easy use and entertaining to read. In addition to a traditional table of contents from "Abolition" to "Yoknapatawpha," a second table is arranged by such subjects as arts and culture, colleges and universities, cities and regions, rituals, icons, music, language, and politics. There is also an extensive thirty-one-page, triple-columned index that covers all the names and topics within the listed entries. Readers will find that this volume is a thorough introduction to the culture of the South and a useful companion to their readings of Southern literature.

---

Classification: LC PS261; Dewey 810.

---

319. *African American Writers*, by Valerie Smith, ed.

Publisher: Charles Scribner's Sons/Gale Group, New York, NY (2001)

Price: $240.00/set

Review by Richard Bleiler—Reference Librarian, University of Connecticut, Storrs.

The two volumes of *African American Writers* comprise the 2nd edition of a work first published in one volume in 1991. The 2nd edition contains fifty-five essays, fifty-two of which are biocritical and twenty-one of which are new to these volumes. All essays are lengthy and signed; many are written by top scholars in the field. Researchers will find such names as Thadious M. Davis, Henry Louis Gates, and Arnold Rampersad among the contributors. Each essay concludes with a lengthy bibliography of primary and secondary sources, and the set concludes with a lengthy index. The 2nd edition of *African American Writers* is excellent, but it is not perfect. On a trivial level, only the first volume has a table of contents. Equally seriously, the ideas of balance and criticism are almost absent from the pages of this set, and many of the essays are no more than extended appreciations—panegyrics rather than assessments. Indeed, so glowing are virtually all the essays that it comes almost as a surprise to read a blunt "she lied" in Cheryl Wall's discussion of Zora Neale Hurston's life. Finally, for all that it is an excellent set, it is also a set that concentrates on an established canon rather than attempting to expand and redefine the canon, and nowhere is this more evident than in the presentation of the writers known for their genre work. Octavia Butler, Samuel R. Delany, and Chester Himes—all safe choices—are discussed, but Clarence Cooper, Veronica Johns, Ernest Tidyman, Frank Yerby, and such relatively new voices as Walter Mosley are not accorded mention, although their accomplishments are perhaps greater than some of the writers profiled. The 2nd edition of the *African American Writers* set belongs in all public, high school, and academic libraries. One nevertheless hopes for a 3rd edition.

> *African-American Writers* by Philip Bader and Catherine Reef (2011) is a shorter work, also widely held. Classification: LC PS153; Dewey 810.

320. *Encyclopedia of the Harlem Renaissance*, by Aberjhani and Sandra L. West

Publisher: Facts on File, New York, NY (2003)

Price: $65.00

Review by Charmaine Ijeoma—Assistant Professor of English and African and African American Studies, Penn State Abington College, Abington.

The *Encyclopedia of the Harlem Renaissance* provides a wealth of information in minute detail on a literary and cultural time period significant not only for

Americans generally but for African Americans specifically. The entries are clear, concise, and alphabetized, thereby making this reference source easy to use. Additionally, this is a thorough and rigorously comprehensive work that constitutes an eclectic selection of elements spanning the entire spectrum of contributions made by intellectuals, artists, critics, and musicians in New York City during the 1920s and 1930s. For example, Aberjhani and Sandra L. West include surprising and refreshing details concerning such cities as Philadelphia and its pivotal connection to the black renaissance. In fact, West asserts, "With its cultured black writers, artists, educators, and publications, Philadelphia added important talent and creative substance to the Harlem Renaissance" (p. 263). Further, scholars, students, and members of the general public who are either seeking a deeper understanding of the literary history of the Harlem Renaissance or unfamiliar with the era will discover many helpful sources at the end of each entry. This useful text also contains several appendixes that include items such as a four-page list of additional resources, a chronology to keep the literary history in perspective, and a glossary of slang from the period. The in-depth discussion of the personalities as well as the events that ushered in the Harlem Renaissance reveals an important and an intricate part of the African American literary canon. This book is an enjoyable read.

---

A 2004 work with the same title by Cary D. Wintz and Paul Finkelman is also widely owned. Classification: LC PS153; Dewey 810.

---

## World Literature

321. *The Cambridge Guide to Literature in English*, by Dominic Head, ed.
Publisher: Cambridge University Press, New York, NY (2006)
Price: $50.00
Review by John T. Gillespie—College Professor and Writer, New York, NY.

As with the two previous editions, this impressive, one-volume work has as its purpose "to provide a handy reference guide to the literature in English produced by various English-speaking cultures throughout the world" (editor's note). Most of the 5,000 entries average about 25 to 35 lines each and are biographical in nature. As well as literary authors there are some entries for writers in other fields (e.g., Darwin in science, Gibbon in history). A lesser number of entries deal with synopses of important novels and plays; literary movements, groups, and genres; critical terms and poetic forms; and more specialized subjects like the most important theaters, literary periodicals, and libraries. Except for the Booker and Pulitzer, book awards and prizes are not covered.

The editor, a professor of English literature at Nottingham University, was helped by 200 contributing scholars, each of whom is listed (without identifying credentials) in a preface. Articles are unsigned. Almost 90 percent of the entries are reprinted intact from the 2nd edition. The remaining 10 percent are either new to this edition or updated revisions of entries from the previous edition (coverage ends usually at 2004). Most of the new entries are for 280 "new" authors, such as Nick Hornby, E. Annie Proulx, and Paul Auster. With such a wide field to cover selectivity in topics is essential, but it is unfortunate that there is not more extensive coverage on contemporary writers. For example, such established modern American playwrights as Gurney, Guare, and Mamet are held over from the 2nd edition, but only Tony Kushner is new to this edition, while such important emerging talents like LaButte, Shanley, and Lucas are ignored. Literary genres like children's literature and detective fiction are covered primarily thorough three- to four-page articles. Individual entries in these areas are also highly selective. Cross-references are indicated by the use of italics within entries. There are no bibliographies. The occasional black-and-white illustration enlivens the text. Of particular interest are the witty caricatures of contemporary writers by the cartoonist Jonathan Wateridge. In spite of some questionable editorial decisions, this is a worthy addition to a general reference collection with only the out-of-date *Benet's Reader's Encyclopedia* approaching it in scope and treatment.

---

Classification: LC PR85; Dewey 820.

---

322. *The Oxford Companion to English Literature*, by Dinah Birch and Margaret Drabble, eds.

Publisher: Oxford University Press, New York, NY (2009)

Price: $125.00

Review by Michael Adams—Reference Librarian, City University of New York Graduate Center.

The 7th edition of this venerable work finds Dinah Birch succeeding Margaret Drabble as editor and attempting to reconcile her text to the changing world of reference resources and to new phenomena such as the growing number of reading clubs. Birch has eliminated entries on cultural figures and topics only tenuously related to literature and has reduced the number of items about characters because of the proliferation of studies of individual writers and their major works. To create needed space, plot summaries have been truncated. Hundreds of figures have been added or had their entries replaced since the 6th edition in 2000, including Martin Amis, James Ellroy, Neil Gaiman, Alfred Hitchcock, Alice James, Bharati Mukherjee, J. K. Rowling, Zadie Smith, and Christa Wolf. Entries related to black British writing, children's literature, fantasy, post-colonial literature, science fiction, travel writing, and the relationships between literature, film, and television have been expanded, and there are four introductory essays, including "Literary Culture and the Novel in the New Millennium." An index of new and heavily revised entries is included, as is a chronology from 1000 through 2008, lists of poet laureates, children's laureates, and major British literary awards. As with any such undertaking, omissions are easy to spot, as with the failure to mention film and television adaptations in the entry for *Pride and Prejudice*, and the brevity of entries devoted to American writers, as with the one-sentence summary of Neil Simon. The general strength of its scope, however, makes the volume indispensable, and the print version is also much easier to browse than its Gale Virtual Reference Library counterpart.

Classification: LC PR19; Dewey 820.

323. *Encyclopedia of World Literature in the 20th Century*, by Steven R. Serafin, ed.
Publisher: St. James Press/Gale Group, Farmington Hills, MI (1999)
Price: $575.00/set
Review by Staff, Libraries Unlimited.

Previous editions of this important reference work have been favorably reviewed in ARBA. This latest revision continues the tradition of excellence, offering users a comprehensive guide to world literature of the century. The 4-volume set covers more than 2,300 authors, with more than 250 new names added. It provides users with a wealth of information on authors from around the world, as well as on specific national literatures (e.g., Turkish literature, Austrian literature) and on the major literary and intellectual movements of the century (e.g., postmodernism, futurism). Each author entry provides vital statistics, a biographical and critical essay, a list of the author's publications, and a bibliography of other sources of information. Biographies have been written by qualified subject specialists, and generally speaking the content is accurate and complete. Black-and-white photos accompany many of the biographies, and critical excerpts are appended to some essays. To enhance access, the volume is amply cross-referenced and indexed. It is also worth noting that a nationality index has been added to this edition. As in previous editions, the coverage of European and North American authors is strongest. However, representation of Asian and South American authors is also substantial in this edition. It would be beneficial if subsequent editions continue the effort to achieve a more balanced representation. Although the revisions and additions to this edition are not as extensive as to the last, the book maintains its position as an essential reference for public and academic libraries.

Classification: LC PN771; Dewey 803.

324. *The Companion to African Literatures*, by Douglas Killam and Ruth Rowe
Publisher: Indiana University Press, Bloomington, IN (2000)
Price: $49.95
Review by Bernice Bergup—Humanities Reference Librarian, Davis Library,
   University of North Carolina—Chapel Hill.

Billed as a comprehensive guide, Killam and Rowe's bio-bibliography dictionary provides a convenient, encompassing introduction to the major African literatures and African authors writing in English or in non-African languages
available in English translation. Among those featured are well-known writers
such as Nobel Prize winner Wole Soyinka and Chinua Achebe and lesser-known
writers such as Charity Waciuma of Kenya. In addition to author entries there
are title entries for more prominent works. A selective list of topics discusses the
major languages and literatures such as Gikuyu, Pidgin, and Xhosa as well as
Afrikaans, Francophone, and Lusophone literatures. Thematic entries include
articles on Onitsha popular market literature, black consciousness, feminism
and literature, writing systems in Africa, women in literature, apartheid, and
oral tradition and folklore. The entries, contributed by more than 170 scholars
and critics, are critical rather than descriptive, often comparing similarities
among authors and works and citing other sources. Bibliographic references are
identified within entries by year of publication, eliminating the need for an additional comprehensive bibliography. However, given the range of literatures, the
suggestions for further reading are extremely minimal. The companion includes
a useful country and author guide and two maps, one showing African nations
with their dates of independence and the other identifying locations for the
major languages treated in the entries. This valuable resource belongs in academic and public libraries, both those with major African Studies collections
and those with limited resources given its broad scope.

Classification: LC PR9340; Dewey 820.

325. *The Dictionary of Imaginary Places*, by Alberto Manguel and Gianni
   Guadalupi
Publisher: Harcourt Brace Jovanovich, San Diego, CA (2000)
Price: $40.00
Review by Edmund F. SantaVicca—Librarian, Phoenix College, Phoenix, AZ.

Newly revised and updated from the 1987 edition, this work takes readers through some of the most intriguing and beguiling imaginary countries and locations that never existed except in the mind of the authors that created them. More than 1,200 entries are alphabetically arranged, profiling the geography and customs of the locations in question. Entries range from brief paragraphs to four or five pages (or more). In some cases black-and-white maps are included, while in others illustrations of landmarks or buildings are included. New to this edition are such places as Alifbay, City of the Blind, Deads' Town, Eastwick, Forest, Green-Man Land, Hogwarts, Imagination, Iounalao, Jurassic Park, Monomotapa, Moor, Neverwhere, Ouidah, Sasania, Women's Island, and Youkali. These complement older entries such as Oz, Narnia, Never-Never Land, and Middle-Earth. For all entries, the basic identification of author, work of fiction, and place and date of publication are given. A comprehensive index provides easy access to information. This work is highly recommended for public library reference collections and academic reference collections with strong literature collections. Students and researchers alike will enjoy the informative and entertaining explanations and descriptions.

---

Classification: LC GR650; Dewey 809.

---

326. *Encyclopedia of Rhetoric*, by Thomas O. Sloane, ed.

Publisher: Oxford University Press, New York, NY (2001)

Price: $150.00

Review by John B. Romeiser—Professor of French and Department Head, University of Tennessee—Knoxville.

Oxford University Press's massive new *Encyclopedia of Rhetoric* is a veritable treasure trove of information from the earliest beginnings of the discipline to its most current incarnations. The more than 830-page volume offers concise and readable essays by North American and international specialists in the field on an incredibly wide range of topics from the most ancient (pathos, logos, and ethos) to the post-modern (new rhetoricians, contingency, and probability). In addition, an exhaustive list of entries related to figures of speech from the seemingly obscure (auxesis and chiasmus) to the more mundane (metaphor and synecdoche) is included. The majority of entries contain a decent-sized bibliography of related works. The readers who will be attracted to this impressive and handsomely bound work will be primarily advanced undergraduate students; postgraduates; and university faculty of classics, English, foreign languages, and literatures. Moreover, law students, faculty, and even practicing attorneys will be especially interested in the sections of the book dealing with argumentation strategies. Encyclopedia of Rhetoric concludes with a synoptic outline of its contents, a valuable resource that will help the reader more easily identify areas of interest. Owing to its international scope and the depth and range of its essays, this commendable work will be a must-purchase for interested scholars and university libraries.

Classification: LC PN172; Dewey 808.

## Children's Literature

327. *The Oxford Encyclopedia of Children's Literature*, by Jack Zipes, ed.

Publisher: Oxford University Press, New York, NY (2006)

Price: $495.00/set

Review by Rosanne M. Cordell—(formerly) Head of Reference Services, Franklin D. Schurz Library, Indiana University–South Bend.

Editor Jack Zipes and his over 800 contributors have compiled the most extensive English-language encyclopedia available on children's literature. The approximately 3,200 entries in 4 volumes cover the history of children's literature worldwide, from the medieval period to the present, which is a longer time period than many works recognize. Entries on authors, illustrators, publishers, educators, developments throughout the world, and special topics are included. Many entries are about 100 words, with those on some topics or major figures running three to four pages. The concise, factual style may seem sparse to some readers, but the breadth of coverage far exceeds any other work of its type. The appearance is uncluttered, with well-spaced type, large bold entry names, and heavy lines between entries. Some entries have short bibliographies, and many include *see also* references. The 400 black-and-white illustrations are too few to be a significant feature. Volume 1 has a list of entries as well as a historical background on children's literature in its introduction. Volume 4 includes a selected bibliography; a list of major international children's book awards; a list of significant children's literature collections; a topical outline that has sections on the geographically focused articles, genres, characters, titles, authors, and illustrators; a directory of contributors with their entries; and an extensive general index. Other recent works on children's literature are far more limited in coverage. Zipes's work will be the first stop for information on this subject. This work is an essential purchase for any academic library supporting literature or teacher preparation programs and is highly recommended for public libraries as well.

Classification: LC PN1008; Dewey 809.

328. *The Cambridge Guide to Children's Books in English*, by Victor Watson, Elizabeth L. Keyser, Juliet Partridge, and Morag Styles, eds.

Publisher: Cambridge University Press, New York, NY (2001)

Price: $50.00

Review by Vang Vang—Reference Librarian, Henry Madden Library, California State University–Fresno.

*The Cambridge Guide to Children's Books in English* is an authoritative reference tool. Its author and title headings are arranged in alphabetic order, with authors by surname. Legendary and fictional figures, such as Robin Hood and Bugs Bunny, are listed according to their first used name. Cross-references between authors, titles, and series are successfully interwoven in the text. The Guide covers children's books from Britain and the United States to successful children's books written in English in Canada, New Zealand, Australia, India, and Africa. Each of the entries in the Guide is critically and appreciatively well written. Additionally, topics such as neglected authors, disabilities in children's books, playground rhymes, and illustrations are included as well as the various folktales and myths around the world that have found their way into children's stories. The Guide also contains entries on television, comics, annuals, and the growing range of media texts. There is even a selection of notable awards and previous winners of awards such as the Caldecott Medal and the Children's Book Award in the appendix. The Guide is well written and easy to read, and the many illustrations scattered in the text provide wonderful reading breaks when browsing. It is highly recommended for all libraries with a children's collection.

> Classification: LC PR990; Dewey 820.

## Performing Arts

### Film

No guide to film reference tools should omit the free *Internet Movie Database* website, now IMDb.com, which includes coverage of television and has some elements of a wiki for adding content and reviewer ratings. *Wikipedia* (entry 38)—which is often strong on popular culture topics—offers detailed information about many films and also television series, sometimes with lists of episodes by season.

329. *Schirmer Encyclopedia of Film*, by Barry Keith Grant, ed.

Publisher: Schirmer Books/Gale Group, New York, NY (2007)

Price: $370.00/set

Review by Jim Agee—Assistant Director and Technical Services Manager-Acquisitions/Serials, James A. Michener Library, University of Northern Colorado, Greeley.

This 4-volume set of encyclopedias from Schirmer, an imprint of Thomson Gale, contains 200 alphabetically arranged articles. A list of examples from the article headings (Direction, Disaster Films, Distribution, Documentary, Dubbing and Subtitling, Early Cinema, Editing, Egypt, Epic Films) shows the breadth of coverage, the attention to cinematography, but also the inclusion of geographic influences from across the globe. Most articles are 8–10 pages and have one, or often two, highlighted biographical cameos. Articles pan broad expanses of cinema to thoroughly introduce the topic. Many references to films or individuals are included in each article, references that can give context for a reader's understanding of the topic as well as guide further study. Volume 4's article, "Stars," serves as a typical example. Ten pages, with four subheadings such as "Star Performance" and "Stars and Moviegoers," provide historical perspective, discussion of character type, moviegoer assumptions, and insights into technical viewpoint shots, psychological concepts, and theoretical aspects of the perception and identity that binds moviegoers to particular stars. Half-page color photographs, one of Tom Cruise and two of Clint Eastwood, are balanced by a quarter-page black-and-white of Lillian Gish. Both Eastwood and Gish are given three-quarter page boxes that highlight their careers and give lists of recommended viewing and recommended reading for more insight into each of these stars. The end of the article, as with most of the entries, lists *see also* headings and further reading lists. Photographs liberally illustrate these volumes, as well as a limited number of diagrams and charts. A well-designed and extensive index of nearly 150 pages is reproduced in each volume. These sturdily constructed books will withstand heavy use. Editor-in-Chief Grant, and the 200 contributing authors, should be proud of this encyclopedic film resource. This set is highly recommended for libraries in high schools or universities that support film study programs. These volumes are an excellent quick resource for film industry offices. While topics are easily found, the scholarly compilation of perspectives result in a perceptive explanation of many human, technical, and creative processes that are the essence of cinema and film.

---

Classification: LC PN1993; Dewey 791.

---

330. *The New Biographical Dictionary of Film*, by David Thomson
Publisher: Alfred A. Knopf/Random House, New York, NY (2004)

Price: $22.95

Review by Lucy Heckman—Reference Librarian (Business-Economics), St. John's University Library, Jamaica, NY.

Author David Thomson, who has written extensively on film, including books about David O. Selznick and Orson Welles, has compiled an entertaining biographical dictionary of film. The author includes profiles of notables in film from early stars and pioneers including Sir Charles Chaplin, Mary Pickford, Lon Chaney, D. W. Griffith, and Lillian Gish, through representatives of the "Golden Age of Hollywood," including Clark Gable, Gary Cooper, Joan Crawford, Norma Shearer, Greta Garbo, and Cary Grant, through stars of today, among which are Renee Zellweger, Meryl Streep, Nicole Kidman, Mel Gibson, Michael Douglas, and Johnny Depp. Character actors and actresses are also given their due and include such notables as Jane Darwell, Claude Rains, Charles Coburn, and Ward Bond. Coverage is international in scope, and in addition to American stars there is a large selection of profiles of individuals from various parts of the world, such as Emil Jannings, Anton Walbrook, Andrzej Wajda, and Anna Magnani. Each entry contains the date of birth of the subject, the year of birth and date of death (when applicable), and birth name. For instance, Vivien Leigh's entry lists her birth name, Vivian Mary Hartley. Each entry provides an entertaining read as in Miss Leigh's entry. It opens with a description of how Vivien Leigh was "discovered" for her role of Scarlett O'Hara, dramatically taking place during filming of the burning of Atlanta. It describes her various film roles pre- and post-Scarlett, names the films she starred in and the years released, and her personal life is briefly treated. The *New Biographical Dictionary of Film* is more than a reference book; it provides a very interesting read about each film personage and some critique of their notable works. The author also intersperses interesting bits of trivia in the profiles, for instance, actress Betty Hutton being Ludwig Wittgenstein's favorite actress. The source is arranged alphabetically by name with some interesting cross-references, including a cross-reference from actress Sharon Stone to a combined article on Miss Stone and Frances Farmer. The *New Biographical Dictionary of Film* is highly recommended for public and academic collections. It can be used to answer movie trivia questions and also to learn more about favorite film personages. It provides lively reading.

---

The 5th edition appeared in 2010. Classification: LC PN1998; Dewey 791.

---

331. *The Anime Encyclopedia: A Guide to Japanese Animation since 1917*, by Jonathan Clements and Helen McCarthy

Publisher: Consortium, Minneapolis, MN (2006)

Price: $29.95

Review by Staff, Libraries Unlimited.

This revised edition of *The Anime Encyclopedia* provides users with over 3,000 entries on anime titles, studios, creators, and history of the art form. As interest has exploded in the United States in the past several years, an update of this title is both timely and needed. This revised edition provides 40 percent more entries as well as 150 illustrations and screen captures. The book begins with an introduction on the current state of anime (both in Japan and in the United States) and a very thorough discussion of how the book is arranged. The authors write in a very clear, conversational style that discusses the great things about anime in the twenty-first century as well as some of the not-so-great aspects (e.g., lack of originality). The book then goes on to list the entries in alphabetic order. Each anime title includes the date, information on director and crew, number of minutes, and a summary of the plot and comparisons to other relevant anime movies. Terms that can be cross-referenced to other entries in the book have been bolded. Especially useful for parents, teachers, and librarians, the authors have included icons for films that include violence, obscene language, and nudity. A two-page bibliography and an extensive 110-page index conclude the volume. The index is especially noteworthy as it is heavily cross-referenced, especially between Japanese and English titles. This work continues to be an essential purchase for medium and large public libraries, school libraries that deal extensively with anime, and film and media collections of college and university libraries.

---

The 3rd edition appeared in 2015 as *The Anime Encyclopedia: A Century of Japanese Animation*. Classification: LC NC1766; Dewey 791.

---

## Theater and Dance

332. *The Oxford Companion to Theatre and Performance*, by Dennis Kennedy, ed.

Publisher: Oxford University Press, New York, NY (2010)

Price: $45.00

Review by Charles Neuringer—Professor of Psychology and Theatre and Film, University of Kansas, Lawrence.

This reference work is a new and concise revision of the 2003 two-volume edition of *The Oxford Encyclopedia of Theatre and Performance*. It is a more concise and updated version of its predecessor. There are 689 pages containing 2,000 alphabetically arranged entries starting with "Abbey Theatre" and ending with

"Stefan Zweig." The entries deal mainly with actors, playwrights, directors, styles, companies, and organizations. Some peripheral subjects such as paratheatrical events, sports, public executions, and censorship receive some minor attention. Non-theatrical performance activities such as opera, film, dance, radio, and television are also referenced. The reference work is international in scope but concentrated mainly on English-speaking theater and performance. The editors point out that in their revised work they have downplayed literary aspects, theatrical issues, and regionalism in favor of performance aspects of the theatrical enterprise. The editors provide a very useful side-by-side timeline comparing historical and cultural events with theater's historical events. Suggestions for further readings organized by particular topics and historical eras are also provided. Finally, the editors list a series of Web resources that have direct and indirect applications to the theater (e.g., Shakespeare, theater companies, theater history). Instruction on how to access the sites is also given. There is no name or subject index. This volume is a pleasure to read and to randomly dip into. Although it is a concise and supplemental version of its massive two-volume predecessor, it can and does function as a useful standalone reference work. Since it is a concise version there will be complaints about what has been excised.

---

Classification: LC PN2035; Dewey 792.

---

333. *The Oxford Dictionary of Plays*, by Michael Patterson
Publisher: Oxford University Press, New York, NY (2005)
Price: $45.00
Review by Charles Neuringer—Professor of Psychology and Theatre and Film, University of Kansas, Lawrence.

Oxford University Press has published what it describes as a concise and useful reference to the most important 1,000 plays of the Western world. They are presented in alphabetic order, starting with Abie's *Irish Rose* and concluding with *The Zoo Story*. Each entry is composed of the title (and/or alternative title), author(s), date of composition, date of first performance, genre, setting, cast size, a brief synopsis, and a brief commentary. Although there are occasional minor errors, the entries are usually informative and well written. Certain plays that are felt by the author to be particularly important are dealt with in greater detail than the other entries. The author supplied an index of characters and the plays in which they appear, which allows the reader to follow the path of those characters that have appeared in multiple works. An index of playwrights also appears, which gives the title and dates of their creations. For those fans of Shakespeare, a useful family tree of characters in the historical plays is presented by the author. These are preceded by a listing of the elected works according to country of origin, period, and genre. The plays selected for special attention appear in bold face. A somewhat modest selected bibliography is also provided. Readers may disagree about the selection of the "Best 1,000." No criteria for selection are given. The selection procedure seems to be an intuitive process coupled with consultation with others. No criteria, such as "number of world performances," was used. However, if one wants good information about a play or its characters, one will probably find it in this volume. Academics, professionals, and lovers of the theater will want to have access to this reference work.

Classification: LC PN1625; Dewey 809.

334. *The Oxford Companion to American Theatre*, by Gerald Bordman and Thomas S. Hischak

Publisher: Oxford University Press, New York, NY (2004)

Price: $75.00

Review by Richard D. Johnson—Director of Libraries Emeritus, James M. Milne Library, State University College, Oneonta, NY.

The 3rd edition of this valued reference work has been updated by Thomas S. Hischak. Hischak (SUNY Cortland) has several reference works to his credit: *Stage It with Music* and *American Musical Theatre Song Encyclopedia*. The new edition has approximately 3,100 entries arranged in one alphabet. Individual entries range from 70 words to a few with more than 1,000 words (e.g., "Scene Design" has 1,200 words). Hischak notes that to retain the work's size it was necessary to condense and edit some entries so as not diminish the volume's overall scope. An excellent system of cross-references links entries. The work covers individuals, plays, theaters, organizations, and awards, as well as entries on such general subjects as feminist theater and Asian-American theater. The work includes not only the professional Broadway stage, but Off and Off-Off Broadway, and regional theaters throughout the nation. Individuals featured are those who have had a major relationship with the live stage, such as playwright, director, set designer, producer, reviewer, or performer. Thus, although she is at times principally associated with television, there is an entry for Carol Burnett, but there are none for Mary Tyler Moore or Dick Van Dyke. Although Gene Kelly is cited in the entries on *The Time of Your Life* and *Pal Joey*, he merits no separate entry. There are some judgment calls: Glenn Close is in; Meryl Streep is out. Numerous individuals from other nations are included (e.g., Shakespeare, Chekhov, Gilbert & Sullivan, Noël Coward, Laurence Olivier) with information on their relation to the American stage. The entries for individual plays are most useful in that they give capsule plot summaries and list principal performers and production history. Coverage goes back to the eighteenth century (the actor-manager Lewis Hallam) and continues through early 2003 (the Tony award-winning *Take Me Out*). The volume includes currently reigning stars, as well as continuing stalwarts. The next edition will undoubtedly include rising stars. A few entries include a bibliography. This work is recommended for all collections. It serves as a complement to *The Cambridge Guide to American Theatre*, which has special features such as illustrations, a lengthy bibliography, and an excellent index listing individuals not included with entries of their own.

Classification: LC PN2220; Dewey 792.

335. *The Oxford Companion to the American Musical*, by Thomas Hischak

Publisher: Oxford University Press, New York, NY (2008)

Price: $39.95

Review by Richard D. Johnson—Director of Libraries Emeritus, James M. Milne Library, State University College, Oneonta, NY.

Hischak (SUNY Cortland) has an impressive list of publications, many of them reference works related to the performing arts. A recent example is his revision of the 3rd edition of *The Oxford Companion to American Theatre*. In this new volume he furnishes a separate guide to American musicals, but with a difference: he does not limit himself to the stage but also includes film and television musicals. There are approximately 2,000 entries arranged in one alphabet: by name of individual or organization; title of show; or subject (e.g., "Revue Musicals"). Individual entries range in length from 250 to some more than 1,000 words. Hischak cross-references items by use of "caps and small caps" for words or names within entries to show there is a link to another entry. Small icons indicate whether the show discussed is a stage, film, or television musical. The scope is broad, ranging from the earliest musicals (a production of Gay's *Beggar's Opera* in 1750 to 2008s *In the Heights*). One finds performers from Lillian Russell (1861–1922) to Sutton Foster (b. 1975), composers from John Philip Sousa (1854–1932) to Adam Guettel (b. 1964), and producing organizations like Playwrights Horizons and the Ohio Light Opera. Performers identified with screen musicals (Joan Blondell and Nelson Eddy) are featured as are those with the stage (Karen Ziemba and Alfred Drake), not to mention those who found careers on stage, screen, and television (Danny Kaye and Bob Hope). As the work is not limited to one medium, the reader can follow the course of a particular show. For *Oklahoma!* information is given on casts of four major stage productions as well as the film. In a few cases the show began as a film. For *Singin' in the Rain* you first have information and cast of the 1952 movie and then the 1986 stage version. There are some productions that had life only on the screen (*Gold Diggers*,

*Moulin Rouge*). Hischak does a fine job treating the individual versions a particular show might have. With *Peter Pan* there is a basic story but two different stage versions plus a movie and then a television production. Or consider O'Neill's *Ah, Wilderness!* It had one incarnation as a film musical, *Summer Holiday*, and then a completely different life on stage as *Take Me Along*. Hischak adeptly handles what might otherwise be confusing situations. The subject entries give an extra dimension to this work; for example, "Business and Politics in Musicals" and "Shakespeare Musicals" address these very specific topics. Unfortunately, those using the work solely as a ready-reference tool may miss these valuable additions. Hischak enlivens many entries with his own personal comments, which give this work particular warmth. The volume concludes with several appendixes: a chronology of the musicals (1750–2008), a chronological list of Academy and Tony Awards, a guide to recordings, a comprehensive bibliography, and an index. For many shows Hischak features as a sidebar lists of casts (original and revival productions and movie and television versions). For some musicals he also includes a sidebar with musical numbers. The photographs throughout the volume are a good addition. Aficionados may question a few statements or regret the omission of some favorite performers and shows; but they should take a cue from those South Pacific Seabees, singing about the "dames" they miss, "Be grateful for the things they got." Like the latest edition of Gerald Bordman's *American Musical Theatre: A Chronology*, this volume is an essential reference work on the shelves of all performing arts collections, large public libraries, academic libraries, and the personal libraries of individuals committed to the American musical.

---

Classification: LC ML102; Dewey 782.

---

336. *The Oxford Companion to Shakespeare*, by Michael Dobson and Stanley Wells, eds.

Publisher: Oxford University Press, New York, NY (2001)

Price: $45.00

Review by Charlotte Lindgren—Professor Emerita of English, Emerson College, Boston, MA.

This comprehensive, attractively produced, single-volume encyclopedia contains three thousand alphabetic entries as well as maps, copious illustrations from Elizabethan woodcuts and portraits to modern photographs, genealogical charts of the Houses of York and Lancaster, and a lengthy chronology of Shakespeare's life, work, and reception from 1564 to 1999. Seventeen pages list by theme Shakespeare's works, principal characters, literary contemporaries, and theatrical and publishing history, followed by a listing of his plays in alphabetic order. Articles by major Shakespearean scholars of his plays and sonnets discuss sources, texts, synopsis, artistic features, critical history, and stage and screen history, and each ends with a list of recent major editions and representative criticism. Sonnets cover the mystery of the Dark Lady and Mr. W. H. Each article is in its alphabetic position but set apart by decorative margins. Entries are well cross-referenced (i.e., Cinema "See Shakespeare on Sound Film; Silent Film"). Together these two give a history of cinematic productions from the 1899 death scene of *King John* to the 1999 film "A Midsummer Night's Dream." Cross-references within entries are marked by an asterisk before the pertinent names. Definitions of terms are both literary (e.g., iambic) and historical (e.g., tireman [Elizabethan carer of costumes]). The list of further readings is divided by topics. The encyclopedia is inexpensive for such a handsome and useful volume. Not only should it be in every academic library, but the students, actors, general readers, and serious scholars for whom it was designed should add it to their shelves.

---

The 2nd edition appeared in 2015. Classification: LC PR2892; Dewey 822.

---

337. *All Things Shakespeare: An Encyclopedia of Shakespeare's World*, by Kirstin Olsen

Publisher: Greenwood Press/ABC-CLIO, Santa Barbara, CA (2002)

Price: $150.00/set

Review by Christopher Baker—Professor of English, Armstrong Atlantic State University, Savannah, GA.

There has not been a factual account of the details of daily life in Shakespeare's England since the Oxford publication of *Shakespeare's England* (repr. ed., 1966), as R. E. Pritchard's recent *Shakespeare's England: Life in Elizabethan and Jacobean Times* (2001) is an anthology of period writings on society. Olsen's two volumes succeed in offering a wealth of information on a wide variety of topics found in the plays, and they should satisfy the ready-reference needs of a popular audience. There are 205 general entries presented, covering topics such as alchemy, farming, news, poetry, and transportation. Experienced Shakespeareans may find some generalizations misleading. To say that "there were no banks" in the Renaissance (v. 1, p. 113) bypasses the founding of the Bank of Venice in 1171 or of Amsterdam's in 1609. Some recent developments in Shakespearean culture are noted, including the excavation of the Rose Theatre in 1989; the entry on women reflects the contemporary interest in gender, but the statement that "women, were, in most respects, treaded badly by Shakespeare"

(v. 2, p. 681) is an opinion rather than accepted scholarly fact. The bibliography and topic guides present selected books for further reference, although the intended audience is unlikely to have access to the Latin 1st editions of Gesner, Fludd, or Vesalius cited there. The extensive "Chronology of Historical Events" is an excellent supplement for the study of Shakespeare's history plays. The index is detailed, with helpful subheadings, and frequent black-and-white maps, photographs, and line drawings enhance the text.

Classification: LC PR2892; Dewey 822.

338. *The Oxford Dictionary of Dance*, by Debra Craine and Judith Mackrell
Publisher: Oxford University Press, New York, NY (2010)
Price: $18.95
Review by Lizbeth Langston—Reference Librarian, University of California—Riverside.

The 2nd edition of the *Oxford Dictionary of Dance* updates the resource published in 2000. Newly added entries include those for dance forms such as krumping and various contemporary dancers or composers. Recent choreographies update the entries for many individuals and dance companies, including those outside Europe or the United States. Death dates and career summations update entries for deceased dancers and choreographers. While some new entries for dance forms have been added, missing are contemporary sociocultural, popular, and athletic types such as folklorico, bhangra, and zoomba. Except for a few classic films (such as *The Red Shoes*), movies and television shows with a dance theme are excluded. Overall, the thousands of entries cover the field of dance. This paperback (with paper quality to match the modest price) is appropriate for reference collections of all libraries and is fun to browse.

Classification: LC GV1585; Dewey 792.

## Music

339. *The Harvard Dictionary of Music*, by Don Michael Randel, ed.
Publisher: Harvard University Press, Cambridge, MA (2003)
Price: $39.95
Review by Bradford Lee Eden—Dean of Library Services, Valparaiso University, Valparaiso, IN.

This reference work has always been an indispensable guide to the music professional and amateur. Known as the best 1-volume music dictionary available, the 4th edition has over 220 drawings and 250 musical examples throughout. Numerous changes from the previous edition, including outright additions and deletions of subjects and composers as well as new developments in musical scholarship, are reflected in its content. Many of the standard entries have revised bibliographies that do not cite larger standard reference works, given the enormity of the topics and the number of entries. This book has always been a staple of study for musicians studying for their comprehensive graduate examinations, performers looking for beginning source materials for research on composers, and music amateurs looking for a quick source to determine language translations of music terms and composer directions in musical scores. The 4th edition of *The Harvard Dictionary of Music* is a must for every music library and an essential component of any general reference collection.

Classification: LC ML100; Dewey 780.

340. *The Oxford Companion to Music*, by Alison Latham, ed.
Publisher: Oxford University Press, New York, NY (2002)
Price: $60.00
Review by Ian Fairclough—Cataloger, Marion Public Library, Marion, OH.

No edition statement appears with this work, even though a note states that this volume was first published in 2002—so a little explanation is in order. Percy A. Scholes wrote the 1st edition, published in 1938, in one volume. The 10th edition appeared in 1970 with John Owen Ward as editor, but was still predominantly the work of Scholes. The *New Oxford Companion to Music*, in two volumes, came in 1983; Denis Arnold was general editor, and a team of scholars prepared the signed entries. Nineteen years have transpired between that work and the current one, which reverts to the original title and one-volume format while still being the work of numerous individuals. All of this information is elaborated in the preface; however, a summary publication history would help, and the absence of an edition statement is lamentable. Most of the entries are dictionary length, while others are encyclopedic. Users will find numerous biographies, accounts of individual musical works, translations of foreign terms, as well as topical articles with bibliographies. The entry for "Opera," set off on a gray-shaded background, is 27 pages long. The work is extensively self-referenced using asterisks within articles. In the back of the volume is a 35-page "Select Index of People" who do not have their own entries. There is also a list of contributors with a key to their initials, some of whom have a brief biography following (it is frustrating that not all of them do).

The scope of the volume is focused on Western art music. A British orientation is evidenced in the entry for "Copyright" that has sections headed "International Perspective" and "Essentials of UK Copyright Law," but not one on U.S. law. Some entries have references to longer articles. The Low Countries and Latin America are treated as a unit. Some entries are quite obscure, such as "Eis" (German for E sharp, a note rarely used). This title can serve as a handy, quick reference tool, but may duplicate other materials in collections. The preface refers readers to the 29-volume *New Grove Dictionary of Music and Musicians* (entry 342) for further, more specialized articles. Other notable titles from this publisher include *The Oxford Dictionary of Music* (2nd ed.), which is similar in scope and arrangement.

---

Classification: LC ML100; Dewey 780.

---

341. *Baker's Biographical Dictionary of Musicians*, by Nicolas Slonimsky and Laura Kuhn, eds.

Publisher: Schirmer Books/Gale Group, New York, NY (2001)

Price: $595.00/set

Review by Dorothy Jones—Reference Librarian, Founders Memorial Library, Northern Illinois University, De Kalb.

A 100-year-old classic reference book, with 1,000 new classical entries and massive additions that reflect a new policy of full inclusion for jazz and popular musicians, is cause for celebration. Theodore Baker's 1st edition of *Baker's Biographical Dictionary of Musicians* was published in 1900. Nicolas Slonimsky was editor of the 5th through the 8th editions. Slonimsky died in 1995 at the age of 101. The centennial, or 9th edition, of Baker's is a work authored and revised by many people. Laura Kuhn, Baker's Series Advisory Editor, and Dennis McIntire expanded classical entries. The contributions of about 2,000 entries about popular and jazz musicians by William J. Ruhlmann and Lewis Porter have vastly expanded the scope and size of the centennial edition. Rock entries adapted from Brock Helander's Schirmer work, *The Rock Who's Who*, and recent rock entries by Hand Bordowitz have also been incorporated into the centennial edition. In the short "Preface to the Centennial Edition," written by Kuhn and Ruhlmann, Ruhlmann describes some of the challenges presented by the differing nomenclatures of classical musicians and popular musicians. The challenges are well met by means of compromise and additional terminology, which does not detract from the unity of the whole. Almost all of the classical entries from the past have been revised to reflect new research into the lives of deceased musicians as well as changes in the lives and works of living musicians. New classical entries include the noteworthy people and events of the final decade of the twentieth century. Slonimsky's long and chatty prefaces to the 5th, 6th, 7th, and 8th editions are included in volume 1 and are both historically interesting and a fine tribute to the man. Entries in the body of the dictionary range in length from a paragraph to several pages. The lists of works or discs at the end of composer or performer entries is of major value. It is notable that even small entries often contain "stories" to make their reading a pleasure. For example, the entry on George Bridgetower, one of the small entries and the only Abyssinian-Polish musician in the dictionary, was a violinist but is historically important because he gave the first performance of the Kreutzer Sonata, with Beethoven himself at the piano, in Vienna on May 24, 1803. The indexes included at the end of volume 6 include a genre index, a nationality index, and an index of women composers and musicians. The genre index is divided into classical, jazz, and popular sections. The classical section is subdivided into early music, Renaissance, Baroque, classical, Romantic, and modern. Jazz is subdivided into early, swing, bebop, and avant-garde. The popular section is subdivided into country, pop, R&B/rap, and rock. This index is particularly useful considering the expansion of the scope of this edition. The centennial edition of *Baker's Biographical Dictionary of Musicians* is built on the older editions but contains so many new entries and revisions and so great a change in scope that it will be a necessary addition to any library or personal collection in which a solid, basic music section is important.

Classification: LC ML105; Dewey 780.

342. *The New Grove Dictionary of Music and Musicians,* by Stanley Sadie, ed.
Publisher: Macmillan Publishers Limited, New York, NY (2001)
Price: $4,580.00/set
Review by Staff, Libraries Unlimited.

This authoritative and massive (twenty-nine volumes) work covers a vast array of people, places, and things. The first twenty-seven volumes are arranged in classic A to Z format; the twenty-eighth volume includes appendixes and the twenty-ninth volume is an index. Entries vary in length. Some can be a short paragraph and some can be dozens of pages (e.g., the entries for Acoustics and Bach). Tables, diagrams, figures, and black-and-white photos are used throughout the volumes. Bibliographies follow many entries. In all volumes, the front matter contains General Abbreviations, Bibliographical Abbreviations, Discographical Abbreviations, Library Sigla, and A Note on the Use of the Dictionary. The first volume additionally contains a Preface, a Preface to the 1980 Edition, an Introduction, Acknowledgments, a Publisher's Note, and a Preface to the First

Edition. The introduction covers, among other topics, alphabetization, usages, authors, article headings, article structure, cross-references, transliteration, bibliographies, and appendixes. The front matter of volume 28 starts with general abbreviations, special abbreviations, library sigla, and a note on the use of the dictionary. The first appendix covers collections (private), Congress reports, dictionaries and encyclopedias of music, editions (historical), libraries, periodicals, and sound archives. The second appendix has illustration acknowledgments and music example acknowledgments; a contributor list comprises the third. Volume 29, at eight hundred pages, contains the index for the entire set and a separate list of composers, performers, and writers. This volume has its own introduction and an extensive system of *see* and *see also* references. Highly recommended for public and academic libraries.

> All twenty-nine volumes are included in the digital Grove Music Online: see http://www.oxfordmusiconline.com/. Classification: LC ML100; Dewey 780.

343. *The NPR Listener's Encyclopedia of Classical Music*, by Ted Libbey
Publisher: Workman Publishing, New York, NY (2006)
Price: $19.95
Review by Staff, Libraries Unlimited.

Libbey designed this A to Z collection of more than 1,500 entries to be broad and inclusive and to appeal to a general readership without being simplistic. With such an undertaking, the selection process posed the biggest challenge. Inside the encyclopedia, readers will find entries on composers, performers, instruments, named pieces, institutions and organizations, and concepts. The length of each varies, from one paragraph (see toccata) to several pages (see Mozart). Many entries conclude with recommended readings. There are more than 2,000 recommendations in all, though there is no further readings list at the end of the book. Users can be sure of the accuracy. In addition to the many sources consulted in writing this book, Libbey relied on the 2000 edition of *New Grove Dictionary of Music and Musicians* (entry 342), the leading authority on the subject (all 29 volumes). The most exciting aspect of this work, however, is that it provides access (explained in the front matter) to a website developed by Naxos specifically for this book. More than 500 musical pieces and more than 75 hours of sound are available to readers. A speaker icon within entries indicates those that link to the website. This allows users to hear an example of an aria (e.g., Puccini's Turandot), the overture to Tchaikovsky's Romeo and Juliet, and much more. Highly recommended to public and academic libraries.

Classification: LC ML100; Dewey 780.

344. *Oxford Companion to Jazz*, by Bill Kirchner, ed.
Publisher: Oxford University Press, New York, NY (2000)
Price: $49.95
Review by Staff, Libraries Unlimited.

This addition to the Oxford Companion series provides sixty essays that address the history and importance of jazz, the genre's leading musicians, and more. The sixty essays are roughly arranged in chronological order starting with "African Roots of Jazz" by Samuel A. Floyd, Jr., and ending with "Jazz Improvisation and Concepts of Virtuosity." The book covers such jazz artists as Jelly Roll Morton, Louis Armstrong, Duke Ellington, Ella Fitzgerald, Billie Holiday, Charlie Parker, Miles Davis, and John Coltrane. Other musicians are covered in such chapters as "Pianists of the 1920s and 1930s." Styles and influences are also explained in chapters like "Jazz Composing and the American Song," "Cool Jazz and West Coast Jazz," and "The Avant-Garde, 1949–1967." Various chapters discuss jazz in terms of other countries—Europe, Africa, Japan, Canada, Australia—and certain instruments in relation to jazz—clarinet, saxophone, trumpet, trombone, electric guitar, vibraphone, bass, and miscellaneous instruments. Such topics as jazz and its relationship to literature, dance, and film and television are also represented in this work. Concluding chapters analyze jazz clubs, jazz education, and jazz criticism. The book ends with a selected bibliography and an index that facilitates finding musicians like the Marsalis brothers who do not have a dedicated chapter. Entries are substantial, approximately ten to twenty pages each. Altogether, they achieve the editor's objective of providing a useful reference for everyone from the novice to the expert. Highly recommended for public and academic libraries.

Classification: LC ML3507; Dewey 781.

345. *The New Grove Dictionary of Jazz*, by Barry Kernfeld, ed.
Publisher: Oxford University Press, New York, NY (2002)
Price: $475.00/set
Review by Staff, Libraries Unlimited.

This second edition has doubled in size and broadened in scope to include more international jazz musicians; topical essays on such things as women and jazz and the cultural meaning of jazz in films; discussion of the intersections of the jazz mainstream with popular styles and genres like hip hop; essays on ethnic instruments used in jazz; nightclubs and other venues; and more information on record companies and corporations. Another notable change is the inclusion of URLs in the bibliography. Articles retained from the first edition have in most cases been revised. The work is divided into three volumes, with entries arranged in an A to Z format. The first volume contains a preface and introduction in 14 parts covering the dictionary's alphabetization, article structure, bibliographies, and more. All three volumes include general abbreviations, discographical abbreviations, bibliographical abbreviations, and library sigla in the front matter. The third volume contains three appendixes: "Bibliography," "Calendar of Jazz Births and Dates," and "List of Contributors." Most of the articles are signed; unsigned articles were compiled by the editorial team. Additionally, almost all the entries have one or more bibliographical citations. Black-and-white photographs are sprinkled throughout the text. Articles vary in length from one paragraph to multiple pages, depending on the subject. The new section on nightclubs and other venues occupies the first 155 pages of volume 3. This reference work should be a mainstay on the reference shelves of public and academic libraries. Highly recommended.

Classification: LC ML102; Dewey 781.

346. *The Rolling Stone Encyclopedia of Rock & Roll*, by Holly George-Warren, Patricia Romanowski, and Jon Pareles, eds.
Publisher: Fireside/Simon & Schuster Adult Publishing Group, New York, NY (2001)
Price: $40.00
Review by Staff, Libraries Unlimited.

In this third edition, editors George-Warren and Romanowski revised existing profiles and added groups and individual performers, resulting in an encyclopedia with nearly two thousand entries that cover the history of rock and roll from the 1950s. Since the first edition in 1983, the editors have added seven hundred entries. The introduction explains the selection process and the reasons why some musicians were cut from this edition. It also provides information on the length, which varies from one paragraph to several pages; on sources used; on the entry format; on sources for music chart data; and on what the book is not (a history of rock-and-roll music, a consumer guide, or a collection of critical commentaries). Entries include biographical details, information about when bands formed, and discographies, followed by essays that contextualize the musicians. Black-and-white photographs supplement the information. The encyclopedia starts with ABBA and ends with ZZ Top. Many of the hundreds of bands and musicians in between are just as recognizable—The Beach Boys, The Beatles, Fleetwood Mac, Bob Marley and the Wailers, and Prince. Others are less so—The Beautiful South, The Champs, Snooks Eaglin, Joy of Cooking, and Peaches and Herb. Within the traditional A to Z format, *see* references point users in the right direction. The book concludes with an appendix of cuts made from the second edition, information about the contributors, and an index. This comprehensive and reliable rock-and-roll encyclopedia is highly recommended for public, school, and academic libraries.

---

Classification: LC ML102; Dewey 781.

---

347. *Encyclopedia of Rap and Hip Hop Culture*, by Yvonne Bynoe
Publisher: Greenwood Press/ABC-CLIO, Santa Barbara, CA (2006)
Price: $69.95
Review by Staff, Libraries Unlimited.

Rap and hip-hop music have left an immeasurable mark on both entertainment and culture in the past three decades. Thought to have been started in the 1970s, hip-hop culture has grown to include four major art forms: MCing (or rap); B-boying (break dancing); DJing; and graffiti (the visual aspect of the art). Today these four elements combine to form the unmistakable cultural phenomena known as hip-hop. This volume explores in encyclopedic format the major players, developments, themes, and highlights of this racially diverse culture. The entries vary in length from a few sentences to several pages. Some of the most well-covered topics include East Coast/West Coast Rivalry, Tupac Shakur, Russell Simmons, Bad Boy Entertainment, Sean "P. Diddy" Combs, Rap-Metal, Graffiti, and Run DMC. The majority of the entries focus on well-known artists of hip-hop and rap. After a list of entries and a lengthy introduction focusing on the history and impact of hip-hop, the work goes on to list the entries alphabetically. The work includes *see* references and over one hundred black-and-white photographs. The work concludes with an appendix listing a selected rap discography as well as an appendix that reprints the "Hip Hop Declaration of Peace," which was unveiled at the United Nations on May 16, 2002. A selected bibliography and index conclude the volume. Overall, this is an outstanding volume that impressively covers both the highlights and lesser-known aspects of rap and hip-hop culture and industry. A few aspects of interest were omitted, including the role that fashion has played on the industry. This work will be well received in high school, academic, and public libraries.

Classification: LC ML102; Dewey 782.

## Philosophy

348. *Encyclopedia of Philosophy*, by Donald M. Borchert, ed.

Publisher: Macmillan Library Reference/Simon & Schuster Macmillan, New York, NY (2006)

Price: $995.00/set

Review by Staff, Libraries Unlimited.

The 1st edition of the *Encyclopedia of Philosophy* was considered a premier reference source when it debuted in 1967. The supplement to the Encyclopedia was published in 1996 and was edited by Donald Borchert, the editor of this 2nd edition. Borchert worked with a board of 7 associate editors and 14 consulting editors in the updating of this resource. Each of the associate and consulting editors specializes in a different field of philosophy (e.g., modern, philosophy of science, ethics, metaphysics, philosophy of religion, feminism). As Borchert mentions in the preface to this set, the editors of this volume had a great advantage in updating the encyclopedia due to the fact that the 1st edition was so comprehensive in scope and the substantive articles were written by scholars in the field. Regardless, after a span of 40 years they realized that substantial updates were required to make this edition as scholarly and highly regarded as the first. The work was updated with 450 entirely new entries; 300 entries present in the 1st edition were completely revised by new authors for this 2nd edition. New entries include those on feminism, the philosophy of sex and love, ethics, and biographical entries of those new to the field. Some 90 articles were updated by their original author and an additional 150 have addendums written by new authors. In addition, more than 430 of the original 1,200 entries have new bibliographic citations. Along with providing updated information the editors also have broadened the scope of the encyclopedia by focusing on cultural diversity. New regional and cultural entries include those on Chinese, Buddhist, Islamic, and Indian philosophies. The bulk of the volumes provides an A-Z listing of entries. Entries vary in length from half a page to several pages in length. Each entry includes *see also* references as well a bibliography. Additional materials are provided in volume 10. These include an appendix of additional articles (a list of articles that were unable to be listed in the main encyclopedia due to time constraints in the editorial process); a thematic outline of contents for those who wish to research certain time periods or subfields; bibliographies of philosophical encyclopedias, journals, and bibliographies; and a nearly 500-page subject index. This encyclopedia will be useful to researchers, scholars, and students. It is written in clear, jargon-free English so that even the educated layperson will be able to use it easily. The *Encyclopedia of Philosophy* will find much use in larger academic and research libraries.

Classification: LC B51; Dewey 103.

349. *Concise Routledge Encyclopedia of Philosophy*, by Edward Craig, ed.
Publisher: Routledge/Taylor & Francis Group, New York, NY (2000)
Price: $40.00
Review by Richard H. Swain—Reference Librarian, West Chester University, West Chester, PA.

The *Concise Routledge Encyclopedia of Philosophy* properly presents itself as "a complete introduction to world philosophy." It is a condensation of the 10-volume *Routledge Encyclopedia of Philosophy* (1998), and it is comprised of entries that often are the introductory matter from the more extended, technical entries of the full *Routledge Encyclopedia*. There are over 2,000 entries in the *Concise Routledge Encyclopedia*. They cover the major areas of philosophy (e.g., ethics, metaphysics, epistemology), time periods and schools of thought periods (e.g., medieval philosophy, stoic philosophy), national and ethnic topics (e.g., Chinese philosophy, Yoruba epistemology), definitions, and biographies (including biographies of living philosophers). No entry is more than six two-column pages long, and most are less than two columns. Particularly useful are the annotated lists of further readings that accompany each entry. The entries are authoritative, straightforward, and well written. There is a good one-page introduction, a list of contributors (which, unfortunately, are listed alphabetically by entry and not by contributor name), and an excellent index. Owners of the full *Routledge Encyclopedia* will obtain no new information by purchasing the *Concise Routledge Encyclopedia*, but, since it provides such good nontechnical introductions, definitions, and descriptions, it is valuable for anyone not willing or able to handle the technical content of the full encyclopedia. Owners of the *Encyclopedia of Philosophy* (Macmillan; entry 348) and its supplements should purchase the full *Routledge Encyclopedia of Philosophy* if possible. It is more up-to-date and includes topics of current interest (artificial intelligence, Bell's Theorem, environmental ethics, private language argument). If a library cannot afford the full *Routledge Encyclopedia*, it should purchase the *Concise Routledge Encyclopedia*. This is a superb reference work. It must be numbered among the three best one-volume guides to philosophy in the English language. The other two are the *Oxford Companion to Philosophy* (entry 351) and the *Cambridge Dictionary of Philosophy* (entry 350). It is difficult to decide among them. All are well written, reliable, and provide serious coverage of contemporary issues and non-European philosophy in addition to more traditional topics. The *Cambridge Dictionary* does not include an index, and thus it is the least useful of the three. The *Oxford Companion* stands out because it includes illustrations and because some of the most prominent names in late twentieth-century Anglo-American philosophy are among its contributors (Davidson, Dummett, Dworkin, Searle, and Quine, among others). Nonetheless, the lucid prose and annotated lists of further readings of the *Concise Routledge Encyclopedia* make it the best choice for general readers, including high school and undergraduate students. All libraries should seriously consider buying the *Concise Routledge Encyclopedia*, even those who own the full version.

> The related *Shorter Routledge Encyclopedia of Philosophy* (2005) takes a different tack, sampling about half of the articles from the full *Routledge Encyclopedia of Philosophy* and reprinting the complete original text for about one hundred of those articles. Classification: LC B51; Dewey 103.

350. *The Cambridge Dictionary of Philosophy*, by Robert Audi, ed.

Publisher: Cambridge University Press, New York, NY (1999)

Price: $74.95

Review by Gregory Curtis—Regional Federal Depository Librarian for Maine, New Hampshire, and Vermont, Fogler Library, University of Maine, Presque Isle.

With the revision of this work into a new edition, it becomes only stronger as a reference work and more worthy of inclusion on the library shelf. This 2nd edition includes more than four hundred new entries by fifty additional contemporary philosophers. It also expands the coverage of developing fields, such as applied ethics and philosophy of the mind, while at the same time expanding on non-Western and non-European philosophy. A large selection of entries is devoted to African, Arabic, Islamic, Japanese, Jewish, Korean, and Latin American philosophy. This inclusion is especially gratifying with the world becoming smaller all the time. Inclusion of the non-Western philosophies further exemplifies the breadth of discussion currently undertaken in philosophy. Entries, as the preface to the 1st edition indicates, fall between brief descriptions of the concept and that of an encyclopedic entry consisting of background context and bibliographic information. Each entry attempts to express the nature and content of the concept while illuminating salient related side avenues of the entry. The target of this volume is the well-versed reader in other fields who may need access to definitions of concepts in the field of philosophy to enhance their understanding. A number of philosophers are included in the entries, not as much to define and discuss their biographical information, but to more fully explore the developments of philosophical thought throughout its development as a field of intellectual inquiry. Various related fields and subfields are also included. Some examples include the philosophy of history, computer and artificial intelligence, political philosophy, and the philosophy of science. Modern philosophers are selectively included in the 2nd edition, again weighted toward writers whom many nonphilosophers may want to look up.

The 3rd edition appeared in 2015. Classification: LC B41; Dewey 103.

351. *The Oxford Companion to Philosophy*, by Ted Honderich, ed.

Publisher: Oxford University Press, New York, NY (2005)

Price: $60.00

Review by Alan Asher—Art/Music Librarian, University of Northern Iowa, Cedar Falls.

Originally published in 1995, *The Oxford Companion to Philosophy* has been updated and expanded, and the present 2005 edition contains over 300 new articles. Entries are arranged alphabetically in dictionary style and range from the history of aesthetics to an entry about women and philosophy. Included are biographies of the great thinkers of western civilization, such as Aristotle, Plato, Augustine, Descartes, and Kant and also entries on non-western philosophers, such as Confucius. Written by 249 contributing philosophers under the editorial guidance of University College London philosopher Ted Honderich, the present 2nd edition also contains a chronological table of philosophy and many entries on national philosophies. There are gaps and omissions in this edition. For example, while there are biographical profiles of several thinkers from the political left, there is no mention of Russell Kirk, who was one of the most important conservative thinkers in twentieth-century America. Not all entries are dispassionate or unbiased. For example, the entry on animals is really an article on the importance of animal rights and makes many references to the importance of the works of philosopher Peter Singer to the animal rights movement. It comes as no surprise then that the author of this particular entry is none other than Peter Singer. Interestingly, although there are entries for Buddhist philosophy, Hindu philosophy, and Islamic philosophy, there is no corresponding entry on Christian philosophy. Despite these shortcomings, *The Oxford Companion to Philosophy* remains a valuable compendium for philosophic inquiry and reference.

Classification: LC B51; Dewey 103.

352. *Stanford Encyclopedia of Philosophy* [digital], by John Perry and Edward N. Zalta

Publisher: Metaphysics Research Lab, Center for the Study of Language and Information (CSLI), Stanford University, Palo Alto, CA

Price: Free online. Date reviewed: 2017.

URL: http://plato.stanford.edu/

Review by Steven W. Sowards, Associate Director for Collections, Michigan State University Libraries, East Lansing.

*SEP* is an online Open Access resource with content contributed by leading academic philosophers from around the world. Grants, support from Stanford University, and monetary contributions from member libraries cover costs and allow fee-free use by all readers. Content is added or updated on a wiki model, but all entries and revisions are refereed by an editorial board before posting. *SEP* was conceived in the 1990s and since has grown to more than 1500 articles. Entries can be browsed in alphabetical order, and keyword or phrase searching covers the full text. Entries include biographies of major thinkers, schools of thought, terms, and concepts. Examples include Albert Camus, Seneca and Socrates; Stoicism and Chan Buddhism; and democracy, critical theory, sovereignty and envy. Coverage is global, with entries about thought from China, India, and Africa, although there is an emphasis on European and American traditions. Coverage extends from the classical period into the twenty-first century with discussion, for example, of ethical aspects of social networking and moral issues in terrorism. Each signed entry begins with a short summary and an outline of the longer text and ends with a substantial bibliography and links to related texts, both within *SEP* and from outside sources. Articles can be quite long—a length of 20,000 words is not unusual—and are written by and for an academic audience. The introductory summaries are more accessible for general readers. A less technical alternative is the *Internet Encyclopedia of Philosophy*, also free and online at http://www.iep.utm.edu/.

---

Classification: LC B51; Dewey 100.

---

353. *Encyclopedia of Ethics*, by Lawrence C. Becker and Charlotte B. Becker, eds.

Publisher: Routledge/Taylor & Francis Group, New York, NY (2001)

Price: $350.00/set

Review by Hans E. Bynagle—Library Director and Professor of Philosophy, Whitworth College, Spokane, WA.

The 1st edition of this work filled, and filled well, a need for a reasonably current comprehensive encyclopedia on philosophical ethics. It has since been joined by a small cadre of other encyclopedic works in its field, including the three-volume *Ethics* in Salem Press's Ready Reference series, edited by John Roth (1993); the *Encyclopedia of Applied Ethics*; and the namesake *Encyclopedia of Ethics* by Susan Terkel. Nonetheless, the Beckers' volume remains a top choice for academic and large public libraries, and most of those should acquire the 2nd edition. New features include approximately 30 percent more content, expanding the two original volumes to three; some 150 new entries; moderate revision and occasional reorganization of the original articles; updated bibliographies; and improved cross-referencing. New entries represent not just topics that are new or newly prominent since the early 1990s (such as genetic engineering), but more often older topics previously neglected (e.g., conservation ethics) or now given more expansive treatment (e.g., the original article on risk is now joined by separate articles on risk analysis and risk aversion). Aspects that remain the same are, most significantly, the intent to serve primarily "scholars, university students, and readers with a serious interest in philosophy" (introduction); a focus on ethical theory coupled with substantial attention to applied ethics, biographical material, religious traditions, and history of ethics; and a distinct, but by no means exclusive, emphasis on philosophical ethics of the Western and English-speaking worlds. Other continuities include a distinguished cast of contributors (326) and a peer-review process applied to most of the contributions.

Classification: LC BJ63; Dewey 170.

354. *Encyclopedia of Philosophy and the Social Sciences*, by Byron Kaldis, ed.

Publisher: SAGE, Thousand Oaks, CA (2013)

Price: $350.00/set

Review by Margot Note—Information Manager and Archivist, World Monuments Fund, New York, NY.

The studies of philosophy and the social sciences have long been interconnected but rarely has their interdisciplinary nature been examined so thoroughly as it is in this multivolume set. This comprehensive two-volume encyclopedia covers the major theories, research, and issues in the interdisciplinary and multidisciplinary study of the links between philosophy and the social sciences. Many of the topics discussed are at the cutting edge of this topic, and some are controversial in nature. Editor Byron Kaldis from the Hellenic Open University in Greece assembled international experts in the field to write more than 150 entries. The work contributes to the renewal of the philosophy of the social sciences and will help to promote new modes of thinking about classic problems of society. The entries are diverse in nature, touching on economics, sociology, ethics, genealogy, and more. Entries range from about 600 to 2,000 words, with related entries, further readings, and websites noted. Entries are listed alphabetically and by theme, and an index completes both volumes. Several longer-framing essays provide an overview of contemporary research. Addressing complex philosophical topics, the *Encyclopedia of Philosophy and the Social Sciences* is a cohesive, usable reference source for both public and academic libraries and is well worth its high price.

---

Classification: LC B63; Dewey 103.

---

## Religion and Beliefs

### Antiquity

355. *The Oxford Dictionary of Classical Myth and Religion*, by Simon Price and Emily Kearns, eds.

Publisher: Oxford University Press, New York, NY (2003)

Price: $39.95

Review Susan Tower Hollis—Associate Dean and Center Director, Central New York Center of the State University of New York, Syracuse.

This volume, derived from the 3rd edition of *The Oxford Classical Dictionary* (entry 228) by the two area advisors for that volume, provides a reasonably priced and accessible reference work that interested nonspecialists and specialists in related fields will surely find useful. It opens with a brief discussion of mythology as interpreted by classicists and then follows with short discussions of religious pluralism and the reception of myths. After another short section on how to use the book, the editors provide an extremely brief bibliography followed by a most useful thematic index. This last resource makes it easy for the user to see the volume's entries on particular topics, including different types of ancient authors, different kinds of religions, and various types of deities. As a tool to make using the dictionary easier, this thematic index proves to be invaluable. The dictionary entries not only include mythological references but also topics such as religious places, officials, organizations, and rituals. In addition, among the entries, one finds discussions of "regional religions and 'mystery cults'" along with entries related to "Judaism and Christianity in the Hellenistic and Roman periods" (p. xvii). Many of the entries also provide cross-references as well as include references to appropriate primary texts. The volume concludes with three related maps and six genealogies, including one outlining the deities in Hesiod's *Theogony*. The modest price of this volume along with its extensive coverage makes it an appropriate acquisition for every college and high school library as well as most public libraries and many private collections.

---

Relevant content also appears in *Brill's New Pauly* (entry 229). Classification: LC BL715; Dewey 292.

---

356. *Encyclopedia of Ancient Deities*, by Charles Russell Coulter and Patricia Turner

Publisher: McFarland, Jefferson, NC (2000)

Price: $75.00

Review by Susan Tower Hollis—Associate Dean and Center Director, Central New York Center of the State University of New York, Syracuse.

This extensive volume provides much information for the interested individual looking for fairly complete information about a particular deity from a variety of mythologies and cultures. There is a vast number of entries, the largest number covering deities, with a small additional number of nondeities such as Odysseus, Achilles, Perseus, and places and concepts (e.g., Babylonian Esagila and the Ancient Egyptian Negative Confession). The authors also include some figures who continue as part of living religions such as Mohammed and Jesus. The immense index and extensive cross-referencing of names make finding the desired entry fairly straightforward, but some of the varied spellings reflect translations from the original, especially the ancient Egyptian. The volume's bibliography will assist the interested user in finding additional resources, although the lack of some resources, most notably Yves Bonnofoy's *Mythologies*, is a curious omission. Nevertheless, the inclusiveness of the entries can provide a very nice entry point for the student or layperson seeking information on a particular figure related to religion and mythology. Thus, this volume should be seriously considered as a good resource for any public library and perhaps for the community college library as well. Some colleges and universities may also wish to include it in their collection.

---

Classification: LC BL473; Dewey 291.

---

357. *The Complete Gods and Goddesses of Ancient Egypt*, by Richard H. Wilkinson

Publisher: Thames and Hudson, New York, NY (2003)

Price: $39.95

Review by Susan Tower Hollis—Associate Dean and Center Director, Central New York Center of the State University of New York, Syracuse.

In this lavishly illustrated volume (338 illustrations in 243 text pages), following a brief but solid introduction to Egyptian religion and deities, the author presents a comprehensive catalog of 387 deities, including the major and significant minor deities of this ancient culture. He also includes sections on the rise and fall of the divinities, including their births, lives, and deaths; the nature of these deities with their forms, appearances, and manifestations; how they were worshipped and tended, both formally and informally, with everything from magnificent temples to home altars and personal stelae; and the key concepts surrounding kingship and the deities. The numerous fine-quality illustrations and the many sidebars with details only serve to enhance the clear and well-written text that generally captures accurately the salient issues around the various concepts addressed, be they creation, manifestation of the deities, popular religion and piety, or any of the many other significant concepts that help clarify the complexities of ancient Egyptian religion. For example, the author very clearly unpacks the persistent challenge of divine kingship by noting that for the deities the king represented his people and was, therefore, human in the eyes of the divine world, while for the people, the king represented the divine world. In the end, among the current books available addressing the same or similar topics, this volume should be the first choice for the general, school, and undergraduate college library (and the Egyptophile's as well). The excellent bibliography, which is not limited to works only in English (although works in English predominate), even allows the interested reader to truly extend his or her knowledge with reference to most of the most important materials in the field.

---

Classification: LC BL2450; Dewey 299.

---

## Judaism and Christianity

### *General Works*

358. *Encyclopaedia Judaica*, by Fred Skolnik and Michael Berenbaum
Publisher: Macmillan Reference USA/Gale Group, New York, NY (2007)
Price: $1,995.00/set
Review by Staff, Libraries Unlimited.

This 22-volume set is a revision of the 1st edition published in 1972. The CD-ROM version was released in 1997 and was reviewed in ARBA 1998. It provided updated material; however, users were unable to tell what material was new. This latest edition has been long awaited and much anticipated by the library and research communities. The editor in chief, Fred Skolnik, who served as the co-editor of the 1st edition, has worked in cooperation with some 50 contributing editors, all of whom are experts in their areas of expertise. In addition to the 50 contributing editors a group of 1,200 contributors wrote or rewrote entries articles for this new edition. The volumes cover information on the Jewish people, the Jewish faith, and the state of Israel. Areas of study that have been expanded upon for this new edition are Jewish women, the Bible, Jews in popular culture, community life, Jewish law, and new scholarship on the Holocaust. The last topic in particular is covered more thoroughly, especially with the new abundance of literature, film, art, and museums covering the topic in the past 30 years. This 2nd edition provides updates to nearly 10,000 of the original entries, sometimes with an addendum and other times with just an updated bibliography. It also includes 2,200 new entries, and 30,000 new bibliographic entries. The entries vary in length, but most run several paragraphs to several pages in length. All entries are signed, and nearly all provide bibliographic information. Supplemental materials to this new edition include 600 maps, tables, and illustrations, including eight pages of four-color inserts within each volume. These color inserts depict such images as archaeology, art, the life cycle, synagogues, and the Sabbath and festivals. Gale offers this volume in e-book format as well as in print format. Users can search the text by keyword, article title, or full-text. Libraries that subscribe to the PowerSearch platform from Gale can include other Gale resources in their search as well, which could provide curriculum-related articles or current events not covered in this encyclopedia but that show up in other Gale resources. This updated edition of the classic *Encyclopaedia Judaica* will be an essential purchase for large academic libraries and some public libraries. With 22 large volumes (over 17,000 pages in all) and weighing in at over 70 pounds, libraries with limited space may choose to go with the e-book only. Regardless of the format selected, this resource remains an essential purchase for the study of the history and current condition of Judaism around the world.

Classification: LC DS102; Dewey 909.

359. *The New Encyclopedia of Judaism*, by Geoffrey Wigoder, Fred Skolnik, and Shmuel Himelstein, eds.

Publisher: New York University Press, New York, NY (2002)

Price: $99.95

Review by Janet J. Kosky, Mukwonago Community Library, Mukwonago, WI.

Following the greatly applauded 1st edition, a 1989 American Libraries Association Outstanding Reference Book, this 2nd edition contains 250 new articles beyond the original 1,000 and updated information to reflect current issues and developments in the religious life of all the major branches of Judaism. As before, there is an emphasis on liturgy, and the influence women have had, from ancient times to the feminist movement. Biographical entries have been expanded to cover later rabbinical authorities; biblical, Hasidic, academic, and popular figures; and more of the Talmudic sages. Other fortified areas include biblical and Second Temple history, the Apocrypha and Pseudepigrapha, and Zionism. Since the work is intended for both laypeople and students, and for non-Jews as well as Jews, cross-referencing of Hebrew words to English facilitate its use. A new feature of this volume aimed at the goal of accessibility is an annotated bibliography of basic works on Judaism for the general reader. Further, related articles are noted by capital letters within each entry. Completing the user's tools is a key to abbreviations, a glossary, and rules of transliteration. Numerous sidebars of useful information add interest and helpful tips for further study. Editorially speaking, the qualifications of the compilers and the 80 writers are impressive. The late Geoffrey Wigoder's previous credits include chief editor of the multivolume *Encyclopaedia Judaica* (entry 358), and more recently, a comprehensive work on the Holocaust. The contributors represent an international authority of Reform, Conservative, and Orthodox Jewry. Even taken alone, the more than 300 black-and-white and color illustrations tell a fascinating story of Jewish history and customs and folk traditions. They do much to augment the written material at an emotional and artistic level. This work offers a thorough, one-volume reference for Jews and those interested in the Jewish religion and way of life. With continued Middle East conflict, many people are questioning the beliefs and history of Islam and Judaism that underlie the struggle. This book should be available in libraries to aid the public in this quest.

---

Classification: LC BM50; Dewey 296.

---

360. *Oxford Companion to Christian Thought*, by Adrian Hastings, Alistair Mason, and Hugh Pyper, eds.

Publisher: Oxford University Press, New York, NY (2000)

Price: $55.00

Review by Dorothy Jones—Reference Librarian, Founders Memorial Library, Northern Illinois University, De Kalb.

Planned and written over a period of eight years, this is a truly grand book. It is imposing in its scope, its depth, and the quality of its contents. Here is a rich resource for scholars who want to better visualize how their own personal research fits into the context of the whole panorama of Christian thought. It is equally appropriate for laypersons exploring ideas in a study group or spiritual searchers of any faith who are eager to understand concepts and ideas heard but never explained. The mission or objective of the book, crucial to its best use, is presented in the fine introduction by Hastings. He reminds the reader that "thought" is not "fact," and, while the articles may be described as authoritative, they are also expressions of the individual author's personal scholarship and convictions. The contributors, 260 scholars from all over the world, include Catholics, Protestants, Orthodox, and "agnostics of various sorts," and, at most points, the editors "have deliberately attempted to balance one writer with another so that a diversity of viewpoints could be reflected without forcing each contributor to maintain an absolute balance" (p. ix). Entry headings include biblical subjects, theological and philosophical subjects, persons who have had an outstanding influence on Christian thought, places that carry uncommonly strong symbolic power, and the list goes on. The choice of subjects treated is diverse and exciting. Hastings writes: "While it would be impossible to cover the wider sea of thought at all adequately, we have put a toe bravely in here and there, not only with considerable general articles on science, music, art, poetry, and novels, but with particular studies of Shakespeare, Dante, Bach, and Milton, among other figures" (p. xi). The organization and indexing of the book is meticulous and reader-friendly, traits readers have come to expect from Oxford University Press. Articles are arranged in the traditional encyclopedic manner, in alphabetic order by entry title. Within articles, cross-references to other articles are indicated by means of asterisks. Numerous asterisks may have a somewhat jarring effect on the reader, but the usefulness of the cross-references is certainly great enough to justify them. Almost all of the articles end with a list of books to guide the reader in further exploration. Preceding the articles are three lists: Contributors, Entries, and Abbreviations. The list of contributors includes each person's professional position, the name of the institution in which he or she teaches or works, and the headings of the encyclopedia article(s) contributed. The alphabetic list of entry headings serves as a quick-search table of contents. The list of abbreviations used in the book is delightfully short, a relief from the multitudinous abbreviations and acronyms present in many reference books. There is a name index in the back of the book for people who are discussed within articles but who do not have their own entries. Each of the names is followed by the titles of entries in which that person is discussed. This book is recommended without reservation for public and academic libraries, and for any individuals, groups, or institutions interested in "humanity's long march across the centuries in search of the meaning of things" (p. xiii).

Classification: LC BR95; Dewey 230.

361. *New Catholic Encyclopedia*

Publisher: Gale/Cengage Learning, Farmington Hills, MI (2003)

Price: $1,195.00/set

Review by Staff, Libraries Unlimited.

This 2nd edition of the *New Catholic Encyclopedia* is a revision of the 1st edition published in 1967. Since its inception there have been several supplement volumes, including the Jubilee volume published in 2001 to celebrate the beginning of the new millennium. This new edition has updated many of the entries that originally were published in the 1967 edition and has added hundreds of new entries. Consisting of fifteen volumes (all of which are close to nine hundred pages in length), the scope of this work is vast. It covers the history of the eastern churches, the churches of the Protestant Reformation, and other ecclesial communities as well as the Christian roots based in ancient Israel and Judaism. No comprehensive resource on Catholicism can be complete without touching on other world religions as well, including Islam, Buddhism, and Hinduism. This resource provides entries not only on the doctrine, organization, and history of the church, but also on the people, institutions, and social changes that have affected the church over the years. Arranged alphabetically, the entries run in length from half a page to several pages in length. All entries provide the name of the contributor and a bibliography. Cross-references to related articles are located throughout the work. Adding to the usefulness of the set are more than three thousand black-and-white photographs, maps, and charts that complement the scholarly articles. The editorial board has also provided what they call "Subject Overview Articles" throughout the volumes. These articles outline the scope of major fields; "Jesus Christ, Articles on" and "Theology, Articles on" are two examples. This impressive fifteen-volume set will serve as a prominent reference source in Catholic studies as well as religious studies in general. Certainly large university libraries should consider its purchase as well as larger public libraries.

Classification: LC BX841; Dewey 282.

362. *Encyclopedia of Protestantism*, by Hans J. Hillerbrand, ed.

Publisher: Routledge/Taylor & Francis Group, New York, NY (2004)

Price: $495.00/set

Review by Hans E. Bynagle—Library Director and Professor of Philosophy, Whitworth College, Spokane, WA.

Perhaps Protestantism will never have the benefit of an encyclopedia rivaling in comprehensiveness and depth the monumental *New Catholic Encyclopedia*

(2nd ed.; entry 361) and its predecessors. But the work under review, even if far less ambitious and imposing, now offers a substantial and worthy complement covering one of Christianity's two other major branches. (Eastern Orthodoxy awaits its turn.) The *Encyclopedia of Protestantism* boasts an impressive roster of over 600 contributing experts, international although predominantly American and British, including such prominent scholars as David Barrett, Edith Blumhofer, Edwin Gaustad, Geoffrey Wainwright, and editor Hillerbrand himself, a leading reformation specialist and previously editor of the 4-volume *Oxford Encyclopedia of the Reformation*. Contributors often evidence personal affinities—in terms of denominational affiliation or theological conviction—for the subjects of their articles, but not uncritical fervor that I could find. The thematic range of some 1,000 entries is handily displayed in a categorized list at the front of volume 1. About half are biographical, encompassing mainly theologians, ministers, and other religious leaders, but also a few Protestant literary figures and philosophers. Theological topics, generally treated to reflect the diversity of Protestant views, account for some 135 entries. A roughly equal number represent denominations or broad traditions such as Anabaptism, Calvinism, and Wesleyanism. The remaining entries divide over the smaller categories of creeds, confessions, and religious works; cultural and social issues; geographical entries; historical events; institutions and organizations; and trans- or non-denominational movements as diverse as the civil rights movement, Jews for Jesus, Liberal Protestantism, the Moral Majority, and seeker churches. Protestantism is demarcated in broad terms as "whatever is not Catholic (or Orthodox)," thus including some strains (e.g., Mormonism, the Unification Church) that some would resist counting as part of the Protestant family (preface). By its own description, this encyclopedia accentuates the historical dimension of its subject. It also "favors" North America, an emphasis justified with the observation that there "the rich diversity of Protestantism has come to bear its most meaningful fruit" (preface). But these emphases should not mislead one into underestimating the encyclopedia's topical breadth and global scope. This set belongs in most college and university libraries, many larger public libraries, and of course all seminary and other substantial theological libraries.

---

There is also a single-volume 2005 work with the same title, edited by the well-regarded scholar J. Gordon Melton. Classification: LC BX4811; Dewey 280.

---

363. *Contemporary American Religion*, by Wade Clark Roof, ed.

Publisher: Macmillan Reference USA/Gale Group, New York, NY (2000)

Price: $225.00

Review by John W. Storey—Professor of History, Lamar University, Beaumont, TX.

Whereas formal religion revolves around churches, synagogues, mosques, and related institutions, popular religion deals more broadly with the seemingly infinite ways ordinary people make sense of their lives. As this suggests, popular religion is remarkably fluid and difficult to pin down, so much so that scholars cannot agree whether they are grappling with "folk religion," "invisible religion," "common religion," or merely what is left over from the traditional studies. Although this study does not resolve the matter of definition, an entry on popular religion notwithstanding, it nonetheless is an outstanding guide to America's increasingly pluralistic landscape. Written by recognized authorities from numerous academic disciplines, the five hundred or so entries treat everything from Peyote, Star Trek, and UFO cults to magic, feminist theology, and hell. Some of the features are brief, meriting only one-half page or so, but others run three to four pages, such as those on African-American religions, church and state, and God. Little more than a page is allotted to the evangelist Billy Graham, but a photograph accompanies his sketch. Because of its alphabetic arrangement, along with cross-references and an exhaustive fifty-eight-page index, the material is readily accessible. Admittedly, a work on a subject this vast cannot include everything. Yet some of the omissions are puzzling. Football, sports, Bear Bryant, and Super Sunday certainly have religious meaning for multitudes, but are ignored. And if there is room for Norman Vincent Peale and televangelism, why not Fulton J. Sheen and Cecil B. DeMille? Such quibbles aside, this fine study should be added to high school and university reference collections. It will be of interest to students and scholars of contemporary American religion.

> See entry 215 for the *U.S. Religion Census 1952 to 2010* online. Also useful is *Melton's Encyclopedia of American Religions* (9th ed., 2016). Classification: LC BL2525; Dewey 200.

364. *Encyclopedia of Fundamentalism*, by Brenda E. Brasher, ed.

Publisher: Routledge/Taylor & Francis Group, New York, NY (2001)

Price: $125.00

Review by Henry E. York—Head, Collection Management, Cleveland State University, Cleveland, OH.

Two observations provide a background for approaching this most interesting one-volume encyclopedia of religious fundamentalism. First, the emphasis and orientation is on Protestant fundamentalism that, according to the introduction, emerged in the early twentieth century, especially in the United States. It is organized around a literal interpretation of the Bible with an absolutist claim to truth and an emphatic intolerance to others. From this base in American

Protestantism, the volume turns to the other religions where it finds variations of fundamentalism that create the global phenomenon of fundamentalism. The treatments of fundamentalism in Catholicism, Judaism, Islam, Hinduism, and so on are all seen from this Protestant starting point. Another notable feature is the attitude of the editor toward fundamentalism. In the introduction she explains that fundamentalism was "a popular means to revolt against modernism by traditional Christians at odd with the dominant values of a rapidly developing, modern, technological, capitalistic society." It attempts to "fence off adherents from the influence of contemporary culture." This evaluation of fundamentalism is shared by at least a good number of the contributors of the entries. This encyclopedia provides a very useful and readable discussion of the phenomena of fundamentalism, with articles covering major denominations, historical events, theological concepts, and cultural flash points such as abortion, biblical criticism, biblical inerrancy, and America as a Christian nation. Relevant materials, such as sections from the Bible or such documents as *Roe v. Wade*, are included. The volume is very useful in documenting some of the areas of controversy involving fundamentalism. In this regard, the comparison between fundamentalism and Evangelicalism, and that between the old Latin and the new vernacular masses, is very clear and informative. This volume includes entries on Islamic Fundamentalism and the Taliban that give a historical sketch of the development of these forces, including the recent destruction of the statues of Buddha in Afghanistan.

Classification: LC BL238; Dewey 200.

### The Bible

The following entries deal with secondary works, but it is not unusual for reference collections to include various versions of the Old and New Testaments of the Bible. A large variety of English-language translations are in print, and digital editions of the *King James Bible* and the *New International Version* (which are among the best-selling translations) can be found on the Web. Multivolume series such as the *Anchor Bible* and the *Interpreter's Bible* combine text with commentary based on current scholarship. The Judaeo-Christian Bible is a key source not only in religion, but also for topics in philosophy and literature.

365. *Eerdmans Dictionary of the Bible*, by David Noel Freedman, Allen C. Myers, and Astrid B. Beck, eds.

Publisher: William B. Eerdmans, Grand Rapids, MI (2000)

Price: $45.00

Review by Craig W. Beard—Reference Librarian, Mervyn H. Sterne Library, University of Alabama at Birmingham.

As the *Anchor Bible Dictionary* (*ABD*) differs from other multivolume Bible dictionaries and encyclopedias, so does *Eerdmans Dictionary of the Bible* (*EDB*) differ from its peers among one-volume dictionaries. This is not surprising, given that Freedman (a professor of Hebrew biblical studies at the University of California, San Diego) is the driving force behind both. Also, like the *ABD*, this is a new work rather than an updating of an earlier one (although the publisher's original intention was to revise and update the 1987 *Eerdmans Bible Dictionary*), providing users with the results of cutting-edge biblical scholarship. The *EDB* comprises approximately five thousand entries written by an international and interconfessional team of some six hundred scholars, many of whom are acknowledged experts in their respective fields. The articles deal with all matters that bear directly or indirectly on interpreting and understanding the Bible. Every book of the Bible (including the Old Testament apocryphal/deuterocanonical books) and all the persons, places, and significant terms mentioned in them (based on the *New Revised Standard Version*) receive entries. In addition, related subjects, such as biblical theology, cultural and historical background, geography, Near Eastern archaeology, textual and literary studies, and noncanonical writings (including the Old Testament Pseudepigrapha, New Testament Apocrypha, and Dead Sea Scrolls), are treated. The large number of articles equates to more specific access points than in comparable works, such as the *New Bible Dictionary* (3rd ed.). Yet it is odd that *EDB* does not have individual entries for most of the well-known Dead Sea Scrolls texts, among them the Copper Scroll, Miqtsat Ma'asei ha-Torah, and Rule of the Community. One of Freedman's goals was to provide a balanced presentation of subjects, especially where there are substantially differing viewpoints. Through the diversity of the team of contributors, an overall balance is achieved for the volume. However, within some of the articles it is lacking, as can be seen in "Conquest: Biblical Narrative," which exhibits an extremely negative view of the historicity of the narrative material in the Old Testament. Primarily because of this, balanced reference collections should place *EDB* alongside the dictionary mentioned above on their shelves.

---

Classification: LC BS440; Dewey 220.

---

366. *The Oxford Guide to People & Places of the Bible*, by Bruce M. Metzger and Michael D. Coogan, eds.

Publisher: Oxford University Press, New York, NY (2001)

Price: $30.00

Review by Craig W. Beard—Reference Librarian, Mervyn H. Sterne Library, University of Alabama at Birmingham.

This is a handy one-volume reference, derived from the *Oxford Companion to the Bible*, to most of the major characters and places in the Old and New Testaments and a few of the characters in the Apocrypha. The people presented include named individuals (Jesus, Moses, and Paul), literary characters (Dives, the traditional name of the rich man in Jesus's parable about the beggar Lazarus—for whom, incidentally, there is no entry), pagan deities (Asherah and Baal), and groups (Israel, the tribe of Judah, and Pharisees). Places presented include geographical locations and features (the Arabian and Sinai peninsulas, the Jordan River, and the Red Sea), nations and cities (Assyria and Egypt, Babylon, and Jerusalem), and even a few structures (the Temple and the Tower of Babel). In addition to the people and places, the guide also contains a substantial amount of information on the books of the Old and New Testaments and the Apocrypha. This material is found in the articles on the authors of the books (Jeremiah, Solomon, and John the Apostle), persons who are featured in those books (Nehemiah and Timothy), or places to which those writings—especially the letters of Paul—were addressed (Corinth, Ephesus, and Galatia). A brief bibliography, a subject index, and a set of maps round out the volume. In spite of its excellent pedigree and the useful information contained in it, the guide's existence is questionable. Certainly it is not intended to provide information otherwise unavailable or to update what is available, since most of what is within its pages can be found in expanded form in the Oxford companion. Apparently, it is also not intended to present a compact edition of its parent, since numerous topics treated in the companion do not fall under the umbrella of "people and places." However, libraries looking for a volume on people and places in the Bible, and who do not want to spend $60 on the companion, will probably find that the guide meets their needs. Libraries that own the former can pass on this one.

Classification: LC BS570; Dewey 220.

367. *Women in Scripture: A Dictionary of Named and Unnamed Women in the Hebrew Bible, the Apocryphal/Deuterocanonical Books, and the New Testament*, by Carol Meyers, Toni Craven, and Ross S. Kraemer, eds.

Publisher: Houghton Mifflin Harcourt, New York, NY (2000)

Price: $45.00

Review by Bernice Bergup—Humanities Reference Librarian, Davis Library, University of North Carolina–Chapel Hill.

A meticulous, scholarly work of feminist biblical scholarship, *Women in Scripture* recruits some eighty men and women experts from America, Europe, and Israel to examine biblical texts. The purpose of the work is to analyze how texts represent women "and also to evaluate whether sexism is encoded in the text, its traditional interpretation or both" (p. ii). Based on both the Jewish and the Christian canons, the 1st part covers more than two hundred named historical or literary figures. Next in the work appear entries for unnamed women representing both individuals and groups, either as generic roles or as types. A good example is the entry for "women deacons" in I Timothy 3:11. Finally, the third part looks at female deities and personification. Here users find entries for female images of God in the Hebrew Bible and the Canaanite goddesses Astarte, Anath, and Asherah. Each entry critically examines the particular woman or group, or the literary figure, in its historical and literary context, using the most authoritative knowledge gleaned from the late 1960s as well as more recent feminist scholarship. Cross-references are indicated at the ends of articles along with suggestions for further reading. The introductory essays providing framework are as valuable as the entries themselves. An essay by Carol Meyers discusses the state of critical biblical scholarship, while another by Alice Ogden Bellis outlines the history of feminist biblical scholarship. An essay by Karla Bohmback also elucidates the biblical tradition of names and naming practices. Other scholars contribute important discussions of the Hebrew Bible, the Apocryphal/Deuterocanonical books, and the New Testament. An annotated list of additional ancient sources is appended, as is a complete bibliography of the sources listed as suggestions for further reading in the individual entries. Singular in its approach, this landmark work deserves a place in academic libraries supporting religious studies or biblical literature programs. Large public libraries as well will want to add this to their reference collections in religion.

Classification: LC BS575; Dewey 220.

368. *Encyclopedia of the Dead Sea Scrolls*, by Lawrence H. Schiffman and James C. VanderKam, eds.
Publisher: Oxford University Press, New York, NY (2000)
Price: $295.00/set
Review by Staff, Libraries Unlimited.

The editorial board, led by Schiffman (professor of Hebrew and Judaic Studies at New York University) and VanderKam (professor of Theology at Notre Dame), and the contributors (listed in the back of volume 2) are a virtual "who's who" of Qumran scholarship. Notably absent is Robert Eisenman, some of whose radical ideas have not been accepted by the majority of Scrolls scholars. These scholars represent a variety of opinions regarding controversial issues: dating of the texts, identity of the inhabitants of Qumran, and so on. The editors apparently went to no great pains to ensure either agreement with themselves or uniformity among the contributors. Readers will indeed encounter diverse and even conflicting ideas as they peruse related articles. The articles in this encyclopedia (and it is an encyclopedia rather than a two-volume dictionary) are arranged alphabetically and are signed by the authors. The categories of articles cover places, material remains, written materials, related texts, history, beliefs and practices, figures of ancient history, and Scrolls research. Most articles conclude with at least a brief bibliography, many of which include helpful annotations. An appended "Provisional List of Documents from the Judean Desert" helps identify the documents in spite of changes in their naming and numbering. The index is limited to major topics and cannot be used to locate all occurrences of terms. One of the disappointments in this work is that there are no illustrations. Maps, line drawings, and photographs of some of the scrolls would have been a welcome addition. Nevertheless, the *Encyclopedia of the Dead Sea Scrolls* has already established itself as the standard reference work—alongside the texts and translations—and should be in all academic and public libraries serving those interested in the Scrolls.

Classification: LC BM487; Dewey 296.

## Islam

369. *Encyclopaedia of the Qur'an*, by Jane Dammen McAuliffe, ed.

Publisher: Brill Academic, Boston, MA (2001–2006)

Price: $228.00 per volume

Review by Linda L. Lam-Easton—Associate Professor, Department of Religious Studies, California State University–Northridge.

*The Encyclopaedia of the Qur'an* is a highly prestigious and competent volume from a superb publisher with contributions by the world's leading experts. If readers were to own one volume on this topic, this work would be the encyclopedia to own. The first volume is carefully and masterfully crafted and provides the expectation of valuable work to come. With the desire to take stock of Qur'anic studies at the turn of the century, and the growing interest in this field, the work was planned in 1993. The entries are designed to stimulate further research as well as present the state of research to this point. The particular need for a work in a language other than Arabic, which has several excellent encyclopedias, was pressing. The key words in its formulation were "rigorous" and, most importantly, "academic." The editors have admirably succeeded with their stated task in the first volume, and the scholarly community looks forward to future volumes.

> The six-volume set was completed in 2006. The older spelling "Koran" reflects superseded methods of transliteration from Arabic. Classification: LC BP133; Dewey 297.

370. *Encyclopedia of Islam and the Muslim World*, by Richard Martin, ed.

Publisher: Macmillan Reference USA/Gale Group, New York, NY (2016)

Price: $489.00/set

Review by Mark Schumacher—Art and Humanities Librarian, University of North Carolina, Greensboro.

This encyclopedia of over 540 articles, prepared by over 350 scholars from around the world, explores the religious, social, political, and cultural realms of Islam over the last 14 centuries. There appears to be considerable "evolution" from the 2004 edition. For example, the articles "American culture and Islam," "Americas, Islam in the," and numerous biographies are no longer present, while many new entries, such as "Australia and New Zealand," "Byzantines," "Damascus," "ISIS," and "Intifada," now appear. Broad articles exploring art, architecture, and literature exist alongside specialized topics of the Islamic faith and Muslim history. Numerous maps and color photos enhance the work considerably, as do the bibliographies at the end of each article. Students and scholars of the Muslim world will find much useful information here. Academic and public libraries will benefit from having this set, as could high school libraries. Librarians might consider retaining the 2004 volumes as well.

> *See also* the *Encyclopedia of the Modern Middle East and North Africa* (entry 277). Classification: LC BP40; Dewey 909.

371. *The Oxford Dictionary of Islam*, by John L. Esposito, ed.

Publisher: Oxford University Press, New York, NY (2003)

Price: $76.50

Review by Staff, Libraries Unlimited.

The editor designed this readable and accessible dictionary in collaboration with an editorial board. The more than two thousand entries focus on the nineteenth and twentieth centuries and are geared toward those readers with only a very basic understanding of Islam. The dictionary combines material from *The Oxford Encyclopedia of the Modern Islamic World* with a large number of new entries provided by approximately one hundred U.S., European, and Islamic scholars (the full list is provided in the front matter). In a nod to its intended audience, the dictionary uses standard transliteration without diacriticals. Exceptions are made for words like al-Qaeda, which has "achieved currency in non-standard transliteration in English." Moreover, the editors chose to list words in this A to Z work in the place readers would most likely search. Examples of this include the decision to list the "Palestine Liberation Organization" rather than "Harakat al-Tahrir al Filistin" and the use of "fasting" instead of "swam." An extensive system of cross-references within the entries and *see also* references at the end of entries ensures that readers will find the terms they seek. Entries vary in length from a short paragraph for a topic like "Camel, Battle of" to a whole column of text for "Christianity and Islam." There are also authoritative and lengthy entries for "Shii Islam," "Sunni Islam," "Women and Islam," and other important topics. A chronology that begins with the birth of Muhammad in 570 C.E. and ends in 2001 C.E. rounds out the work. Highly recommended for school, public, and academic libraries.

---

*See also* the multivolume *Oxford Encyclopedia of the Islamic World* (2009; entry 278) by the same author. Classification: LC BP40; Dewey 297.

---

### Buddhism

372. *A Dictionary of Buddhism*, by Damien Keown

Publisher: Oxford University Press, New York, NY (2003)

Price: $35.00

Review by Nadine Salmons—(retired) Technical Services Librarian, Grant Library, Fort Carson, CO.

Primarily written by Damien Keown, a senior lecturer in Indian religion at the University of London and an author of other books, *A Dictionary of Buddhism* is an encyclopedic dictionary with over two thousand entries that covers both historical and contemporary issues and includes all the major Buddhist sects and cultures. It also includes coverage of contemporary issues in Buddhism such as abortion, marriage, and the role of women. The author has chosen a selection of terms, phrases, texts, countries, and personages related to

Buddhism using modern thought without prejudice, giving a fairly even distribution of explanations on all major sects of Buddhism. *A Dictionary of Buddhism* begins with a preface, then provides the body of the dictionary, three appendixes (with maps), a pronunciation guide for difficult names and terms, an informative guide to Buddhist scriptures, and a chronology of Buddhism. Additionally, there are small but clear line drawings, frequent use of *see* and *see also* references, the use of asterisks when another entry is first used in an entry, and the sometimes disconcerting use of English spelling of some words (e.g., centre). While some descriptions are exceedingly short (e.g., zendo), others are extensive, such as the descriptions of various schools of Buddhism (e.g., Pure Land). Where appropriate, Keown includes in each entry the origin of the term, how to pronounce it, references to other terms (asterisks), and a brief Buddhist history of individual countries or regions. This lexicon is an authoritative tool to be used by the scholar, researcher, neophyte, or anyone interested in learning more about Buddhism.

---

Classification: LC BQ130; Dewey 294.

---

373. *Encyclopedia of Buddhism*, by Robert E. Buswell Jr., ed.

Publisher: Macmillan Reference USA/Gale Group, New York, NY (2004)

Price: $265.00/set

Review by Philip G. Swan—Head Librarian, Hunter College, School of Social Work Library, New York, NY.

The two-volume *Encyclopedia of Buddhism* offers a comprehensive view of the topic with a generalist Western audience in mind. The preface makes the case for a resource that helps Westerners relate Buddhism to the larger cultures of its diverse adherents, and the encyclopedia does this job admirably. Signed articles, written by over two hundred scholars in the field, are arranged alphabetically by subject and include individual bibliographies as well as cross-references. Articles vary from half-column biographies to discussions of topics like the "Four Noble Truths" that range over several pages. The articles do not avoid controversial issues, such as Buddhism's sometimes contradictory stance on war and sexuality, and this gives the work a compellingly nuanced tone that is in keeping with such a complex topic. Each volume includes illustrations in an eight-page color insert and numerous black-and-white illustrations scattered throughout the text. Following the preface in volume 1 is an alphabetic list of article topics along with their authors, who have their names and credentials listed in a separate list of contributors. Volume 1 also includes an excellent synoptic outline of articles, which helps with cursory cross-referencing. Maps of

Asia follow this outline, which illustrate the spread of Buddhism from India to the rest of the region. There is a timeline of Buddhist history at the close of volume two covering the major regions of Asia, and this is followed by a tremendously detailed subject index. This is an appropriate addition to public or undergraduate libraries.

Classification: LC BQ128; Dewey 294.

## World Religions and Belief Systems

Aspects of world belief systems can overlap with concepts covered by works on ethnography, mythology, folklore, and popular culture in Chapter 2 "Social Sciences."

374. *Encyclopedia of Religion*, by Lindsay Jones, Mircea Eliade, and Charles J. Adams

Publisher: Macmillan Reference USA/Gale Group, New York, NY (2004)

Price: $1,295.00/set

Review by Staff, Libraries Unlimited.

This edition of *The Encyclopedia of Religion* is a long-awaited update of the original set published in 1988. This volume continues the tradition of the 1st edition by focusing on the role of religion in the everyday lives of people around the world as well as focusing on the unique ways cultures experience religion and how it affects their societal values. An international team of nearly 2,000 scholars worked with the publisher to determine what additions should be made to this 2nd edition to reflect our changing world and religion's unique role in it. The 15-volume set includes more than 3,300 articles, 600 of which are new to this edition. The articles range from one paragraph to several pages. Articles that are new or updated for this edition include anticult movements, bioethics, ecology, and religion, Mary Magdalene, Nation of Islam, Rastafarianism, transculturation and religion, and feminist theology. Many of the articles include black-and-white photographs and illustrations, cross-references to relevant articles, and updated bibliographies. The volumes also include full-color inserts depicting religious practices, sacred places, and religious events. A comprehensive index concludes the volume. This updated set will be a valuable addition to large public libraries and university reference collections. The articles are written in a scholarly yet easy-to-understand style that will appeal to many readers. It can also be used to support other areas of study, such as history, gender studies, and anthropology. This set is highly recommended.

Classification: LC BL31; Dewey 200.

375. *Religions of the World: A Comprehensive Encyclopedia of Beliefs and Practices*, by J. Gordon Melton and Martin Baumann, eds.

Publisher: ABC-CLIO, Santa Barbara, CA (2010)

Price: $595.00/set

Review by Megan W. Lowe—Reference/Instruction Librarian, University Library, University of Louisiana at Monroe.

Calling itself a "comprehensive encyclopedia of beliefs and practices" might be stretching it just a little, but *Religions of the World* is indeed thorough and wide-ranging enough to just warrant using the world comprehensive. In addition to the entries covering religions, people, practices, concepts, organizations, cults, and geographies, the Encyclopedia provides a goodly selection of quantitative data pertaining to religion and religious practice in the world in the form of data sets and graphs in its introductory pages. The "A-Z List of Entries" provides users with a quick look of the Encyclopedia's coverage. Like a standard encyclopedia, this title provides cogent *see also* lists and reference lists that contain a good mix of historical and up-to-date resources. The illustrations and photographs are greatly appreciated, although in the case of this title, color would have been recommended, when one considers the significance of colors in many religions. The entries are uniformly well written and are as objective as one could hope when discussing a hot-button issue like religion. Entries pertaining to organizations or groups (and sometimes individuals) also contain contact information. This encyclopedia does not seek to critically analyze its topics; rather, it prefers to present the facts as well as it can. It pursues neutrality in its presentation of information, although it does not hesitate to raise questions, such as medical issues related to exorcism. The title's careful and specific approach to geography and religion is appreciated; it does not simply say "China" and have done with it. It digs further into regions and the relationship between different religions and regions. This precise method acknowledges that a church or religious movement may vary from country to country, and even within a country or region. The main issue this reviewer has with regard to this title is its price. Although it is a four-volume set, the volumes themselves are not remarkably thick, so the nearly $600 price tag seems unwarranted. With regard to the content, however, this title is highly recommended for academic libraries, particularly at institutions with significant religion/philosophy programs, and public libraries.

Classification: LC BL80; Dewey 291.

376. *Encyclopedia of Religious Rites, Rituals, and Festivals*, by Frank A. Salamone, ed.

Publisher: Routledge/Taylor & Francis Group, New York, NY (2004)

Price: $195.00

Review by Staff, Libraries Unlimited.

Under the editorship of anthropologist Frank A. Salamone, this encyclopedia provides broad and inclusive coverage of religious rituals while acknowledging that ritual itself is hard to define and not a static concept. The encyclopedia begins with a list of entries and an introduction and concludes with a list of contributors and an index. The 130 articles are arranged in an A to Z format and are supplemented by 60 photographs and 60 sidebars mainly comprised of primary text. The entries vary in length from about three pages to approximately 10 pages; entries are signed and include *see* and *see also* references as well as suggestions for further reading. Contributors hail from a variety of academic backgrounds and countries, though a majority of scholars are affiliated with academic institutions in the United States. The entries themselves are international in scope and fall into four categories laid out in the introduction: those that provide context and understanding of rituals in general, with a focus on key concepts that apply across all or most forms of ritual, like magic and taboo; specific types of rituals and their diversity and similarities across cultures (agricultural rituals, identity rituals, rituals of rebellion, and naming rituals); overviews of key rituals of major world religions, cultural regions, and specific cultures; and specific rituals like Christmas. Highly recommended for public and academic libraries.

Classification: LC BL31; Dewey 203.

377. *Religious Holidays and Calendars: An Encyclopedic Handbook*, by Karen Bellenir, ed.

Publisher: Omnigraphics, Detroit, MI (2004)

Price: $84.00

Review by Bradford Lee Eden—Dean of Library Services, Valparaiso University, Valparaiso, IN.

This revised and expanded 3rd edition is an authoritative, comprehensive source for information about the holidays and calendars of the world's religions. Concise information is also provided about the practices, history, and beliefs of over twenty major religions. Some of the new features of this edition include more than one hundred new entries on holidays not previously covered (bringing the total to nearly five hundred sacred holidays, fasts, feasts, and festivals); new illustrations that highlight important places, concepts, and symbols; and the information on Christianity that has been expanded into three chapters titled "Roman Catholic and Protestant," "Orthodox," and "Non-Trinitarian and Non-Traditional." The book is divided into three sections. "The History of Calendars" includes explanations of lunar and solar calendars along with calendar reforms. "Calendars and Holidays for Religious Groups" is divided into seventeen chapters that cover the world's major religions and many smaller religious organizations. And the appendixes and index cover sources for more information and a bibliography; a chronological list of holidays for 2004–2008; and a holiday, calendar, and master index. Overall, this is an essential reference work on religious holidays and calendars for any library.

---

Classification: LC CE6; Dewey 529.

---

378. *The Oxford Companion to World Mythology*, by David Leeming

Publisher: Oxford University Press, New York, NY (2005)

Price: $65.00

Review by Neal Wyatt—Collection Management Librarian, Chesterfield County Public Library, Midlothian, VA.

David Leeming, author of *From Olympus to Camelot: The World of European Mythology* and *Jealous Gods and Chosen People: The Mythology of the Middle East*, has created a solid introduction to the mythical expressions of our global culture. The expected entries of Celtic, Norse, Egyptian, Greek, and Roman mythology are augmented by entries covering a huge range of times, cultures, and countries, including Tibetan, Prehistoric, and Phoenician. This global perspective is nicely balanced in the one-volume companion, offering users enough coverage of the more frequently cited mythic figures and themes as well as introducing a range of less-well-studied traditions. Leeming is very loose with his definition of mythology and includes in this work entries on folklore, fairy tales, and literary texts, such as the Iliad, which are deeply dependent on mythic understanding. Also included in this companion are religious figures, including entries on the central figures of most faiths. While this may raise the eyebrows of some users, Leeming maintains that to the believers of one religion, "the stories—especially the supernatural ones—of another religion tend to be seen as myth rather than history." Leaving aside this debatable point, the companion offers users a rich resource on the culture of myth, summaries of mythic stories, and a contextual overview of the mythic traditions of almost every country. Additionally, three very useful elements to the companion include a listing of mythological entries arranged by country or culture, family trees of major pantheons, and equivalency translations between the deities of Greek and Roman mythology and Sumerian and Babylonian mythology. The companion includes a lengthy bibliography, close to 100 black-and-white illustrations as well as several color plates, and a strong index, which makes a nice addition to a work arranged in alphabetic order. On the whole, this companion will make a great addition to general collections.

Classification: LC BL312; Dewey 201.

379. *Medieval Folklore: An Encyclopedia of Myths, Legends, Tales, Beliefs, and Customs*, by Carl Lindahl, John McNamara, and John Lindow, eds.
Publisher: ABC-CLIO, Santa Barbara, CA (2000)
Price: $175.00/set
Review by Staff, Libraries Unlimited.

Taking nearly ten years to complete, this two-volume set on medieval folklore will enhance any library's folklore collection. There are more than three hundred entries, which focus on a wide variety of topics—customs and activities, religious beliefs (Christian, Muslim, Jewish, and Pagan), oral and written literature, music and art, holidays, and plants and animals. The well-written entries range from one to several pages in length, and many offer black-and-white photographs to enhance the reader's understanding. All entries end with *see also* references and a list of further reading. Many of the over one hundred contributors to this project are well known in their field and all of their entries are signed. There are three indexes that conclude the volume: an index of tale types, an index of motifs, and a general index. This set is highly recommended for the reference collections of public and academic libraries.

Classification: LC GR35; Dewey 398.

380. *Handbook of Mesoamerican Mythology*, by Kay Almere Read and Jason J. González
Publisher: ABC-CLIO, Santa Barbara, CA (2000)
Price: $55.00
Review by Lori D. Kranz—Freelance Editor, Chambersburg, PA.

*Handbook of Mesoamerican Mythology* is ABC-CLIO's sixth volume in their Handbooks of World Mythology series. Geographically, Mesoamerica is defined as Mexico and Central America, an area that encompasses several countries and many languages and cultures historically. The focus of this book is limited mostly to the Mexican highland and Maya areas and to popular mythology in this region. An introduction provides historical background and is followed by a chapter entitled "Mythic Timelines," which includes descriptions of the area's two primary mythic histories: the Maya Popol Vuh and the Nahua "Legend of the Suns." Nearly one-half the book is devoted to "Deities, Themes, and Concepts," a noncomprehensive, alphabetically arranged selection of the most important and, to the authors, most interesting facets of Mesoamerican myth. The last section of the volume is devoted to annotated resources (print, video, and Internet), a lengthy list of references, and a glossary. The index appears to be thorough, and page numbers for the alphabetic entries are set in bold typeface. Scattered black-and-white photographs add interest to this fascinating introduction to Mesoamerican mythology.

---

Classification: LC F1219; Dewey 398.

---

381. *Encyclopedia of Native American Religions*, by Arlene Hirschfelder and Paulette Molin

Publisher: Facts on File, New York, NY (2000)

Price: $65.00

Review by G. Edward Evans—University Librarian, Charles Von der Ahe Library, Loyola Marymount University, Los Angeles, CA.

"Updated edition" is the correct label for this volume. Locating what is new in the main text is something of a challenge. There is a new general index of names, places, and ceremonies that supplements the revised subject index of the 1992 edition. There are also additional entries in the further reading section. Overall, this edition is twenty-three pages longer, but the typeface appears somewhat smaller so the actual total increase in new material is greater than the page count might suggest. The basic format remains the same as in the previous edition. A person might be somewhat misled by the marketing material—both a flyer included in the review copy and a mailed flyer covering both this and several other Native American titles from Fact on File. For example, the marketing material uses the phrase "updated edition features" and lists seven items. One of the items relates to legal decisions regarding prisoners' religious rights. Some people might take that to mean this is a new subject area in the updated edition. The reality is that the topic existed in the first version and what took place was the addition of one new entry under that topic. A side-by-side review of five sections of the two versions showed there were a few new entries in each section, such as "Bear Dance, Calif." and "Stillday, Thomas, Jr." Since the first edition appeared, several other works have come on the market dealing with some of the same subject matter; for example, *Dictionary of Native American Mythology*, *Encyclopedia of Native American Healing*, and *Encyclopedia of Native American Shamanism*. For information on a wide variety of people, ceremonies, and issues related to Native American religions, this is still the best source. If the reference budget is tight and one has the earlier edition in the collection, no harm would be done by passing on this update. However, if one passed on the 1st edition, one should give serious consideration to purchasing this one.

Classification: LC E98; Dewey 299.

382. *The Encyclopedia of Caribbean Religions*, by Patrick Taylor and Frederick I. Case, eds.

Publisher: University of Illinois Press, Champaign, IL (2013)

Price: $250.00/set

Review by Ralph Hartsock—Senior Music Catalog Librarian, University of North Texas, Denton.

This reference source lies at the juncture of religion and regional geography. It employs varied approaches to provide data about the various religions in the Caribbean. This area includes the islands of the West Indies, the greater and lesser Antilles, and select portions of the northern coast of South America (Guyana, Guyane, and Suriname). The editors and contributors approach the subject through ethnic groups (Maya, Nago), geography of nations (Cuba, Guyana, Bahamas, Jamaica), religions (Christianity, Islam, Judaism, Hinduism, Krishna, and Kumina), denominations (Lutheran Church, Methodist Church), and ceremonies and culture (African Caribbean Funerary Rites, Carnival, Nation Dance, Quimbois, Vodou). Many topical articles are subdivided geographically, sometimes with separate contributors. These include detailed descriptions of rituals and sacred practices by Maya, and tables illustrating the varied Orisha rites of the Santeria. Articles devoted to geographic territories present an overview of the religions, indigenous and currently used languages, culture, and societies of the country or island, followed by some specific religious rites or traditions practiced there. In the entry on Cuba, for instance, in twenty-six pages five contributors discuss government relations to churches, various popular religions and rituals, and how art, film, and music manifest themselves in the country. Many of the articles explain their historical background, such as the entry on

Mennonites, and clarify its differences with other religions. Entries are followed by substantial bibliographies, with some sources written in Spanish. Linkage is achieved through several cross-references (indicated by bold font) and a quality index. Volume 1 concludes with sixteen color plates, mostly art works, with high image quality. The only downside is the presence of but one map, prior to the title page of each volume. This encyclopedia serves as an in-depth resource for those interested in Caribbean geography, religions, or languages.

Classification: LC BL2565; Dewey 200.

383. *Encyclopedia of African and African-American Religions,* by Stephen D. Glazier, ed.
Publisher: Routledge/Taylor & Francis Group, New York, NY (2001)
Price: $188.00
Review by Fred J. Hay—Belk Library, Appalachian State University, Boone, NC.

With 452 pages (145 articles by 72 scholars), this work hardly supplants Garland's 1993 *Encyclopedia of African American Religions* (926 pages and 1,200 articles by 32 scholars). Yet, it expands on Garland's excellent and still essential work. There is some overlap, but for the most part, new information and different perspectives are presented. Glazier, Levinson, and several of the associate editors are anthropologists (as are nearly half of the contributors) and have conducted ethnographic fieldwork in the context of African or African-derived religions—adding a new dimension to the heavily historical treatment of the Garland book. Unlike the Garland book, Routledge's work is global and includes entries on major African ethnic groups and religious movements, African-derived religions in various (but not all) countries of the diaspora, and specific denominations and personalities. It is strongly oriented to the diaspora, with Rastafari (4), Santeria (3), and Vodou (2) receiving multiple entries. All articles are signed and accompanied by bibliographies and *see also* references. The encyclopedia includes a thoughtful preface on Du Bois and religion in his hometown by Levinson, an appendix on "The Anthropology of Religion in Africa" by Wyatt MacGaffey, a general bibliography, and a barely adequate index. The greatest problem with the encyclopedia is that there is not more coverage (i.e., entries on Ecuador, Garifuna, Ring Shout, and so on). Nevertheless, this work is essential and should, like Garland's encyclopedia, be found in all respectable reference collections.

Classification: LC 2462; Dewey 299.

384. *Dictionary of African Mythology,* by Harold Scheub, ed.
Publisher: Oxford University Press, New York, NY (2000)
Price: $30.00
Review by Staff, Libraries Unlimited.

In this dictionary, Harold Scheub, professor of African Languages and Literature at the University of Wisconsin, gathers together four hundred myths from countries across Africa. Readers looking for a theological study of African religions; an anthropological, historical, or philosophical survey; or an inclusive set of myths will not find these here. Rather, this work provides a sample that conveys the richness of the African storytelling tradition. Editor Scheub also takes great pains to emphasize the role of the mythmaker as storyteller. This emphasis is reinforced by discrete sections labeled "The Art of the Storyteller." Entries are organized alphabetically by the name of the significant god, hero, etc. depicted in the story. Each myth is followed by the culture or language group and the country of origin. Next, Scheub describes the god, hero, or leading figure in the story and/or provides a description of the belief system. Entries can include related stories or variants. Of the four hundred entries, fourteen are longer so as to include commentaries on some common themes in the myth (heroes, the relations between god and man, creation, tricksters, eternal life, etc.). Especially useful are the three appendixes. The first is self-explanatory, "Myths by Country." The second lists myths by language and culture. The third "The Grand Myth" explains some common threads in the myths: beginnings, first connections, separation, struggle between god and man, second connections, and endings (all of these are briefly explained). For example, under beginnings, users will find "cosmic egg." Next to cosmic egg is "Mebege," the name of the myth where readers will find the idea of a cosmic egg discussed. Fifteen pages of sources and a twenty-seven-page bibliography round out the work. Highly recommended for academic libraries.

Classification: LC BL2400; Dewey 299.

385. *A Dictionary of Asian Mythology,* by David Leeming
Publisher: Oxford University Press, New York, NY (2001)
Price: $27.50
Review by Staff, Libraries Unlimited.

This handy dictionary of Asian mythology provides entries on mythological terms for the countries that now make up India, China, Tibet, Central Asia, Southeast Asia, and Japan. The entries range from a couple of sentences in length to a full page and cover such complex things as deities, sacred places, key events and epics, and traditions. As such, one can find definitions for deities such as Gautama Buddha and the Hindu god Ganesa and sacred sites such as the Cambodian ruins of Angkor. The book also has entries for basic terms, including afterlife, sacrifice, and hero quests (a common theme in all mythology). A short list of resources and an index (providing entry terms in boldface) conclude the volume. This resource will be very easy to use for those who are somewhat educated in Asian mythology. For those who are new to the study, however, it may be difficult to navigate because there are so few cross-references to guide the user. This book provides a lot of information for such a small price and will be a welcome addition in the reference collections of Asian religion, philosophy, and history.

---

Classification: LC BL1005; Dewey 291.

---

386. *Encyclopedia of Taboos*, by Lynn Holden

Publisher: ABC-CLIO, Santa Barbara, CA (2000)

Price: $75.00

Review by Bronwyn Stewart—Reference Librarian, Sam Houston State University, Huntsville, TX.

The *Encyclopedia of Taboos* examines the use of taboos in human culture from ancient times to the present. Holden, a postdoctoral fellow at the University of Edinburgh, includes in her examination those topics typically associated with taboos, such as necrophilia, suicide, and transvestism, as well as lesser-known taboos. She has created a suitably diverse presentation of the subject by including taboos from a variety of cultures and religions. Entries, arranged alphabetically, include theoretical analysis by major scholars in the field, along with cross-references and a short list of further reading. Also included are entries for the foremost writers on the subject of taboos, such as Sigmund Freud and Mary Douglas. Although *see* references are lacking, the book features a comprehensive index and a list of headwords to enhance navigation. Written in an engaging style, this fascinating book is sure to interest both those with a special interest in the field and general readers. It is recommended for academic and public libraries.

---

Classification: LC GN471; Dewey 390.

---

387. *The New Encyclopedia of the Occult*, by John Michael Greer

Publisher: Llewellyn, Saint Paul, MN (2003)

Price: $29.95

Review by Kennith Slagle—Collection Development Librarian, Northern Michigan University, Marquette.

Reading or using material on the occult is fraught with pitfalls. Too many editors and authors trade on the gullibility, ignorance, and wishful thinking of their readers. It is refreshing to review a book that has useful information on this subject and is still mindful of the humbug that permeates many publications in this area. While admitting he is a pagan, Greer does not get caught up in justifying every detail as metaphysical truth. In many cases, he points out the historical inconsistencies and claims that are less than accurate. Greer's encyclopedia has 531 pages of entries encompassing explanations of aspects of all the occult sciences, astrology, numerology, necromancy, and more, while other essays put the subjects in historical context and with biographical material on the major players in this arcane field. While there are no pictures of witches, there are diagrams and illustrations of pertinent symbols that explain pagan practices. Each essay has entries that reference the 22-page bibliography. If users were to read the titles in this list, they would come away with a balanced view of modern occultism. There is no separate index, but there are *see* references to other essays within each section. In fact, the only lacuna in this book is that it contains only modern, twentieth-century information on the occult. The bibliography has few entries from before 1900 and those are the standard classical works and the books written by the various members of the Golden Dawn group. However, for those wanting to know what is currently of interest to the modern pagan and how the occult is viewed, this is the book of choice.

Classification: LC BF1407; Dewey 133.

# CHAPTER FIVE

# Sciences

## General Sources

### Dictionaries and Encyclopedias

388. *McGraw-Hill Dictionary of Scientific and Technical Terms*
Publisher: McGraw-Hill, New York, NY (2003)
Price: $150.00
Review by Laura J. Bender—Librarian, University of Arizona, Tucson.

This large tome is the latest edition of the *McGraw-Hill Dictionary of Scientific and Technical Terms* that has evolved over the past 30 years. The 1st edition was intended for the communities of scientists, engineers, and researchers. This 6th edition supports nonscientists as well. It covers the language of science to include words that have permeated our culture in our endeavor to answer questions about the environment and our world. Each of the 110,000 terms has a pronunciation guide, and the 125,000 definitions include synonyms, acronyms, and abbreviations. The chosen pronunciation scheme is thoroughly explained in the preface, showing why all American dialects are not represented. Each entry falls into one of 104 listed fields, the abbreviation of which is included immediately after the item name. The scope of each field is defined, giving the reader needed context and explanation of the publisher's placement of included items. This edition also features 3,000 black-and-white illustrations located on the outside margin of the appropriate term. There is a "How to Use This Dictionary" page, as well as a 35-page appendix that includes chemical nomenclature, mathematical signs and symbols, the periodic table of elements, and biographical listings, plus 12 more sections of scientific information. As the Dictionary continues to grow, the editors of future editions may want to break it up into multiple volumes to facilitate use. The telephone book style (i.e., A–K and L–Z) would work well, or perhaps dividing the book into the physical and life sciences would be another possibility. This dictionary is an excellent reference tool for most libraries. It is especially recommended for academic and large public libraries.

> The 7th edition appeared in 2011. Classification: LC Q123; Dewey 503.

389. *The American Heritage Science Dictionary*
Publisher: Houghton Mifflin Harcourt, New York, NY (2005)
Price: $19.95
Review by Christina K. Pikas—Technical Librarian, Johns Hopkins University, Applied Physics Laboratory, Laurel, MD.

*The American Heritage Science Dictionary* is a small dictionary aimed at the lay-person. It covers all areas of science, from anthropology to zoology, and contains longer explanatory notes for some terms of interest, photographs and diagrams, and thumbnail biographies of about 40 scientists. Several of the definitions are imprecise. For example, magnetosphere is defined as applying only to the Earth when it actually applies to all planets and stars. Common terms like remote sensing, photogrammetry, detonation, nosocomial, biometrics, and creep are omitted, while phrenology is defined. This dictionary does have nice drawings, charts, and photographs sprinkled throughout that do lead to a greater understanding of the term defined. It is enjoyable to browse through and learn terms from a wide variety of fields. It is difficult to place this work in a proper collection. It is too basic for academic or public library reference collections, but too complex for children's collections. The biographies are better found in any of the reference collections of biographies of scientists, and the terms are better explained in most encyclopedias. This work is, however, much smaller, more portable, and more enjoyable to browse than most of these standard reference works, so it might find its proper home on the desk of a nonscientist or in home collections.

> An updated edition appeared in 2011. Classification: LC Q123; Dewey 503.

390. *McGraw-Hill Encyclopedia of Science & Technology*
Publisher: McGraw-Hill, New York, NY (2008)
Price: $3,495.00/set
Review by Staff, Libraries Unlimited.

The *McGraw-Hill Encyclopedia of Science & Technology* has held the reputation of being a premiere source of information for the most up-to-date information in the sciences. Updated every five years, the 10th edition proves to be just as valuable as past editions. This new edition provides more than 7,100 entries in all areas of science, including biomedical sciences, information technology and computing, chemistry and chemical engineering, industrial engineering, environmental sciences, physics, and astronomy, just to name a few. The entries are edited by an impressive list of specialists, who are listed at the beginning of the volume along with their areas of expertise. More than 5,000 specialists have contributed to the entries, including Nobel Prize winners. Looking at the impressive list of scientists and scholars associated with this work, there is no doubt it is an authoritative resource. Entries within the Encyclopedia are listed alphabetically, and headwords are provided at the top corner of each page for ease of searching. Each entry begins with a definition of the subject, which is then followed by a more in-depth discussion. The larger entries conclude with *see also* references and a bibliography. Supplementing the text are 12,000 black-and-white illustrations, 14,000 tables charting useful data, 90 full-color plates, and mathematical equations where appropriate. Volume 20 provides an appendix that explains scientific notation and the systems of units of measurement used in the text. The remainder of the volume is a complete index. Scientific topics that are stable have remained the same since the 9th edition; however, scientific fields that have changed rapidly (e.g., health sciences, genetics, nanotechnology) have had significant updates and new entries. This set remains an important reference tool for academic libraries and large public libraries. An online version of this encyclopedia is available that provides the same valuable information along with 11,000 enhanced illustrations, 62,000 hyperlinked cross-references, 2,000 hyperlinks to external websites, a dictionary with more than 115,000 terms, and a student center. The publisher plans to keep the articles updated on a yearly basis, which in itself makes the online version worthwhile as the fields of science and technology change so rapidly. For larger institutions the online subscription can run significantly higher than the cost of the print edition. Libraries will need to base their decision on the needs of their patrons as well as their budgetary constraints. For libraries building their digital collections this encyclopedia is available online via Access Science at http://www.accessscience.com.

> The print-format 11th edition appeared in 2012. McGraw-Hill increasingly emphasizes digital versions through its "Access" platform and products. Classification: LC Q121; Dewey 503.

391. *Van Nostrand's Scientific Encyclopedia*, by Glenn D. Considine and Peter H. Kulik, eds.

Publisher: Wiley-Blackwell, Hoboken, NJ (2008)

Price: $395.00/set

Review by Peter Larsen—Physical Sciences and Engineering Librarian, University of Rhode Island Libraries, Kingston.

This venerable resource has grown to fill three volumes in its current incarnation. Many previous editions (print and electronic) have been reviewed in

ARBA, and the overall evaluation remains the same: this is a solid compact general science resource that falls somewhere between a brief dictionary and a full-sized encyclopedia. The entries range from very short (a sentence or two) to longer (five to eight pages). The longer entries generally have suggestions for further investigation, including print and electronic sources. Illustrations (including charts, graphs, and chemical structures) are used extremely sparingly. Each volume begins with a list of contributors, and the final volume has an index. The overall quality of the entries is good, although the reasoning behind some of the entry choices is opaque. For example, there are entries for Beer and Wine but also Vodka, Whiskey, and Gin, which are all essentially distilled beverages (the bulk of the information on distilling can be found in the Whiskey entry). Similarly, whether an animal is described at the species level or higher seems somewhat arbitrary. This is not a critical issue, but hints that the selection of topics was not entirely rigorous. A more significant problem is the quality of the paper, which seems flimsy for a resource that is likely to receive a lot of use. Despite these caveats, this tool will likely find a home in most collections that deal with general science inquiries.

---

Classification: LC Q121; Dewey 503.

---

392. *The Oxford Companion to the History of Modern Science*, by J. L. Heilbron and others, eds.

Publisher: Oxford University Press, New York, NY (2003)

Price: $110.00

Review by Joseph W. Dauben—Professor of History and History of Science, City University of New York.

This volume is designed to set the context for appreciating the ramifications of modern science, from the Renaissance to the present, in such diverse areas as industry, literature, religion, war, and entertainment (including television and film). More than two hundred scholarly authorities have contributed to make this a very readable and informative volume. It covers historiography, major time periods, institutions, philosophy of science, epistemology, methods, theories, apparatus, and computers among the more than six hundred entries it provides. The only aspect of the history of science not covered in detail is the section on biographies. Some one hundred scientists are included, making it a complement to the very useful *Dictionary of Scientific Biography* (DSB), which is beginning to show its age. The *Oxford Companion*, when it includes biographies, seeks to provide coverage that goes beyond what may be found in the DSB, although the omissions in the *Oxford Companion* are at times surprising; there is a biography of Newton for example, but none for Leibniz. Another omission concerns the coverage of academies, which includes the major Italian, French, and British societies, but not the Leopoldina, The German Academy of Natural Scientists, the oldest in continuous existence in Europe (and which includes an active section for History of Science). Photographs help enliven the text. The extensive cross-references are useful, and extensive lists of works of "further reading" are also included with each article. This is ready-reference work for anyone interested in knowing the major implications of modern science for world history. It will serve as an invaluable source of concise but detailed information.

Classification: LC Q125; Dewey 509.

## Biography

393. *The Biographical Dictionary of Scientists*, by Roy Porter and Marilyn Ogilvie, eds.
Publisher: Oxford University Press, New York, NY (2000)
Price: $125.00/set
Review by Julia Perez—Biological Sciences Librarian, Michigan State University Libraries, East Lansing.

The 3rd edition of this reference tool includes more than 1,280 in-depth biographies of scientists from across the major scientific disciplines. A comparison of the new edition to the 2nd edition finds an increase of 80 new biographies, new sections on chronologies, new tables of scientific discoveries, and an enlarged glossary. Arranged in 2 volumes, volume 1 begins with historical reviews of the major sciences and includes the disciplines of astronomy, biology, chemistry, earth sciences, engineering and technology, mathematics, and physics. Each topic describes its major developments throughout history up to the present in an 8- to 10-page essay. The reviews offer a good introduction for those unfamiliar with these scientific fields. The biographical section takes up the majority of the text. New in this edition are the inclusion of more contemporary scientists and the addition of more women scientists. Each entry ranges in length from around 500 to 1,200 words. Basic biographical information is included, along with the scientist's major contributions to his or her field. A few photographs and illustrations are scattered throughout. As with the previous edition, the criteria for inclusion in the dictionary is not included, none of the biographies are signed, nor are the sources consulted indicated. The appendixes include useful information on scientific discoveries, a list of Nobel Prize winners, chronologies arranged by discipline, an extensive glossary, and an index. Despite some minor drawbacks, the amount and variety of information contained in the 3rd edition make it a very useful tool. It is recommended for public and academic libraries.

Classification: LC Q141; Dewey 509.

**394.** *Biographical Encyclopedia of Scientists*, by John Daintith
Publisher: CRC Press, Boca Raton, FL (2009)
Price: $210.00
Review by Staff, Libraries Unlimited.

This 3rd edition, two-volume set by well-known author and scholar John Daintith provides A to Z access to biographies of more than 2,400 scientists from antiquity through the late 2000s, focusing on each individual's important contributions to science. Entries include life and death dates followed by nationality and scientific field: e.g., Bacon, Roger (1220–1292) English philosopher and alchemist. Entries vary in length from one paragraph to several paragraphs. Taken as a whole, the scope of this dictionary makes it as much a place to learn about great schools of scientific thought and scientific discovery as it is a place to find biographical details. Following the entries is a chronology from the 6th century B.C.E. to the present. The chronology is not a typical timeline; rather, it has a notation below important dates (e.g., under the date 1637 readers will see "Mathematics" and under this it says "Cavileri introduces his method of indivisibles"). Next comes a "Useful List of Web Sites" that includes URLs for some open access sites. In the concluding index, a scientist's last name follows the indexed scientific discovery or concept. This comprehensive and reliable work is highly recommended to public and academic libraries.

Classification: LC Q141; Dewey 509.

**395.** *The Biographical Dictionary of Women in Science: Pioneering Lives from Ancient Times to the Mid-20th Century*, by Marilyn Ogilvie and Joy Harvey, eds.
Publisher: Routledge/Taylor & Francis Group, New York, NY (2000)
Price: $195.00/set
Review by Christopher W. Nolan—Assistant University Librarian, Elizabeth Huth Coates Library, Trinity University, San Antonio, TX.

Ogilvie's 1986 publication of *Women in Science: Antiquity through the Nineteenth Century* (MIT Press) was a major addition to science biographical sources that had almost ignored women's contributions up to that point. But the past decade has seen the publication of a considerable number of biographical sources on women in science, many of them building upon Ogilvie's work. Her current 2-volume dictionary, co-edited with Joy Harvey, once again reclaims center stage as the most comprehensive reference source on women scientists. This title includes approximately 2,500 women scientists who lived from antiquity through the mid-twentieth century. Science is defined broadly to include related fields like anthropology and sociology. Unlike many competing sources, this one moves beyond North America and Europe to include women from many other countries. Entries begin with a brief biographical description, with birth and death dates, educational background, and area of professional work. The essays, typically 250 to 750 words long, give only brief early life history before focusing on the subjects' principal scientific contributions. Every entry includes a bibliography that usually contains a list of primary, secondary, and standard sources. Indexing is excellent and permits simultaneous searching by more than one concept (e.g., early twentieth-century biochemists). The well-written articles are aimed at older readers but should be accessible to middle school students (although the editors avoid any attempt at inspiring future scientists found in many of the current youth-oriented titles). This source has five times the number of entries found in the well-done *Notable Women Scientists*, although the latter title frequently has photographs and lengthier entries. Overall, Ogilvie and Harvey's work is a must-have reference tool.

Classification: LC Q141; Dewey 509.

## Biology

### General Topics

396. *Encyclopedia of Evolution*, by Mark Pagel, ed.

Publisher: Oxford University Press, New York, NY (2002)

Price: $325.00/set

Review by John Laurence Kelland—Reference Bibliographer for Life Sciences, University of Rhode Island Library, Kingston.

This two-volume encyclopedia covers evolution from Darwin's original discoveries to its current applications in biology as well as those in other fields. It covers fundamental concepts and evolution as it relates to behavior, systematics, developmental biology, disease, language, sociology, and the evolution of man. The articles are listed alphabetically and by subject in the front matter. There are a preface and nine overview essays. Each of these essays is written by the principal authority in that field. An introduction summarizes the essays. The essays cover such topics as the history of evolutionary thought, the rapid evolution of man, culture in chimpanzees, the role of females in evolution, genomics and proteomics, and more. Articles are arranged alphabetically. Each one is illustrated, has sidebars and an extensive bibliography, and has cross-references to other related articles. There are many types of illustrations: cladograms, maps, taxonomic relationship charts, and classification outlines, as well as pictorial material. There are also cross-references from unused topic headings to used ones. Since cladograms are fairly numerous among the illustrations, it would have been useful to have an article about cladistics, given the breadth of topics covered. There is a directory to the approximately 350 contributors as well as an index. Prominent authorities, such as John Maynard Smith, Jane Goodall, Sarah Hardy, Daniel Dennett, and Stephen Jay Gould, write the overview essays. The contributors generally show distinguished credentials as well. Articles are excellent and well written. Unfortunately, there are no color illustrations, which would have been useful in a few cases. This work is highly recommended for academic libraries.

A 2007 work with the same title, by Stanley A. Rice, is less widely owned. Classification: LC QH360; Dewey 576.

397. *The Cambridge Dictionary of Human Biology and Evolution*, by Larry L. Mai, Marcus Young Owl, and M. Patricia Kersting

Publisher: Cambridge University Press, New York, NY (2005)

Price: $60.00

Review by John Laurence Kelland—Reference Bibliographer for Life Sciences, University of Rhode Island Library, Kingston.

This dictionary covers many aspects of human biology: anatomy, growth, physiology, genetics, paleontology, physical anthropology, primatology, and zoology. It has 13,000 definitions, with cross-references and synonyms but no pronunciation. The entries are often much more than mere definitions, with some discussion. The 1,000 most common terms are marked. In addition to the terms there are boxes covering special subjects, such as an explanation of the dating of paleontological specimens, blood group factors, and nutritional deficiencies. A notable feature is the 10 appendixes. These cover taxonomy of extinct and living primates, a geological time scale, a chronology with the Pleistocene epoch (giving that epoch more detail), marine oxygen isotope chronology (a clue to climate variations), anatomy, and a timeline of the events in the history of human biology as a science. Also included are a hominid phylogeny and the Greek alphabet. There is a list of 1,000 word roots. This is a scholarly work that is suitable for students and professionals. It covers a particular area that is not often covered and contains some terms not found in medical or general biology dictionaries. Therefore, it fills a need. This work is strongly recommended for academic libraries.

Classification: LC QP34; Dewey 612.

398. *A Dictionary of Genetics*, by Robert C. King, William D. Stansfield, and Pamela K. Mulligan

Publisher: Oxford University Press, New York, NY (2006)

Price: $75.00

Review by Staff, Libraries Unlimited.

Published originally in 1968 to answer a need for a reliable reference in an expanding field, this dictionary provides users with approximately 6,500 definitions (nearly 400 of these include diagrams, illustrations, or tables). The entries are presented in an A to Z format and vary in length from one sentence to a substantial paragraph. The dictionary makes generous use of see references. Following the main entries are a series of appendixes. Appendix A presents a classification of living organisms that includes all of the species entries in the dictionary. Appendix B "Domesticated Species" groups alphabetically the scientific names of approximately 240 domesticated species. Appendix C summarizes the history of genetics breakthroughs in an annotated chronology with 920 entries from 1590 to 2001. This appendix includes an alphabetic list of the scientists discussed and a bibliography of over 140 books. Appendix D presents a bibliography of periodical literature, as well as a list of publishers and foreign words often used in titles. Appendix E includes references to Internet sites, and the final appendix is a one-page list of genome sizes and gene numbers. Appendixes A and C are most crucial to this dictionary as main entries cross-reference to the information in the appendixes. For example, the definition for "biometry" reads: "the application of statistics to biological problems. See Appendix C, 1889, Galton." Highly recommended for public and academic libraries.

The 8th edition appeared in 2012. Classification: LC QH427; Dewey 576.

399. *Encyclopedia of Bioethics*, by Stephen G. Post, ed.

Publisher: Macmillan Reference USA/Gale Group, New York, NY (2004)

Price: $595.00/set

Review by Diane Schmidt—(Retired) Biology Librarian, University of Illinois, Urbana.

Over half of the nearly 550 articles in this 3rd edition of a highly regarded encyclopedia are new or have been completely revised, increasing its relevance in a fast-moving field. New topics include bioterrorism, stem cell research, cloning, and dementia, but the encyclopedia keeps its broad coverage. Topics from agriculture, biotechnology, medicine, environmental issues, animal rights, psychology and psychiatry, and basic research are all included, and the issues are discussed from an equally broad range of points of view including religious, philosophical, and financial. The authors provide an even-handed, thorough discussion for even the most contentious topics, leaving readers to make up their own minds about the issues. The essays are aimed at a fairly sophisticated audience rather than school children. Each article includes cross-references and often lengthy bibliographies, most of which were updated for this edition. The last volume of the set also includes nearly 300 pages of the full text of directives and codes in bioethics as well as a list of additional resources, an annotated bibliography, and an index. In all, this is a major resource for public, academic, and medical libraries.

---

Classification: LC QH332; Dewey 174.

---

400. *World Atlas of Biodiversity: Earth's Living Resources in the 21st Century*, by Brian Groombridge and Martin D. Jenkins

Publisher: University of California Press, Oakland, CA (2002)

Price: $54.95

Review by Marvin K. Harris—Professor of Entomology, Texas A & M University, College Station.

*The World Atlas of Biodiversity* is chronicled from the inception of the biosphere to the present in a lucid, succinct, and entertaining manner. Insights are provided into fascinating subjects of biology, systematics, paleontology, biogeography, evolution, ecology, natural resources, agriculture, and politics, providing a prodigious database for the concluding chapter on human endeavors to respond to changing biodiversity. Color illustrations, including pictures, maps, graphs, and tables, allow easy comprehension of sometimes difficult concepts. Original works are referenced in the text with unobtrusive superscripts. The discussion of science, policy issues, and proposed solutions endeavor to objectively inform the reader on the current status. The passive documentation of the propensity of humans to first understand and then to exploit the biosphere is thorough. Most biologists agree every species follows a biological imperative to increase density until the carrying capacity of the environment externally exerts limits. Are humans different? This book aids the understanding of our place in the biosphere and describes efforts to redirect exploitation. This is an excellent reference for those unafraid of jeopardizing their views with facts on this complex and often contentious subject. The attractive appearance qualifies the book for display purposes, and the academic rigor commends it for the college classroom and reference shelf.

---

Classification: LC QH541; Dewey 333.

---

## Animals in General

401. *Encyclopedia of Animals: A Complete Visual Guide*, by Fred Cooke and Jenni Bruce

Publisher: University of California Press, Oakland, CA (2004)

Price: $39.95

Review by Frederic F. Burchsted—Reference Librarian, Widener Library, Harvard University, Cambridge, MA.

This attractive book highlights the diversity of form and color in the animal kingdom. Each section features several color paintings or photographs of several members of each taxonomic group, usually family (e.g., Felidae: cats) for mammals and order (e.g., Anura: frogs and toads) for others. There are brief descriptions of the characteristics and natural history of each group and "Fact File" boxes giving numbers of families, genera, and species within each order and examples of particular species with range maps and natural history and conservation data. Special pages and marginal boxes describe and illustrate particular aspects of natural history: primate conservation, hermaphroditism in fish, aerial mating in swifts, and more. Introductory chapters discuss classification, evolution, biology and behavior, habitats and adaptation, and conservation. This book serves to counteract the tendency for biological textbooks to repetitively illustrate certain standard creatures while ignoring diversity. Here we have pictures of five different sturgeons. There is a strong emphasis on the "higher" animals. Mammals start the book with 181 pages, then birds (109 pages), reptiles (61 pages), amphibians (31 pages), and fish (65 pages). The invertebrates, including insects, which comprise the majority of animals, occupy 73 pages. Minor orders of insects are relegated to three pages, with embiopterans, strepsipterans, and zorapterans omitted. Several of the smaller phyla have only one picture with no text (e.g., gastrotrichs, rotifers), and some are omitted entirely (e.g., nematomorphs, nemerteans, gnathostomulidans). This book is not intended as a comprehensive treatise and the omitted groups are obscure. They are listed in the introductory section on classification. This is an excellent visual overview of animal natural history, which should be of wide interest. This book is highly recommended for secondary school, college, and public libraries. It should be useful for art libraries as well.

Classification: LC QL7; Dewey 590.

402. *Grzimek's Animal Life Encyclopedia*, by Bernhard Grzimek, Neil Schlager, and Donna Olendorf, eds.

Publisher: Gale/Cengage Learning, Farmington Hills, MI (2003–2004)

Price: $1,595.00/set

Review by Staff, Libraries Unlimited.

It was more than 30 years ago that Dr. Bernhard Grzimek edited the 1st edition of *Grzimek's Animal Life Encyclopedia*. This past year the Encyclopedia has been completely revised under the supervision of Michael Hutchins, with 16 volumes and this cumulative index to the series. The main volumes in the series cover metazoans and lesser deuterostomes, protostomes, insects, fishes, reptiles, amphibians, mammals, and birds. The final volume is a 278-page, triple-column cumulative subject index to the entire set. Species are listed by both their common names (in Roman letters) and their scientific name (in italics) and provide both the volume and page numbers. Libraries can purchase the entire set as a whole for $1,595 or can purchase each species volume or set individually.

The complete set includes these volumes: volume 1 on the lower metazoans and lesser deuterostomes; volume 2 on protostomes; volume 3 on insects; volumes 4–5 on fishes; volume 6 on amphibians; volume 7 on reptiles; volumes 8–11 on birds; and volumes 12–16 on mammals; with a cumulative index in volume 17. Classification: LC QL7; Dewey 590.

403. *Encyclopedia of Animal Behavior*, by Marc Bekoff, ed.

Publisher: Greenwood Press/ABC-CLIO, Santa Barbara, CA (2004)

Price: $349.95/set

Review by Diane Schmidt—(Retired) Biology Librarian, University of Illinois, Urbana.

With over three hundred entries written by nearly three hundred contributors, this encyclopedia covers a wide range of areas in animal behavior. The topics are drawn from comparative psychology, ethology, behavioral ecology, sociobiology, and all of the other subdisciplines that study this fascinating subject in all its ramifications, both controversial and well-established. While the focus is not on animal welfare, there are several entries on this and related subjects. The encyclopedia is arranged by broad subjects, such as cognition or reproductive behavior, with narrower entries clustered within these subjects. This clustering works in some cases but may not serve other users. There are cross-references within each article, a table of cross-references at the beginning of the first volume, and an index. Users may need to use all three resources to find all relevant articles on a topic. For instance, there is a valuable discussion of the domestication of foxes in an article on dog cognition that is not repeated in the domestication cluster, cannot be found in the index under the term domestication or the term foxes, and is cross-referenced only within one of the domestication entries. The entries range from fairly brief, simple articles clearly aimed at high school or advanced grade school students to lengthier and more substantive entries. Many of the briefer articles deal with careers or are first-person descriptions of a project by individual researchers, so they are clearly aimed at piquing the interest of students. Some of them, especially the ones that mention personal encounters with animals, do this better than others. There is a great deal of variation among the more in-depth articles as well. They range from scientific articles discussing animal behavior in carefully non-anthropomorphic terms to an article by Rupert Sheldrake advocating for the existence of telepathy in animals. Besides articles on specific behaviors or animals, the encyclopedia also includes biographies, historical articles, descriptions of methods used in studying animal behavior, and a very extensive list of animal behavior organizations and websites. There are black-and-white photographs scattered throughout the text and a separate section of color plates in each volume. Overall, the quality of the entries is very high, striking that difficult balance between being easy to understand and being accurate and detailed, between being personal and being scientific. The encyclopedia is recommended for academic and public libraries and large high schools.

Classification: LC QL750; Dewey 591.

404. *Walker's Mammals of the World*, by Ronald M. Nowak

Publisher: Johns Hopkins University Press, Baltimore, MD (1999)

Price: $99.95/set

Review by Elaine F. Jurries—Coordinator of Serials Services, Auraria Library, University of Colorado, Denver.

Since the 1st edition of *Walker's Mammals of the World* was published in 1964, it has been considered by many to be the most comprehensive reference work on mammals ever written. The 6th edition continues that tradition. A comparison of the latest edition to the 5th edition finds a 25 percent increase in text length,

95 percent of previous generic accounts significantly modified, and 81 new generic accounts added. A goal of the work since the beginning has been to provide a quality photograph of a living representative of every genus of mammal. The black-and-white photographs are excellent in quality. Each genus entry contains information on the number of species known, key literature references, physical description, comparison of characteristics of representative species, description of habitat, general behavior, breeding and care of young, and information on the species' endangered status. This edition takes great care in noting whether a species is endangered or in decline based on the International Union for Conservation of Nature's (IUCN) list of threatened animals. Close to one-half of all of the world's living mammal species are in serious to critical decline. The high quality of scholarship of this work is evidenced not only in the careful descriptions of each genus, but also in the extensive 172-page bibliography of references. The only other reference work on mammals that approaches the excellence of this set is *Grzimek's Encyclopedia of Mammals*. Grzimek's work is nearly as comprehensive as Walker's and includes color photographs and more information on behavior, ecology, and conservation, but with a much higher price tag. As there has been a significant amount of additional and revised material added since the 5th edition, this latest edition of *Walker's Mammals of the World* is recommended for every academic and public library.

Classification: LC QL703; Dewey 599.

405. *Guide to Marine Mammals of the World*, by Pieter A. Folkens and Randall R. Reeves
Publisher: Alfred A. Knopf/Random House, New York, NY (2002)
Price: $32.50
Review by ARBA Staff Reviewer.

This reference work to worldwide marine mammals begins with an introduction that provides basic data about the definition of marine mammals; their range, habitats, and behavior; reproduction; food and foraging habits; status and conservation; and tips for watching marine mammals (some of which are difficult to observe and to identify). Also included in the introduction is information about the organization of the guide, which makes it ideal for quick and easy access to facts about 118 species, divided into 10 groups, with each section starting with its own introduction. Covered are Polar Bears and Others; Pinnipeds (eared seals, walrus, and true seals); Cetaceans (baleen whales, sperm whales, beaked whales, river dolphins, beluga and narwhal, ocean dolphins, and porpoises); and Sirenians (dugong and manatees). Entries vary in length and detail as different amounts of information are known about different species. There is generous use of color photographs throughout, which enhances the work's usefulness, as do the maps included on the inside of the front and back covers. The guide concludes with a series of indexes: "Regional Assemblages," "Marine Mammal Morphology," "Illustrated Glossary," "Photo Credits," "Index," "Contributors," and "Acknowledgements." This authoritative work is highly recommended for public, school, and academic libraries.

> Sometimes identified as the *National Audubon Society Guide to Marine Mammals of the World*. Classification: LC QL713; Dewey 599.

## Dogs and Cats

406. *Encyclopedia of Dog Breeds*, by D. Caroline Coile
Publisher: Barron's Educational Series, Hauppauge, NY (2005)
Price: $29.95
Review by Mary Ellen Snodgrass—Freelance Writer, Charlotte, NC.

Barron's Educational Series has managed to make a superb, low-price reference work as gorgeous as it is useful. In artistically designed facing pages, the text defines and characterizes each canine breed. Entries feature elegant portraiture and a black-and-white drawing of distinguishing skeletal and posture traits, for example, the aloof grace of the borzoi and the stamina of the herding class. Alongside are action shots of neatly coiffed dogs at play and at work. The only detail lacking from the layout are pictures of dogs in infancy and during training. Commentary is precise without being pedantic. Back matter offers the researcher and dog fancier specifics of constitutional malformation and disease, such as joint dysplasia. Indexing supplies common names as well as proper names. Coile's book combines the function of a reference book in the guise of a handsome coffee-table compendium. The 2nd edition of the *Encyclopedia of Dog Breeds* is highly recommended for schools and public libraries.

> The 3rd edition appeared in 2015. Classification: LC SF422; Dewey 636.

407. *The New Encyclopedia of the Dog*, by Bruce Fogle
Publisher: DK Publishing, New York, NY (2000)
Price: $40.00
Review by Mary Ellen Snodgrass—Freelance Writer, Charlotte, NC.

A royal treasure for the dog lover, this new dog compendium is a superb collaboration between noted veterinarian-author Bruce Fogle and the art and publishing whizzes of Dorling Kindersley. Anecdotal photographs highlight details of toy selection, grooming tools, and essential leashes and tags as well as shiny eyes and sleek or rough coats. Expressions, such as the engaging smile on the Manchester Terrier, the posture of the Puli, and the spunk of the Norwegian Elkhound, elevate chapters from a status-conscious American Kennel Club parade to a delightful and informative text on dogs in general. Contributing to the book's success are boxed "key facts" entries; color range of coats; and labels noting physique, stamina, and performance. A balance of pure breeds with casual photographs of dogs at play or work, nursing young, and relaxing in the wild rounds out a magnificent color layout. Charts such as the dog's family tree, "How Hormones Work," and "Development of the Fetus" contribute to the book's worth as a reference guide for families, breeders, veterinarians, pet shops, schools, and public libraries. Editing is generous in its lineup of chapters on dog history, choosing and caring for a dog, and dog behaviors. In the section on feeding and nutrition, the author ignores the trend toward pricey designer food to laud home-cooked meals as well as canned, dry, and semi-moist foods. Pictures of dogs in service flesh out the picture of human dependence on animals. Additional commentary on canine collectibles and dogs in art, film, sports, and literature round out the reader's knowledge of the dog's place in human society. Oversights are few. Missing from the entry on birth are any mention of the runt and any behavioral or breeding problems with the last born. A diagram illustrating nerve endings in nails would aid home groomers in sparing dogs a slice to the quick, and a chart on correct methods of medicating dogs with pills and liquids would end standoffs between owners and pets. The one-page glossary covers anatomical terms and such details as estrus, pointing, and inbreeding, but omits under bite, flea and tick control, senility, and dysplasia—all pervasive problems. The author sensibly overlooks the dog as human food, even though that aspect of dog rearing is common in some parts of the world.

Classification: LC SF422; Dewey 636.

408. *The New Encyclopedia of the Cat*, by Bruce Fogle
Publisher: DK Publishing, New York, NY (2001)
Price: $34.95
Review by Staff, Libraries Unlimited.

In this 2nd edition of *The New Encyclopedia of the Cat*, veterinarian and author Bruce Fogle expands the text to include more information and more lavish photographs. The general layout of this "encyclopedia" is not really encyclopedic at all. It is more a handbook about domestic cats covering everything from their ancestry (descendants from the North African wildcat) to their current status as the most popular household pet in North America, and everything in between. The first two chapters discuss the early beginnings of the cat family and their evolution, their larger cat relatives, and the process of domestication as well as the human relationship to cats as it pertains to religion, folklore, superstition, and entertainment. Chapters 3 and 4 discuss the physical description of cats and the particulars of their behavior (e.g., social behavior, hunting, mating, communication style). Chapter 5, which makes up the bulk of the work, lists the different breeds of cats—first shorthairs and then longhairs. More than 275 breeds of cats are listed here with information on each breed's history, date and place of origin, weight range, temperament, coloring and markings, and any other key information. The book concludes with an in-depth chapter on caring for cats, which includes information on choosing a cat, selecting the right food, maintaining health, grooming, and correcting behavioral problems. An index concludes the volume. The more than 1,400 photographs and illustrations greatly enhance a very readable and informative text. Public libraries will want to consider this work for their general readers.

---

Classification: LC SF422; Dewey 636.

---

## Birds

409. *Firefly Encyclopedia of Birds*, by Christopher Perrins, ed.

Publisher: Firefly Books, New York, NY (2003)

Price: $59.95

Review by Charles Leck—Professor of Biological Sciences, Rutgers University, New Brunswick, NJ.

Noted ornithologist Christopher Perrins has coordinated writings from more than 100 bird experts from around the world. The product is this truly authoritative, but very readable, review of the more than 9,800 bird species on our planet, organized by the natural groups of families (e.g., parrots, waterfowl, owls, warblers, penguins). Each of the 172 families is reviewed in a dual format: there are a concise "fact file" that briefly summarizes distinctive features of the group (number of species and genera; world distribution with maps; basic details of plumage, size, voice, nest, and eggs; diet; and conservation status) and a more lengthy discussion of noteworthy species and biological highlights of the group (e.g., specialized migrations, feeding methods, courtship behavior). Throughout there are a great many excellent illustrations and color photographs showing selected species in their natural habitats. The text has given particular attention to recent ornithological discoveries and to important environmental/conservation issues. This well-done reference should be useful for the academic library but also for the general public with its easy-to-read text. Indeed, many serious birders may well want to have this hefty volume on their home shelves.

Classification: LC QL672; Dewey 598.

410. *The Sibley Guide to Birds*, by David Allen Sibley

Publisher: Alfred A. Knopf/Random House, New York, NY (2001)

Price: $35.00

Review by Charles Leck—Professor of Biological Sciences, Rutgers University, New Brunswick, NJ.

While there are many field guides to North American birds, this is the first that illustrates all plumage variations recognizable in the field. There are 6,600 full-color illustrations of the 810 species showing the spectacular diversity of plumage variety, including male and female differences, immatures as well as adults, seasonal changes, and geographic races. The author and gifted artists of this handbook literally spent decades in fieldwork throughout the continent to make study observations, sketches, and identification notes that went into this definitive work. The text that accompanies the illustrations is concise and dedicated to identification, including comments on the bird's habitat and detailed song descriptions. Important field marks are indicated directly, with notations on the illustrations. Each species also has an up-to-date range map showing its distribution (e.g., winter, summer, migrational) across North America. As the design and organization of the book is entirely user-friendly it has already become a widely used reference, especially appreciated by experienced birders.

The 2nd edition appeared in 2014. Classification: LC QL681; Dewey 598.

411. *The Sibley Guide to Bird Life & Behavior*, by Chris Elphick, John B. Dunning Jr., and David Allen Sibley, eds.

Publisher: Alfred A. Knopf/Random House, New York, NY (2001)

Price: $45.00

Review by Charles Leck—Professor of Biological Sciences, Rutgers University, New Brunswick, NJ.

Three ornithological editors have coordinated the writing of 48 expert bird-ers and biologists to make a superb handbook on North American bird life. Organized by accounts of each avian family (79 total), the book guides the reader beyond identification by discussions of taxonomy, ecology, and behavior. A family account typically includes sections on classification (taxonomic rela-tionships), diet diversity and feeding methods of species in the family, breeding behavior (including courtship displays), and conservation concerns. The author-itative accounts are current, clearly written, and informative. Throughout the work almost 800 full-color illustrations (by Sibley) show important features mentioned in the text. A 100-page introduction actually forms an independent part of the book—a popular overview of five major topics in modern ornithol-ogy, again contributed by appropriate experts. These broad topical reviews cover avian flight, evolution, behavior, distribution, and population regulation. The birding public has a great new source of information on the biology of North American birds.

---

Classification: LC QL681; Dewey 598.

---

412. *Birds of North America*, by Kenn Kaufman

Publisher: Houghton Mifflin Harcourt, New York, NY (2000)

Price: $20.00

Review by Staff, Libraries Unlimited.

This guide by renowned birder Kenn Kaufman is designed for ease of use. The front matter includes a pictorial table of contents and a quick guide to the range maps. The introduction details birding basics, including where and when to look, bird topography and field marks, notes on bird distribution, looking for different birds at different times of the year, habitat, and more. The book covers, in order, ducks, geese, and swans; other swimming birds; aerial waterbirds; birds of prey; chicken-like birds; wading birds; shorebirds; medium-size land birds; hummingbirds, swifts, and swallows; flycatchers; typical songbirds; war-blers; tanagers and blackbirds; sparrows; and finches and buntings. These groups of birds are color-coded, which facilitates use. The key to the color cod-ing also appears in the front matter. There is abundant information for each bird group. The birds of prey section, for instance, begins with two pages that intro-duce readers to the different types of raptors—buteos, osprey, eagles, owls, and more. In the following pages, these groups are broken down into subspecies. Under buteos, for example, readers will find the red-tailed hawk next to its sci-entific name, *Buteo jamaicensis*, and a range map. The accompanying description describes its habitat, its markings, and its voice. The illustrations (more than 2,000) in the book are noteworthy, as Kaufman has digitally enhanced all the photographs for clarity and color. The book concludes with an index of birds by English names and a short index. The breadth and scope of this guide (which is also compact enough to go on any birding outing) makes this a highly recommended resource for public and academic libraries.

> The 2007 *Field Guide to Birds of North America* by the same author is a later work covering similar content. Classification: LC QL681; Dewey 598.

413. *National Geographic Complete Birds of North America*, by Jonathan Alderfer, ed.

Publisher: National Geographic Society, Washington, DC (2006)

Price: $35.00

Review by Charles Leck—Professor of Biological Sciences, Rutgers University, New Brunswick, NJ.

A large team of ornithologists and artists have created a remarkable resource covering all 962 species of birds known from North America. Because this desk reference is much larger and longer than standard field guides it provides notably more comprehensive information for each bird. The typical species account includes comments on behavior and ecology, field identification, geographic variations in plumage, vocalizations, and distribution (including migration periods for arrivals and departures). There are also important conservation comments on the species populations, especially with modern risks (e.g., habitat losses and fragmentation, pesticides). Throughout, the birds are all superbly illustrated, with 4,000 paintings and 150 photographs, in full color. The book also includes well-written reviews of the 80 families of North American birds, and hundreds of up-to-date range and migration maps. This systematically organized compendium will be a definitive reference for years, welcomed by novice birders as well as experts.

> The 2nd edition appeared in 2014. A companion volume, *National Geographic Complete Birds of the World*, is less widely owned. Classification: LC QL681; Dewey 598.

414. *Peterson Field Guide to Birds of Eastern and Central North America*, by Roger Tory Peterson

Publisher: Houghton Mifflin Harcourt, New York, NY (2010)

Price: $19.95

Review by Charles Leck—Professor of Biological Sciences, Rutgers University, New Brunswick, NJ.

The classic *Peterson Field Guide* that started so many on their way to bird identification and nature appreciation has now reached its 6th edition—with major updates, innovations, and additions. While keeping Peterson's outstanding paintings for the 150 full-color plates (with arrows highlighting distinguishing fieldmarks) this new work has important improvements. A team of 6 field ornithologists brought 512 new distribution maps with annotations of range changes, touch-ups, and additions in artwork; fine-tuned the text with new information and taxonomy; and included a URL where readers can get Internet access of sets of video podcasts on birding. (The 33 podcasts provide selected species profiles with birdsongs, tutorials for the field guide, and other products particularly helpful for beginners.) The book's editorial staff also provided excellent enhancements in design and format for this noteworthy edition. Birders rejoice!

---

Peterson's guides have set a standard since 1934. There is a companion volume: the *Peterson Field Guide to Birds of Western North America*. Classification: LC QL681; Dewey 598.

---

## Fish and Reptiles

415. *Encyclopedia of Aquarium & Pond Fish*, by David Alderton

Publisher: DK Publishing, New York, NY (2005)

Price: $35.00

Review by Frederic F. Burchsted—Reference Librarian, Widener Library, Harvard University, Cambridge, MA.

This attractive book is an introduction to fresh and saltwater aquariums and fish ponds for amateurs and enthusiasts. It is well illustrated with color photographs of aquariums, ponds, plants, and fish. After an introduction on fish biology, there are sections on freshwater and saltwater aquariums and on fish ponds, each with information on tank set-up and maintenance, health, and breeding, followed by descriptions of individual species of plants and fish, and in the saltwater section, some invertebrates. These directory sections offer, for each species, a photograph and information on origins, size, diet, water temperature and pH preferences, and temperament (e.g., "Aggressive and quarrelsome"). The text is clear and well written. The introductory section on fish taxonomy and biodiversity is very well done. This work will be a good choice for any public library.

---

Classification: LC SF456; Dewey 639.

---

416. *Firefly Encyclopedia of Reptiles and Amphibians*, by Tim Halliday and Kraig Adler, eds.

Publisher: Firefly Books, New York, NY (2002)

Price: $40.00

Review by Edmund D. Keiser Jr.—Professor of Biology, University of Mississippi, University, MS.

Editors Tim Halliday and Kraig Adler utilized the artwork of David M. Dennis and Denys Overden and the writings of thirty-eight specialists to achieve a superbly attractive, authoritative, and highly informative sourcebook on amphibians and reptiles. The volume is presented as a 1st edition. Although ignored, the obvious progenitor was a 1986 book with a similar title by the same editors titled *The Encyclopedia of Amphibians and Reptiles* (Facts on File and Equinox). The 16 contributors produced works for both books, and much artwork and a number of photographs are repeated. The Firefly Encyclopedia, however, is updated, greatly expanded, and much more attractive. It is organized into a preface; major units titled "Amphibians," "Reptiles," "Pollution and Hormone Mimics," and "Unisexuality: The Redundant Male?"; and a glossary, bibliography, and index. "Amphibians" has a series of general topics on amphibian biology, natural history, and conservation followed by subunits on caecilians, salamanders and newts, and frogs and toads. Each subunit covers introductory systematics, natural history, and distribution of included taxa. The "Reptiles" section begins with fossils and reptilian history and continues with general information on the group as a whole. Included subunits follow on turtles and tortoises, lizards, wormlizards, snakes, tuatara, and crocodilians, with systematics, natural history, distribution, and interesting aspects covered on each. A chapter on pollution and hormones and another on unisexuality complete the narrative. "Factfile" panels with summaries and distribution maps are provided for many taxa. Discussions throughout are supported by superb color photographs and vividly rendered artwork. Technical terminology is minimal, and the text can be easily comprehended by anyone with a high school education. This work is highly recommended for general purchase by high school, municipal, and college and university libraries.

The 3rd edition appeared in 2015. Classification: LC QL640; Dewey 597.

417. *The New Encyclopedia of Snakes*, by Chris Mattison

Publisher: Princeton University Press, Princeton, NJ (2007)

Price: $35.00

Review by Edmund D. Keiser Jr.—Professor of Biology, University of Mississippi, University, MS.

Chris Mattison, accomplished United Kingdom author and herpetologist, has produced an attractive and informative reference work on snakes of the world. This is an expanded and thoroughly revised version of the author's 1995 *The Encyclopedia of Snakes* (Facts on File). The narrative is organized into an introduction and ten chapters. Chapter 1 details snake definitions, classification, origins, and evolution. Function and anatomy are addressed in chapter 2. Thermoregulation, respiration, water and salt balance, and other life style information are covered in chapter 3. Snake habitats and distribution are focal topics in chapter 4, feeding in chapter 5, defense in chapter 6, and reproduction in chapter 7. Interactions with humans are stressed in chapter 8 and general taxonomy in chapter 9. The final chapter concerns family-level classification and concise summaries of snake genera within the families. A geographically oriented bibliography, index, acknowledgments, and photographic credits complete the volume. Nearly all topics are superbly illustrated. Illustrations include about two hundred high-quality color photographs, plus distribution maps, graphs, and drawings, also in color. Mattison has a talent for presenting scientific information in a manner that is both entertaining and educational. The cover and text arrangement are attractively designed, and the narrative is appealingly written and easy to comprehend. This is an excellent source of accurate general information about snakes, a topic of widespread public interest. The book will especially appeal to animal breeders and amateur naturalists. While the text passages contain little new information for technically advanced ophidian specialists, the fantastic color plates alone will make this book an excellent addition for their libraries. The *New Encyclopedia of Snakes* is highly recommended for general purchase by municipal, high school, college, and university libraries.

Classification: LC QL666; Dewey 639.

## Insects

418. *Encyclopedia of Insects*, by Vincent H. Resh and Ring T. Cardé
Publisher: Elsevier Science, San Diego, CA (2009)
Price: $120.00
Review by Staff, Libraries Unlimited.

This second edition contains updates and new entries, totaling 273 articles that fall into 12 categories: anatomy, physiology, behavior, evolution, reproduction, development and metamorphosis, major groups and notable forms, interactions with other organisms, interactions with humans, habitats, history, and methodology. Articles are alphabetical within categories. Articles utilize figures, tables, and illustrations; suggestions for further readings and *see also* references to other articles within the encyclopedia appear at the end of each article. A glossary of 800 words based on terms used in the encyclopedia follows the 12 sections. Comprised of entries by leading experts worldwide, this encyclopedia is the most reliable and comprehensive resource on the creatures that account for 70 percent of species on the planet. A must-have for academic and public libraries.

---

The 2nd edition appeared in 2009. Classification: LC QL462; Dewey 595.

---

419. *Firefly Encyclopedia of Insects and Spiders*, by Christopher O'Toole, ed.

Publisher: Firefly Books, New York, NY (2002)

Price: $40.00

Review by Frederic F. Burchsted—Reference Librarian, Widener Library, Harvard University, Cambridge, MA.

This book covers insects, chelicerates (spiders, mites and ticks, and scorpions and their relatives), and myriapoda (centipedes, millipedes, and related groups). Christopher O'Toole, a bee specialist at Oxford University's Museum of Natural History, and a distinguished group of mostly British contributors very successfully provide an overview of insect natural history. There is a chapter on each order; for example, the entry on beetles provides information on phylogeny, body plan, and other general characteristics, concentrating on ecology, behavior, and conservation rather than anatomy and systematics. Each chapter has a "Factfile" box that gives numbers of species, families and suborders, a range map, and basic biological data. The numerous photographs and paintings are splendid. The organization is very clear, and the writing is highly readable and accurate. There is a glossary, short bibliography, and index. The bibliography seems rather slapdash. Especially for more general books, early editions are listed where recent ones are available, and there are more recent treatments of several of the subjects included. This is a fine book and an excellent purchase for high school, college, and public libraries.

---

Classification: LC QL462; Dewey 595.

---

420. *Insects: Their Natural History and Diversity*, by Stephen A. Marshall

Publisher: Firefly Books, New York, NY (2006)

Price: $95.00

Review by Frederic F. Burchsted—Reference Librarian, Widener Library, Harvard University, Cambridge, MA.

The great problem of insect identification for the nonspecialist is the vast number of species; there are far more than for birds, mammals, for instance. Two types of books have evolved to meet this need. Large manuals use dichotomous keys accompanied by drawings to exhaustively identify families or subfamilies: e.g., *Borror and DeLong's Introduction to the Study of Insects* by Triplehorn and Johnson (7th ed., Thompson Brooks/Cole, 2005), and Ross Arnett's *American Insects: A Handbook of the Insects of America North of Mexico* (2nd ed.). Small field guides use photographs and/or drawings to selectively illustrate the major families: e.g., *The Audubon Society Field Guide to North American Insects and Spiders* by Lorus and Margery Milne, and Borror and White's *A Field Guide to Insects: America North of Mexico* (Houghton Mifflin, 1987). In his magnificent book on the insects of northeastern North America (north of Georgia, east of the Mississippi), Stephen Marshall presents thousands of photographs that allow identification of almost any insect to family and many to genus or species. Groups for which this approach is not useful (e.g., ichneumon flies) or for which abundant photographs are available elsewhere (e.g., butterflies, dragonflies) receive less attention, but for amenable groups coverage is rich. There are fifty-five photographs of Robber flies and twenty-two of Tiger beetles—many more than in White's *A Field Guide to the Beetles of North America* (Houghton Mifflin, 1983). This level of coverage is possible because of the geographical restriction. Most of the photographs show living insects and are aimed at allowing identification by the noncollector. The beetle field guide and Covell's *A Field Guide to Moths of Eastern North America* (Houghton Mifflin, 1984) emphasize use of dead specimens. For each order, the photographs are preceded by family-by-family natural history descriptions. What might have been a dry assemblage of facts is a delight to read due to Marshall's wry sense of humor and idiosyncratic enthusiasms. He allows himself digressions on points of peculiar interest: we learn of Sphaerocerid fly larvae specializing on millipede dung. The other source of family-by-family descriptions is *Borror and DeLong's Introduction to the Study of Insects*, which, however, emphasizes structure and is more formal. There are specialized photographic guides to some of the groups (e.g., butterflies, dragonflies, damselflies), but for most of the smaller orders plus the mighty hosts of bugs, flies, wasps, and bees, this book is an unprecedented boon. The price is modest given the size and richness of the book. This will be an excellent purchase for any public or academic library.

---

Classification: LC QL473; Dewey 595.

---

## Botany, Plants, and Trees

421. *The American Horticultural Society A-Z Encyclopedia of Garden Plants*, by Christopher Brickell and H. Marc Cathey, eds.

Publisher: DK Publishing, New York, NY (2004)

Price: $80.00

Review by Diane M. Calabrese—Freelance Writer and Contributor, Silver Springs, MD.

Equal parts gem and tool, this book is like a diamond. Clear, concise, and thoroughly useful, it fits the needs of all gardeners. Knowledgeable sorts can easily confirm tolerances, size, and soil preferences for potential plant introductions. Novices can review the essentials of botany, such as how a raceme differs from a panicle, or how a pinnatisect leaf (think dandelion) looks compared to a pinnatifid one (think white oak). A simple pruning guide details the when and how for particular species. Learn the methods for taking cuttings or how to grow cacti, ferns, or tropicals. Build a successful aquatic garden or a well-ventilated shed for alpine plants. An index of common names ensures readers find *Cornus alba*, even if they remember only red-twig dogwood. Text and visual glossaries make all terms understandable. The heat-zone and hardiness-zone maps are large and easy to interpret. The cautionary sidebar on chemicals is great. All plants likely to be tapped by U.S. gardeners are treated as equals, so marigolds get as much attention as delphiniums. Sheer beauty rounds out the book with photographs that simultaneously depict and tempt. Put this book in the hands of nongardeners and they will likely start hoeing.

---

Classification: LC SB403; Dewey 635.

---

422. *Mabberley's Plant-Book: A Portable Dictionary of Plants, Their Classification and Uses*, by D. J. Mabberley

Publisher: Cambridge University Press, New York, NY (2008)

Price: $90.00

Review by Staff, Libraries Unlimited.

Selected as one of *Choice*'s outstanding titles of 2009, the 3rd edition of *Mabberley's Plant-Book* is truly one of the most practical and authoritative texts on the market for botany students and scholars. The title features 20,000 entries on every family and genus of seed-bearing plant, as well as ferns and clubmosses. Entries include taxonomic details and use both English and vernacular names in the definition. For this new edition all entries have been updated, and more than 1,650 new entries have been added, most notably ecologically important genera of mosses. Additional features include instructions for how to use the book, an appendix, and a list of abbreviations and symbols. This title remains one of the most practical botanical texts available.

> The 4th edition appeared in 2017. Classification: LC QK11; Dewey 580.

423. *Taylor's Encyclopedia of Garden Plants*, by Frances Tenenbaum, ed.

Publisher: Houghton Mifflin Harcourt, New York, NY (2003)

Price: $45.00

Review by Susan C. Awe—Assistant Director, University of New Mexico, Albuquerque, NM.

All gardeners, experienced or novice, need a guide to garden plants and will gain new insights from Taylor's. With descriptions of over 1,000 species and 1,200 color photographs, *Taylor's Encyclopedia* is the definitive source for North American gardeners. The easy-to-use format and easy-to-read descriptions are arranged by scientific genus name but supported with a thorough common name index. Entries covering trees, shrubs, vines, bulbs, and perennials include genus name and pronunciation, plant family, the plant's native area, a brief description, cultivation information, number of species, landscape uses, and any pests or diseases. Following the main entry are several species descriptions with pronunciation, size, noteworthy cultivars, and USDA hardiness zones. For example, for Hemerocallis the pronunciation "hem-er-oh-KAL-iss" is given as well as the fact that it is of the lily family with the common name daylilies. It is described as "long-lived perennials grown for colorful, trumpet-shaped flowers carried on erect stalks called scapes" and provides a section on "How to Grow." Four species are described as well as award-winning cultivars. Detailed illustrations and instructions of common techniques accompany a thorough chapter on "Propagating Plants." Editor Tenenbaum has edited the Taylor series for more than 30 years. Entertaining, accurate, and dependable, this resource will provide users with pleasure and answers to a myriad of gardening questions.

> Classification: LC SB403; Dewey 635.

424. *The PLANTS Database* [digital]

Publisher: Natural Resources Conservation Service National Plant Data Team, U.S. Department of Agriculture, Washington, DC

Price: Free online. Date reviewed: 2015.

URL: http://plants.usda.gov/java/

Review by Staff, Libraries Unlimited.

The *PLANTS Database* is the result of a joint effort by the U.S. Department of Agriculture (USDA) Natural Resources Conservation Service (NRCS) National Plant Data Team (NPDT), the USDA NRCS Information Technology Center, the USDA National Information Technology Center, and others. This is a centralized place to find standardized information about the vascular plants, mosses, liverworts, hornworts, and lichens for the United States and its territories and Canada. The database includes names, plant symbols, checklists, distributional data, species abstracts, characteristics, images, crop information, automated tools, Web links, and references. There are several other ways to search the website by state, and there are links to many topics, such as alternative crops, cover crops, and threatened and endangered crops. New material is uploaded regularly. The comprehensive data available through this free website will be useful to a range of users.

---

Classification: LC QK96; Dewey 581.

---

425. *Dirr's Encyclopedia of Trees & Shrubs*, by Michael A. Dirr

Publisher: Timber Press, Portland, OR (2011)

Price: $79.95

Review by Diane M. Calabrese—Freelance Writer and Contributor, Silver Springs, MD.

So much beauty, yet so little time and space to make all the trees and shrubs that capture our imagination part of our landscape. This dream-maker of an encyclopedia helps us narrow our choices, even as we are swayed by more possibilities. Spellbound by the many gorgeous species of cedar (Cedrus), we realize all of them require more growing room that we can provide. As for that statuesque Spanish fir (*Abies pinsapo*), we do not want to supplant or overshadow the vegetable garden. A paperbark maple (*Acer griseum*) is something we ought to try because it will lend texture and color to winter, once it slowly takes root. Anyone planning to add trees and shrubs to their established or new landscape ought to consult this book first. There are a few omissions of tempters, such as cashew (*Anacardium occidentale*). But the luscious and weighty volume is a genuine surfeit of riches. The conversational nugget that accompanies the superb photograph of each tree or shrub includes essential information about size, suitable zones, threats, hardiness, and sources. The separate indexes to scientific and common names are complemented by lists of good selections for everything from salty soil to urban setting. Gardeners who love their snow fountains (*Prunus x yedoensis*) will be surprised to read that it lacks grace. Finally, we could not agree more with his advocating for gardening as the way to find solace during the most difficult times.

Classification: LC SB435; Dewey 635.

426. *The Illustrated Encyclopedia of Trees*, by David More and John White
Publisher: Princeton University Press, Princeton, NJ (2013)
Price: $49.95
Review by Mike Parchinski—Librarian, Brookfield Library, Brookfield, CT.

*The Illustrated Encyclopedia of Trees* covers more than 1,900 trees consisting of natural species and cultivars, which are trees bred for desirable characteristics such as ornamental flowers. The brief descriptions include physical attributes, what the wood is used for, and native region. A specific tree can be found by checking the Index of Scientific Names or Index of English Names sections. Colorful illustrations show unique characteristics that help identify a tree more easily. For instance, depictions of Rauli Beech show the "spiky green" fruit, elliptical leaf shape, and bark pattern. The "Trees for Problem Sites or Special Needs" listings show types that should or should not be considered under certain conditions. For instance, the Sweet Gum provides especially good fall leaf colors and the Ash is better suited for clay soils. The names of natural species are in boldface; cultivars have the scientific name italicized followed by the word "cultivar" but have English names in the written text. For example, the Lawson Cypress is followed by the cultivars "Somerset" and "Pottenni." Separate categories further distinguish features such as height in 10 and 20 years and full grown. The foreword has only the two authors' initials, but the full names should come first to clarify what these letters refer to. The foreword and introduction state trees in Western Europe and/or North America are featured in the book, but many are from other places. For example, the Engler Beech grows in China. The introduction should clarify the geographic areas. The "Unusual Garden Trees" list includes Antarctic Southern Beech, but there is no separate entry. A new entry could include history on why this tree received the name "Antarctic" even though it actually grows in rainforests and is native to Chile. This publication has exceptional illustrations and is a good starting point to find general information on a wide variety of trees.

Classification: LC QK474; Dewey 582.

427. *The Encyclopedia of North American Trees*, by Sam Benvie
Publisher: Firefly Books, New York, NY (2000)
Price: $35.00
Review by Carol L. Noll—Volunteer Librarian, Schimelpfenig Middle School, Plano, TX.

Trees dominate much of the North American continent; even the deserts and prairies are dotted with the occasional tree. They are important sources of food and shelter for native wildlife, and although much of the old-growth forest that once seemed limitless is now gone, forests are still one of our most important natural resources, both for their lumber and paper products and for their recreational uses. This encyclopedia is a comprehensive guide to the individual species of trees that make up these forests, desert oases, and suburban parks. Only trees that are native to North America are included (no gingko or eucalyptus). Trees are listed in alphabetical order by genus. Genera with four or more members feature an introductory section sketching out their worldwide distribution, characteristics, and economic importance. Each of the 278 species is pictured in a full-color photograph, then described in clear, readable prose, emphasizing the tree's distinctive characteristics such as fall color, fruits, preferred soil and habitat, and importance in the ecosystem. The encyclopedia also includes a glossary, a tree-hardiness and climate-zone map of the United States and Canada, a bibliography with tree-related Internet sites, and an index of common tree names. While this is not a field guide, this book makes a valuable companion since it gives much more information than the simple description and range map found in most tree guides. It will be of most interest to landscapers and gardeners, opening their eyes to the great variety of trees native to the North American continent.

---

Classification: LC QK110; Dewey 582.

---

## Agriculture

428. *Dictionary of Agriculture*, by Alan Stephens, ed.

Publisher: Fitzroy Dearborn/Taylor & Francis Books, New York, NY (1998)

Price: $45.00

Review by Elaine F. Jurries—Coordinator of Serials Services, Auraria Library, University of Colorado, Denver.

This is the 2nd edition of a dictionary of agricultural terms written from a British perspective. Approximately 5,000 terms are defined, with some topics supplemented with quotes from farming publications. Phonetic pronunciation is included for the main entry words. Agriculture covers a broad territory, and this book does remarkably well, covering aspects ranging from breeds of livestock, crop varieties, agricultural economics, agrarian terminology, farming equipment and buildings, and agricultural organizations. It not only covers agriculture of temperate regions but also attempts to cover topics related to the agriculture of the tropics. With the British focus, there are naturally some topics of interest to Americans that are omitted. For example, the organizations Future Farmers of America (FFA) and National Farmer's Organization (NFO) are not present. There are several other agricultural dictionaries that can be compared to this one. *The Dictionary of Agriculture: From Abaca to Zoonoisis* provides definitions for 3,400 terms with a focus on U.S. agricultural policy and economics. The *Agriculture Dictionary* defines 10,000 terms, with a slant toward scientific terminology. Any of these dictionaries, solely or in combination, would be useful for public libraries serving a rural population, or academic libraries with an agriculture curriculum.

Classification: LC S411; Dewey 630.

429. *OECD-FAO Agricultural Outlook* [digital]

Publisher: Food and Agriculture Organization of the United Nations, Rome, Italy

Price: Free online. Date reviewed: 2015.

URL: http://www.agri-outlook.org/

Review by Staff, Libraries Unlimited.

This website is the result of collaboration between the Organisation for Economic Cooperation and Development (OECD) and the Food and Agriculture Organization of the United Nations (FAO). It offers access to both the annual reports of this name from 2009 to the present and the related agricultural outlook database. The dual goal of the collaboration is to bring together the commodity, policy, and country expertise from the OECD and the FAO, along with input from collaborating member countries, to provide annual assessment of prospects for the coming decade of national, regional, and global agricultural commodity markets. The website is easy to use and has links to an enormous amount of data. From the Publication link, users can access a free digital version of the printed *OECD-FAO Agricultural Outlook* report. *OECD-FAO Agricultural Outlook 2017–2026* is the most recently posted edition, and there are links to older reports as well. The Database link has a full user manual that guides patrons through the information on commodity, country, and variables. There are also links to sections that focus on a specific commodity like sugar, cotton, or fish.

Classification: LC HD1415; Dewey 338.

430. *FAOSTAT* [digital]

Publisher: Food and Agriculture Organization of the United Nations, Rome, Italy

Price: Free online. Date reviewed: 2017.

URL: http://www.fao.org/faostat/en/

Review by Staff, Libraries Unlimited.

This freely available database offers an abundance of statistics related to the mission of the Food and Agriculture Organization (FAO) of the United Nations. Specifically, it offers "free access to Food and Agriculture data for over 245 countries and territories" as the organization aims to meet the broader objectives of eradicating poverty and ensuring food security for all. The site is well designed in offering several ways to access and use data. Clicking on the central Explore Data tab leads users to a variety of specific indicators (crops, pesticides use, energy use, etc.) grouped into broader categories (agricultural emissions, investments, forestry, prices, etc.). Users can also conduct a search via indicators or commodities attuned to particular nations. The site also employs tabs to help group the data in other ways: a Bulk Download allows access to all updated data, Database Updates highlights all recent changes, and the *FAO Statistical Yearbook* provides data visualizations (graphs, charts, etc.) on selected indicators by country. Users may alternatively choose to access information via a Country Indicator or Rankings tab. Clicking on the former tab will display a nation's map in addition to a sidebar listing of indicators such as Demographics, Food Availability, Land, Economic & Political Stability, and others. The Rankings tab notes export and import data for a country's top commodities such as wheat, milk, vegetables, and meat. Users can also easily access the 2030 Agenda for Sustainable Development which details the most current strategies to advance the FAO's global mission. A Definitions and Standards tab on the menu bar clarifies abbreviations, national and regional identities, currencies and measurements, and more. There is also a Compare Data tool which allows users the ability to compare information gathered over more than 50 years, and a sidebar which displays the FAO's latest tweets, which convey snapshot statistics and other food/agriculture news of the day. The site's information is available in six languages. The abundant data would certainly appeal to students, researchers, policy-makers, activists, and many others.

---

*FAO Statistical Yearbooks* in PDF also are available at http://www.fao.org/economic/ess/ess-publications/ess-yearbook/en/. Classification: LC HD9000; Dewey 131.

## Astronomy

431. *The Firefly Encyclopedia of Astronomy*, by Paul Murdin and Margaret Penston, eds.

Publisher: Firefly Books, New York, NY (2004)

Price: $59.95

Review by Christina K. Pikas—Technical Librarian, Johns Hopkins University, Applied Physics Laboratory, Laurel, MD.

*The Firefly Encyclopedia of Astronomy* is a selection of articles from the celebrated four-volume *Encyclopedia of Astronomy and Astrophysics*. Many of the articles were rewritten for length and to appeal to the amateur astronomer. While the original work stands out for its size and comprehensiveness, this work is the same size as many widely owned and used concise encyclopedias and dictionaries. Unlike the others, however, this work has glossy color prints sprinkled throughout—like a coffee-table book—and has many practical instructional articles on techniques for the amateur. The editors have addressed several of the complaints from reviews of the larger edition by adding new articles such as those on brown dwarves and dark energy; however, they have omitted the signatures from the articles and the index. Cross-references are plentiful, but the lack of a table of contents or index really impedes use. The articles on planets are somewhat less thorough than those found in *Encyclopaedia Britannica* (entry 37) or the *McGraw-Hill Encyclopedia of Science & Technology* (entry 390), but coverage of space missions, equipment, and research organizations is much more complete. Overall, *The Firefly Encyclopedia of Astronomy* is a nice, concise reference book appropriate for branch libraries, smaller collections, and personal or home use. Libraries with astronomy research collections should purchase the 2001 four-volume encyclopedia instead.

Classification: LC QB14; Dewey 520.

432. *Astronomy Encyclopedia: An A-Z Guide to the Universe*, by Patrick Moore, ed.

Publisher: Oxford University Press, New York, NY (2002)

Price: $50.00

Review by Robert A. Seal—University Librarian, Texas Christian University, Fort Worth, TX.

A title search of WorldCat for "astronomy encyclopedia" retrieves more than seventy records. In such a crowded universe of similar titles, why should this revised edition of the 1987 Oxford University Press work command attention? It should for a number of reasons. First, before even opening the covers of this attractive and weighty volume, the reader knows that it is a quality work because it is edited by the prolific and highly respected Sir Patrick Moore, author and editor of scores of astronomical books for general readers and amateur astronomers, and because it is published by Oxford, known for its first-rate astronomical reference works. Inside, the book offers an impressive array of features, including more than three thousand entries, five thousand cross-references, six hundred illustrations, and a set of very fine star maps created by the expert in that field, Will Tirion. Aimed at the student and educated layperson, the work is up to Oxford University Press's usual high standards. Arranged alphabetically and beautifully illustrated with full-color photographs, illustrations, and diagrams, it is a comprehensive look at the universe and the astronomers who have helped us understand it better. In addition to defining a multitude of terms and providing the meaning of a myriad of abbreviations, the book thoroughly covers the expected topics, such as the planets, the Sun, planetary satellites, comets, meteors, asteroids, stars, galaxies, star clusters, nebulae, novae, and other interstellar objects. A particularly useful feature is its approach to the constellations. Each is given its own box placed alphabetically throughout the encyclopedia with various bits of useful data, such as the origin of the name and a description of the brightest stars. This superb collection of astronomical information is the result of contributions by dozens of the world's most preeminent astronomers and is highly recommended for university and secondary school libraries as well as the personal collection of the serious amateur.

---

Classification: LC QB14; Dewey 520.

---

433. *Space Atlas: Mapping the Universe and Beyond,* by James Trefil
Publisher: National Geographic Society, Washington, DC (2013)
Price: $50.00
Review by Staff, Libraries Unlimited.

This visually appealing atlas to the planets, stars, and beyond provides full-color photography and computer graphics of our galaxy. Along with the stunning photographs are biographies of leading scientists in astronomy, facts about the planets, and information on stars, galaxies, moons, and nebulae found in our solar system. The index guides readers through the use of bold type to illustrations, scientists' biographies, and facts. A place-name index is also included. This is one of those rare reference titles that can be used to identify fast facts as well as provide users will hours of pleasure as they browse its eye-catching pages. It will be a hit with both students and adults and can therefore be recommended for both school and public libraries.

Classification: LC QB65; Dewey 520.

434. *The Cambridge Encyclopedia of the Sun,* by Kenneth R. Lang

Publisher: Cambridge University Press, New York, NY (2001)

Price: $49.95

Review by Robert A. Seal—University Librarian, Texas Christian University, Fort Worth, TX.

Aimed at scientists, graduate students, and advanced undergraduates, this reference work provides an excellent overview of the sun, from fundamental concepts to more advanced material. After a brief introduction to basic concepts like solar radiation, physical characteristics, and origin, the book quickly delves into the sun's role as a star, both in the Milky Way galaxy and in the universe. This information is followed by a good overview of stellar evolution including where the sun is located on the so-called main sequence of stars. Other topics in the book include solar energy, the internal composition of the sun, the solar atmosphere, solar flares, solar wind, sunspots, and so on. The author also explores the earth-sun relationship and presents an overview of how solar observations are made. Special features include numerous charts and graphs, color photographs, a bibliography, a list of websites, an extensive solar glossary, and an index. This encyclopedia is an excellent work, well written and clearly presented, but it is too advanced for most lay readers. As such, this encyclopedia is appropriate for most university libraries but is too sophisticated for all but the largest public libraries, despite the fact that the cover blurb says that the work will attract the general reader. Perhaps, but unless they have a science undergraduate degree, laypersons may be discouraged by the mathematical equations and complex graphs and charts. They would be better served by a general encyclopedia of the solar system or an introduction to astronomy.

Classification: LC QB521; Dewey 523.

## Earth Sciences

### Geology

435. *The Encyclopedia of Earth: A Complete Visual Guide,* by Michael Allaby, Robert Coenraads, Stephen Hutchinson, Karen McGhee, John O'Byrne, and Ken Rubin

Publisher: University of California Press, Oakland, CA (2008)

Price: $39.95

Review by Mark A. Wilson—Professor of Geology, College of Wooster, Wooster, OH.

"One could make the case that geology, the science of the Earth, is the most critical of all the sciences for the 21st Century." This is the opening line of Walter Alvarez's foreword to this very impressive volume, and the book indeed makes the case. It is comprehensive, well written, beautifully and luxuriously illustrated, very up to date, and, as far as I can tell, scrupulously accurate. To top it, the value for the price is simply unbeatable. This is a visual encyclopedia, so the emphasis is on images, both photographic and diagrammatic. Each page is brilliantly colored, with modest text essentially filling in the spaces between pictures. There are so many images, however, that users still trace a narrative through the captions alone. These illustrations are of the very highest quality. The volume is divided into six elemental sections: Birth, Fire, Land, Air, Water, and Humans. Each has a series of articles within it. Each article has a consistent set of features for easy orientation and navigation. Global and regional maps ensure that the reader can locate the many examples used for the topic. Charts and graphs are often inset to provide critical information but not distract from the photographs and graphic images. These latter are often complex block diagrams with cross-sections showing internal details. Some of the articles are quite detailed, even to the point of describing each major tectonic plate separately. There is a glossary at the end, along with a long index. The coverage of geological topics in this book is so thorough that some teachers and professors will be tempted to use it as a textbook. The publishers might even consider selling the illustrations separately as images for projection in classrooms. This book is highly recommended for all libraries with Earth and environmental sciences collections.

Classification: LC QB631; Dewey 550.

436. *Oxford Companion to the Earth*, by Paul L. Hancock and Brian J. Skinner, eds.
Publisher: Oxford University Press, New York, NY (2000)
Price: $75.00
Review by Staff, Libraries Unlimited.

This companion to the earth sciences is designed for those needing general information on many aspects relating to the Earth. It will be useful in the hands of undergraduate students, journalists, city planners, and those with a general interest in the sciences and how they work together on our planet. There are more than nine hundred entries in this volume, which include a full range of topics, including geology, geophysics, geochemistry, paleontology, soil science, glaciology, oceanography, climatology, environmental sciences, and the history of earth sciences. Written by more than two hundred contributors (each an expert in their field), the entries are thorough and will be understood by the educated lay reader. The work is thoroughly cross-referenced, and many of the entries provide books for further reading. Entries typically range from half a page in length to several pages, and many include black-and-white illustrations, maps, or graphs. Four appendixes complete the volume: a geological time scale; a measurement scale for the earth and the solar system (which includes mass, density, and distance from the sun for all planets); the periodic table; scientific units and notation, conversion tables, and abbreviations. A thematic list of topics found in the volume and an index complete the text. Public and undergraduate university libraries will want to add this volume to their collection. It covers a lot of scientific topics and explains each in an easy-to-understand style. At $75, this work is well worth its price.

---

Classification: LC QE5; Dewey 550.

---

437. *Encyclopedia of Earthquakes and Volcanoes*, by Alexander E. Gates and David Ritchie

Publisher: Facts on File, New York, NY (2007)

Price: $75.00

Review by Danielle Andrea Kane—Science Librarian, University of California–Santa Cruz.

A unique volume that covers historical earthquakes and volcanoes, this volume also includes entries on geologic and seismic principles. This newest edition contains around 1,500 entries, 200 of which are new. These entries reflect all aspects of earthquakes and volcanic eruptions, including the causes, characteristics, and historical accounts, formatted into clear and concise entries. An excellent, descriptive, and brief essay on plate tectonics covers the earth's architecture, including the different sort of plate margins or boundaries that occur when lithospheric plates meet. The main section of the book is an alphabetic listing of terms; a number of entries are supplemented with black-and-white photographs, maps, and charts. Included with the standard geologic terms are major earthquakes. The term earthquake as an identifier follows each name, and a location is listed. At the top of each page are the first and last terms listed in the two-page spread. Some entries have *see also* references and if another term is contained within the entry it is capitalized for emphasis. There are a total of eight appendixes covering the following topics: a "Chronology of Earthquakes and Volcanic Eruptions," "Eyewitness Accounts of

Major Eruptions and Quakes," a selected bibliography of further reading and websites, "The Deadliest Earthquakes," "The Deadliest Volcanoes," "The Highest Magnitude Earthquakes," "The Frequency of Occurrence of Earthquakes," and "Magnitude versus Ground Motion and Energy." At the end of the book is an index. With its organization, the *Encyclopedia of Earthquakes and Volcanoes* would make an excellent reference book for high school students and lower-level undergraduates new to earth science. It will also be useful for public libraries and as a supplementary title for college libraries.

Classification: LC QE521; Dewey 551.

438. *Encyclopedia of Volcanoes*, by Haraldur Sigurdsson, Bruce Houghton, Hazel Rymer, John Stix, and Steve McNutt, eds.

Publisher: Academic Press, San Diego, CA (2000)

Price: $99.95

Review by Bruce H. Tiffney—Associate Professor of Geology and Biological Sciences, University of California–Santa Barbara.

Like dinosaurs, volcanoes are an aspect of earth science that attracts strong interest. However, the curious non-volcanologist quickly finds out that "volcano literature" is dominated by its two end points—popularizations and technical journal articles. This book fills a niche to the technical side of the middle ground, but is a magnificent introduction to the subject that could be read by scientist and nonscientist alike. It is not an encyclopedia in the sense of a long alphabetic list of terms with brief definitions, but rather a collection of eighty-three essays written and reviewed by a variety of experts in the field. The breadth of the book is exemplary. The bulk of the chapters treat the physics and chemistry of magma, and the geologic features involved in its expression on the Earth's surface. While five chapters treat volcanism elsewhere in the solar system, twenty-eight chapters focus on the role of volcanoes in human life, from their threat to civilization to their ecological impact and their role in art, literature, and horticulture. Those wishing for further data will find each chapter ends with a bibliography leading to the technical literature. Nonspecialists will appreciate the glossary of important terms that introduce each chapter. The book is extensively illustrated with both color and black-and-white photographs, a range of line drawings, and tables. The writing is generally clear and accessible to those with serious interest in the subject. While unusual in its presentation, this is an outstanding reference book belonging in public and research libraries alike.

The 2nd edition appeared in 2015. Classification: LC QE522; Dewey 551.

## Climate and Weather

439. *Encyclopedia of Climate & Weather*, by Stephen H. Schneider and Michael D. Mastrandrea, eds.

Publisher: Oxford University Press, New York, NY (2011)

Price: $450.00

Review by Staff, Libraries Unlimited.

While it may be true that "Everyone talks about the weather, but nobody does anything about it," we have certainly had a lot to talk about over the past 15 years since the 1st edition of this title was published in 1996. Every month we are faced with more deadly afteraffects of weather, including hurricanes, tornadoes, flooding caused by rain, blizzards, and extreme drought conditions. This makes this update of a well-received reference on the weather and climatology all the more timely. This new edition has been updated with new articles on such topics as global warming, extreme weather, the Intergovernmental Panel on Climate Change, tradable permits, and the Kyoto Protocol. Overall, it includes some 330 entries that include scientific concepts used in climatology, processes that produce weather, classification of climates, and the history of atmospheric sciences. The editors have used more than 300 maps, photographs, and charts to illustrate the various concepts and topics throughout the text. Each entry is typically several pages in length, has subtopics within that help organize the text, has a bibliography, and is signed by the contributor. The audience for this resource remains high school students, undergraduate students, and the general reader, making this a worthwhile addition for high school, university, and public libraries.

Classification: LC QC854; Dewey 551.

440. *The Encyclopedia of Weather and Climate Change: A Complete Visual Guide*, by Juliane L. Fry

Publisher: University of California Press, Berkeley, CA (2010)

Price: $39.95

Review by Maren Williams—Reference Librarian, University of Louisiana at Monroe.

This comprehensive guide to all aspects of weather and climate includes six sections, each written by a different scientist with expertise in the relevant subject area. The first section, "Engine," provides an overview of Earth's atmosphere, climate systems, jet streams, and seasons. "Action" delves into water formations and cycles as well as various types of clouds. "Extremes" provides in-depth information on thunderstorms, tornadoes, hurricanes, blizzards, and droughts, as well as the coldest, hottest, wettest, and driest places on the planet. "Watching" examines modern storm tracking and forecasting, as well as the history of meteorology. "Climate" describes climate zones in general, as well as specific subregional climates of the world. The final section, "Change," examines all aspects of climate change, including natural cooling and warming cycles, the impact of humans, and effects on the ecosystem. Several locations around the world are featured as "Hot Spots" with explanations of how they impact, mitigate, or may suffer the effects of climate change. The Encyclopedia is illustrated in full color with numerous photographs, illustrations, charts, graphs, and maps. In fact, in some cases it seems that the graphics are featured at the expense of textual content. Nevertheless, the book's clear explanations of meteorological and climatic effects, instruments, and history make it a useful reference to have in middle school, high school, and undergraduate libraries.

---

Classification: LC QC854; Dewey 551.

---

441. *Encyclopedia of Global Change: Environmental Change and Human Society*, by Andrew S. Goudie and David J. Cuff, eds.

Publisher: Oxford University Press, New York, NY (2002)

Price: $275.00/set

Review by Michael G. Messina—Associate Professor, Department of Forest Science, Texas A & M University, College Station.

The term "global change" has been used in a variety of contexts but is usually interpreted as referring to global climate change caused by both humans and nature. *The Encyclopedia of Global Change: Environmental Change and Human Society* interprets global change to refer to natural and human-caused changes in the Earth's physical, chemical, and biological systems and resources, and the effects those changes have on human society. Topic coverage ranges from less than one page to several pages, including photographs, tables, and other illustrations. A directory of contributors is included, showing their current positions and areas of expertise. A synoptic outline of contents helps readers understand quickly the extent of coverage of major areas. The set also includes a large, detailed index with suggested related topics to broaden the set's usefulness. Global change has become an emotionally charged issue leading to books that are decidedly nontechnical and are instead meant to further the political agenda of certain groups. However, content in these volumes appears to be strictly technical. Advanced degrees in various earth sciences are unnecessary to appreciate this encyclopedia. In other words, this is not another doom-and-gloom, nontechnical treatise of how life on Earth will cease in the near future because of the wanton disregard mankind has shown the planet. This encyclopedia will be valued by anyone working in an environmental or earth science area, or just interested in current issues involving global change. It should be contained in the reference section of all public and school libraries.

---

The *Encyclopedia of Global Warming* (Salem Press, 2010) covers similar themes. Classification: LC GE149; Dewey 363.

---

442. *National Weather Service* [digital]

Publisher: National Oceanic and Atmospheric Administration (NOAA), U.S. Department of Commerce, Silver Spring, MD

Price: Free online. Date reviewed: 2017.

URL: http://www.weather.gov/

Review by Staff, Libraries Unlimited.

This site from the National Oceanic and Atmospheric Administration (NOAA) is the essential weather resource. It presents a generous series of maps and subject tabs where users can find a wealth of information on all types of weather affecting the continental United States, Alaska, Hawaii, and territory islands. The site is easy to navigate, with an abundance of tabs linking to regional weather information and specialized features. The home page initially presents the general national outlook statement on all regions and then displays a large national map demarcated by counties which are colored according to any current and/or developing weather pattern. A key below details twenty-seven categories of weather scenarios, such as Flood Warning, Winter Weather Advisory, Gale Warning, and Fire Weather Watch. Clicking links below the map allows users to follow the weather in the American territories of Samoa, Guam, Puerto Rico, and the Virgin Islands. Clicking on a county will redirect users to the National Weather Service page for that weather reporting station and its forecast. From the menu bar, users can select from a variety of tabs. The Forecast can be aimed at a number of individual categories such as Aviation, Marine, Hurricanes, Severe Weather, Sun/Moon, Long Range Forecasts, and more. Past Weather will note Records, Astronomical Data, and twenty-four-hour Temperature Readings. Clicking on the Safety tab links to a listing of topical pages addressing the extreme of tsunamis or tornadoes in addition to the common issues of fog, heat, or wind. Other tabs include Active Alerts, which also relates to various categories (river, flooding, drought, etc.) and can be searched by state. Forecast Maps offer an excellent selection of graphics illustrating a long list of weather variables, such as Temperature, Precipitation, Short or Medium Range

Forecast, Wind Speed & Directions, and Sky Cover. Other maps, including Previous Days, Animated, and High-Resolution, are also available here. Users can also access maps and information exclusive to Rivers, Lakes & Precipitation, or Air Quality, view composite Satellite Image maps (updated every thirty minutes), and much more. Additional resources are plentiful and include Information and Education tabs linking to many Publications, Brochures, a Glossary, the Daily Briefing, Statistics, Initiatives, and many other resources. Well organized and extensive, the material on this site would appeal to students, professionals, and casual weather observers alike. Highly recommended for public, school, and academic libraries.

---

Classification: LC QC875; Dewey 551.

---

443. *Weather Underground* [digital]

Publisher: The Weather Company LLC, Atlanta, GA (2008)

Price: Free online. Date reviewed: 2008.

URL: http://www.wunderground.com

Review by Greg Byerly—Associate Professor, School of Library and Information Science, Kent State University, Kent, OH.

*Weather Underground* goes back to the very early days of the Web and was created at the University of Michigan. It became one of the first hits on the Web in the mid-1990s. It has evolved into a major commercial weather service, even though it gets much of its information from the *National Weather Service* (entry 442). Its cluttered screen offers an incredibly wide range of current and historical weather information. The Education section is worth checking out, especially for climate change and global warming issues.

---

Classification: LC QC875; Dewey 551.

---

## Water and the Oceans

444. *Encyclopedia of the Sea*, by Richard Ellis

Publisher: Alfred A. Knopf/Random House, New York, NY (2000)

Price: $35.00

Review by Julia Perez—Biological Sciences Librarian, Michigan State University Libraries, East Lansing.

Ellis, the author of several books and articles on aquatic life and a celebrated marine artist, has undertaken this new publication on sea life and lore. The author draws upon his own knowledge, research, experiences, and the help of others in the aquatic field to develop the text. Virtually as many significant areas as possible relating to the sea have been touched upon in this one-volume text. Included in the disparate list of topics are entries pertaining to bodies of water and the marine life within them, birds, wildlife, explorers, islands, flora, cities, ships, and so on. The encyclopedia covers 377 pages of entries arranged alphabetically, from "abalone" to "zooxanthellae." Each page includes 2 columns of entries along with 2 to 3 entries per page that average anywhere from 150 to 200 words each. The entries are informational, entertaining, and easy to understand, and most include *see also* references. The work is also illustrated with more than 450 of the author's own black-and-white drawings and color paintings. Disappointingly, neither a bibliography nor sources cited are included. This one-volume compendium of information about the sea offers an informative overview on the topic. Where else can users read about the existence of the vampyroteuthis—a cross between a squid and an octopus that has the ability to turn itself inside out. This encyclopedia is recommended for all libraries.

Classification: LC GC9; Dewey 551.

445. *Encyclopedia of Marine Science*, by C. Reid Nichols and Robert G. Williams

Publisher: Facts on File, New York, NY (2009)

Price: $85.00

Review by Ralph Lee Scott—Professor, Assistant Head of Special Collections for Public Services, and Curator of Printed Books and Maps, East Carolina University Library, Greenville, NC.

This is a handy one-volume encyclopedia that covers concepts in marine science in a series of concise articles. Also included are 20 additional essays covering topics in more depth such as Marine Embedment Anchors; Jacques-Yves Cousteau; Glomar Challenger; Sargasso Sea; Icebreaking; Radioactive Waste Disposal at Sea; Robert D. Ballard; and NOAA's PORTS system. Five appendixes cover further resources (print, Web, and associations); a list of major marine oceans, seas, gulfs, and bays; classification of marine organisms; periodic table of elements; and geologic timescale. Some encyclopedia entries have additional bibliographies appended at the end of the article. The additional essays were written by invited contributors; for example, the essay on Dr. Ballard was written by the president of the Marine Information Resources Corporation in Ellicott City, Maryland. The work is illustrated with numerous black-and-white photographs, line drawings, and tables. The articles and essays are well written and provide basic information on the topic. While not written at an advanced scientific level, the articles will provide most general readers and students with the basic facts.

Classification: LC GC9; Dewey 551.

446. *Freshwater Issues: A Reference Handbook*, by Zachary A. Smith and Grenetta Thomassey

Publisher: ABC-CLIO, Santa Barbara, CA (2002)

Price: $45.00

Review by Michael G. Messina—Associate Professor, Department of Forest Science, Texas A & M University, College Station.

*Freshwater Issues* is part of the Contemporary World Issues series, volumes that address topics vital to modern society such as pollution, food safety, and nuclear proliferation. Written by professional writers, scholars, and subject matter experts, the series provides a good first point of reference for research on these issues. Availability of an ample supply of quality drinking water will be one of the most critical issues facing world society, including the United States. Although 75 percent of Earth is covered in water, 97 percent of that water is in the oceans. Only about 1.5 percent of Earth's water is fresh and fit for human consumption. Distribution and dependable availability of this water will continue to be a public policy issue requiring serious attention. Freshwater Issues begins with three general overview chapters dealing with water supply, demand, development, rights, allocation challenges, management problems, and a history of key people and events. The book then presents a detailed history of U.S. water policy, freshwater facts and data, a directory of government and international agencies, organizations and associations, and selected print and nonprint resources. The book concludes with a useful glossary and an index. Although *Freshwater Issues* is part of the contemporary world issues series, the book deals only with the United States. However, it appears to be complete and current in its coverage. The reader needs no special training in hydrology, geology, or any other earth science to appreciate this book. Anyone interested in America's water resources will gain from referencing it. It should be contained in the reference section of all public and school libraries.

*The Global Water Crisis* by David E. Newton (2016) is a recent publication on related topics. Classification: LC TD345; Dewey 333.

## Mathematics

447. *The Universal Book of Mathematics: From Abracadabra to Zeno's Paradoxes*, by David J. Darling

Publisher: Wiley-Blackwell, Hoboken, NJ (2004)

Price: $40.00

Review by Staff, Libraries Unlimited.

This A to Z title of all things related to math is not intended as a comprehensive, academic dictionary of mathematics. Nevertheless it is a valuable ready reference that includes entries related to myriad areas: algebra, analytical geometry, approximations and averages; arithmetic; biography; board games and chess problems; calculus and analysis; calendars, dates, ages, and clocks; chaos, complexity, and dynamical systems; codes and ciphers; combinatorics; complex numbers; computing, artificial intelligence, and cybernetics; differential geometry; dimension, higher and lower; dissection; fractals and pathological curves; functions; games; geometry, graphs, and graph theory; groups; history of mathematics; illusions and impossible figures; infinity; large numbers; logic; magic squares; mathematics (foundations and miscellaneous); mazes; measuring and units; mechanical puzzles; mirrors and symmetry; number theory; numbers (both special and types); packing; paradoxes; places and buildings; plane curves; polygons; polyominos; prime numbers; probability and statistics; puzzles; science and philosophy; series and sequences; sets and set theory; solids and surfaces; space curves; terminology; tiling; time; topology; and words and word puzzles. Along the way, users will discover expected entries for pi, linear algebra, relativity theory, etc. and such less-expected terms as hairy ball theorem, disme, Lissajous figure, and birthday paradox. The entries vary in length from one line (e.g., Wff—defined as A Well-Formed Formula) to more lengthy articles. There are extensive cross-references within entries, and terms with their own entry are indicated in bold type. Readers will find puzzles and answers at the back of the book, along with a list of references and a category index. Highly recommended for school, public, and academic libraries.

---

Classification: LC QA5; Dewey 510.

---

448. *Encyclopedia of Mathematics*, by James Tanton

Publisher: Facts on File, New York, NY (2005)

Price: $75.00

Review by Holly A. Flynn—Mathematics Librarian, Michigan State University, East Lansing.

According to the author, many primary and secondary students miss out on the beauty of mathematics because of the way they are taught the subject. Mathematics is often taught as a series of facts that need to be memorized in order to solve a particular problem. Students do not question these facts, so they do not develop a deep understanding or appreciation of the subject. This book aims to make mathematics interesting to students by telling its history. The author, James Tanton of St. Mark's Institute of Mathematics in Massachusetts, believes that each mathematical concept has its place in history and when students learn mathematics in context they will understand it better. The eight hundred entries in this encyclopedia are arranged alphabetically and cover the standard undergraduate-level definitions and rules. However, the encyclopedia adds context to these rules with six essays on the history of equations and algebra, calculus, functions, geometry, probability and statistics, and trigonometry. In addition, the author includes lengthy biographies of many mathematicians from all over the world. Overall, the treatment of undergraduate-level mathematical concepts is comprehensive. The text is complemented by numerous charts, graphs, and pictures. The encyclopedia contains a very helpful index and a timeline of the history of mathematics. Finally, a bibliography and webliography of additional resources is included. This encyclopedia is similar in scope to the two-volume *World of Mathematics*, edited by Brigham Narins and published by the Gale Group in 2001. The work under review is a bit more concise and is recommended for libraries that serve high school and undergraduate students.

Classification: LC QA5; Dewey 510.

449. *CRC Concise Encyclopedia of Mathematics*, by Eric W. Weisstein

Publisher: CRC Press, Boca Raton, FL (1999)

Price: $65.00

Review by Margaret F. Dominy—Information Services Librarian, Drexel University, Philadelphia, PA.

This work attempts to define the field of mathematics, no small feat and no small work at nearly two hundred pages. Definitions tend to be concise, usually not much longer than a column page. For clarity, an illustration is often included. Mathematical rigor is maintained in the definitions. For some of the longer entries, references are provided. The cross-referencing is generous to both internal entries and Internet sites. Of particular interest is the effort to relate the mathematical topic to recognizable everyday life through copious examples. This makes for very appealing reading. Mathematicians, scientists, engineers, and students will find this book useful and a delight to use. The book is also available on CD-ROM. This encyclopedia is highly recommended for academic, public, and school libraries.

> The 2nd edition appeared in 2003, and a longer 3-volume *CRC Encyclopedia of Mathematics* in 2009. Classification: LC QA5; Dewey 510.

## Physics and Chemistry

450. *CRC Handbook of Chemistry and Physics*, by David R. Lide, ed.

Publisher: CRC Press, Boca Raton, FL

Price: $125.96

Review by Ignacio J. Ferrer-Vinent—Science Reference/Instruction Librarian, Auraria Library, University of Colorado, Denver.

The *CRC Handbook of Chemistry and Physics* provides a wealth of numerical data, constants, and other scientific information of interest to scientists and engineers. The Handbook is probably the first reference resource to which chemistry students are exposed, and it is often found in the offices of science professionals. It has grown from the thin, 116-page pocket book manual of 1913 to the familiar, authoritative, and massive volume containing a plethora of physical science data distilled from the work of innumerable scientists. David R. Lide has been its editor-in-chief for close to 20 years. A list of current contributors appears at the beginning of the work. The handbook is expanded and updated with every new edition. Additional new tables of data in the 88th edition are on the subjects of ionic liquids, solubility of organic compounds in pressurized hot water, solubility of hydrocarbons in seawater, nutrient values of foods, and properties of organic semiconductors. This essential compendium of physical science data should be in every college and university library as well as in any chemistry, physics, or engineering research lab.

> The 98th edition was published in 2017. Classification: LC QD65; Dewey 540.

451. *The Nature of Science: An A-Z Guide to the Laws and Principles Governing Our Universe*, by James Trefil

Publisher: Houghton Mifflin Harcourt, New York, NY (2002)

Price: $35.00

Review by Adalyn Smith Watts—Librarian, San Joaquin Valley College, Visalia, CA.

This engagingly written tome explains 200 laws and principles fundamental to the understanding of science, alphabetically arranged with an index and a glossary at the back of the book. A color code indicates subject areas. Written by James Trefil, a professor of physics and coauthor of *The New Dictionary of Cultural Literacy* (entry 61), the book is hard to forego with timelines not only listed in a chart in the back of the book, but a history of thought about each principle or law to the side of each entry. Entries are very up-to-date with Mendeleyev's periodic table taken up to 118 elements and the discovery of the 119th mentioned, far better than those found easily on the Web. The book, however, lacks a list of references or bibliography of any kind. This oversight limits the usefulness of the work and hopefully will be corrected in later editions.

Classification: LC Q121; Dewey 503.

452. *Encyclopedia of Physics*, by Joe Rosen

Publisher: Facts on File, New York, NY (2004)

Price: $75.00

Review by James W. Oliver—Chemistry Librarian, Michigan State University, East Lansing.

Facts on File publishes a number of quality encyclopedias and handbooks, and this is certainly no exception. It is a high-quality list of facts, names, and definitions of the history of physics. Each entry is relatively short, but not at the expense of omitting necessary information. For example, the entry for Richard Feynman covers his academic life and career, including his role in the investigation of the Challenger explosion near the end of his life. There is a second entry with detailed information about his Feynman diagrams. This article is longer and very complete. The book also includes eleven essay-length entries that are interspersed throughout the book. The index to the book is necessary for the best use of the book. It cross-references the articles in the book so that the user may find all the information on any given topic. There are three appendixes as well. The first has a bibliography of references and websites. The second is a list of Nobel Prizes in physics listed by year. The third is a periodic table and list of chemical elements. The author, Joe Rosen, is a retired professor who is a Visiting Professor of Physics at the Catholic University of Washington, D.C. This is a book that would be useful for all libraries from high school to academic.

Classification: LC QC5; Dewey 530.

453. *Van Nostrand's Encyclopedia of Chemistry*, by Glenn D. Considine, ed.

Publisher: Wiley-Blackwell, Hoboken, NJ (2005)

Price: $195.95

Review by Robert Michaelson—Head Librarian, Seeley G. Mudd Library for Science and Engineering, Northwestern University, Evanston, IL.

First published in 1957 as *The Encyclopedia of Chemistry*, and most recently in 1984 as *Van Nostrand Reinhold Encyclopedia of Chemistry*, this work has earned a solid reputation. Alphabetically listed entries range from brief paragraphs to multipage articles with diagrams and references, including general topics (e.g., Corrosion), types of reactions (e.g., Esterification), classes of compounds, elements, and brief biographies of notable chemists. Coverage includes chemical engineering and biochemical topics. This edition includes new topics, such as fullerenes, and new articles on hot fields, such as "Molecular and Supermolecular Electronics" and "Nanotechnology (Molecular)." Entries are interspersed with see references; there is an adequate, although sometimes frustrating index; for example "Fullerenes" is not listed and "Buckminsterfullerene" leads to a brief paragraph chiefly giving "see also Carbon Compounds" where substantial information is found. The only real competition in single-volume chemistry encyclopedias is from the *Concise Encyclopedia Chemistry* (Walter de Gruyter, 1994), which includes many entries on individual chemical compounds, absent in Van Nostrand's, and many gems of concision. Van Nostrand's, however, has many valuable discursive articles. Any good chemistry collection should have both. This work is strongly recommended.

The 5th edition appeared in 2010. Classification: LC QD4; Dewey 540.

454. *Periodic Table of Elements: LANL* [digital]

Publisher: Los Alamos National Laboratory, Los Alamos, NM

Price: Free online. Date published: Date reviewed: 2017.

URL: http://periodic.lanl.gov/chem.shtml

Review by Staff, Libraries Unlimited.

The Los Alamos National Laboratory developed this freely available database as a service to the public. The simply designed home page offers several main links: About the Resource, About the Periodic Table, How to Use, Characterizing the Elements, Chemical Properties, Elements List, and Periodic Table Downloads. The information discoverable by clicking on these tabs is geared toward those unfamiliar with the periodic table. So, for example, when the information under How to Use is accessed, users will find straightforward explanations of atomic number, atomic symbol, standard atomic weight, electron configuration, and atomic radius (this last term has external links for those wanting more information). Characterizing the Elements provides a basic explanation for how elements are classified as metals or nonmetals, while Chemical Properties provides basic definitions for an atom, subatomic particle, nucleus, electron, and chemical bonding. The Elements link takes users to the heart of the site. Here each element is listed in alphabetic order; a click on the element name pops up basic information like atomic number, boiling point, atomic radius, etc., along with a history of the element's discovery, the production and properties of the element, isotopes, uses, and handling instructions where necessary (as in the case of Polonium). Some of these element descriptions are enhanced by illustrations. Radium, for instance, features a black-and-white picture of Madame Currie, the scientist who first discovered it. In addition to the periodic table, the site provides links to outside resources like the American Chemical Society and the *CRC Handbook of Chemistry and Physics* (subscription required; entry 450) along with links to current chemistry news. Highly recommended to school and public libraries.

Classification: LC QD467; Dewey 540.

455. *WebElements Periodic Table of the Elements* [digital]
Publisher: The University of Sheffield and WebElements Ltd., Sheffield, UK
Price: Free online. Date reviewed: 2017.
URL: https://www.webelements.com/
Review by Staff, Libraries Unlimited.

Hosted by Professor Mark Winter, University of Sheffield, United Kingdom, *WebElements* offers free and easy access to the periodic table of elements, a visualized organization of all known chemical elements such as oxygen, uranium, or aluminum. The home page is, in fact, the periodic table, by which elements are arranged by group and period. Users can access more detail by either clicking on an element within the table or by clicking on a topic (such as History or Atoms) from the menu above the table. Clicking on the element itself leads to a generous description of the element, including historical information, element properties, and more. Particular points are bulleted, such as atomic number, symbol, color, classification, and other technical information. Users who choose to click on the menu bar will go directly to their chosen topic within the element's broader description (e.g., the Physics tab leads users to information regarding the physical attributes of an element based on several scientific scales). Supplementary features include photographs, audio recordings (pronunciation and facts), and more. The site's navigable structure makes it ideal for secondary school students, but the depth and detail of the content make it suitable for more advanced students as well.

---

Classification: LC QD467; Dewey 540.

---

## Technology

Technology changes quickly, faster than reference books are written and published. Summary works like encyclopedias can be partially out of date by the time that they appear in print (while still recording the state of knowledge at a moment in time, which is one of their purposes). They remain useful for identification of persistent issues, definitions and vocabulary terms, the names of important innovators, chronology, historical background, and fundamental facts.

456. *Scientific American Inventions and Discoveries: All the Milestones in Ingenuity—From the Discovery of Fire to the Invention of the Microwave Oven*, by Rodney P. Carlisle

Publisher: Wiley-Blackwell, Hoboken, NJ (2004)

Price: $40.00

Review by Staff, Libraries Unlimited.

This historical encyclopedia discusses more than 400 inventions and discoveries in the context of their impact on broader society. The text is divided into six parts: The Ancient World through Classical Antiquity, 8000 B.C. to A.D. 330; Middle Ages through 1599; The Age of Scientific Revolution, 1600–1790; The Industrial Revolution, 1791–1890; The Electrical Age, 1891–1934; and The Atomic and Electronic Age, 1935 into the 21st Century. In the introduction, author Carlisle lays out the rationale for the periodization used and points out that inventions and discoveries that cross time periods are located in the section in which they had the most impact. Sections start with short introductions, and entries within sections appear in alphabetic order. Photographs, illustrations, tables, and textboxes supplement the material and add interest to entries that run approximately half a page to several pages in length. Inventions and discoveries covered fall along a broad spectrum from agriculture to corset to flush toilets to matches to diesel engines to the Internet. The book concludes with an extensive index, which is a crucial finding aid in a book that is arranged by period instead of in typical A to Z format. Highly recommended to public and academic libraries.

Classification: LC T15; Dewey 609.

457. *Encyclopedia of Science, Technology, and Ethics*, by Carl Mitcham, ed.
Publisher: Macmillan Reference USA/Gale Group, New York, NY (2005)
Price: $475.00/set
Review by Adalyn Smith Watts—Librarian, San Joaquin Valley College, Visalia, CA.

Reviewing a set of encyclopedic works about the ethics of science and technology is a daunting task. Of necessity the reviewer must consider the arrangement and the selection of entries, and not become overly distracted by individual articles. Since most entries are by different people, they vary in quality and completeness. There are four volumes in this work. The selection of topics is outstanding. The points of entry are imaginative and are varied. There is a list of articles, a topic outline, appendixes, and an index. There are eight separate introductory essays. The list of contributors does not begin until page 89. There are 114 Roman numeral pages before page 1 starts with Abortion. The entry on Abortion may be the best five-page consideration of the logical ethics of abortion this reader has seen, with the headings: "Abortion Definition and Techniques," "Ethical Issues," "Law and Policy in the United States," and "Law and Policy Outside the United States." The 17 pages of topics average about 42 topics per page, so that roughly 714 articles are included in the 4-volume set. Under the letter "T" are the following entries: Three-Mile Island; Tolkien, J.R.R.; Tools and Machines; Tourism; and Tradeoffs, which may give the reader an indication of the breadth of the work. Most college classes incorporate ethics within the curriculum and teach individual courses in ethics. As a starting point for the researcher, this reference work is nearly essential.

The 2nd edition appeared in 2015, as *Ethics, Science, Technology, and Engineering: A Global Resource*, by J. Britt Holbrook and Carl Mitcham. Classification: LC Q175; Dewey 503.

458. *An Encyclopaedia of the History of Technology*, by Ian McNeil
Publisher: Routledge/Taylor & Francis Group, New York, NY (1996)
Price: $151.95
Review by ARBA Staff Reviewer

Designed with both the student and layman in mind, this encyclopedia covers the whole history of technology from antiquity to the present in 22 chapters written by area experts. The book begins with a brief discussion on the place of technology in history and the differences between science and technology. There is also commentary on the archaeological ages and the seven technological ages of man. The main content appears in five parts: Materials, Power and Engineering, Transport, Communication and Calculation, and Technology and Society. Chapters within these sections cover nonferrous metals, ferrous metals, and the chemicals and allied industries; water, wind, and animal power, steam and internal combustion engines, electricity, and engineering; roads, bridges, and vehicles, inland waterways, ports and shipping, rail, aeronautics, and spaceflight; the telegraph, radio and radar, and information storage; agricultural technologies, textiles and clothing, building and architecture, the domestic interior, public utilities, weapons and armor; and much more. These main chapters follow a chronological order, and subsections are clearly indicated. Covering nearly 1,000 pages of text, the chapters are substantial. The written material is supported by 150 tables, illustrations, and drawings and by the inclusion of further reading suggestions. There is also a list of contributors as well as a name index and a topic index. This well-written, well-organized, and well-researched encyclopedia is unparalleled in terms of its depth and breadth of coverage of the history of technology. Highly recommended for public, school, and academic libraries.

Also worth noting are *The Encyclopaedia of the History of Science, Technology, and Medicine in Non-Western Cultures* (Springer, 2008) and *Medieval Science, Technology, and Medicine: An Encyclopedia* (Routledge, 2005). Classification: LC T15; Dewey 609.

459. *McGraw-Hill Dictionary of Engineering*, by Sybil P. Parker, ed.

Publisher: McGraw-Hill, New York, NY (1997)

Price: $17.95

Review by Diane J. Turner—Science/Engineering Liaison, Auraria Library, University of Colorado, Denver.

This paperback dictionary provides the user with 16,700 terms covering the realm of engineering. Based on the 5th edition of the *McGraw-Hill Dictionary of Scientific and Technical Terms* (entry 388), this resource has terms that are fundamental to understanding engineering. Terms are listed alphabetically on a letter-by-letter basis, and each definition provides the field of engineering it is used in. The definitions are brief and understandable even to the layperson. Cross-referencing and a synopsis of each field in engineering are provided. The appendix gives the user conversion factors for the U.S. Customary System, the metric system, and the International System, as well as special mathematical constants and variables, indefinite integrals, and trigonometric identities used in engineering. For more in-depth definitions, researchers and others may wish to use specific reference works in the fields of civil engineering, electrical engineering, and the like. The *McGraw-Hill Dictionary of Engineering* is reasonably priced and recommended for engineering students and public and academic libraries.

---

The 2nd edition appeared in 2002. Classification: LC TA9; Dewey 620.

---

460. *FOLDOC: Free On-Line Dictionary of Computing*, by Denis Howe [digital]
Publisher: London Imperial College, Department of Computing, London, UK
Price: Free online. Date reviewed: 2017.
URL: http://foldoc.org/
Review by Staff, Libraries Unlimited.

FOLDOC is a simple, easy-to-use, and downloadable resource for all computing vocabulary. Offering no bells or whistles, the site allows users to conduct a basic search for a wide range of computer terminology via the bar. Users can also select the Contents tab to access the full-text search function, or begin the browsing process. The site has several browsing capabilities. Users can browse entries by subject area (128 of them), browse by an alphabetical listing of entries, or browse a combined listing of both. FOLDOC currently contains over 15,000 terms, including acronyms and jargon (including numbers and symbols) for companies, individuals, software, languages, locations, applications, programming, networking, and much more. The definitions are as straightforward as the rest of the site and generally note the category/subject area of the term and provide a brief statement which may include cross-referencing links if other FOLDOC terms are included in the definition. The entry may also include a sample of term usage, a listing of nearby terms, and a notation of the date the definition was last updated. Users can additionally submit a comment for each term to suggest an edit, etc. Some of the most referenced subject categories within the site include "programming," "storage," "operating system," "networking," "language," and "hardware." Users will recognize common terms like ".com," "algorithm," "meme," "web browser," "screensaver," "Playstation," etc., alongside highly technical and perhaps less-established words and phrases such as "SAMeDL," "plesiochronus" and "wave a dead chicken." In fact, it may be worth pointing out that some definitions may themselves be highly technical, causing users to extend their research throughout the dictionary or other sources. Fortunately, FOLDOC can link to other search sites if a term is not found in its database or the definition is not sufficient to users. There is definitely a sense of inside humor running throughout the site (see "wave a dead chicken" above). Quite a few of the terms may be pejorative ("kangaroo code," "Stupids," etc.). The Random tab displays a different entry definition every time it is clicked for an element of fun. Commercial advertisements run on the page but do not interfere with the browsing experience of this valuable research tool that would appeal to everyone whether adept with computer technology or not. Recommended to public, school, and academic libraries.

---

Classification: LC QA76; Dewey 004.

---

461. *Dictionary of Media and Communications*, by Marcel Danesi

Publisher: M. E. Sharpe, Armonk, NY (2009)

Price: $89.95

Review by Stephanie Vie, University of Central Florida, Winter Park.

Marcel Danesi's dictionary seems ideal for undergraduate students enrolled in courses relating to media and communications theory and practice. The dictionary is a handy pocket reference that spans common terms, concepts, and practitioners of media and communications theory; for example, there are definitions for Facebook, MySpace, Marshall McLuhan, Adbusters, and information society, among many others. A short introduction prefaces the reference entries themselves. At the end there is an abbreviated timeline of major events in mass media theory (split up by books and magazines; newspapers; advertising; radio and sound recording; film and video; television; and the Internet, World Wide Web, and data transmission). Also included are a bibliography and list of suggested Web resources. Each definition is brief and to the point; it is here where the breadth of the dictionary takes precedence over depth, thus the recommendation for undergraduates. As a reference work for beginning students, this will help them understand basic concepts and figures. For graduate students and beyond, this material would likely be too brief and they would need to consult additional works to gain a fuller picture. This work is best suited as an adjunct to an undergraduate course in media theory.

---

Classification: LC P87; Dewey 302.

---

462. *The Audio Dictionary*, by Glenn D. White and Gary J. Louie

Publisher: University of Washington Press, Seattle, WA (2004)

Price: $29.95

Review by Robert L. Wick—Professor Emeritus, Auraria Library, University of Colorado, Denver.

*The Audio Dictionary* is becoming a standard source for libraries and for individuals in the area of audio technology. In the introduction to the 3rd edition the authors point out that this book "is aimed at dispelling some misinformation and is intended to supplement textbooks for courses . . . and also to serve as a source of information for the general reader who has an interest in reproduced music and/or musical acoustics" (p. xi). The new edition has more than four hundred new entries. And all of the previous entries have been evaluated for accuracy. Entries cover both technical and more common terms and concepts. Definitions are brief but clear, and cross-references are provided when appropriate. In most cases definitions requiring mathematical information are kept as simple as possible. In addition to the dictionary there are a number of useful appendixes, including "The Art and Science of Good Acoustics," "Some Frequently Used Symbols and Units," "Musical Scales and the Tuning of Musical Instruments," "Some Notes on the History of High Fidelity," and even one entitled "How to Subdue a Hi-Fi Salesperson." *The Audio Dictionary* is highly recommended for all public and academic library collections, and for individual purchase for musicians who are involved in recording and acoustical engineers.

Classification: LC TK7881; Dewey 621.

463. *The Music Tech Dictionary: A Glossary of Audio-Related Terms and Technologies,*
     by Mitch Gallagher
Publisher: Gale/Cengage Learning, Farmington Hills, MI (2009)
Price: $24.99
Review by Staff, Libraries Unlimited.

This extensive dictionary is an indispensable guide for anyone who makes music, either live or in the studio. In this straightforward book, people will find the meanings of obscure terms like A-weighting, ogg vorbis, and humbucking coil. Acronyms like RTZ (return to zero) and abbreviations like "U" (which stands for modular unit) are spelled out. Helpfully, figures are used throughout, as are *see* references. The alphabetical sections are followed by terms that start with 0–9, in numeric order. Here are found definitions for such things as 37-key or 8 bit. This is not a book for everyone, but there is no equivalent resource. This extremely reasonably priced title is highly recommended for public and academic libraries.

Classification: LC ML102; Dewey 786.

464. *Macmillan Encyclopedia of Energy*, by John Zumerchik, ed.

Publisher: Macmillan Reference USA/Gale Group, New York, NY (2001)

Price: $350.00/set

Review by Robert B. McKee—Professor, Mechanical Engineering, University of
    Nevada, Reno.

The earliest reference of the use of a windmill, we are told, was made by Anti-
pater of Thessalonica sixty-five years before the birth of Christ. Men had used
the wind to propel boats, of course, long before that. In addition to a timeline
and bibliography, this one-thousand-page, three-volume encyclopedia contains
many good plain-language expositions of the history and technology of our use
of energy, plus sixty biographies. The section on Hybrid vehicles provides a good
understanding of the operation of the two such automobiles now on the market.
The section on "Aircraft" is a pretty good short course on aerodynamics. The editor of the encyclopedia himself produced an interesting section on batteries.
A compilation of the work of one hundred different authors will not be uniform;
some of these articles are much better than others. On the whole, however, this
is a very readable and valuable reference.

> Obviously much has happened since 2001, but historical information—
> on steam engines or Thomas Edison—remains useful. The *Encyclopedia of
> Energy* by Morris Pierce (Salem Press, 2013) is newer but less widely
> owned. Classification: LC TJ163; Dewey 621.

465. *Dictionary of Energy*, by Cutler J. Cleveland and Christopher G. Morris

Publisher: Elsevier Science, San Diego, CA (2015)

Price: $111.00

Review by Staff, Libraries Unlimited.

This updated, second edition builds on the format and purpose of the first
(Elsevier, 2005). The editors designed the first edition as an interdisciplinary,
broad dictionary that covered all the disciplines and the multifaceted aspects of
the concept of energy for use by students, researchers, and the general public.
While acknowledging that subject specialists may be disappointed not to find
definitions of discipline-specific terms, the editors explained that other resources
filled this need; more important for the purposes of this dictionary was the need
to provide a compilation of commonly agreed-on terms and definitions to
enhance understanding and communication, particularly in cases in which the
same term can mean different things (e.g., elasticity and efficiency mean

different things to economists and engineers). The second edition increases the number of headwords and entries from 8,000/10,000 to 10,000/13,000. Each subject area has new entries, but the section on oil and gas accounts for the largest percentage of new entries, 175 more, largely due to newer extraction techniques, new fields, modern exploration technology, and industry terms. The effect of energy on the natural world, environmental and alternative energy sources and technology, and other developments account for a number of new entries as well. The second edition has expanded in other ways: there are more biographies, more quotations on energy (a third of which predate 1900), and more color images. Prior to the prefaces, users will find a list of the subject areas covered in the dictionary and dozens of special essays on important energy terms. The subject areas are worth listing as they convey the scope of the dictionary: biographies, biological energetics, biomass, chemistry, climate change, coal, communication, consumption and efficiency, conversion, earth science, ecology, economics and business, electricity, environment, geothermal, global issues, health and safety, history, HVAC, hydrogen, hydropower, lighting, materials, measurements, mining, nuclear, oil and gas, organizations, photovoltaic, physics, policy, refrigeration, renewable/alternative fuels, social issues, solar, storage, sustainable development, thermodynamics, transportation, and wind. A subject area appears in italics after each headword in the dictionary. The special essays section serves the needs of readers who are most likely familiar with terms like cap and trade, solar, carbon footprint, climate change, and smog, but may want to read a succinct and authoritative explanation of the origins of the word or term. There are also essays on terms that are likely less familiar (Otto cycle, Ghawar, Hubbert curve, etc.). An introduction explains the layout of the dictionary, and there is a list of abbreviations commonly used in energy. This is a comprehensive, authoritative, and easy-to-use dictionary that is highly recommended for public and academic libraries.

Cleveland also edited the six-volume *Encyclopedia of Energy* (Elsevier, 2004). Classification: LC TJ163; Dewey 333.

# CHAPTER SIX

# Health Sciences

Medical and health science reference sources present special challenges. Access to the most current information is desirable, while older editions of standard books may remain on the shelf. Access to free online tools helps address this problem because some recent research and clinical findings are available through open access publication. The professional literature of medicine is vast, sophisticated, and expensive to purchase, including as it does of books, journals, online databases, and specialized "point of care" tools intended for physicians. There is some overlap between medical reference books and the textbooks used by medical students in professional programs: many of those books appear in frequent new editions. Of course, librarians do not offer medical advice, but libraries can offer core resources for readers. There also are numerous publications aimed at consumers, including some that are sponsored by organizations coming out of the medical professions and the health-care industry.

## Dictionaries

466. *Dorland's Illustrated Medical Dictionary*, by W. A. Newman Dorland
Publisher: Elsevier Science, San Diego, CA (2011)
Price: $50.95
Review by Staff, Libraries Unlimited.

Saunders (now an imprint of Elsevier) first published this venerable reference work in 1900. Over a century later, its value is undiminished, despite freely available information on the Web. Front matter includes an index to tables, an index to plates, and an index to the appendixes as well as a usage guide and notes on medical etymology. In addition to the approximately 124,000 entries, there are 1,525 illustrations (most in full color); of these, about 500 are new to this edition. The usage guide, comprised of information about the content of entries, pronunciation, related entries, cross-references, abbreviations, and more, is particularly helpful and well worth reading prior to delving into the body of the work. For example, the guide explains the dictionary's policy of using subentries. Users will find, for instance, "alveolar c." and "aneurismal c." under the main entry for "cyst" rather than in the "A" section. The appendixes include the following: "Frequently Used Stems," "Selected Abbreviations Used in Medicine," "Symbols," "Phobias," "Table of Elements," "Celsius and Fahrenheit Temperature Equivalents," "Units of Measurement," and "Reference Intervals for the Interpretation of Laboratory Tests." It is important to note that purchasers of the print edition receive a CD-ROM which has audio phonetics for 35,000 medical terms, a tabular listing of selected terms in anatomy, and a listing of surgical equipment not included in the main dictionary. This broad-based, reliable, and expertly curated dictionary is highly recommended to students and medical professionals and should be in public and academic libraries.

> The 32nd edition was published in 2011; the 33rd edition is announced for 2018. Classification: LC R121; Dewey 610.

467. *Mosby's Dictionary of Medicine, Nursing & Health Professions*, by Mosby Inc.
Publisher: Elsevier Science, San Diego, CA (2017)
Price: $44.95
Review by Staff, Libraries Unlimited.

Following a foreword, list of consultants, and pronunciation key are a series of color atlases of human anatomy: skeletal system, muscular system, circulatory system, endocrine system, lymphatic system, nervous system, respiratory system, digestive system, reproductive system, urinary system, and special senses. The guide to the dictionary provides direction on alphabetization, cross-referencing policies, the elements of an entry, word etymology, and more. Inside users will find more than 56,000 definitions and nearly 2,500 full-color photographs and illustrations that facilitate comprehension of a disease or syndrome. Three hundred of these color illustrations are new to this edition, while new developments in health care have led to 11,000 new terms (some of these are revised from older editions). Unlike *Dorland's Illustrated Medical Dictionary* (entry 466), *Mosby's* does not make use of subentries. Users will also benefit from numerous appendixes such as "Nursing Interventions Classification (NIC) Definitions, 1924"; "Nursing Outcomes Classification (NOC) Definitions, 1934"; "Language Translation Guide, 1949"; "Normal Reference Values, 1961"; "Nutrition, 1966"; "Range of Motion, 1974"; "Infection Control CDC Isolation

Guidelines, 1992"; and "Diagnosis-Related Groups, 1994." This is highly recommended to public and academic libraries as well as medical professionals.

---

Earlier editions had a different title: *Mosby's Medical, Nursing, and Allied Health Dictionary.* 2017 is the 10th edition. Classification: LC R121; Dewey 610.

---

468. *The American Heritage Stedman's Medical Dictionary*

Publisher: Houghton Mifflin Harcourt, New York, NY (2004)

Price: $27.00

Review by Barbara M. Bibel—Reference Librarian, Science/Business/Sociology Department, Main Library, Oakland Public Library, Oakland, CA.

Medical terminology, with its Greek and Latin roots, is a foreign language to most lay readers. A medical dictionary will help them understand the jargon, but many of these are created for professionals. They may be as inaccessible as the literature that they are supposed to interpret. First published in 1997, *The American Heritage Stedman's Medical Dictionary* is designed for general readers and professionals in the allied medical fields, law, and the insurance industry. The editors have used the style of *The American Heritage Dictionary of the English Language* (4th ed.; entry 5). Words have brief definitions that are technically accurate with minimal jargon. They have also avoided the traditional subentry format in most medical dictionaries, which puts a long list of terms under a main entry. For example, Tourette's syndrome would be found under syndrome rather than under Tourette's as it is here. There is an index of these main entries at the beginning of the dictionary. The entries are listed alphabetically, with cross-references for variants, symbols, and synonyms. Some entries have black-and-white line drawings. A user looking up the word leukocyte will find a *see* reference to white blood cell. Those unfamiliar with medical terminology will need further clarification after reading the definition: "Any of the colorless or white cells in the blood that have a nucleus and cytoplasm and help protect the body from infection through specialized neutrophils, lymphocytes, and monocytes." Individual entries for each of these cells do not offer much assistance. A monocyte is "a large, circulating phagocytic white blood cell." The dictionary does include definitions of new terms, such as SARS, virtual colonoscopy, and gamma knife, which may turn up in news reports. The dictionary also has over 300 biographical entries for those who have contributed to medical science. Louis Pasteur, Rene Laennec, Ivan Pavlov, and Marie Curie are examples. These are only one or two sentences long. There are anatomical charts, a periodic table, measurement and metric conversion tables, a chart of first aid for burns, and dietary guidelines and Recommended Daily Allowances (RDAs) at the end of the book. The RDA information is from 1989, rather than the revised 2001 allowances. While this dictionary would be sufficient for a small office or home collection, libraries serving students and the public will find *Mosby's Dictionary of Medicine, Nursing & Health Professions* (entry 467) more useful. It has more entries; clearer, more detailed definitions; and 2,200 color illustrations.

Classification: LC R121; Dewey 610.

469. *The Oxford Illustrated Companion to Medicine*, by Stephen Lock, John M. Last, and George Dunea, eds.
Publisher: Oxford University Press, New York, NY (2001)
Price: $60.00
Review by Staff, Libraries Unlimited.

This guide will serve as an easy-to-use reference for those seeking basic information on the topics of the history of medicine, various diseases, medical practices in other countries, and medical and nursing specialties, just to name a few. Designed primarily for the educated lay reader, this work may also be a welcome addition in consumer health libraries and even academic medical libraries because of its interesting text and illustrative photographs. The more than 500 entries are arranged alphabetically and run from a half page to several pages in length. The editors of this volume have changed the format as compared to previous editions by adding sidebars that highlight key discoveries, diseases, and technologies. At times this interferes with the alphabetic organization; to remedy this there is extensive cross-referencing throughout the volume. For example, the entry on Salerno Medical School is placed within the entry on Italy, but there is a cross-reference to this when one looks under Salerno Medical School. There are four indexes located at the end of the volume to aid those using this tool for research: a topic index, a list of conditions and diseases, a people index, and a general index. This encyclopedic work differs from many others available because of its focus on the history of medicine and the practice of medicine throughout the world. Even the photographs shown here are most often of the historical practice of medicine instead of current photographs. For its easy-to-comprehend style, this work is recommended for public and consumer health libraries, but it should be supplemented with other medical encyclopedias.

Earlier editions appeared as the *Oxford Medical Companion*. Classification: LC R121; Dewey 610.

470. *Taber's Cyclopedic Medical Dictionary*, by Donald Venes and others, eds.
Publisher: F. A. Davis, Philadelphia, PA (2001)
Price: $35.95
Review by Polin P. Lei, Silver Springs, MD.

The 18th edition of this classic nursing dictionary is famous for its nursing appendix and the easy-to-read definitions and graphics. For the revised 19th edition, the addition of complementary and alternative medicine terms and appendixes reflects today's health care practices and usages of information. Not only health care clinicians and students are using this dictionary for their needs, but patients are also taking information from this dictionary as a valuable source of health information. There are more than 56,000 terms in this dictionary, with more than 2,200 new terms included. The extra value of Taber's is its appendixes. The expanded nursing appendix (in red thumb tab) lists 300 disease disorders, nursing interventions classification, nursing outcomes classification, nursing organizations in the United States and Canada, home health care classification, concept models and theories of nursing, and the Omaha System. The original appendixes includes sections on nutrition; integrative therapies; normal reference laboratory values; prefixes, suffixes, and combining forms; Latin and Greek nomenclature; medical abbreviations; symbols; units of measurement; phobias; manual alphabet; interpreter in three languages; medical emergencies; computer glossary; health care resource organizations; professional designations and titles in the health sciences; documentation system definitions; and standard and universal precautions. The body of the work includes 150 new color illustrations that enhance the text of selected definitions. Selected disorder entries include cross-references to an appendix of nursing diagnoses grouped by disorder. Also, caution statements are highlighted in red underscore for readers' considerations. The table of contents lists consultants, Taber's feature finder, features and their use, illustrations, tables, abbreviations used in the text, and vocabulary. The text is completely revised and some of the terms are rewritten from scratch. Taber's, as mentioned above, is a classic health care dictionary, and readability is appropriate for the audience it serves. No library should miss this item on their reference shelves.

> The 23rd edition appeared in 2017. Classification: LC R121; Dewey 610.

## Topical Resources

471. *AHA Guide to the Health Care Field*
Publisher: American Hospital Association, Chicago, IL

Price: $330.00

Review by Steven W. Sowards—Associate Director for Collections, Michigan State University Libraries, East Lansing.

This annual survey and directory covers more than six thousand American hospitals in all fifty U.S. states, the District of Columbia, and American territories such as Puerto Rico, whether or not they belong to the American Hospital Association; and more than four hundred associated health care systems. Included are federal, state, for-profit, and not-for-profit entities; facilities of the VA, through the U.S. Department of Veterans Affairs; and the full range of general, psychiatric, specialized, and rehabilitation hospitals. Through a standard template, information for each hospital includes contact information (address, telephone number, and URL), the names of key administrators, and a summary of operational information (such as FTE staff count, operating costs including payroll, inpatient bed count, the annual number of inpatient admissions, the annual number of outpatient visits, and the number of births per year). Numerical codes indicate accreditation for specific programs such as residencies. A similar set of numerical Facility Codes tracks available specializations and services such as MRI units, HIV-AIDS services, fertility clinics, and certified trauma centers. Paragraphs in an explanatory key define services. Hospital entries are presented state by state, and then by city. There are indexes for hospital names, for the names of key health care professionals such as CEOs or Chief Medical Officers, and for associate AHA members including insurers and pharmaceutical companies. Users will benefit from a one-page detachable AHA Guide Code Chart and a sample hospital entry. There is a key to abbreviations. Entries for systems and alliance list subsidiary hospitals and facilities.

---

The 2018 edition appeared in late 2017. Classification: LC RA977; Dewey 362.

---

472. *Encyclopedia of Sports Medicine*, by Lyle J. Micheli, ed.

Publisher: SAGE, Thousand Oaks, CA (2011)

Price: $995.00/set

Review by Amy B. Parsons—Metadata Librarian/Associate Professor, Courtright Memorial Library, Otterbein College, Westerville, OH.

As baby boomers retire and stay active, and younger folks and children incorporate fitness and sports into their lifestyles, sports medicine is a field that will continue to grow. This is a four-volume encyclopedia that not only focuses on medical issues; it also covers topics in rehabilitation and physical therapy, conditioning and kinesiology, nutrition, psychology, and more. Examining the first volume there is a reader's guide that clusters certain subjects together on related topics. There are *see also* references to cross-reference related terms. The further readings at the end of the entries are not exhaustive bibliographies; they were selected by the author from hundreds of readings and websites and are considered the optimum selections for more information. Subjects included in this encyclopedia include medical topics, such as arthroscopy, which includes a description of the anatomy of a joint, indications for arthroscopic surgery, benefits, limitations, and a description of what will happen after surgery. Another subject, the benefits of exercise and sports, has a more popular science flow and includes some scientific explanations of how exercise benefits the heart and lungs and also new trends in exercise including dance and video games. At the end of the fourth volume there is a glossary of terms. Appendix A includes written instructions and black-and-white photographs of taping and bracing techniques. There is an appendix listing sports medicine organizations and an index. This encyclopedia is recommended for people interested in learning more about the topics in the sports medicine fields. It would also be useful for sports medicine students and professionals already working in the various fields of sports medicine.

---

Classification: LC RC1206; Dewey 617.

---

473. *The Encyclopedia of Genetic Disorders and Birth Defects*, by James Wynbrandt and Mark D. Ludman

Publisher: Facts on File, New York, NY (2008)

Price: $67.50

Review by Caroline L. Gilson—Coordinator, Prevo Science Library, DePauw University, Greencastle, IN.

*The Encyclopedia of Genetic Disorders and Birth Defects* is one of the newest publications in the Facts on File Library (subject-specific titles in this series address modern health issues and social issues). The 3rd edition of this resource offers general information on congenital disorders and birth defects. There are over 1,000 entries, including over 135 new entries and over 60 revised entries. Entries are presented in A to Z order and vary in length, from several paragraphs to one to two pages. The preface states that entries were selected based on the incidence of the disorder, and clinical and historical importance. Information provided includes a description of the condition or disorder, prognosis, prevalence, mode of inheritance, and the ability of carrier screening and prenatal diagnosis. Any terms used within an entry that have their own separate entry are designated with small capital letters. There are no illustrations or photographs. Appendixes include data such as Congenital Defects Surveillance Data, Infant Mortality Statistics, Birth Defects Data (from selected U.S. States and U.S.

Department of Defense), State Agencies and Birth Defect Surveillance Programs, organizations and groups that offer information and support, and a bibliography of books and articles. A subject index is also included. The strength of this source is that it is a good starting point for learning the basics about a known genetic disorder or condition. Users should consult the index to locate entries covering dual topics. As with other medical reference books, this source is not meant to be a substitute for professional medical care. *The Encyclopedia of Genetic Disorders and Birth Defects* offers a good basic introduction and overview to the topics addressed. This work is most appropriate for academic libraries and public libraries that field medical questions.

---

Classification: LC RB155; Dewey 616.

---

## Handbooks

### Consumer Information

474. *American Medical Association Family Medical Guide*
Publisher: Wiley-Blackwell, Hoboken, NJ (2004)
Price: $45.00
Review by Susan E. Thomas—Head of Collection Development/Associate Librarian, Indiana University, South Bend.

The *American Medical Association Family Medical Guide* is intended as a medical reference source but is such a fascinating, well-written resource that it could easily be read cover to cover. The 4th edition has been thoroughly revised and updated with greater coverage of health issues and better organization. The book is divided into six main sections: "What You Should Know: Information to Keep You Healthy"; "Your Healthy Body"; "First Aid and Home Caregiving"; "What Are Your Symptoms"; "Health Issues throughout Life"; and "Diseases, Disorders, and Other Problems." Especially useful is the first section on maintaining health. Topics in this glossy-paged, well-illustrated section include healthy eating, exercise, weight, stress, aging well, cancer, genetics, the dangers of smoking, heart disease, and terrorism. Other useful sections include the "Visual Aids to Diagnosis" (with photographs illustrating visual signs of illness), the section on "Common Examinations and Tests" (which provides relevant descriptions of commonly ordered screening and diagnostic tests), and the "Self-Diagnosis Symptoms Charts" (which may be extremely helpful when describing health concerns to a doctor). The book is easy to use either by a quick scan of the table of contents or a check of the index. The information provided is succinct but informative with relevant illustrations scattered throughout the text. As appropriate, the book indicates that concerns about medical conditions and symptoms should be discussed with a doctor. The resource is written for an average adult reader, with a glossary of terms as well as a drug glossary of frequently prescribed drugs included. While most of the medical conditions presented would be heard in discussions with a health professional or found in mainstream literature sources, a pronunciation guide would have been helpful.

Classification: LC RC81; Dewey 613.

475. *Mayo Clinic Family Health Book*, by Scott C. Litin, MD

Publisher: Time Inc., Des Moines, IA (2009)

Price: $49.95

Review by Steven W. Sowards—Associate Director for Collections, Michigan State University Libraries, East Lansing.

Prepared by physicians with consumers in mind, the preface to this lengthy, revised, and expanded volume asserts that "knowledge is essential in maintaining good health" and that this work can help you "communicate more effectively with your doctor . . . to manage your health." Health care advice includes lifestyle adjustments to promote good health. The content is presented in six sections: Living Well, with information about diet, weight, stress, exercise, and safety; Common Conditions and Concerns through Life's Stages, with chapters on infants, preteens, teens, pregnant women, adult health, and dying; Making Sense of Your Symptoms, briefly noting signs to look for, with references to detailed content elsewhere in the book; First Aid and Emergency Care, including instructions and diagrams for dealing quickly with choking, bleeding, shock, poisoning, stings, injuries from heat and cold, and mental health situations; a very long section on Diseases and Disorders, with summary information about signs and symptoms, diagnosis and discussion, and treatment for numerous conditions; and Tests and Treatments, addressing diagnostic tools, medications, surgery, pain, and alternative medicine. Numerous illustrations and tables assist in identifying conditions, including a forty-page color section of anatomical illustrations and photographs. Some of the health care issues discussed are the many kinds of vaccinations, end-of-life planning, suicide prevention, bullying, living with HIV-AIDS, management of medications including common side effects, and the potential contributions of alternative or complementary medicine such as herbs, meditation, and acupuncture. There is a twenty-page glossary, and a directory of resources such as medical boards, associations and foundations, with contact information and URLs. The index is more than fifty pages long, with cross-references and a mix of vernacular and technical terms (such as entries for both "heel pain" and "plantar fasciitis"). Medical advances can supersede older information: for updates, "Patient Care and Health Information" from the Mayo Clinic website at https://www.mayoclinic.org/patient-care-and-health-information is freely available.

> The same author has written the *Mayo Clinic A to Z Health Guide* (2015), with entries organized in alphabetical order. For more on health problems that can be treated at home, *see* the *Mayo Clinic Book of Home Remedies* (entry 477). Classification: LC RC81; Dewey 613.

476. *American Medical Association Complete Medical Encyclopedia*, by Jerrold B. Leikin and Martin S. Lipsky, eds.

Publisher: Random House, New York, NY (2003)

Price: $45.00

Review by Elaine Lasda Bergman—Bibliographer for Reference and Gerontology, Dewey Graduate Library, University at Albany, Albany, NY.

This single-volume encyclopedia provides information on many medical topics, including diseases, medical terminology, types of drugs, functions of the body, and medical procedures. The entries are usually several paragraphs long and explain basic information on the topic. There are many clear diagrams and illustrations, ranging from how to burp a baby to the structure of the hand. The bulk of the book is the alphabetic encyclopedia, but the book also includes symptom charts that will help the user get an idea of a diagnosis for such symptoms as breast pain, vision loss, and depression. In addition, there is an atlas of the body with a page devoted to each of the major systems of the body that includes an explanation and diagram. There is also an essay on twenty-first-century medicine. The back of the book includes first aid instructions, a sample legal form, and an important section on the new HIPAA privacy laws that affects patients. This volume is a good first resource for finding information on a wide variety of medical and health topics. It is recommended for consumer health sections of any type of library.

> Classification: LC RC81; Dewey 610.

477. *Mayo Clinic Book of Home Remedies: What to Do for the Most Common Health Problems*, by Philip T. Hagen and Martha Millman

Publisher: Oxmoor House, Birmingham, AL (2010)

Price: $25.95
Review by Staff, Libraries Unlimited.

This authoritative reference from the Mayo Clinic provides guidance on everything from acne to the common cold to wrinkles. While much of this information can be found in other places, this is a convenient, trustworthy, and easy-to-use reference that covers many topics in one handy location. The book is arranged in an A to Z format. Each entry describes the condition and associated problems. Home remedy suggestions follow. In a separate textbox within each entry, users will find medical help information. The book also contains a list of those supplies every person should have to cope with accidents or common illnesses, as well as items that are necessary in an emergency like medical histories and medical consent forms for each family member. The coverage is broad. Topics covered include blisters, sunburn, back pain, canker sores, bites and stings, allergies, chronic pain, and exercise as a remedy for a variety of different conditions. In addition to this, there are more than 20 pages of guidance on what to do in emergencies ranging from allergic reactions to shock. This is followed by an extensive index with *see* and *see also* references. As a ready reference guide to basic home remedies and more, this book is highly recommended to public and academic libraries.

Republished in 2013 as the *Mayo Clinic Book of Alternative Medicine & Home Remedies*, with the addition of the full text of the *Mayo Clinic Book of Alternative Medicine* (2007). For more extensive discussion of diseases and disorders, see the *Mayo Clinic Family Health Book* (entry 475). The Mayo Clinic posts "Patient Care and Health Information" on a free website at https://www.mayoclinic.org/patient-care-and-health-information. Classification: LC RC81; Dewey 615.

## Online Resources

478. *Merck Manual Consumer Version*, by Merck Sharp & Dohme [digital]
Publisher: Merck & Co., Inc., Kenilworth, NJ
Price: Free online. Date reviewed: 2017.
URL: http://www.merckmanuals.com/home
Review by Staff, Libraries Unlimited.

The comprehensive *Merck Manual* brings a wealth of information regarding a large range of medical topics to online consumers. This version differs from the

Professional version (http://www.merckmanuals.com/professional; entry 483) in that it specifically targets patients, nonprofessional caregivers, and others with a general interest in the information. The site employs simplified, nonspecialized language to examine a wide range of topics from a consumer-friendly perspective. The website, available in several languages, is easy to navigate and explore. Users can conduct a basic search from the bar, scroll through featured topics within the page, or browse several categories through the menu. Medical Topics lists over two dozen general categories such as Blood Disorders, Children's Health Issues, Fundamentals, Infections, and Immune Disorders. Selecting a category under this tab leads to a summary "textbook" presentation with related topics presented in a section/chapter format. For example, the category Blood Disorders is separated into sixteen sections offering both basic educational and specific disorder material, such as Biology of Blood, Blood Clotting Process, Blood Transfusion, Leukemias, and Anemia. These sections (e.g., Anemia) are then further divided into individual topical chapters of varying length. Chapters (e.g., Overview, Anemia of Chronic Disease, Iron-Deficiency Anemia, etc.) are well organized and make excellent use of headers, bullet points, links to affiliated information, illustrations, and more. The tone, language, and detail of the material is clearly geared toward the average consumer. The left sidebar will simultaneously scroll through chapter headers as users read through it for easy reference. The right sidebar notes the chapter subject within the context of the main section. Affiliated quizzes, videos, news, and other material may also be included within the article page. The Symptoms tab allows users to browse a list of roughly one hundred medical symptoms. Symptoms can be general (e.g., pain) or specific (e.g., joint pain, single joint) and are organized into categories such as Chest & Respiratory, Children's Symptoms, Abdomen & Digestive, and Eye. Selecting a specific symptom will provide information organized similarly to that under the Medical Topics tab, with ample and effective use of headers, links to affiliated information, and other tools. Common topics addressed with symptoms include causes, treatment, warning signs, and when to see a doctor. The Emergencies tab allows for quick access to twenty topics which reflect incidents which may necessitate immediate medical response, such as drowning, choking, burns, cardiac arrest, wounds, and more. The information here is similarly organized to material in other areas of the website and also found underneath the broader Medical Topics tab. The Drug Information tab allows users to conduct a basic search for downloadable and printable information within the categories of drug information, natural products (e.g., ginseng), and drug interactions. Users can also browse an extensive alphabetized list of generic and brand names to access ample material regarding dosage, storage, warnings, and side effects. The Pill Identifier searches medications by imprint, shape, color, or generic drug name. News & Commentary links to a variety of topical articles and current commentary on medical and health information relevant to consumers, such as the "Use of Acetaminophen during Pregnancy" or "Keep Halloween Spooky, but Safe." These articles are also featured throughout the homepage, in addition to a topical Infographic which illustrates a particular health issue (male breast cancer as of this review). The Resources tab links to an extensive collection of self-assessment tools, quizzes, pronunciations, videos, medical terms, first aid information, and much more, all geared toward the consumer. As the site is directed to consumers, it is important to note that the information within it is meant for educational purposes only and would not take the place of individual medical advice. Nonetheless, the quality and range of the material, in conjunction with the site's easy-to-navigate format, makes this an excellent online resource for consumers. Recommended for public and academic libraries.

---

For a digital version of the *Merck Manual of Diagnosis and Therapy* for health care professionals, *see* entry 483. Classification: LC RC81; Dewey 610.

---

479. *MedlinePlus: Trusted Health Information for You* [digital]

Publisher: U.S. National Library of Medicine, National Institutes of Health, Department of Health & Human Services, Bethesda, MD

Price: Free online. Date reviewed: 2013.

URL: https://medlineplus.gov/

Review by Staff, Libraries Unlimited.

*MedlinePlus* offers a wide variety of health information for consumers, including current health news, a medical dictionary, a medical encyclopedia, information about diseases and conditions, drug information, and directories of health professionals and institutions. There are also tutorials and real-time videos of diagnostic and surgical procedures, information in many languages, and easy-to-read articles. It is an excellent starting point for almost all medical questions. This tool is not the same as *MEDLINE* (also a product of the National Library of Medicine), which is very much a professional tool. Medical librarians can go through weeks of training learning all of *MEDLINE*'s functions and what they mean. For general consumer health queries, however, *MedlinePlus* is a much better option and will fill most reference librarians' needs.

---

*MEDLINE*, the bibliographic tool provided by the U.S. National Library of Medicine as part of *PubMed* at https://www.ncbi.nlm.nih.gov/pubmed/, has its own content, layout, and mission: searching the medical literature. Classification: LC RA776; Dewey 613.

480. *Household Products Database: Health and Safety Information on Household Products* [digital]

Publisher: U.S. National Library of Medicine, National Institutes of Health, Department of Health & Human Services, Bethesda, MD

Price: Free online. Date reviewed: 2014.

URL: https://householdproducts.nlm.nih.gov/

Review by Staff, Libraries Unlimited.

This is a great website to discover whether any given household product can be hazardous to your health. This database includes product information for auto products, pet care, pesticides used in landscape/yard work, and more, with coverage of manufacturers, health effects, first aid, handling/disposal, and ingredients. Useful and enlightening information can be found here by browsing either by category (such as Pesticides), product names in an A-Z listing, manufacturers (with contact information such as toll-free numbers if available), ingredients in an A-Z list, or health effects. There is also a Quick Search option for keyword or phrase searching. This site is supported by the National Library of Medicine.

---

*TOXNET* at https://toxnet.nlm.nih.gov/ is a related web resource with more complex information. Classification: LC TS175; Dewey 615.

---

## Women's Health

481. *The New Harvard Guide to Women's Health*, by Karen J. Carlson, Stephanie A. Eisenstat, and Terra Ziporyn

Publisher: Harvard University Press, Cambridge, MA (2004)

Price: $24.95

Review by Elaine Lasda Bergman—Bibliographer for Reference and Gerontology, Dewey Graduate Library, University at Albany, Albany, NY.

This updated volume contains useful information for health care consumers interested in women's health. It includes records on items one would typically think of as women's health issues, such as uterine fibroids and breast reduction, but also contains entries on such diverse and general topics as headaches, occupational hazards, and coffee. The topics covered generally include diseases and conditions, different types of tests and procedures, and items that can affect health. Many of the longer entries have a question-and-answer format, and there are related entries providing cross-references to other topics contained in the book. There are a fair number of diagrams and illustrations for various entries as well. In the middle of the book are sections on nutrition, vitamins and minerals, and systems of the body and a place to record one's personal medical history. The book may already be dated in some places: the entry for "Diet" stated that the government was considering restricting or labeling ephedra, whereas ephedra has now been banned in the United States. Overall, this is a worthwhile addition to library collections that serve the general public.

Classification: LC RA778; Dewey 616.

482. *Our Bodies, Ourselves,* by the Boston Women's Health Book Collective
Publisher: Simon & Schuster, New York, NY (2011)
Price: $28.00
Review by Staff, Libraries Unlimited.

This 2011 title is the ninth edition of this seminal work first published in the 1970s. The content is divided into seven sections: Bodies and Identities; Relationships and Sexuality; Sexual Health and Reproductive Choices; Childbearing; Postreproductive Years; Medical Problems and Navigating the Health Care System; and Major Factors Affecting Women's Sexuality and Reproductive Health. Topics covered in these sections include body image, sexual pleasure, birth control, infertility, menopause, violence against women, and politics and women's health. According to the introduction, this edition omits some information on health issues, emotional issues, and nutrition issues that disproportionately affect women in favor of adding more material on reproductive rights, violence against women, and environmental health. While rights, issues, and contexts have changed since *Our Bodies, Ourselves* first published, this guide remains a leading place to find factual information on women's health and on social justice topics. Highly recommended for public and academic libraries.

Classification: LC RA778; Dewey 613.

### Professional Information

The literature of clinical medicine is extensive and complex. While non-physicians may wish to consult the professional literature, librarians at a general reference desk need to be aware of the ethical and legal limits on providing medical information. Many articles are freely available through open-access publishing and can be identified using *MEDLINE* and *PubMed*, a high-quality, freely available bibliographic resource available at https://www.ncbi.nlm.nih.gov/pubmed/ thanks to the National Center for Biotechnology Information of the U.S. National Library of Medicine.

483. *Merck Manual Professional*, by Merck Sharp & Dohme [digital]

Publisher: Merck & Co., Inc., Kenilworth, NJ

Price: Free online. Date reviewed: 2017.

URL: http://www.merckmanuals.com/professional

Review by Staff, Libraries Unlimited.

This site represents the Professional version of the comprehensive *Merck Manual*—the online resource that defines and discusses a large range of medical topics. This version differs from the Consumer version (http://www.merckman uals.com/home; see entry 478) in that it specifically targets the medical community of doctors, medical students, and other health care professionals via relevant topics, specialized language, and an industry point of view. Regardless of this difference, the website, available in several languages, is easy to navigate and explore. Users can conduct a basic search from the bar, scroll through featured topics within the page, or browse several categories through the menu. Medical Topics lists two dozen broader categories such as Clinical Pharmacology; Hematology and Oncology; Infectious Diseases; and Nutritional Disorders. Selecting a category under this tab leads to a summary "textbook" description with related subtopics presented in a chapter format. For example, the category Critical Care Medicine is separated into six chapters, which are further divided into individual topical articles of varying length. Articles are well organized and may incorporate headers, bullet points, cross-reference links, videos, and illustrations. The tone, language, and detail of the articles are clearly geared toward the medical community. The left sidebar will simultaneously scroll through section headers as users read through the article for easy reference. The right sidebar notes the chapter subject within the context of the main topic. Affiliated quizzes, videos, news, and more may also be included within the article page. The Drug Information tab allows users to browse an extensive alphabetized list by generic or brand name. Selecting a drug brings up ample information organized by topic, such as Pregnancy Risk Factor, Medication-Safety Issues, Administration, Use, Dosing, and Brand Names. The Pill Identifier searches medications by imprint, shape, color, or generic drug name. News & Commentary links to a variety of blog posts, articles, and current event commentary on the latest procedures, environmental factors, medical devices, therapies, and other research. Several of these items are featured on the home page under the Latest News banner. The Resources tab links to an extensive collection of audio recordings, figures, images, podcasts, abbreviations, and much more. Medical students, in particular, would greatly benefit from several features on the page, including the searchable video collection of 125 of the latest Procedures & Exams (e.g., How to Apply a Knee Immobilizer). The Quizzes & Cases tab offers 10 case studies of real-life medical scenarios and over 300 short quizzes ideal for the student. A featured Med Student Stories link to the Merck Manual Student Stories site offers a genuinely appealing look at the novice experience. And the site's social media connections, quick access to Popular Resources, and other features establish it as a bona fide learning hub. Even as the site is directed to professionals, the information within it is meant for educational purposes only. The quality and range of the material, in conjunction with its solid organization, makes this a vital online resource for the medical community. Recommended to public and academic libraries.

---

The print-format *Merck Manual of Diagnosis and Therapy* is still widely held by libraries, but ceased in print format with the edition of 2011. Merck now emphasizes its online publications. Classification: LC RC55; Dewey 615.

---

484. *Diagnostic and Statistical Manual of Mental Disorders, Fifth Edition: DSM-5*, by the DSM-5 Task Force

Publisher: American Psychiatric Association, Arlington, VA (2013)

Price: $110.00

Review by Staff, Libraries Unlimited.

The DSM is the standard reference for information supporting mental health clinical practice, organized through a system of classification. A list of DSM-5 classification codes and a preface open this volume. There are two codes provided for each disorder. The first is the ICD-9-CM code in use until September 2014 and the second is an ICD-10-CM code in use after October 2014. Following this are three sections. The first, DSM-5 Basics, includes the introduction, instructions on how to use the manual, and a cautionary statement about the forensic use of DSM-5 by courts and legal professionals. The second, Diagnostic Criteria and Codes, is the largest portion of the book. It covers such conditions as neuro-developmental disorders, obsessive-compulsive and related disorders, anxiety disorders, feeding and eating disorders, personality disorders, and much more. These are not in alphabetic order. Once a disorder like obsessive-compulsive and related disorders are accessed, users will find specifiers, diagnostic features, associated features supporting diagnosis, prevalence, development and course, risk and diagnostic factors, culture-related diagnostic issues, gender-related diagnostic issues, suicide risk, functional consequences of OCD, differential diagnosis, and comorbidity. The same information is supplied for all the related disorders like hoarding disorder and body dysmorphic disorders. The third section, Emerging Measures and Models, contains "Assessment Measures," "Cultural Formulation," "Alternative DSM-5 Model for Personality Disorders," and "Conditions for Further Study." A series of appendixes come next: "Highlights of Changes from DSM-IV to DSM-5," "Glossary of Technical Terms," "Glossary of Cultural Concepts of Distress," "Alphabetical Listing of DSM-5 Diagnoses and Codes (ICD-9-CM and ICD-10-CM)," "Numerical Listing of DSM-5 Diagnoses and Codes (ICD-9-CM)," "Numerical Listing of DSM-5 Diagnoses and Codes (ICD-10-CM)," and "DSM-5 Advisors and Other Contributors." An index concludes the work; it includes references to tables, which are indicated by boldface page numbers. This is the leading authority in its field and is highly recommended to public and academic libraries.

The first edition of the *DSM* appeared in 1952. Classification: LC RC455; Dewey 616.

## Drug Information

485. *The Merck Index Online—Chemicals, Drugs and Biologicals* [digital]

Publisher: The Royal Society of Chemistry, London, UK; and Merck & Co., Inc., Whitehouse Station, NJ

Price: Price negotiated by site. Date reviewed: 2017.

URL: https://www.rsc.org/merck-index

Review by Staff, Libraries Unlimited.

*The Merck Index Online*, a project devised in conjunction with the United Kingdom's Royal Society of Chemistry, presents a searchable database of over eleven thousand monographs related to chemical, drug, and biological information. The online edition is based on the 15th print edition of the extensive index, but subject to regular updates. The site offers two types of paid subscriptions: individuals can "Pay-Per-View" of selected monographs, or institutions can inquire about other pricing options. The most significant content is available to subscribers; however, some information is free of charge. First-time users may choose the Get Started with The Merck Index Online button in the middle of the home page to access a video tutorial and information on how to register for the site to access the extensive, specialized material. When conducting a search, there are a number of options available. Users can enter a name, Chemical Abstracts Service (CAS) Registry number, Molecular Weight, or Molecular Formula into the Quick Search bar. Users can also connect several parameters or search by chemical structure. A separate Search tab guides users to search via text or properties, and the Structure Search tab allows users to draw a chemical structure as the basis for a Substructure or Similarity Search. Users can alternatively Browse through an alphabetical directory of elements, compounds, and more, from the possibly complex Fagarine, Cacodylic Acid, Palitantin, Karaya Gum, or Nadoxolol to the humble Water. The Named Reaction tab alphabetically organizes over 500 selected reactions such as the Hammick Reaction, the Wacker Oxidation, and the Castro-Stephens Coupling. All site users are able to view a basic profile of the element, compound, reaction, etc. The profile for an element may generally include a monograph identification number, molecular formula, molecular weight, percent composition, or structure illustration. Paid subscribers may view an individual, full monograph at a cost of £5 (roughly $6.64 U.S.) each. For the reactions, all users can view a reaction scheme and brief description of the transformation, while subscribers can access other information such as key contributors and key references. The Reference Tables are also available only by subscription, although all users can view a listing of the supplemental information included here, such as a Glossary, a Chemical Terms Translator, a Company Register, Thermometric Equivalents, a Table of Minerals, the Periodic Chart of Elements, Latin Terms, and International Patent Country Codes. The free content on the site would certainly give potential users— various researchers, professionals, students, educators, and others—a good sense of the complete information, and thus they would be able to make a well-informed decision as to whether to subscribe. The "Pay-Per-View" Option is certainly a flexible method with which to explore more content. All things considered, the nature of the information and the relative ease of online access make *Merck Index Online* a valuable reference.

---

This is an online successor to *Merck Index: An Encyclopedia of Chemicals, Drugs, and Biologicals*: the 15th edition in print appeared in 2013. Classification: LC RS51; Dewey 615.

---

486. *Physicians' Desk Reference (PDR)*

Publisher: Physicians' Desk Reference, Philadelphia, PA (2013)

Price: $110.90

Review by Staff, Libraries Unlimited.

The *Physicians' Desk Reference (PDR)* is standard equipment in physicians' offices, clinics, and hospitals throughout the United States. Every student in any discipline of health care quickly learns the incomparable value of the *PDR*. This three-thousand-page annual drug reference provides essential information on the efficacy, possible adverse effects, clinical pharmacology, recommended use, and dosages of literally thousands of commonly used drugs. The first three sections of the volume are divided into color-coded indexes: manufactures index, brand and generic name index, and product category index. The remaining three sections include a product identification guide, diagnostic product information, keys to controlled substances categories, keys to FDA used-in-pregnancy ratings, and a national directory of poison control centers. The U.S. Food and Drug Administration telephone numbers and sample "Adverse Event Report" forms are appended at the end of the book. Each of the indexes provides valuable information. The index of manufacturers furnishes contact information and a list of products for individual pharmaceutical companies. The brand and generic name index is a particularly helpful cross-reference, allowing the location of an individual drug by either its brand or generic name. The "Product Identification Guide," organized alphabetically by manufacturers, supplies a full-color, actual-size photograph of tablets and capsules, while inhalers and other dosage formats are shown smaller. This pictorial guide is an invaluable asset to those who may need to identify an unlabeled medication. The heart of the *PDR* is the "Product Information" section. Organized alphabetically by manufacturers, there is in-depth information on the clinical pharmacology; indications for use; contraindications; warnings and precautions; adverse reactions; the signs, symptoms, and treatment for overdosages; dosage and administration; and how the drug is supplied. The only caveat is, all of the information in the *PDR* is supplied by the pharmaceutical manufacturer and may therefore have a bias. This fact notwithstanding, this is a classic and very useful book, recommended for all academic and public libraries.

The online PDR.net site recasts the acronym as "Prescribers' Digital Reference." The publisher states that the 71st edition of 2017 will be the last print-format edition. A consumer-oriented version—*PDR+ for Patients*—is online at http://www.pdr.net/browse-by-consumer-monograph-name/. Classification: LC RS75; Dewey 615.

487. *PDR for Nonprescription Drugs, Dietary Supplements, and Herbs: The Definitive Guide to OTC Medications*

Publisher: Thomson Healthcare, Montvale, NJ (2012)

Price: $59.95

Review by Caroline L. Gilson—Coordinator, Prevo Science Library, DePauw University, Greencastle, IN.

The 33rd edition of *PDR for Nonprescription Drugs, Dietary Supplements, and Herbs* provides entries and information on hundreds of over-the-counter medications, supplements, and herbal remedies. Entries are presented according to therapeutic categories, and both by scientific name and common name. The guide provides complete descriptions of the most common OTC drugs, with additional information on ingredients, indications, interactions with other drugs, and recommended dosages for symptomatic relief. Also included are a listing of devices, diagnostics, and nondrug products and two full sections on dietary supplements and herbs (fully cross-referenced and alphabetically organized for ease of use). Indexing herbs by both botanical name and common name is appreciated for the academic as well as general public audiences. Language within can get technical, so a cautionary note to public libraries considering this source: have a chemistry or medical dictionary handy. *PDR for Nonprescription Drugs, Dietary Supplements, and Herbs* is becoming a standard reference source in the medicinal field. This new edition is recommended to college and university libraries supporting medical and botanical collections and to public libraries supporting advanced alternative medicine information.

> The 35th edition of 2014 was the last to appear in print as *PDR for Nonprescription Drugs*; copies remain widely held by libraries. Classification: LC RM671; Dewey 615.

488. *PDR for Herbal Medicines*

Publisher: Thomson Healthcare, Montvale, NJ (2007)

Price: $59.95

Review by Caroline L. Gilson—Coordinator, Prevo Science Library, DePauw University, Greencastle, IN.

The 4th edition of *PDR for Herbal Medicines* provides entries and information on over 700 generic medicinal herbals. Entries are presented alphabetically, both by scientific name and by common name. Multiple cross-indexing categories include therapeutic category, homeopathic indications, Asian indications, and side effects. A drug-herb interaction guide and a safety guide are also included. The herb identification guide has over 380 small color photographs of various botanicals covered in the monographs. The volume concludes with nutritional supplement monographs. The heart of this volume, the herbal monographs, is where entries are found on herbal and medicinal plants. Each monograph contains up to 10 standard sections, describing the plant and its habitat, and then provides information on the effect the herbal has on the human body. Clinical trial information is given, along with usage, precautions, dosage, and literature for further reading or research information. Length of individual entries varies from a half page to several pages. Indexing herbs by both botanical name and common name is appreciated for the academic as well as general public audiences. Placing the photograph with the monograph would be useful; each entry should have a photograph. Language in the monographs can get technical, so a cautionary note to public libraries considering this source: have a chemistry or medical dictionary handy. *PDR for Herbal Medicines* is becoming a standard reference sources in the medicinal plant field. This new edition is recommended to college and university libraries supporting medical and botanical collections and to public libraries supporting advanced alternative medicine information.

---

This 2007 edition is the last to appear in print, but copies remain widely held by libraries. PDR.net online is the publisher's preferred venue. Classification: LC RS164; Dewey 615.

---

## Anatomy

489. *Gray's Anatomy for Students*, by Richard L. Drake, Wayne Vogl, and Adam W. M. Mitchell

Publisher: Churchill Livingstone, St. Louis, MO (2005)

Price: $64.95

Review by Barbara Delzell—Librarian, St. Gregory's University, Shawnee, OK.

This edition of the well-known, time-tested standard, *Gray's Anatomy*, is simply excellent. It is a reorganized, student-oriented version of *Gray's Anatomy* with a clinical focus, exceptional indexing, and system cross-referencing. The illustrations and clinical images are superb. It also features electronic integration. Full-text online access is extended to the purchaser, along with six months' free access to *Gray's Anatomy* (39th edition). The book consists of eight chapters: anatomy and imaging; back; thorax; abdomen; pelvis and perineum; lower limb; upper limb; head and neck. Each chapter consists of four sections: conceptual overview; regional anatomy; surface anatomy; clinical cases. The conceptual overview section can be utilized independently by anyone who wishes to acquire detailed basic-level information. It also functions nicely as a summary review for medical students. Ease of use is enhanced first by thoughtful organization of material and second by subtle color coding. The cases presented with each chapter are integrated smoothly with the related material. Overall, this title should certainly be on every beginning medical student's gross anatomy resources must-have list. It is highly recommended for academic reference collections supporting any type of health-related curriculums and is also a useful supplement to *Gray's Anatomy*. Its user-friendly accessibility makes it a valuable general collection recommendation to public, school, and academic libraries.

---

*Gray's Anatomy: The Anatomical Basis of Clinical Practice* is a classic source, first printed in 1858 and still in print today. Classification: LC QM23; Dewey 611.

490. *Grant's Atlas of Anatomy*, by Anne M. R. Agur and Arthur F. Dalley
Publisher: Wolters Kluwer, New York, NY (2016)
Price: $89.99
Review by Staff, Libraries Unlimited.

Now in its 14th edition, *Grant's Atlas of Anatomy* has upgraded the material in response to the needs of students and educators without sacrificing its easy-to-use layout and its tried-and-true organization. The most important changes to the 14th edition are in the realm of illustrations. The entire collection of carbon-dust illustrations has been remastered and recolored leading to high-resolution images. The schematic illustrations have also been overhauled with a modern uniform style and consistent color palette. This is in addition to the pictures of real cadavers in the classic illustrations. In terms of written material, users will find clinical comments in blue next to illustration legends. These clinical notes provide information about real-life medical applications of the anatomical concepts being presented. The work has also reordered body regions to correspond to the sequence used in the more recent editions of *Grant's Dissector*. What has not changed is the uncluttered presentation of material and the excellent organization. The detailed table of contents is followed by a list of tables that are grouped by chapters. Chapters themselves begin with a table of contents, and chapters follow the same format, moving from more general overviews to specific information, and concluding with diagnostic images. There are nine chapters on the following regions: back, upper limb, thorax, abdomen, pelvis and perineum, lower limb, head, neck, and cranial nerves. For those who prefer to search a specific topic without going to the table of contents or individual chapters, the extensive index has *see* and *see also* references; tables are also indexed and clearly marked as such. Highly recommended for public and academic libraries.

---

While not as well known among the public as *Gray's Anatomy* (entry 489), this work is highly regarded in medical circles. First published in 1943. Classification: LC QM23; Dewey 611.

---

491. *The Oxford Companion to the Body*, by Colin Blakemore and Sheila Jennett, eds.
Publisher: Oxford University Press, New York, NY (2001)
Price: $65.00
Review by Lynn M. McMain—Instructor/Reference Librarian, Newton Gresham Library, Sam Houston State University, Huntsville, TX.

Any publication from Oxford University Press produced in conjunction with the Physiological Society (United Kingdom) carries an expectation of quality, and *The Oxford Companion to the Body* does not disappoint. Editors Blakemore and Jennett are of outstanding ability and reputation, as are the section editors and the more than 350 contributors. Entries are alphabetically arranged and have *see*, *see also*, and further reading references. A detailed index incorporates commonly used synonyms, thus providing for expanded access. Lastly, a section of plates illustrate various human organ systems. Beautiful full-page photographs decorate the text intermittently, and there are more than 150 illustrations, some quite historic and interesting, such as the line drawing by Christopher Wren of the base of the human brain found in the entry under the headword "Vision." The use of British spelling will be confusing for readers outside the United Kingdom. For example, to locate the entries on estrogen and edema readers must look under oestrogens and oedema. However, this does not detract from the overall superior quality of this book, which is highly recommended for secondary school, college and university, and public libraries.

Classification: LC QM7; Dewey 612.

## Alternative Medicine

492. *The Gale Encyclopedia of Alternative Medicine*, by Laurie Fundukian, ed.

Publisher: Gale/Cengage Learning, Farmington Hills, MI (2014)

Price: $714.00/set

Review by Barbara M. Bibel—Reference Librarian, Science/Business/Sociology Department, Main Library, Oakland Public Library, Oakland, CA.

The use of alternative medical therapies is increasing as people seek more holistic care. Many insurance providers now cover chiropractic and acupuncture. The fourth edition of *The Gale Encyclopedia of Alternative Medicine* reflects this with an article about the Patient Protection and Affordable Care Act (Obamacare) and how it will impact alternative care practitioners. This edition of the encyclopedia contains 800 signed, alphabetical entries. Fifty are new. All have resource lists and definitions of key terms in colored text boxes. The entries cover therapies (acupuncture, chiropractic), herbs/remedies (milk thistle, vitamins), and diseases/conditions (breast cancer, osteoarthritis). Articles about therapies include their history, description, benefits, precautions, and side effects. Those about herbs and remedies include their general use, types of preparation, side effects, and interactions. Entries for diseases and conditions contain a definition, description, causes and symptoms, diagnosis and treatment, allopathic treatment, expected results, and prevention. The contributors provide evidence-based information about the effectiveness of the therapies. A list of organizations and a glossary help readers find further information. *The Gale Encyclopedia of Alternative Medicine* is an excellent resource for health information collections in public and consumer health libraries.

---

Classification: LC R733; Dewey 615.

---

493. *The Encyclopedia of Medicinal Plants*, by Andrew Chevallier
Publisher: DK Publishing, New York, NY (1996)
Price: $39.95
Review by Staff, Libraries Unlimited.

Featuring more than 550 plants that are put to therapeutic use around the world, this book introduces readers to the rich traditions and resources of herbal medicine. With a refreshing combination of folkloric and scientific material, it brings together each plant's history and tradition with research-based information about its active constituents, key actions, and potential new uses. After a general overview of the global development of herbal medicine, the book's focus shifts to major continents, tracing traditions within each. A colorful and well-illustrated index of herbs follows. This is divided into two broad sections—"Key Medicinal Plants" (which covers 100 herbs) and "Other Medicinal Plants" (which covers more than 400 herbs). Within the sections, herbs are listed alphabetically by their scientific name, below which appear—in large typeface—their common name or names. The following information is given for each herb: name (scientific and common), habitat and cultivation, related species, key constituents, key actions, traditional and current uses (including self-help uses), parts used, and key preparations and their uses. This same type of information is offered in each section, but it is given in greater detail in the first section. Final chapters in the book are devoted to growing, harvesting, and processing herbs; making herbal remedies; and consulting a herbal practitioner. A glossary, a bibliography, a general index, and an index of ailments conclude the book. If this book has a weakness, it is in the sheer ambition of covering the globe with a rather slippery language. Because general readers are for the most part unaware of scientific names of herbs, they may have difficulty locating specific plants. A thorough index could make up for this problem, but although this book's index does list common names, it does not always list all common names for an individual herb. Hence, the Chinese herb *Angelica sinensis*, commonly known as dong quai in the United States, is listed under its Latin name and under a variation of the common name that one supposes is used in the United Kingdom, dang gui. Other herbs seem simply to be excluded. Osha root (or chuchupate), a Native American remedy for cough relief, does not appear, nor does the Asian Indian digestive ajwain (or ajawan). Another fine work on this topic is *Rodale's Illustrated Encyclopedia of Herbs*, which focuses more on North American and Western European herbs and traditions. The Rodale volume also emphasizes cultivation and herb lore, rather than modern herbal medicine. In fact, these two books complement one another and should not be considered substitutes. In spite of inevitable omissions and weaknesses of this book, it is a rare find. Used in conjunction with other herbal guides, it is a worthwhile reference book. One can always hope that in subsequent editions, the author will expand the index to provide easier access to this abundant information. For collections covering this subject area, the book is highly recommended.

---

The 2nd edition appeared in 2001. Classification: LC RS164; Dewey 615.

---

494. *Native American Medicinal Plants: An Ethnobotanical Dictionary*, by Daniel E. Moerman

Publisher: Timber Press, Portland, OR (2009)

Price: $29.95

Review by Kenneth M. Frankel—Associate University Librarian, Florida Atlantic University, Boca Raton.

This work, focusing on the traditional medicinal use of plants by Native American groups, is an abridged version of the author's *Native American Ethnobotany* (Timber Press, 1998), a larger volume that also included plants used for nonmedicinal purposes, such as for food or shelter. This volume covers the uses of more than 3,000 plants by 218 Native American tribal groups. It was compiled by analyzing and indexing over 170 different ethnobotanical publications including both journal articles and monographs. The work opens with a brief essay on plant use by Native Americans, along with lists of drug usage categories (e.g., analgesic, expectorant) and the Native American groups included. The following "Catalog of Plants" lists the plant species alphabetically by their scientific names. Each entry also includes the popular name, followed by an alphabetic listing of the groups that use it, the medicinal purpose(s) they use it for, and a cross-reference to the bibliography of sources. The length of the entries can vary considerably based upon the number of groups using a plant as well the number of purposes the species is used for. Entries for some species include a black-and-white botanical line drawing. An index of tribes lists each Native American group followed by the categories of drug usage and the species they use for them.

An index of plant uses lists the drug use categories, followed by the species and which tribal group uses them. An index of common plant names provides the nonspecialist with the scientific name for each species. This volume is recommended for academic libraries serving institutions that offer programs in ethnobotany, Native American studies, or pharmaceutical sciences.

Classification: LC RS171; Dewey 615.

## Nutrition

Additional works about food and food practices can be found in the section "Popular Culture" in Chapter 2 (entries 174–177).

495. *Encyclopedia of Foods: A Guide to Healthy Nutrition*, by Robert A. Rizza and V.L.W. Go, eds.

Publisher: Academic Press, San Diego, CA (2002)

Price: $29.95

Review by Staff, Libraries Unlimited.

The *Encyclopedia of Foods* is much more than just an encyclopedia. Prepared by Academic Press and with assistance from the Mayo Clinic, the University of California-Los Angeles, and the Dole Food Company, this resource gives a lot of information surrounding all aspects of healthy living and healthy eating. The first part of the book discusses how good food relates to a healthy lifestyle in five chapters: "Optimizing Health," "The Nutrients and Other Food Substances," "The Food-Health Connection," "Planning Meals: Selecting Healthful Foods, Plus Two Weeks of Menus," and "Preparing Healthful Meals." The chapters are not encyclopedic in nature but instead provide detailed information in textbook format. Such topics as dietary guidelines and the food pyramid are discussed as well as how foods can contribute to and prevent such diseases as obesity, diabetes, and cancer. The chapter on preparing healthful foods not only discusses healthy cooking techniques but also gives tips on food safety and how to clean certain foods to prevent bacteria from spreading. Part II, "Encyclopedia of Food," describes a variety of foods. They are listed first by category (e.g., fruits, vegetables, high-protein food) and then alphabetically within each category. Each fruit and vegetable is presented on one page and has a thorough description, a list of its varieties, botanical facts, uses, and nutrient composition. The grains, protein foods, and dairy sections are not arranged in strict encyclopedic order but instead read more like a textbook. They provide interesting sidebars with helpful information on such topics as lactose intolerance, different meat grades, and soy products. The book concludes with a glossary and a list for further reading. The appendixes at the end of the volume provide tables on recommended dietary intakes for children and adults as well as nutrients and calories in foods. Because this book is not entirely encyclopedic in nature, the index is essential. Luckily, it is easy to use and provides easy access to the important topics found within the volume. Because of the popularity of this topic to both laypersons and the health community, this volume is recommended for public, academic, and consumer health libraries of all sizes.

Classification: LC TX349; Dewey 641.

496. *The Encyclopedia of Vitamins, Minerals and Supplements*, by Tova Navarra

Publisher: Facts on File, New York, NY (2004)

Price: $65.00

Review by Denise A. Garofalo—Systems and Catalog Services Librarian, Curtin Memorial Library, Mount Saint Mary College, Newburgh, NY.

Containing a full range of consumer information on vitamins, minerals, food supplements, and herbs, the 2nd edition of *The Encyclopedia of Vitamins, Minerals and Supplements* is an interesting and informative source for sound information on these options for supplementing nutrition. Topics are arranged via A-Z entries and include dieting, cancer prevention, and options to enhancing nutrition beyond vitamins, minerals, and supplements. Also included are various appendixes that contain helpful information such as the food pyramid, a nutrition chronology, clinically important drug and nutrient interactions, and food and drug misinformation. Overall, it is an easy-to-use reference for consumers of all ages.

Classification: LC QP771; Dewey 612.

497. *The Encyclopedia of Obesity and Eating Disorders*, by Dana K. Cassell and David H. Gleaves

Publisher: Facts on File, New York, NY (2006)

Price: $75.00

Review by Caroline L. Gilson—Coordinator, Prevo Science Library, DePauw University, Greencastle, IN.

*The Encyclopedia of Obesity and Eating Disorders* is one of the newest publications in the Facts on File Library of Health and Living series. Over 40 subject-specific titles in this series address modern health issues and social issues. The 3rd edition includes over 450 entries on topics related to the economic, sociological, legal, psychological, and medical aspects of obesity and eating disorders. The Encyclopedia begins with a historic overview of eating disorders and obesity. Next, topical entries are arranged alphabetically and vary in length from one to two paragraphs to several pages. Topics covered include artificial sweeteners, childhood obesity, food addiction, as well as dual topic entries such as depression and eating disorders, elderly and obesity, and males and anorexia nervosa. New areas addressed in the 3rd edition include how multicultural populations are affected by eating disorders and obesity, and newer information on topics related to bariatric surgery. Over 150 entries are new to this edition; remaining entries have been revised or rewritten. Any terms used within an entry that have their own separate entry are designated with small capital letters; longer entries end with references to articles and books cited in the entry. There are no illustrations or photographs. Appendixes include a chronology of key events, research, and breakthroughs; lists of organizations and groups that offer information and support; websites providing further information; and bibliographies of books, articles, and audiovisual sources. The Encyclopedia concludes with a subject index. The strength of this source is the wide range of information given about eating disorders and obesity. Like other medical reference books, it is not meant to be a substitute for professional medical care. Users should consult the index to locate entries covering dual topics. *The Encyclopedia of Obesity and Eating Disorders* offers a good introduction and overview to the topics addressed. This work is most appropriate for academic libraries and public libraries that field medical questions.

Classification: LC RC552; Dewey 616.

498. *USDA National Nutrient Database for Standard Reference*, by the Nutrient Data Laboratory [digital]

Publisher: Agricultural Research Service, United States Department of Agriculture, Beltsville, MD

Price: Free online. Date reviewed: 2016.

URL: https://ndb.nal.usda.gov/ndb/

Review by Staff, Libraries Unlimited.

The *National Nutrient Database* is a project run by the USDA's Nutrient Data Laboratory. There are several ways to search this comprehensive, free, and regularly updated database: Food Type, Nutrients List, and Ground Beef Calculator.

To search by food type, a user can enter a basic search term like flour tortillas. This search can be further refined by manufacturer name and/or source (Branded Food Products or Standard Reference). The list produced by this search will allow direct comparisons of the nutrients and ingredients in, for example, the organic flour tortillas from Buenatural and the regular flour tortillas from La Tortilla Factory (the latter has fewer grams of carbohydrates per 100 grams). Those who want to search by nutrients rather than type of food can search up to three ingredients in an individual search and further refine the search by food type group (baby food, baked products, beef products, beverages, and breakfast cereals), food name, or measurement (household or 100 grams). The inclusion of the Ground Beef Calculator as a major search screen makes sense because ground beef is the most commonly consumed beef product in the United States (according to information at www.ars.usda.gov). The calculator allows users to generate nutrient profiles for ground beef products containing any level of fat between three and thirty percent. The site also includes a tab for Documentation and Help as well as a Contact Us tab. Under the latter, researchers will find a sample citation, links to articles by Nutrient Data Laboratory staff; Food Composition and Nutrition Links; instructions for submitting data to USDA Nutrient Databases; and a list of FAQs that includes answers to questions on copyright, the difference between calories and kilocalories, and much more. Results are all printable and downloadable, and all data is in the public domain. Data is regularly updated (a list of updates appears on the site) so users can keep their own information current. Highly recommended.

> The *National Nutrient Database* makes up one part of the USDA Food Composition Databases website: the other part is the *USDA Branded Food Products Database*. Classification: LC TX551; Dewey 613.

## Veterinary Medicine

499. *Merck Veterinary Manual* [digital]
Publisher: Merck & Co., Inc., Kenilworth, NJ
Price: Free online. Date reviewed: 2017.
URL: http://www.merckvetmanual.com/
Review by Staff, Libraries Unlimited.

The *Merck Veterinary Manual* is an extensive online resource covering a wide range of topics relevant to the health care of numerous and varied animals from the domesticated to the exotic. Matching closely to the 11th print edition, the online version offers additional multimedia content and continually updated information, such as new research on heart disease, wound management, and aquaculture. The use of specialized language and a trade point of view mainly targets site material to professionals and students in the veterinary field. However, there is a fair amount of information here that would appeal to regular pet owners as well. Even with its abundance of information, the site is easy to navigate. Users can conduct a basic search from the bar, scroll through the featured items within the page, or select from several tabs on the menu bar. Veterinary Content lists twenty-two general categories such as Behavior, Digestive System, Exotic & Laboratory Animals, Pharmacology, and Poultry. Selecting a category under this tab leads to a summary "textbook" layout with related topics presented in a section/chapter format. For example, the category Exotic & Laboratory Animals is separated into 22 sections related to specific (e.g., ferrets) and nonspecific (e.g., marine mammals) animal types and issues pertaining to them. These sections are then further divided into individual topical chapters of varying length. For example, the section on Pet Birds contains fourteen chapters including an Overview of Pet Birds, Bacterial Diseases of Pet Birds, Nutritional Diseases of Pet Birds, Toxicoses of Pet Birds, and more. Chapters are well organized and may incorporate headers, bullet points, links to affiliated information, illustrations, and video content. The left sidebar will simultaneously scroll through chapter headers as users read through it for easy reference. The right sidebar notes the chapter subject within the context of the main section. The information included underneath the Pet Health tab is similarly structured to Veterinary Content; however, its categories and topics are more attuned to the pet owner/consumer. Categories here are simplified and include Dog, Cat, Horse, Bird, All Other Pets, and Special Subjects. Sections within each category generally address an animal's Description and Physical Characteristics, Routine Care and Breeding, Behavior, and individual disorders. A user guide provides important information about the organization of the material, and an A to Z glossary assists with frequently used terms and specialized language. Quizzes & Cases presents a searchable listing of quick subject quizzes on a number of topics from animal behavior to disease. Users can also read one case study which follows the examination, testing, diagnoses, treatment, and more of a dog with external wounds. Hopefully, more case studies will be added in the future. The Resources tab links to an extensive collection of audio recordings, videos, images, figures, tables, reference guides, abbreviations, and other material. News & Commentary links to a variety of topical articles and current commentary on veterinary information relevant to the field, such as "AHS Recommends Best Practices to Prevent Heartworm Transmission" or "Rates of Food Allergies in Pets Are Not Generally Known." These articles and others are also featured throughout the homepage, in addition to a topical Infographic, a listing of Trending Veterinary Topics, a listing of Popular Resources, and a link to the Veterinary Student Stories website which offers personal impressions of veterinary student life. While the site offers ample information, it is meant for educational purposes only and would not take the place of individual veterinary counsel. Nevertheless, the quality, range, and presentation of the material make the site a valuable resource for professionals, students, and consumers alike.

This online text reflects the 11th edition of the print-format *Merck Veterinary Manual*, published in 2016. The *Merck/Merial Manual for Pet Health: Home Edition* (2007) is found in many libraries as well. Classification: LC SF413; Dewey 636.

## Health Statistics

500. *Health, United States*, by the National Center for Health Statistics [digital]
Publisher: U.S. Department of Health and Human Services, Washington, DC
Price: Free online. Date reviewed: 2017.
URL: https://www.cdc.gov/nchs/hus/index.htm
Review by Staff, Libraries Unlimited.

This compendium of national health statistics is published annually as a report to the president and Congress from the Department of Health and Human Services. The 150 tables give data over multiple-year periods on health status measures, utilization of ambulatory and inpatient facilities, availability of medical professionals by job category, and national expenditures for health care. A representative sampling of table headings are low-weight births by age and race of mother, ambulatory care visits, active physicians in the United States by specialty and state, hospital occupancy rates, and national health costs by category of expense and more. *Health: United States* includes a chartbook, which focuses on a different topic with each edition. Injury is featured in the 1996–97 volume. There are 33 figures presented, and accompanying text provides data on injury mortality, hospitalization, emergency room usage, and other statistics. This subject was selected . . . because injuries account for 12 percent of all U.S. medical spending. In 1991 the cost for medical treatment and work time lost associated with injuries was $325 billion. The chartbook concludes with suggestions for using this information to design injury prevention programs. The report is indexed by subject, and appendixes describe the agencies reporting data as well as definitions of the terms used in the tables. The material in this book is also available electronically on disk and on the National Center for Health Statistics Web page. This reference provides useful trend data on a wide variety of health care statistics.

The chartbook section of this annual has a different focus each year: for example, long-term trends in health (2016), racial and ethnic health disparities (2015), the health of adults aged 55–64 (2014), and prescription drugs (2013). Classification: LC RA407; Dewey 362.

# Subject Index

Note: Reference is to the entry number.

# Title Index

Note: Reference is to the entry number.

## About the Editors

**Steven W. Sowards** is associate director for collections and past head of reference at the Michigan State University Libraries. He has written scores of reviews of reference works and multiple articles on reference sources, the reference world, and the print-to-digital migration of library resources. He sits on the board of *American Reference Books Annual* (ARBA) and was on the editorial review board of the American Library Association's Guide to Reference series. His publications include *Guide to Reference in Business and Economics* and "Reference Collections, Reference Services, and the Change from Text to Technology," *New Library World*.

**Juneal Chenoweth** is an historian and long-time editor of *America: History and Life* and *Historical Abstracts*. Now managing editor of *American Reference Books Annual* (ARBA) and *ARBAonline*, Chenoweth works with an advisory board to track and make sense of the reference world for librarians. Chenoweth and her extensive network of reviewers, librarians, and editors annually review hundreds of reference books, websites, and subscription databases for inclusion in ARBA.